THE MOOSEWOOD COLLECTIVE

Moosewood Restaurant Cooking for Health

More than 200 new vegetarian and vegan
recipes for delicious and nutrient-rich dishes

SIMON & SCHUSTER PAPERBACKS
NEW YORK LONDON TORONTO SYDNEY

Simon & Schuster Paperbacks
A Division of Simon & Schuster, Inc.
1230 Avenue of the Americas
New York, NY 10020

First Simon & Schuster trade paperback edition November 2009

SIMON & SCHUSTER PAPERBACKS and colophon are registered trademarks of
Simon & Schuster, Inc.

For information about special discounts for bulk purchases, please contact Simon & Schuster
Special Sales at 1-866-506-1949 or business@simonandschuster.com.

The Simon & Schuster Speakers Bureau can bring authors to your live event.
For more information or to book an event contact the Simon & Schuster Speakers Bureau
at 1-866-248-3049 or visit our website at www.simonspeakers.com.

Designed by Joel Avirom and Jason Snyder
Illustrations Copyright © 2009 by Scott McKowen

Manufactured in the United States of America

2 4 6 8 10 9 7 5 3 1

Library of Congress Cataloging-in-Publication Data

Moosewood Restaurant cooking for health : more than 200 new
vegetarian and vegan recipes for delicious and nutrient-rich dishes /
The Moosewood Collective—1st Simon & Schuster ed.
p. cm.
1. Vegetarian cookery. 2. Cookery (Natural Foods). 3. Functional Foods.
I. Moosewood Restaurant. II. Moosewood Collective.
TX837.M67435 2009
641.5'636—dc22
2009010689

ISBN 978-1-4165-4886-7
ISBN 978-1-4165-4887-4 (pbk)
ISBN 978-1-4391-6046-6 (ebook)

*We dedicate this book to organic farmers and small farmers
the world over, including backyard and balcony gardeners.*

ACKNOWLEDGMENTS

Arnold and Elise Goodman have been our agents and steadfast friends since 1983, when we knocked on their door asking for guidance. Thank you, Elise and Arnold, and bon appétit!

Sydny Miner, our editor, is smart, funny, responsive, flexible, efficient, and fair. We feel confident that our book is very well taken care of by Sydny and her assistant, Michelle Rorke. Thank you both.

We also thank everyone else at Simon & Schuster who has helped refine the book and shepherd it all along the way. We appreciate the enthusiasm with which you've been behind this book from the beginning: David Rosenthal, publisher; Nancy Singer, design director; Michael Accordino, art director; Patti Ratchford, cover designer; Mara Lurie, copy editing supervisor; and Suzanne Fass, our copy editor.

We owe a debt of gratitude to the talented designers Joel Avirom and Jason Snyder for creating the handsome look of this book and an especially heartfelt thank you to the artist, Scott McKowen, who deftly labored to make our fantasies visible.

Karen Uber was careful and always agreeable while preparing the nutritional analyses of the recipes. And the technical assistance of Emilio Del Plato was, as always, invaluable. We're grateful to you both.

We're also thankful, as always, for our long-time Moosewood partners and friends and all the wonderful people who work in the restaurant.

CONTENTS

INTRODUCTION

The Moosewood Collective has written a dozen cookbooks filled with recipes for flavorful, interesting vegetarian food from soups to desserts. We've covered quick and easy meals and cooking for celebrations. One of our books is about the world of ethnic cuisines; another teaches you how to cook from your own kitchen garden. Many of our early recipes are loaded with cheese, and one of our most popular cookbooks is all about low-fat fare. Sometimes we think we've said everything we have to say, but then we find new ingredients, new cuisines, and new information, and ultimately we find we have new perspectives. Today we want freshness and integrity of ingredients. Our food must be attractive and delicious, but we also want it to contribute to good health. Really, we want it all.

We read and hear a lot about nutrition. We are bombarded with information on food, and the media definition of healthful food changes from week to week. Bits of nutritional information can be blown out of proportion, taken out of context, or viewed in isolation without considering the complexity of interactions in the body. Sometimes studies are poorly interpreted in the media. Too much of what we learn comes from advertising. Sometimes it seems that we receive more nutritional advice (and some of it contradictory) than we can process.

However, science continues to advance. New and better findings supplant the old, and nutritional recommendations change. So we are careful to heed only the advice of reputable sources, and we deliberate and then proceed with caution before changing our eating habits or making recommendations of our own.

One thing we know is that the surest source of nutritious and delicious food is your own kitchen. And we've noticed that all the experts we trust agree on a few things: eat more plant foods—fruits, vegetables, beans, whole grains, nuts and seeds; avoid processed foods, refined sugars and carbohydrates, additives and preservatives; cut back on fats, especially trans fats and saturated fats. Many essential vitamins, minerals, and other phytonutrients are found abundantly—sometimes exclusively—in the plant world, and most people will be healthier longer if they pack their diets with plant foods. Well, that's what we're good at. Moosewood has been focused on making delicious vegetarian whole foods for years.

Judging by our customers' questions and requests, and by scanning the magazine covers while waiting in the supermarket checkout line, we think our health concerns are probably similar to yours: achieving wellness, enhancing fitness, maintaining a healthy weight, and managing chronic illness with a conscious diet.

Most people are aware of the role food plays in good health—the five-a-day message has been heard—yet it is believed that fewer than a third of Americans come close to this goal. Newer guidelines from the National Cancer Institute call for seven servings of fruit and vegetables a day for women and nine a day for men. Oldways recommends twelve servings of antioxidant-rich foods a day. It seems that although we acknowledge the nourishing and healing powers of plant foods, most of us still need help getting enough vegetables and fruits into our diets to enjoy these positive effects.

There are a number of things we've kept in mind while creating recipes for this book. First of all, we want to cook with real, whole, natural foods, and we want to avoid processed and refined ingredients. So we started with the basics: whole grains rather than refined grains; olive oil instead of the "bad" fats; sweetness from the fruits and vegetables themselves; and lots and lots of dark green, red, orange, yellow, purple, and blue. We've included refined carbohydrates and sugars in scant amounts only or not at all, and we've completely avoided the "white foods": white bread, white pasta, white rice, and white potatoes. Not all fruits and vegetables are created equal, it turns out; some are phytonutrient superstars. So we looked for new ways to use blueberries, sweet potatoes, kale, seaweed, cherries, nuts, and pomegranates.

Then we looked at cooking techniques. We played with all of the methods the kitchen has to offer—steaming, sautéing, roasting, baking, braising, grilling, boiling, simmering, and stewing—to come up with healthier ways to prepare some of our old favorites. Healthier not only in terms of our bodies, but also better for the environment. For example, we've baked tofu in the oven for years. That's fine when it's cold out and the heat from the oven helps warm the house or when the oven is on anyway for some other dish. But what about when it's hot out and the house needs to be cooled down, not heated up? In this book, we have several recipes for stove-top tofu, like Pomegranate-glazed Tofu, that cook more quickly over direct heat, using less energy.

We also explored some of the intriguing ways to prepare raw "living" food dishes, such as Winter Squash "Rice Mexicali"; and we came up with more healthful but still satisfying ways to attain certain qualities. For example, we thickened creamy Watercress and Cauliflower Soup with cauliflower rather than potatoes or a flour-and-fat roux, and we made a delicious Sweet Potato Pie lighter by whipping the egg whites and using buttermilk.

Another way to make a dish more healthful is to reverse the usual proportions of ingredients, adding more vegetables than usual and maybe less cheese or eggs. For example, we've been making our Pasta with Broccoli for a long time but it has evolved over the years; now it probably ought to be called Broccoli with Pasta. The pasta is whole wheat and there's just enough olive oil and cheese to make it flavorful with a good mouth feel.

It also occurred to us to boost the nutrition in some dishes by tucking in a couple of little extras not strictly necessary in the recipe. For instance, our Breakfast Muffins are made with whole wheat flour, oat bran, and fruits, and are further enhanced with a little wheat germ or flaxseeds. For more protein, we added edamame (fresh green soybeans) to a classic stir-fry of noodles with vegetables and tofu and called it Three-Soy Sauté with Soba.

Our primary inspiration all along at Moosewood Restaurant has been ethnic grain-based cuisines that are low in saturated fats and high in plant foods. The traditional bean and corn dishes of Latin America, vegetable stews of West Africa, and tofu and vegetable sautés of Asia are all brimming with nutritious vegetables. Sometimes we adjust these dishes to accommodate ingredients that are close at hand, and sometimes we tinker with the traditional recipes and cooking methods to make them vegetarian, quicker, easier, lower

in fat, or just plain tastier. Our fascination with both traditional ethnic foods and the multicultural synthesis of eclectic dishes is represented in foods as diverse as Quinoa Tabouli, New World Pizza, Thai Red Curry, Tempeh Bourgignon, and Mushroom Barley "Risotto."

We've included information we came upon in answering our own questions: Why are whole grains so much better than refined ones? What are phytonutrients? Which fats and oils are more nutritionally beneficial? Shouldn't our interest in healthful eating go beyond what's on the plate to the relationships among food, sustainable farming practices, and the environment? Is it more important to choose organic food or locally grown food?

It's a great time to eat well. Farmers' markets filled with local and organic vegetables are sprouting up everywhere, and supermarkets are spilling over with whole grain choices, bigger and better produce sections, and a variety of more healthful convenience foods.

Cooking for both health and pleasure has made creating this, our twelfth cookbook, a wonderful experience. What always remains fresh and constant is the joy we find in cooking and delight in eating. And now, we can't imagine separating the enjoyment of food from its healthfulness. Eating well feels good.

ORGANICS

Proponents of organic farming think that making healthy food choices involves intelligent, even ethical decisions. Every mouthful of food is more than an action to satisfy hunger. It is an action that affects the health of communities, the environment, and the planet.

Soil, rainfall, sunlight, farming methods, and pest control all affect the nutrition of fruits and vegetables. Crop scientists at University of California, Davis, compared the nutrition in a selection of organically grown and conventionally grown blackberries, strawberries, and corn, and found that the organics had more antioxidants, including vitamin C. Organically grown tomatoes had more flavonoids, a compound that may protect against both heart disease and cancer.

Organic farmers use manure, crop rotation, and cover crops to enrich the soil, encouraging helpful microbes to nourish plants, replenishing organic compounds each season, and allowing the soil to remain productive year after year. Organically enriched soil has greater water absorption than soil dependent on chemical fertilizers, which reduces erosion and dependence on irrigation. When pesticides are not used, birds, insects, and wildlife thrive. There is productive pollination and a balance between predator and prey populations, and the groundwater remains free of toxic chemicals.

Organic farmers support biodiversity. Many are starting seed banks to preserve varieties of plants that have long been a part of our culinary heritage. Those plants that thrive and taste delicious become prized local varieties that work their way into regional cuisines. At our local farmers' market, each season brings new, exciting vegetables. Last summer it was round, pink watermelon radishes; this year, tender kale raab. Whereas organic farmers use their (and our) taste buds to decide what to grow, conventional farmers choose mainly varieties that can be grown as monocrops and shipped easily across the country. And comparing organic and conventional crop yields reveals some encouraging results. Organic apple orchards in the Pacific Northwest, for instance, are now producing about the same yield as conventional orchards. More studies are in the works. Meanwhile, some farmers compromise by using a combination of organic and low-residue conventional techniques.

"Buy local" is a motto for many community-conscious citizens who consider how their purchases affect the health of their local economy. In Ithaca, for instance, some shoppers buy salad greens produced in local greenhouses in the winter and by local farms in the summer, instead of purchasing salad mixes flown in from California. Some supermarket produce departments designate clearly where the produce is grown so consumers have a choice between local and "imported" fruits and vegetables.

It's a common belief that organic products are expensive and that organic foods are affordable only for the wealthy. In the United States, farm subsidies can give the illusion that conventionally grown crops are much cheaper than organically grown crops. When one considers the cost of petrochemicals, processing, shipping, and the taxes we pay to finance subsidies, it becomes very difficult to figure out what the true cost is. Organic farmers receive very minimal subsidies, if any. Instead of subsidizing large factory farms that grow crops for biofuels, corn syrup, and canola oil, it may be smarter to support small local organic farms that feed a regional population and grow the food we want to eat.

None of us wants to ingest pesticides, but many of us can't buy organic produce all the time. When choosing between buying organic and conventional fruits and vegetables, a useful source for information is the Environmental Working Group. Its website (www.foodnews .org) presents a lot of helpful information, and they have ranked forty-five fruits and vegetables according to the amount of pesticide residue each most likely contains (see page 6). When you know which fruits and vegetables usually carry the most pesticides and which are cleanest, you can more effectively decide when it is most important to buy organic.

Organic labeling on food product packaging is regulated by the USDA. Products labeled "100 percent organic" must contain (excluding water and salt) only organically produced ingredients and processing aids. Products labeled "organic" must consist of at least 95 percent organically produced ingredients (excluding water and salt). Processed products that contain at least 70 percent organic ingredients can use the phrase "made with organic ingredients" and list up to three of the organic ingredients or food groups on the principal display panel. For example, soup made with at least 70 percent organic ingredients and only organic vegetables may be labeled either "soup made with organic peas, potatoes, and carrots," or "soup made with organic vegetables." Processed products displaying any of these organic labels cannot be produced using excluded farming methods, sewage sludge, or ionizing radiation.

Although organic labels tell you whether a food may contain pesticides and herbicides,

PESTICIDE LEVELS IN FRESH PRODUCE

This produce ranking was developed by analysts at the Environmental Working Group (EWG) based on the results of nearly 43,000 tests for pesticides on produce collected by the U.S. Department of Agriculture and the U.S. Food and Drug Administration between 2000 and 2005. EWG is a not-for-profit environmental research organization dedicated to improving public health and protecting the environment by reducing pollution in air, water, and food. A detailed description of the criteria used in developing the rankings can be found on their website: www.ewg.org.

In this chart, fruits and vegetables are ranked according to pesticide residue. A ranking of 1 (score of 100) indicates the highest pesticide load. So peaches and apples are the most important to buy organically grown, and avocados and onions are the safest to buy conventionally grown.

RANK	FRUIT/VEGETABLE	SCORE	RANK	FRUIT/VEGETABLE	SCORE
1	Peaches	100	24	Cantaloupe	34
2	Apples	96	25	Lemons	31
3	Sweet bell peppers	86	26	Honeydew melon	31
4	Celery	85	27	Grapefruit	31
5	Nectarines	84	28	Winter squash	31
6	Strawberries	83	29	Tomatoes	30
7	Cherries	75	30	Sweet potatoes	30
8	Lettuce	69	31	Watermelon	25
9	Grapes, imported	68	32	Blueberries	24
10	Pears	65	33	Papayas	21
11	Spinach	60	34	Eggplant	19
12	Potatoes	58	35	Broccoli	18
13	Carrots	57	36	Cabbage	17
14	Green beans	55	37	Bananas	16
15	Hot peppers	53	38	Kiwis	14
16	Cucumbers	52	39	Asparagus	11
17	Raspberries	47	40	Sweet peas, frozen	11
18	Plums	46	41	Mangoes	9
19	Oranges	46	42	Pineapple	7
20	Grapes, domestic	46	43	Sweet corn, frozen	2
21	Cauliflower	39	44	Avocados	1
22	Tangerines	38	45	Onions	1
23	Mushrooms	37			

there are many things the label doesn't tell you. It doesn't specify if the workers who harvested and packaged the foods were fairly paid, if the animals were treated humanely, if the farmers are protecting the wildlife and plant diversity on their land, or if the farming practices are environmentally sound.

Could organically grown food feed the world? Most often the way we assist undernourished people around the world involves producing, processing, shipping, and distributing our own surplus crops, especially corn, wheat, soy, and canola oil. The costs are high. Organic farming techniques can be applied anywhere food is grown, and with the kind of assistance that supports practical technology for sustainable farming, communities can grow their own food. Growing crops for local markets allows farmers to pursue their livelihoods and communities to preserve their culinary traditions and continue eating their traditional foods.

EATING LOCALLY

Across the United States many people are looking beyond the shelves of their supermarkets to find out more about the food they eat. They're asking questions that aren't answered by the information on package nutrition panels: Where does our food come from? How is it grown, processed, packaged, and shipped? What are we supporting when we hand our money to the cashier at the supermarket?

Like most Americans, we Moosewood cooks have access to well-stocked supermarkets that provide aisle after aisle of foods we've known all our lives, familiar foods repackaged with a new twist: crackers with rosemary and olive oil, herbed pizza crusts, and chocolate bars with new fruits and flavors; grains and fruits from all over the world; and unfamiliar cheeses from cows, goats, and sheep. A passage in a novel, a scene in a movie, a great dish in a restaurant, a cookbook, a magazine article—all inspire us to hunt down ingredients so we can make the same dish at home. Trying a new recipe or discovering a new cuisine can mean trying fruits, vegetables, grains, and spices from far away. Yet, it's also pleasurable to create dishes made from ingredients grown closer to home, to taste something new from a local or regional farm or market.

According to Slow Food USA, a consortium of farmers, purveyors, and consumers concerned about "eco-gastronomical conservation" and "creating a good, clean fair food system," 93 percent of North American food diversity has been lost in the past century, and worldwide, 30,000 vegetable varieties have become extinct. We lose another plant food every six hours! Cowpeas from the southeastern United States, Gravenstein apples from California, and Manoomin wild rice from Minnesota are examples of the many foods currently on the endangered list. The diversity of our food plants is threatened by the loss of natural habitats, small farms, and arable land, and by our own lack of awareness.

U.S. agribusiness concentrates mostly on cultivating varieties of vegetables and fruits that grow easily, travel well, and behave well on the grocer's shelf. Many farmers, scientists, and ordinary citizens who love to eat good food are concerned. We're grateful for small-scale farmers and home gardeners who preserve a diversity of plant foods.

Many of us are now looking closely at the foods we have taken for granted and asking questions. Those packages of baby lettuces looking bright and perky in the vegetable bin: where did they come from? How much did it cost to ship them here? Who harvested them out in the field? What is in the soil that produced them? What about the farmer down the road who may be growing less well-known but equally delicious varieties? Does organically grown also mean cleanly and fairly grown? What can I get locally that will taste better and be more nutritious?

In recent years some people have decided to challenge themselves to consume only locally grown or produced products. Some call themselves "locavores." A locavore chooses to eat food produced within 100 miles of home, seeking out all the foods possible for a balanced, varied, and interesting diet. All of us can eat seasonal produce, taking advantage of fruits and vegetables at their peak ripeness and flavor. In the Northeast, from the first asparagus, baby lettuces, and peas of early spring, to the bounty of summer, on to autumn's bulging squashes and pumpkins, and finally to the long-keeping root vegetables, it's possible to enjoy a seasonal harvest all year round.

The explosion of farmers' markets around the country brings us an eye-popping variety of fruits and vegetables that may come from places a few miles away. Who would have thought that shiitake mushrooms could grow in our own backyard? Or a rainbow of colored peppers both sweet and hot, and pink, yellow, orange, black, and green-striped heirloom tomatoes? And mâche, cardoons, celeriac, tatsoi, bok choy, and heirloom apples, each variety with its own unique juiciness, tartness, sweetness, and texture? It is a joy to be introduced to these foods, as well as to the extended family of so many common everyday garden varieties.

Most farmers' markets are more than rows of stalls selling produce. It's not unusual to find local artisanal cheeses, breads, pastries, jams, mustards, honey, free-range eggs, and takeaway food. At our local farmers' market in Ithaca, it's possible to sample dishes from the cuisines of Cambodia, India, Tibet, Cuba, Thailand, Hungary, and Vietnam. At this community hub, local farmers, cooks, artists, and people who love food have the opportunity to resurrect and reinvent local cuisine.

When you seek out locally grown and produced foods, you support farmers, bakers, and tofu makers in your community. Pay for a bunch of locally grown spinach, and the money goes directly to the farmer. Purchasing shares in a CSA (community supported agriculture), benefits both the farmer and the consumer. The farmer has an income at the beginning of the planting season and the consumer enjoys fresh, nutritious, local produce that is often organically grown. Farmers and consumers exchange recipes, growing tips, and information about the food. Everyone knows exactly where, how, and when the food they eat is grown. It's a neighborly affair.

In addition to eating locally, we can be more conscious of the origins of the imported foods we love. Fair trade products are becoming more available. Fair trade products come through companies that support equitable practices: the farmers receive a fair wage for their work and the crops are grown using cultivation techniques that are healthy for the food and the land. For several years now, we've been able to consistently access fair trade coffee and chocolate for the restaurant. It feels good.

The writer and poet Wendell Berry, who still lives and farms where he was raised in Kentucky, said, "[H]ow we eat . . . determines . . . how the world is used." Even small changes in our food choices can have an important impact on the survival of our local food culture. When we eat closer to home, we reduce processing, packaging, and transportation, and so send fewer molecules of carbon into the atmosphere. We get to know our neighbors, rural ecology, and local foods a little better. We cook and eat delicious, fresh, healthy food, while contributing to the preservation of a diversity of food plants and to a healthier planet. As the Slow Food people say, "Eat It To Save It."

ABOUT THE RECIPES

We try our very best to make each of our recipes accurate, easy to follow, and delicious, so that if you follow a recipe exactly, you'll get a dish very similar to the one we liked and wanted to pass on. That said, we have to admit that we're not very good at closely following recipes ourselves: not at home, and not in the restaurant kitchen. We often make adjustments to compensate for vagaries in flavor and texture, or because we don't have one of the ingredients, or just to satisfy our own personal whims. Maybe the most difficult task when we're developing recipes for a cookbook is the job of testing a new recipe for accuracy; to do that we have to follow the recipe exactly, measuring amounts, keeping time, and *not* making all the little changes we might normally make. Not one of our recipes is sacrosanct: we hope you'll mess around with them just as we would.

All of the authors of this book are both restaurant cooks and home cooks. We realize that in our cookbooks sometimes we say that we do this or that, or that one thing or another works best, without indicating whether we're talking as home cooks at that moment, or from our experience in making large amounts of food with which to feed our customers. Usually it wouldn't matter, but we want you to know that when we're working on a cookbook, we're thinking about it from a basic-home-kitchen and shopping-in-the-local-supermarket point of view. Of course, we draw on all we've learned through experience and from each other while cooking in the restaurant, but we're writing this book for all you home cooks out there.

Not all ingredients are equal, just like our tastes are not all the same. We use organically grown vegetables and fruits when they are available and affordable. See "Pesticide Levels in Fresh Produce" (page 6) to help you avoid the most pesticide-laden produce. Because it generally tastes better and is more environmentally friendly, we use locally produced food whenever we can. Dan, our wonderful produce delivery man, picks out the very best fruits and vegetables from the regional market all year round, based on his years of experience and good intuition, and drawing on his relationships with many small farms and businesspeople. Basically, we recommend that you use the best ingredients you can find and afford.

At Moosewood and at home, we love to cook and we love to eat, to taste new ingredients and combinations, and to experiment and change recipes and techniques. But when we write a cookbook, we develop new recipes. Then, we follow those recipes precisely, thinking of ourselves as kitchen chemists ensuring that the experiment can be replicated. We hope that you'll come to know our new book well, and after you are familiar with a recipe, you won't always measure, but will elaborate and substitute with abandon. Bon appétit!

Before you start to cook, here are some thoughts, suggestions, and clarifications.

- There are many kinds of salt available in the marketplace. In the restaurant we use finely granulated sea salt that comes in a 55-pound bag, and each Moosewood cook has her own favorite kind: sea salt, kosher salt, coarse, fine, freshly ground. Especially if you are watching your sodium intake, you might find it interesting that there are different sodium levels in different kinds of salt, so check the label. For calculating the nutritional analysis of our recipes, we used table salt with 2,325 mg of sodium per teaspoon.

- You may notice that we don't list "preheat the oven" as the first step in the cooking procedure for dishes that will be baked, except when you'll get the best results if the oven is fully up to temperature at the moment the dish is ready to go into the oven, as with muffins and quick breads.

For other baked dishes it won't really matter if you put the dish into a cold or warm oven, although the baking time may increase. It's in the interest of saving energy and with the assumption that you probably know your oven and how long it takes to heat up that we leave it up to you to decide at what point you should turn it on.

- When we say that a finished dish will keep refrigerated for a few days, we assume that you will store it in a clean, well-covered container that will not compromise food safety or quality.

- At Moosewood, in our home kitchens, and in these recipes, we usually cook with olive oil or soy or canola oil and prepare dressings and marinades with extra-virgin olive oil.

- Accurately measuring "packed" or "lightly" or "loosely" packed greens (spinach, kale, collards, etc.) is difficult, and we think it usually doesn't really matter if you add a little less or a little more. Of course, in the interest of health, err on the side of more not less, and in a soup or a stew, just add a little more liquid if you need to.

- When we use soymilk or yogurt in a recipe we always use unflavored, plain products.

- We use sugar in limited quantity in these recipes. When we call for brown sugar, use whatever you have on hand, light or dark, it doesn't matter.

- When we're making a soup or a stew and the onions or carrots or celery we're using yield more than the amount called for in the recipe, we usually throw it all into the pot and add more broth or water if we need to. (Too many times we've had the experience of finding, at the back of the refrigerator, that quarter of an onion from a couple of weeks ago.) And if we come up a little short, we don't worry.

- We generally peel sweet potatoes, winter squash, and most root vegetables such as carrots, turnips, beets, and parsnips. Sometimes we peel eggplant and cucumbers, sometimes we don't, and sometimes we peel them in strips as a compromise.

- Those of us who love garlic put in double the amount of garlic called for in a recipe; others don't put in any. Some of us *always* cook the garlic, others look for ways to use it raw.

- We use a lot of fresh chiles in our cooking, and because they vary so much in spicy heat, our recipes generally call simply for fresh chiles without specifying exact quantities. We leave it up to you to decide which variety of chiles and the amount to use and whether to seed them or not.

- We like our black pepper freshly ground and our herbs fresh whenever possible. We generally buy spices whole and grind them when we're ready to use them, because we think the flavors and aromas are so much better that way.

ABOUT THE NUTRITIONAL ANALYSIS

For each of our recipes, we've provided a standard nutritional analysis that includes calories, protein, carbohydrates, dietary fiber, total fat, saturated fat, monounsaturated fat, cholesterol, and sodium. This information can be useful, especially for people with specific dietary concerns, but it doesn't tell you everything. In other places throughout this book, we've included discussions and information about other nutrients, such as vitamins, minerals, and antioxidants, and which foods are especially rich in them.

A recipe's nutritional analysis gives you a good indication of the levels of calories, protein, and so on, but it can't be exact. If you visit a supermarket and compare the same ingredient from different manufacturers, you'll find significant differences in the nutritional measures. The figures provided by different nutritional databases may vary also. We used the United States Department of Agriculture database as the baseline for the nutritional analysis of our recipes. The USDA database provides generic values and values by brand. Several ingredients included in some of our recipes are not included in the USDA database, and for those we went to other sources.

The actual nutritional content of an ingredient you use in a recipe may be different from the values supplied by the USDA database for that generic ingredient. For example, King Arthur flour lists different nutritional values than Gold Medal, and the values for other flours are different from these two. The numbers for various forms of tofu cover a wide range and sometimes seem to be contradictory. The same goes for canned beans; the actual values are also affected by whether or not you drain and rinse the beans. For salt sodium levels, we used "table salt" (2,325 mg sodium per teaspoon), but the salt you use may be higher or lower. Coarse kosher salt is usually listed at about 1,920 mg sodium per teaspoon, and the amount in various sea salts ranges considerably.

Cooking methods can also make a difference in the nutrition of the finished dish. Obviously, asparagus that has been steamed for a short time is going to have different nutritional values from asparagus that has been slow-roasted in the oven, boiled until very soft, or sautéed and then simmered for some time. The USDA database usually provides a nutritional analysis for raw and cooked foods, but it does not list all forms of cooking, and it is sometimes difficult to match the recipe procedure with the data available. Further, the nutritional values of fruits and vegetables are affected by variety, growing conditions, ripeness at harvest, time elapsed since harvest, and storage conditions.

All of this is, in a sense, a disclaimer for the accuracy of any nutritional analysis: none can be absolutely exact for the dish that ends up on your table. We've used our best judgment, and trust that the analysis is a good indication of the qualities of what you are eating when you prepare our recipes.

In this cookbook, a "per serving" analysis is usually based on the largest number of servings when a range is given, but to avoid any confusion we list both the total serving number and, when it makes sense, the volume, for example, "Per 1 serving (of 4), 2 cups." When a serving size is discretionary, we give the amount for which the analysis was calculated in cups, tablespoons, ounces, and so on. When several choices are given in the ingredient list, the calculations are based on the first choice that appears. Optional ingredients and garnishes for which no quantity is given are not included in the analysis. When a range is given for the amount of an ingredient, such as 2 to 4 tablespoons soy sauce, the analysis is calculated on the lesser amount.

Throughout this book, we talk about our idea of what constitutes a healthy diet, and we think it bears repeating here. Eat more plant foods—fruits, vegetables, beans, whole grains, nuts, and seeds. Cut back on fats, especially trans fats and saturated fats. Avoid synthetic, artificial, and highly processed foods that are filled with additives, preservatives, and refined sugars and carbohydrates. Don't rely on supplements— many essential vitamins, minerals, and other phytonutrients are found abundantly, sometimes exclusively, in the plant world, and most people will be healthier longer if their diet consists mostly of plant foods.

FISH OR NO FISH

Our focus in this cookbook is on natural foods that are good for our bodies and that are produced in ways that are safe and kind to the earth, air, and marine environments. At Moosewood Restaurant, more than 80 percent of the entrées on our menu are vegan or vegetarian, and while our expertise and leanings have always been toward plant foods, we have also served fish since we opened. Most of our eleven previous books contain some recipes that include fish. So why are there no recipes for fish in this book? Because the cases for and against the consumption of fish generate both good news and bad, and the information is constantly shifting, so we've decided to stick to recipes with ingredients we're more sure of.

There are many studies about the benefits and risks of eating fish and seafood. Information about the impact of various fishing methods on the environment is also available. However, because of complicated interactions, new information, discoveries that stimulate a new or different focus for study and investigation, and a host of other factors, conclusions and recommendations are often contradictory. Many people who want to eat fish and seafood are understandably confused about what kind of fish consumption is both beneficial to their health and environmentally responsible.

Given all of this conflicting information and and the frequency of updates, we don't want to recommend a particular fish that may be considered a questionable choice in a year or two. We hope that people who eat seafood will regularly look into which fish are currently considered healthful and are raised or caught by environmentally responsible methods.

An optimistic Harvard study recently published in the *Journal of the American Medical Association* said that consumption of fish reduces the risk of coronary death by 36 percent, and that the benefit of eating fish high in omega-3s strongly outweighs the risk from contaminants like PCBs and dioxins found in fish such as farm-raised salmon. A more cautious study published at the same time by the Institute of Medicine of the National Institutes of Health says that the consumption of fatty fish such as salmon and mackerel *may* reduce the risk of cardiovascular disease.

Salmon is favored by consumers in the United States for its flavor, convenience, protein, and omega-3 fatty acids, but it takes six and a half pounds of other seafood to produce one pound of farm-raised salmon. Farm-raised salmon are fed a diet of fish oil, primarily from plentiful anchovies and herring, and in the process they also ingest significant amounts of environmental contaminants such as PCBs.

Recent industry innovations reduce the environmental contaminants passed on to consumers by replacing fish oil fed to farm-raised salmon with vegetarian canola oil (which also happens to be less expensive). The jury is still out as people wait to assess the taste and quality of "vegetarian" salmon raised on canola oil feed. If the taste and quality of the fish appeal to shoppers, the cost of feeding farm-raised salmon could be reduced, making salmon not only more healthful but also less expensive.

There are also recent studies that reveal high levels of mercury in some larger fish. According to the Food and Drug Administration and the Environmental Protection Agency, fish tested at mercury levels of one part per million or greater can be removed from the market. High levels of mercury have been found in bluefin and bigeye tuna, while yellowfin tuna tends to show lower levels. Tuna and sushi fans should ask fish markets and restaurants about whether they test for mercury levels.

In addition to consumers' health, there's the health of the seafood species and the environment to consider. We want to avoid fish and seafood that are caught or farmed in ways that are harmful to the marine environment, or that seriously deplete endangered species. The best choices are fish and seafood that are abundant and well-managed, but assessing that could be a full-time job! Currently, trolling is a method of fishing that is considered environmentally friendly, because it causes less habitat destruction and by-catch (other animals and immature juveniles of the target species unintentionally caught in fishing gear).

For more information about fish and seafood, go to the NOAA Fisheries Feature at www.nmfs.noaa.gov/bycatch.htm, which is regularly updated and contains a wealth of reliable information. The website of the Environmental Defense Fund (www.edf.org) includes a section called Seafood Selector that lists the current Eco-Best, Eco-OK, and Eco-Worst species to buy.

GUIDE TO INGREDIENTS

AGAR AGAR *See also page 163.*

Agar agar is a gelling agent, generally available as powder or flakes, made from agar seaweed. It is unflavored and produces a firm, clear jelly. Agar agar forms a gel at 88°, and after gelling, it doesn't melt below 136°, so agar-gelled liquids will stay firm at room temperature.

The basic agar agar rule of thumb is 1 teaspoon of powder or 1 tablespoon of flakes to 1 cup of liquid. Stir the agar agar into the liquid, bring to boil, and simmer, stirring until the agar completely dissolves. You can test firmness by placing a small amount of the cooked gel on a cold saucer. It should set within 30 seconds. If not firm enough, add more agar and recook. If too firm, add more liquid and repeat the cooking steps. One of the beauties of agar is that it can be boiled and remelted if necessary.

Agar agar may not set when mixed with vinegar or foods high in oxalic acid, like spinach, chocolate, and rhubarb. Its gelling ability is also affected by the acidity or alkalinity of the ingredients it is mixed with. More acidic foods, such as citrus fruits and strawberries, may require higher amounts of agar agar. Some foods will prevent the agar from setting at all, such as kiwi, pineapple, fresh figs, paw paws, papaya, mango, and peaches, which contain enzymes that break down the gel, although cooked fruit seems to lose this effect.

Agar's setting properties are different from those of unflavored gelatin, but generally, powdered agar can be substituted in equal measure for powdered plain gelatin (which is not vegetarian), but make adjustments in the recipe's cooking procedure.

AVOCADOS

A ripe avocado yields slightly to thumb pressure. When perfectly ripe, the soft flesh can be easily separated from the pit and the peel. We usually use Hass avocados. Avocados are rich in minerals and B vitamins and most of their fat is monounsaturated.

BARLEY *See also page 276.*

Google barley and read about its remarkable health benefits, and you may start eating it for breakfast every morning. Barley is a powerhouse of antioxidants and dietary fiber. Some barley supplies up to three times the beta-glucans found in most varieties of oats (researchers think beta-glucans are responsible for lower serum cholesterol, especially LDL cholesterol).

Hulled barley is more nutritious than pearled barley, but it takes longer to cook. To cook hulled barley: Rinse the barley and then soak it for 2 to 12 hours in about 3 cups of water for each cup of barley. The longer it soaks, the more quickly it cooks. Simmer in the soaking liquid, covered, for about an hour, until tender. If you cook hulled barley without soaking it first, use 4 cups of water to 1 cup of barley and expect it to take about 1½ hours. To cook "natural" brown pearled barley, follow the same directions except for cooking time, which varies greatly with different pearled barleys: when soaked, 15 to 45 minutes; when not soaked, 25 to 60 minutes.

BEANS *See pages 212–215 for descriptions and more information.*

Beans are little nuggets of good nutrition, handy pantry items, and very versatile in the kitchen. For the most part, any bean variety can be substituted for another, although cooking times may differ when substituting one kind of dried beans for another. Various types of dried beans and peas expand two to almost three times when cooked.

Keep dried beans in an airtight container in a dry, cool, dark place. Do not store in the refrigerator. Beans can be stored indefinitely, but are best when used within a year. Cooked beans can be refrigerated for up to 5 days in a covered container and frozen for up to 6 months in a freezer container.

Canned beans are convenient since they don't have to be presoaked and cooked. According to the American Dry Bean Board, one drained 15-ounce can of beans equals one and one-half cups of drained cooked dried beans, and we've found that to be mostly true, although occasionally we've been surprised when a 15-ounce can yielded a scant cup of beans. In our recipes that call for cooked beans, canned beans can be substituted for cooked dried beans and vice versa.

Unless canned without salt, precooked canned beans are generally pretty high in sodium. Usually, we thoroughly drain and rinse canned beans in a colander under cold running water before using them in a recipe. But sometimes the bean liquid is added to the dish; just be careful about how much more salt you add.

BREAD CRUMBS

If you buy bread crumbs, look for whole grain and organic. But it's easy to make a batch and freeze it, and so handy to have it there when you need it. Whirl chunks of your favorite whole grain bread in a food processor or blender. Dry out the bread crumbs in a moderate oven. When they're cool, put the crumbs in a freezer bag and then into the freezer until needed.

BROWN RICE *See* RICE, BROWN.

BUTTERMILK

Despite its name, buttermilk is virtually free of fat. It contains only 1 gram of fat per ½-cup serving. Originally it was the liquid left after cream was churned into butter. When the butter solidified and was removed, the "buttermilk" left behind was almost fat-free. Natural bacteria in the air gave it a tangy flavor and thick consistency. Today's buttermilk is made with a culture that produces a similar taste and consistency.

CELERIAC

Celeriac, also known as celery root and knob celery, is the swollen stem base, or corm, of one type of celery (different from our common stalk celery). Peel the knobby tuber; its creamy white flesh resembles a turnip and has a mellow heart-of-celery flavor that blends well with other foods. As you slice or chop celeriac, place it in a bowl of water with a little lemon juice to prevent discoloration.

Half a cup of celeriac has 30 calories and no fat, and is an excellent source of fiber. It aids digestion and supports the function of the bladder and kidneys. Favor firm, smaller celeriac, since larger ones tend to be pithy.

CHEESES

Cheese making is thought to be ancient, dating back more than 10,000 years. There is a legend about the discovery that cheese could be made from milk: An Arabian traveler placed milk in a canteen made from a sheep's stomach and carried it during his journey across the desert. To his surprise, after several hours he found that the milk had changed into cheese curds, due to the combination of the sun's heat and the coagulating enzyme, rennin, that was present in the sheep's stomach.

The cheese-making process is an art, akin to wine making. There are probably thousands of different varieties of cheese throughout the world, all of which feature unique tastes and textures. The type of cheese produced depends on the milk used and the cheese-making process. The milk may be full fat, low-fat, or no-fat; it may be pasteurized or unpasteurized; and it may come from cows, sheep, goats, or water buffalo.

Cheeses differ in their water, fat, calorie, sodium, and nutrient content, as well as in flavor, color, aroma, and mouth feel. In general, an ounce of cheese provides 200 to 300 mg of calcium, and the sodium content tends to be high. Cheese is a very good source of protein and a good source of zinc, vitamin B_{12}, phosphorus, iodine, and selenium.

The longer a cheese is aged, the less lactose it contains. Therefore some lactose-intolerant people will have no trouble, and some will have less trouble, eating aged cheeses, which include Asiago, cheddar, Gruyère, Parmesan, and pecorino romano.

Vegetarian cheeses made with non-animal rennet are widely available in supermarkets and health food stores. There are also many vegan cheese alternatives that are made with soy, rice, almond, or oat milk, or with nuts. Various gums, cornstarch, and tapioca are added to provide a cheese-like texture. Generally, vegan cheeses have no cholesterol and fewer calories, less protein and fat, and more sodium than dairy cheeses.

CHILES
There are lots of kinds of chiles, from the everyday jalapeños to hot habaneros to lesser known varieties you can find in seed catalogues and from local farms. Among chiles of the same type, the heat varies wildly, depending (we suppose) on growing conditions. In our recipes, we usually call simply for "fresh chiles," and leave it to you to choose the variety you like best or find at hand. To tone down the heat, remove the seeds and membrane.

CHINESE CHILI PASTE
Most well-stocked supermarkets offer a selection of Chinese chili pastes to choose from. Read the ingredient lists: we've found that usually, the simpler the ingredient list, the better the chili paste. Most include crushed fermented chiles, salt, soy oil, and garlic. Chili paste will keep indefinitely in the refrigerator.

CHIPOTLES IN ADOBO SAUCE
Chipotles are smoked jalapeños; there are several brands of canned chipotles packed in a fragrant, thick tomato purée called adobo sauce. Transferred to a glass jar, they keep well in the refrigerator, and are handy to have around.

CHOCOLATE
People who love chocolate already know that chocolate makes us feel better. The reason? Eating chocolate stimulates the release of serotonin and endorphins, both of which are mood elevators. Chocolate also contains quite a bit of phenylethylamine, the chemical produced by the brain when we fall in love, which might explain why it's so closely associated with Valentine's Day. And dark chocolate is a rich source of antioxidants.

Some dark chocolates now boast on the wrapper about their high polyphenol content, and it's often very easy to find the percentage of cacao (the cocoa solids) on the label, too. A chocolate that is 50% cacao, for instance, will contain 50% other ingredients, such as sugar and oil, that you don't want to consume in excess. Most health claims are linked to chocolate containing 70% or more cocoa solids. The higher the percentage of cacao, the richer, deeper, and more bitter the taste, and the more good-for-you stuff is in there. However, chocolate of 70% or higher cacao tends to be less creamy in mouth feel and may be too bitter for some tastes. You may have better luck finding good-quality chocolate with a high cacao content in the candy aisle than in the baking aisle of the supermarket.

Coconut milk

Coconut milk is a smooth, thick, flavorful liquid made from water and grated coconut that has been puréed and strained. Thai Kitchen brand coconut milk has no preservatives and is rich-flavored. Many brands include preservatives, so check ingredient labels.

Cooking spray

Cooking spray is made with various oils. It is applied to cookware to prevent food from sticking, and also sprayed on foods to be roasted or baked to encourage browning and crisping. Many cooking sprays have fewer calories per ounce than straight oil, and they're applied in a much thinner layer, reducing the added fat in cooking.

In most commercial cooking sprays, the oil is combined with lecithin, an emulsifier, and a propellant such as food-grade alcohol, nitrous oxide, carbon dioxide, or propane. But it's easy to make your own with the oil you prefer. Buy a mister, available in most kitchen supply stores, or even a plant mister, and wash it thoroughly before using. Fill it with oil, or with oil and water in any proportion up to one part oil to six parts water. Be sure to shake oil-and-water sprays well before each use. Use homemade sprays the same way you would use commercial cooking sprays.

Cornmeal

There are various colors and mills of cornmeal. Unless we specify otherwise, in our recipes we're calling for yellow, whole grain cornmeal. Polenta is Italian cornmeal mush, and some cornmeals are labeled "polenta," but most polenta cornmeals are pretty highly refined; we make polenta with the same cornmeal we bake with.

Curry paste

Thai curry paste is available in supermarkets, natural foods stores, and Asian markets. Thai Kitchen brand is good and widely available, but there are lots of brands: check the ingredient list to avoid MSG and preservatives. The level of heat and the flavor varies, so add to taste.

DAIRY PRODUCTS

When you can buy organic or locally produced hormone- and antibiotic-free dairy products, do.

DRIED FRUIT

Drying fresh fruit from a bountiful harvest is one of the oldest ways of preserving for the year ahead. When fruits are dehydrated, by heat, air, or both, the color darkens, the texture thickens, and the sugars, minerals, and flavors are concentrated. For example, six pounds of fresh apricots yields one pound dried. Dried fruit is a delicious snack, alone or with nuts, and is also delicious in salads and baked goods. There are lots of health claims for various types of dried fruits. For example, dried cherries are touted as a cure for jet lag (go to www .choosecherries.com and search on keyword "jet lag"). At Moosewood, we've found a host of uses for our favorite dried cranberries sweetened with maple syrup.

Look for organic dried fruits, because not only are the minerals concentrated, but so are chemical contaminants, and most commercial fruit is grown with pesticides, herbicides, and fertilizers. It's also prudent to buy domestic dried fruit, because most imported dried fruits have been fumigated. Avoid light-colored dried apricots, peaches, golden raisins, and pineapple if sulfites have been added to preserve color.

DULSE *See pages 162–163.*

EDAMAME *See also page 174.*

Edamame are young, tender, green soybeans. They have a fresh, somewhat sweet flavor. Steamed in the pod and salted, many people find them addictive. You can often find them fresh, both shelled and in the pod, or look for them in the grocer's freezer case.

EGGS *See pages 56–57.*

FENNEL, FRESH

Fresh fennel bulb is a curious-looking vegetable: a large, white, bulbous bottom with long stalks of feathery fronds. The bulb has an anise-like flavor and crunchy texture.

FILO

We like Fillo Factory brand organic whole wheat filo dough. A pound package contains at least 12 sheets of filo.

GINGER ROOT

Select ginger roots with light brown, papery, smooth outer skins. The freshly broken end should be yellow, release a strong, fresh fragrance, and feel moist. Older ginger may be quite fibrous with a shriveled or thick skin. If the skin is thin and unblemished, it may not be necessary to peel fresh ginger before grating. Depending on how much you need and how you're going to use it, either hand-grate ginger root with a Microplane grater or the side of a box grater with small cup-shaped holes, or whirl it with some oil in a mini processor. Refrigerated in a brown paper bag inside a sealed plastic bag, fresh ginger often lasts 4 to 6 weeks.

GRAINS *See pages 274–278 for descriptions and more information. Also see* BARLEY, QUINOA, *and* RICE, BROWN, *for cooking information.*

Store most grains in tightly covered glass containers in a cool, dry place. If you have room, store in the refrigerator during periods of warmer weather.

GREENS *See pages 294–297 for descriptions and more information.*

Eat your greens, love your greens. Eat a variety of different dark leafy greens: each type is high in different essential amino acids, and rotating your greens ensures that your body gets all it needs to build protein. Most leafy greens are available year round, and some can be found in the supermarket freezer case. Organic greens are preferable for all the usual reasons, and wild greens have an even higher mineral content than organically farmed greens.

The nutrient value of greens is maintained, and in some cases improved, when cooked. Most greens have the best flavor and mouth feel when cooked for a shorter time than is generally instructed in cookbooks and recipes. The more tender greens, such as chard, spinach, beet greens, and collards, need little more than blanching. For a quick, simple, nutritious supper, we often add chopped fresh greens during the last few minutes when cooking pasta. (If you have frozen greens, thaw them first, so they won't cool off the water and affect the pasta cooking.) Or stir-fry various greens in a little oil, which makes the fat-soluble nutrients like vitamin K more available, sampling as you go to catch them when tender and with the best mild flavor.

To prepare fresh greens: Cut off tough stems (kale, collards, mustard greens) or trim the ends but leave on tender stems (chard, bok choy, turnip greens). Remove bruised or yellowing leaves. Wash and wash again: some bunches of greens are particularly sandy, so soak in a sink full of water and then rinse well, checking the curls and grooves for bits of sand. If you have any doubt that all the sand is gone, rinse again; a little bit of grit may not be harmful, but it sure does intrude upon that delightful mouth feel. Drain and then chop or slice and spin dry in a salad spinner.

When selecting greens, look for freshly cut stems and leaves with vibrant color. A big bunch of fresh kale or chard can look like a massive amount, but most greens cook down considerably. Most greens can be stored in the refrigerator for several days. Wrap collards or kale in a damp towel and place in an open plastic bag in the crisper drawer (or coldest section) of your refrigerator. Store chard, escarole, chicory, broccoli rabe, and mustard greens in a perforated plastic bag. Tender, delicate leaves, such as beet greens, wilt very quickly, so use them as soon as possible or purchase them on the day you plan to prepare them.

HERBS

An herb is the friend of physicians and the praise of cooks. —CHARLEMAGNE

Herbs are the fragrant leaves of various annual or perennial plants; spices are pungent or aromatic seasonings obtained from the seeds, buds, fruit, roots, stems, or barks of various plants and trees. Herbs have nutritive value, but maybe they contribute the most to good health by giving pleasure. Fresh herbs transform an ordinary meal into something delectable. Many culinary herbs, both fresh and dried, contain antioxidants that may help protect against such diseases as cancer and heart disease. Flavoring with herbs can be helpful when cutting back on salt, fat, and sugar.

Fresh herbs are expensive, so don't let the rest of that bunch of dill you bought for a particular dish languish in the refrigerator until it's slimy and you have to throw it away. Take a few minutes to freeze it so you can use it next week or next month. The easiest way we know to freeze herbs and then use them later in cooking is to purée them in a blender with a small amount of water. Pour the purée into ice cube trays and freeze until solid. Transfer to a freezer bag. (Remember to label it: a parsley ice cube looks pretty much like a basil ice cube.) Then just drop a frozen cube or two directly into a pot of soup or sauce.

A little bit about the three fresh herbs we use most at Moosewood:

Parsley: At Moosewood, we always have fresh parsley on hand, and we don't just sprinkle it on serving plates to make them pretty. We think parsley could be classified as a tonic as well as an herb. Parsley is rich in iron, vitamin C, vitamin A, folate, potassium, and calcium. What's more, parsley is touted for its cancer-fighting potential, because it contains polyacetylenes, coumarins, flavonoids, and monoterpenes. In herbal medicine, it is valued as a diuretic, and used for treating kidney and bladder inflammations, irritable bladder, and edema. So eat your parsley!

Cilantro: Cilantro is said to be the most-consumed fresh herb in the world, more than double all other fresh herbs combined, thanks largely to the delicious role it plays in Chinese, Southeast Asian, Indian, Middle Eastern, African, and Latin cuisines. Cilantro is a very good source of fiber, vitamins A, C, E, and K, riboflavin, niacin, vitamin B_6, folate, pantothenic acid, calcium, iron, magnesium, phosphorus, potassium, copper, and manganese. Also a good source of thiamin and zinc. People tend to either love or hate cilantro; we love it.

Basil: What would Italian, Thai, Vietnamese, and Laotian cuisines be without basil? Basil is highly fragrant and one of the most recognizable fresh herb flavors. Basil leaves are roundish and often pointed. They are green in color, although some varieties tend toward red or purple. There are more than sixty varieties of basil, all of which differ somewhat in appearance and taste. The flavor of sweet basil is bright and pungent; other varieties, such as lemon basil, anise basil, and cinnamon basil, have flavors that subtly reflect their names. Basil is a very good source of fiber, vitamins A, C, K, and B_6, folate, calcium, iron, magnesium, phosphorus, potassium, zinc, copper, and manganese. It is also a good source of protein, vitamin E, riboflavin, and niacin.

KEIFFER LIME LEAVES

Also known as kaffir, Thai, and wild, Keiffer lime leaves have a unique lemon-lime perfume and flavor familiar in Southeast Asian cuisines. They're used to impart that scent and zing to soups, sauces, curry pastes, and other dishes. Like bay leaves, the leaves are usually not eaten, but discarded after cooking. However, fine shreds, cut with kitchen scissors, are sometimes left in and also added raw to salads. Keiffer lime leaves are dark green and hourglass-shaped (comprised of the leaf blade plus a flattened, leaf-like stalk or petiole). The leaves can be used fresh or dried, and can be stored frozen.

The Oxford Companion to Food recommends that the name "kaffir lime" be avoided in favor of "makrud lime" (the Thai name for it) because "kaffir" is an offensive term in some cultures, and also there is no clear reason for its being attached to this plant. (For this reason, some South Africans refer to the fruit as "K-lime.") We, along with many others, refer to it as Keiffer lime; however, kaffir lime remains much more common.

KASHA *See also page 277.*

Kasha is the common name for roasted buckwheat groats. It has an earthy flavor and sturdy texture.

KETCHUP

Back in the early years of the Reagan administration, ketchup was classified as a vegetable for the purpose of satisfying school lunch nutritional requirements. Who knew that all these years later, given ketchup's lycopene content, this might actually make sense? Lycopene, an antioxidant that may help prevent some forms of cancer, is the nutrient that makes tomatoes, and ketchup, red. Pound for pound, ketchup is its richest dietary source, two and a half times better than fresh tomatoes, because cooking releases the lycopene. Ergo, ketchup is more, much more, than a mere condiment. And this is particularly true of organic ketchup. In fact, the darkest red organic brands were found to contain three times as much lycopene as conventional brands. Enjoy your ketchup in a meal that also provides a little fat. Lycopene, like other carotenoids, is fat soluble, which means it is not absorbed well without fat.

LEMONGRASS

Amazingly and delightfully aromatic, lemongrass stalks are prized more for their fragrance than their flavor. They range in color from pale yellowish green to green-gray. To prepare lemongrass, cut off the roots, peel away any dried-out or thick outer layers, and chop or mince the tender core. You can simmer the tougher outer and upper stalks when you make stock.

LENTILS *See page 214 for descriptions and more information.*

Lentils are a staple in the cooking of India, Europe, the Middle East, and the Mediterranean. In our recipes, we call for three types of lentils: brown (the most ordinary; they really should be called "hazel" because they're a beautiful green-brown), red (which cook quickly and break down with cooking to become a golden color), and French, also known as de Puy (green, small, firm, and nutty

when cooked). Generally, brown lentils take 25 to 40 minutes, red lentils 15 to 25 minutes, and French lentils 25 to 45 minutes.

LIME LEAVES *See* KEIFFER LIME LEAVES.

MILLET *See page 277.*

MIRIN

Mirin is a low-alcohol sweet Japanese cooking wine made by fermenting rice. Mirin is clear and light gold in color, and is usually sold in a bottle. It's a perfect seasoning to add a mild sweetness to Japanese cooking. The sweetness of mirin is different from that of sugar, and it also gives cooked dishes luster and a nice aroma. It's available in Asian markets and most supermarkets. If you don't have mirin, substitute brown sugar (two-thirds the amount of mirin called for) or brown sugar and dry sherry (two-thirds brown sugar and one-third sherry).

MISO *See page 176 for descriptions and more information.*

Miso is a flavorful paste used in Japanese cooking that is widely available in the United States, and creative cooks use it in a variety of dishes to enhance flavor. We often put it in lentil and split pea soups for added flavor, aroma, and richness. Miso is made by fermenting soybeans and rice, barley, or wheat.

Its flavor and aroma are determined by the grain used and factors in the fermentation and aging process. Different varieties of miso have been described as salty, sweet, earthy, fruity, and savory. We most often use an amber-colored rice miso with a definite presence but a mild, slightly sweet flavor. Miso typically comes in a sealed container and should be refrigerated after opening. It can be eaten raw. Cooking changes its flavor and nutritional value; most cooks do not allow dishes with miso to come to a full boil. Miso is quite high in sodium (1 ounce contains 52 percent of the recommended daily allowance of sodium), but a little miso goes a long way toward providing your daily needs for the trace minerals zinc, manganese, and copper. A single tablespoon of miso contains 2 grams of protein with just 25 calories. Use miso in your cooking instead of plain old salt and reap a variety of benefits in addition to enhanced flavor.

NUTS *See pages 156–157 for more information.*
Most nuts are available year-round. Look for nut meats that are plump, unblemished, and with good color. Look for shells that are uniform in color and not cracked. Nuts in the shell should feel heavy; if one seems light, it may signal a shriveled nut meat within. Because nuts have high oil content and are prone to rancidity, store shelled nuts in the refrigerator or freezer. Unshelled nuts are

usually fine for up to six months when stored in a cool, dry place.

OATS *See also page 277.*
The oats we call for in our recipes are rolled oats: steamed and flattened oat groats, often called regular oats or old-fashioned oats.

OILS *See page 104–107 for descriptions and more information.*
All oils should be kept in a glass bottle or jar in a cool, dark location to maintain freshness. Refrigerate if you use them at a slow rate. Avoid heating any oil to the point of smoking; it affects the flavor of cooked foods, and also its health value.

PASTA *See pages 226–227.*

POLENTA *See* CORNMEAL.

QUINOA *See also pages 277–278.*
Relatively new to the United States, quinoa (pronounced KEEN-wah) has been cultivated in the Andean mountain regions of Peru, Chile, and Bolivia for more than 5,000 years, and it has long been a staple food in the diets of the indigenous people. The Incas considered it a sacred food and referred to it as the "mother seed."

Quinoa is not a true cereal grain but the botanical fruit of an herb plant; however, it is treated as a grain in cooking. Quinoa is mild tasting, and it cooks to a light, fluffy texture. The grains are small flattened spheres, and there are several varieties of quinoa, ranging in color from pale yellow through red and brown to nearly black. The larger lighter varieties are most common. As it cooks, the external germ, which forms a band around each grain, spirals out, forming a tiny crescent-shaped tail. The grain itself is soft and creamy, and the tail is crunchy, providing a unique mouth feel.

Quinoa supplies a host of health-building nutrients. Not only is quinoa high in protein, but the protein it supplies is complete protein: it includes all nine essential amino acids. And not only is quinoa's amino acid profile well balanced, making it a good choice for vegans concerned about adequate protein intake, but quinoa is especially rich in the amino acid lysine, which is essential for tissue growth and repair. Quinoa is a very good source of manganese and a good source of vitamins B_2 and E, magnesium, iron, copper, and phosphorous.

Quinoa's quick cooking time is another bonus. Because some of the bitter saponin covering on the grain can still be present even if the quinoa is washed before being sold, thoroughly rinse the dry grain until the water runs clear. Combine ½ cup quinoa with 1 cup water and simmer for 15 minutes or until tender. For a nuttier taste, toast the quinoa in a hot dry pan for about 5 minutes before cooking. During cooking, quinoa increases about three to four times in volume.

Quinoa is available in many well-stocked groceries and in health food stores. Quinoa should be stored in the refrigerator or freezer if you'll have it longer than a month.

RICE, BROWN *See also page 277.*
The bran and germ are retained in brown rice; only the hull is removed. Look for long-, medium-, or short-grain; the shorter the grain, the more plump, moist, and chewy the cooked rice.

To cook brown rice, rinse and drain the rice, put it in a pot and stir in a little oil and salt, add cool water, cover, bring to a boil, lower the heat to a low simmer, and cook without disturbing until all of the water has been absorbed, about 40 minutes. For 1 cup of rice, use 2 cups of water; for greater amounts of rice, use less water—4½ cups for 3 cups rice).

SEAWEED *See pages 161–163 for descriptions and more information. See also* AGAR AGAR.
Also called sea greens and sea vegetables.

SEEDS *See also pages 156–157.*
Seeds are not only nutrient-rich, but also add interest and richness to baked goods, salads, snacks, and all sorts of dishes. Here's a little health information about the four seeds that appear most often in our recipes.

Flaxseeds: Just four tablespoons of ground flaxseeds provide 6 grams of protein and 8 grams of fiber. Flaxseeds are also a rich source of lignans, an important antioxidant. And they're loaded with essential fatty acids, minerals, and vitamins. Whole flaxseeds can't be digested, so grind them before use. But don't go overboard with flaxseeds; they have a pronounced laxative effect. We store flaxseeds in the refrigerator or freezer and grind them just before use.

Pumpkin seeds (pepitas): A good source of iron, zinc, polyunsaturated fatty acids (including the essential fatty acids omega-3 and omega-6), potassium, and magnesium. Roast pumpkin seeds lightly; excessive heat destroys some of their nutritive value.

Sesame seeds: Maybe the oldest condiment known to man, dating back to as early as 1600 BC. Sesame seeds were brought to the United States from Africa during the late seventeenth century. Varieties of these tiny, flat, oval seeds are white, yellow, brown, black, or red. Of the nuts and seeds commonly eaten in the United States, sesame seeds have the highest total phytosterol content. Phytosterols are known to lower cholesterol, enhance the immune response, and decrease risk of certain cancers. And sesame seeds are rich in the rest of the nuts-and-seeds nutrients. At Moosewood, we use brown sesame seeds.

Sunflower seeds: An excellent source of linoleic acid (an essential fatty acid), dietary fiber, protein, vitamin E, B vitamins, and minerals such as potassium, magnesium, iron, phosphorus, selenium, calcium, and zinc. They are also rich in the cholesterol-lowering phytosterols.

SEITAN

Seitan is made by forming a dough from wheat flour and water, then kneading and rinsing the dough under running water to remove the wheat starch, a lengthy process that produces a mass of stretchy gluten. The gluten is then simmered in broth, which produces a chewy, "meaty" product. Seitan is a protein-rich food. It can be found in natural foods stores and in Asian markets, where it is often called "wheat gluten."

SESAME OIL, DARK

Dark sesame oil is extracted from toasted sesame seeds and imparts a wonderful, rich aroma and flavor not quite like anything else. It's not a cooking oil; it has a very low smoking and scorching point, and so should generally be added near the end of cooking. Find it just about anywhere you find soy sauce. When stored at room temperature too long after opening, it may become rancid, but it keeps indefinitely in the refrigerator.

SOY SAUCE *See pages 175–176 for more information.*

There are a multitude of soy sauces, each with its own flavor. The best have only four ingredients: soybeans, water, wheat, and salt. Good wheat-free and low-sodium soy sauces are also available.

SPELT *See page 278 for more information.*

Spelt is an ancient grain that hasn't been hybridized the way that wheat has been, and so it has a broader spectrum of nutrients compared to many of its more inbred cousins in the wheat family. Spelt does not seem to cause sensitivities in many people who are intolerant of wheat. It can be used in most of the same ways as wheat, including bread and pasta making.

STEVIA *See also page 325.*

Stevia is a small shrub native to Paraguay that has been used as a sweetener for 1,500 years. Today, it is in widespread use in South America, Japan, and China. It has no calories or carbohydrates; its Glycemic Index rating is zero. The taste of stevia is different from other sweeteners, and it can take some getting used to, but many people grow to prefer it.

Stevia is good in almost any recipe using fruit or dairy products, but presents a challenge in baking because it lacks sugar's abilities to add texture, help soften batter, caramelize, enhance the browning process, and feed the fermentation of yeast. Sweetening with stevia requires a learning curve; the most important thing to remember is to not use too much, which can result in excessive sweetness and an aftertaste. There are a number of different companies that process stevia, and the quality, flavor, and sweetening power vary from product to product. In our experience, the amount of stevia powder equivalent to a teaspoon of sugar ranges from a smidgen to ¼ teaspoon. When cooking with stevia, start with less than the amount called for in the recipe, and then taste before you add more.

Anecdotal health claims for stevia (some supported by scientific studies) include regulation of blood sugar in people with diabetes and hypoglycemia; control of hypertension; antibacterial and antifungal properties (both internally and through external application) with particularly beneficial effects on oral health and various skin conditions including acne and eczema; mild laxative effects; and relief from upset stomach. People say that it helps control weight not only because it has zero calories, but also because it contributes to a feeling of satiety.

The FDA has approved stevia as a supplement, but not as a food source. There has been much speculation about the FDA's actions and policies in connection with stevia, but evidence suggests that its position may be the result of lobbying pressure from chemical companies that produce synthetic sugar substitutes.

SUGARS *See pages 323–325.*

SWEET POTATOES

We're giving sweet potatoes a space here because we love them and because there are so many misconceptions about them. First of all, sweet potatoes (*Ipomoea batatas*) are only distantly related to potatoes (*Solanum tuberosum*) and, although they are often called yams, they are even more distantly related to the true yam (*Dioscorea* species), which is native to Africa and Asia. They are, however, closely related to morning glories, and some cultivars of *Ipomoea batatas* are grown as ornamental plants. Sweet potatoes are native to the tropical parts of the Americas, and were domesticated at least 5,000 years ago.

Sweet potatoes are long and tapered tuberous roots with smooth skin whose color ranges between red, purple, brown, and white. The flesh ranges from white through yellow, orange, and purple.

Besides containing simple starches, sweet potatoes are rich in complex carbohydrates, dietary fiber, beta-carotene, vitamin C, and vitamin B$_6$. In 1992, the Center for Science in the Public Interest compared the nutritional value of sweet potatoes to that of other vegetables, and considering fiber content, complex carbohydrates, protein, vitamins A and C, iron, and calcium, the sweet potato ranked highest in nutritional value. Sweet potato varieties with dark orange flesh have more beta-carotene than those with light-colored flesh. Despite the name "sweet," they may be a beneficial food for diabetics; preliminary studies on animals have shown that sweet potatoes help stabilize blood sugar levels and lower insulin resistance.

TAMARIND CONCENTRATE

Tamarind concentrate is a tart, dark brown paste made from the pods of a tropical tree. It usually comes in jars. Look for it where you find Indian or Asian foods.

TEMPEH *See page 175.*

THAI CURRY PASTE *See* CURRY PASTE.

TOFU *See pages 174–175.*

TOMATOES

Tomatoes are an excellent source of vitamin C, vitamin A, and vitamin K. They are also a very good source of molybdenum, potassium, manganese, dietary fiber, chromium, and vitamin B$_1$. In addition, tomatoes are a good source of vitamin B$_6$, folate, copper, niacin, vitamin B$_2$, magnesium, iron, pantothenic acid, phosphorus, vitamin E, and protein. Cooked tomatoes are a better source of lycopene than raw tomatoes.

UMEBOSHI

Umeboshi are a traditional, naturally processed, pickled fruit used throughout Japan, China, and Korea for its health-promoting properties. Although in Japanese the word *umeboshi* means "dried ume," umeboshi is actually pickled, and *ume* is a fruit that is often called a plum but is actually more closely related to the apricot.

Umeboshi plums are usually round, and vary from unwrinkled to very wrinkled. They taste salty, and are extremely sour due to high citric acid content. Besides their dramatic flavor, umeboshi have remarkable medicinal qualities, and could be called both "Japanese aspirin" and "Japanese apples": not only are they a potent hangover remedy, but an umeboshi a day is regarded as one of the best preventive medicines available. Many Japanese people have umeboshi for either breakfast or lunch.

Umeboshi usually comes packed in small glass jars. Before cooking, rinse to remove some of the salt. It also comes in a paste, particularly delicious on hot fresh corn on the cob. Look for umeboshi plums and paste in Asian markets, well-stocked supermarkets, and natural foods stores.

VEGETABLE BROTH

When we call for vegetable broth in our recipes, we mean either a rich, homemade vegetable stock, or our favorite short cut product for home cooking: quart boxes of organic vegetable, mushroom, or "mock chicken" broth found on the shelves of natural foods stores and supermarkets. For flavor, our favorite for most dishes is Imagine Organic No-Chicken Broth.

ZEST

Zest is the outer, colored skin of citrus fruit, particularly oranges, lemons, and limes. Zest is bright and tangy with a strong flavor of the fruit within. To remove the zest for cooking, use a Microplane grater, zester, vegetable peeler, or paring knife. The pith, the white membrane under the zest, is unpleasantly bitter, so be careful not to go too deep.

GUIDE TO COOKING METHODS

Cooking methods are classified as either dry or moist depending on—guess what?—whether or not water is involved. Dry heat cooking methods include baking, roasting, sautéing, and stir-frying. Moist heat cooking methods include boiling, simmering, steaming, and slow cooking. Braising is a combination of dry and moist heat.

The first cooking step in many of our recipes is "cook," meaning, cook the food at medium-high heat, sometimes covered, and stir occasionally. We want you to do something that falls between sautéing and sweating.

BAKING AND ROASTING

In baking and roasting, the food is cooked by surrounding it with heat in either a conventional or convection oven. Baking and roasting tend to brown the outside of foods and seal in moisture. What's the difference between baking and roasting? Roasting used to mean cooking over an open fire, but today it means basically the same thing as baking. In our recipes, we use "baking" to refer to cooking casseroles, breads, stuffed vegetables, etc., and "roasting" to refer to cooking pieces of vegetables in the oven, usually at relatively high heat.

BOILING AND SIMMERING

What's the difference between boiling and simmering? Water boils at a temperature of about 212°. When water reaches a rolling boil, there are big, breaking bubbles and a lot of motion. In simmering, small bubbles break on the surface, with just a little motion. Water simmers at 140° to 185°.

BRAISING

In braising, foods are first cooked with oil on medium to high heat, and then simmered in a liquid.

SAUTÉING

In sautéing, foods are cooked quickly, stirred very frequently, using high heat and a small amount of oil.

STEAMING

Steaming is one of the easiest and most nutritious ways to cook vegetables. In steaming, vegetables are cooked gently over, not in, hot water. The vegetables are put in a perforated steaming basket, which is then placed in a pot containing simmering water at a level below the bottom of the steaming basket. You can use a pot specially designed for steaming, but you don't really need one. In our home kitchens, we've set up all sorts of steaming contraptions. The important things are that the steam must be able to circulate freely, the water should never touch the food, and the water should never boil dry.

STIR-FRYING

In stir-frying, food is cooked on very high heat, usually in a wok, although you can also use a skillet. Stir-frying is a very healthy cooking method: food cooks quickly, without water (allowing it to retain vitamins), and with very little oil. Vegetables are cut into small pieces and added to a preheated wok containing a small amount of oil. The vegetables must be stirred constantly to ensure even cooking and to prevent burning. The key to stir-frying is organization: have everything chopped and near at hand.

SWEATING

Sweating is a means of cooking vegetables until they are tender but not browned. Place a little oil in a saucepan and add the chopped vegetables, cover, and cook gently until the vegetables are tender and releasing juices. This is a good first step in making soups or sauces.

BREAKFAST
& BAKED GOODS

Whole Grain Pancakes

SERVES 4 TO 6 | YIELDS ABOUT 8 LARGE PANCAKES | TIME: 25 MINUTES

These pancakes are light and flavorful. They freeze well and can be warmed in a toaster oven for a quick, satisfying breakfast.

¼ CUP WHOLE FLAXSEEDS

½ CUP ROLLED OATS

1 CUP WHOLE WHEAT FLOUR OR WHOLE WHEAT PASTRY FLOUR

¼ TEASPOON SALT

½ TEASPOON BAKING SODA

2 TEASPOONS BAKING POWDER

2 LARGE EGGS

1 CUP BUTTERMILK OR PLAIN NONFAT YOGURT

¼ CUP OLIVE OIL

1 CUP WATER

---

1 In a blender or spice grinder, whirl the flaxseeds and oats until they reach a consistency like cornmeal. Place in a mixing bowl. Sift in the whole wheat flour, salt, baking soda, and baking powder and mix well.

2 In a separate bowl, beat together the eggs, buttermilk, oil, and water. Make a well in the dry ingredients and pour in the wet ingredients. Stir just until combined.

3 Warm a lightly oiled skillet or griddle on medium-high heat. When a drop of water "bounces" on the hot surface, ladle on about ¼ cup of batter for each pancake and cook until bubbles appear on the top, a minute or two. Turn the pancakes and cook on the second side until golden brown, about a minute.

NOTES: If the batter thickens before all of the pancakes are cooked, add a few tablespoons of water to thin it. To freeze, place a stack of cooled pancakes in a freezer bag. When you're ready for them, separate the pancakes while they're still frozen.

SERVING AND MENU IDEAS: Serve the pancakes topped with fresh fruit such as strawberries or blueberries and/or warm maple syrup, or serve with Simply Baked Fruit (page 319).

WHOLE GRAIN PANCAKES—PER 1 SERVING (OF 6)
Calories: 258, Protein: 10 g, Carbohydrate: 25 g, Dietary Fiber: 5 g, Total Fat: 15 g, Saturated Fat: 2 g, Monounsaturated Fat: 8 g, Cholesterol: 71 mg, Sodium: 424 mg

Southwestern Scramble

SERVES 4 | YIELDS ABOUT 3 CUPS SCRAMBLE, ABOUT 2 CUPS SALSA | TIME: 40 MINUTES

A rich and spicy salsa gives these golden, fluffy scrambled eggs and tofu an appealing Southwestern twist. The tofu adds a healthy dose of fiber and soy protein.

AVOCADO AND CHIPOTLE SALSA

1 RIPE AVOCADO, CUBED

1 CUP CHOPPED FRESH TOMATOES

1 TABLESPOON LEMON OR LIME JUICE

1 TEASPOON MINCED CANNED CHIPOTLES IN ADOBO SAUCE

2 TABLESPOONS CHOPPED FRESH PARSLEY OR CILANTRO

SALT

3 LARGE EGGS

SALT AND GROUND BLACK PEPPER

2 TABLESPOONS OLIVE OIL

1 CUP CHOPPED ONIONS

½ CUP CHOPPED RED BELL PEPPERS

2 GARLIC CLOVES, MINCED OR PRESSED

8 OUNCES FIRM TOFU, CRUMBLED

½ TEASPOON GROUND TURMERIC

½ TEASPOON GROUND CUMIN

½ TEASPOON MINCED CANNED CHIPOTLES IN ADOBO SAUCE

SOY SAUCE (OPTIONAL)

1 To make the salsa, in a bowl, stir together the avocados, tomatoes, lemon or lime juice, chipotles, and parsley. Add salt to taste and set aside.

2 In a separate bowl, beat the eggs with a sprinkle of salt and pepper. Set aside.

3 In a skillet on medium heat, warm the oil and cook the onions and bell peppers for about 5 minutes, until the onions have softened. Stir in the garlic and cook for a minute more. Add the tofu, turmeric, cumin, and chipotles and cook for 4 or 5 minutes, stirring constantly. Add the eggs and cook, stirring a couple of times to scramble, until the eggs are set, about 2 minutes. Add soy sauce to taste.

4 Serve topped with the salsa.

VARIATION: Add some chopped scallions and/or chopped Spanish olives to the salsa.

SERVING AND MENU IDEAS: Serve with toast or wrap the scramble in warm corn or whole wheat flour tortillas. Add some grated cheddar or Jack cheese. Serve as a change-of-pace supper paired with Winter Squash "Rice Mexicali" (page 270), or Roasted Sweet Potatoes (page 299), and have Cantaloupe with Fresh Raspberry Sauce (page 313) for dessert.

TOFU SCRAMBLE—PER 1 SERVING (OF 4), ¾ CUP *Calories: 174, Protein: 9 g, Carbohydrate: 7 g, Dietary Fiber: 1 g, Total Fat: 12 g, Saturated Fat: 2 g, Monounsaturated Fat: 6 g, Cholesterol: 156 mg, Sodium: 82 mg*

AVOCADO AND CHIPOTLE SALSA—PER 1 SERVING (OF 4), ½ CUP *Calories: 91, Protein: 2 g, Carbohydrate: 7 g, Dietary Fiber: 4 g, Total Fat: 7 g, Saturated Fat: 1 g, Monounsaturated Fat: 5 g, Cholesterol: 0 mg, Sodium: 13 mg*

Granola

YIELDS ABOUT 8 CUPS | HANDS-ON TIME: 15 MINUTES | BAKING TIME: 30 MINUTES

This hearty breakfast cereal or snack is easy to make and can be adapted to individual tastes and preferences. Use rolled oats, not quick or instant.

¼ CUP VEGETABLE OIL

½ CUP HONEY OR PURE MAPLE SYRUP

1 TEASPOON SALT

1 TABLESPOON PURE VANILLA EXTRACT

2 CUPS COARSELY CHOPPED NUTS (ALMONDS, WALNUTS, CASHEWS, HAZELNUTS)

6 CUPS ROLLED OATS

½ CUP SUNFLOWER OR PUMPKIN SEEDS

2 TABLESPOONS BROWN SESAME SEEDS

---

1 In a small saucepan on low heat, warm the oil, honey or syrup, and salt. Stir in the vanilla.

2 Place the nuts, oats, and seeds in a large bowl and stir together. While stirring, gradually pour in the warm oil and honey, and stir until all of the ingredients are evenly coated.

3 Spread the granola on an un-oiled baking sheet. In a preheated 325° oven, bake for 30 minutes; stir after about 20 minutes. Remove from the oven and, to prevent clumping, stir every 10 minutes or so, until cool. Store in a closed container at room temperature.

VARIATION: Add ½ cup unsweetened coconut and/or 1 teaspoon cinnamon.

SERVING AND MENU IDEAS: Serve granola topped with fresh or dried fruit and with milk or soymilk, or sprinkle granola on yogurt. Make a special breakfast, brunch, snack, or even dessert by layering vanilla yogurt, fresh fruit such as peaches and raspberries, and granola in a parfait glass.

GRANOLA—PER 1 SERVING (OF 16), ½ CUP
Calories: 316, Protein: 10 g, Carbohydrate: 34 g, Dietary Fiber: 6 g, Total Fat: 17 g, Saturated Fat: 2 g, Monounsaturated Fat: 9 g, Cholesterol: 0 mg, Sodium: 148 mg

Maple Banana Oatmeal

SERVES 4 | YIELDS ABOUT 4 CUPS | TIME: 15 MINUTES

A steaming bowl of this oatmeal is exponentially better than oatmeal made from a package of insipid instant, both in flavor and nutrition. Oats are high in fiber, iron, and B vitamins and may help reduce LDL (bad) cholesterol.

1½ CUPS ROLLED OATS
(NOT QUICK COOKING OR INSTANT)

1 TEASPOON BUTTER (OPTIONAL)

¼ TEASPOON SALT (OPTIONAL)

3 CUPS WATER

½ CUP SOYMILK OR MILK

1 RIPE BANANA

2 TABLESPOONS PURE MAPLE SYRUP

½ TEASPOON GROUND CINNAMON

CHOPPED TOASTED ALMONDS OR OTHER
NUTS (OPTIONAL)

1 In a pot, combine the oats, butter, and salt, if using, and water and bring to a boil. As soon as the mixture begins to bubble vigorously, reduce the heat to low, stir well, cover, and continue to cook for 5 minutes, stirring if needed to prevent sticking.

2 Meanwhile, in a blender, whirl the soymilk and banana until smooth. Stir the banana purée, maple syrup, and cinnamon into the oatmeal and continue to cook on low heat, stirring frequently, for 3 or 4 more minutes. Top each serving with nuts, if you wish.

VARIATIONS: Use another fresh or frozen fruit such as peaches, blueberries, or cherries in place of the banana.

Top the oatmeal with dried cranberries, raisins, chopped figs, or currants.

For orange, date, and almond oatmeal, cook the oats in a combination of 2 cups orange juice and 1½ cups water, and add ½ cup finely chopped dates and ½ teaspoon vanilla before serving. Top with chopped toasted almonds.

SERVING AND MENU IDEAS: Mildly sweet Maple Banana Oatmeal goes great with a cup of hot, spicy Ginger Orange Tea (page 44).

MAPLE BANANA OATMEAL—PER 1 SERVING (OF 4), 1 CUP *Calories: 194, Protein: 6 g, Carbohydrate: 36 g, Dietary Fiber: 4 g, Total Fat: 4 g, Saturated Fat: 1 g, Monounsaturated Fat: 1 g, Cholesterol: 3 mg, Sodium: 20 mg*

Four Fruit Smoothies

Depending upon the ingredients, smoothies vary in health value from high-fat, sugar-laden, and chock-full of calories, to nonfat and low-cal with no added sugar. The best way to know your smoothie is to make it yourself. These four smoothies have fresh flavor and velvety, full-bodied texture. In three of the smoothies, the velvety smoothness comes from oatmeal. When you make too much oatmeal for breakfast, you have a way to use up the leftovers.

Fruit smoothies make a quick breakfast on the run, an after-school snack, or a dessert.

Strawberry

SERVES 2 | YIELDS ABOUT 3 CUPS
TIME: 5 TO 10 MINUTES

This smoothie will be at its best when sweet, juicy, fresh strawberries are in season where you live. At other times, frozen strawberries are okay, too.

2 CUPS CHOPPED FRESH STRAWBERRIES

½ CUP COOKED OATMEAL

1 CUP ALMOND MILK

1 TABLESPOON SUGAR OR OTHER SWEETENER, OR TO TASTE (OPTIONAL)

Whirl all of the ingredients except the sugar in a blender until smooth. Add sugar to taste.

STRAWBERRY SMOOTHIE—PER 1 SERVING (OF 2), 1½ CUPS *Calories: 149, Protein: 4 g, Carbohydrate: 30 g, Dietary Fiber: 4 g, Total Fat: 2 g, Saturated Fat: 0 g, Monounsaturated Fat: 0 g, Cholesterol: 0 mg, Sodium: 71 mg*

Blueberry Peach

SERVES 2 | YIELDS ABOUT 3 CUPS
TIME: 5 TO 10 MINUTES

In the heat of summer, when blueberries and peaches are at their peak of perfection, this cooler is a fabulous thirst quencher. Its color is a beautiful magenta.

1 CUP FRESH OR FROZEN BLUEBERRIES

1 CUP FRESH OR FROZEN PEACH SLICES

1 CUP PEACH JUICE

½ CUP PLAIN NONFAT YOGURT

½ CUP COOKED OATMEAL

1 TABLESPOON PURE MAPLE SYRUP, OR TO TASTE

Whirl all of the ingredients in a blender until smooth.

BLUEBERRY PEACH SMOOTHIE—PER 1 SERVING (OF 2), 1½ CUPS *Calories: 274, Protein: 6 g, Carbohydrate: 63 g, Dietary Fiber: 6 g, Total Fat: 1 g, Saturated Fat: 0 g, Monounsaturated Fat: 0 g, Cholesterol: 1 mg, Sodium: 129 mg*

Melon Berry

SERVES 2 | YIELDS ABOUT 3 CUPS
TIME: 5 TO 10 MINUTES

Use ripe, sweet fruit for this pure-fruit smoothie spiked with fresh ginger.

⅔ CUP CHOPPED FRESH OR FROZEN STRAWBERRIES

1½ CUPS CANTALOUPE CHUNKS

1 CUP UNSWEETENED APPLE JUICE

2 TEASPOONS GRATED PEELED GINGER ROOT

1 TABLESPOON HONEY OR OTHER SWEETENER

Whirl all of the ingredients in a blender until smooth.

MELON BERRY SMOOTHIE—PER 1 SERVING (OF 2), 1½ CUPS *Calories: 149, Protein: 1.5 g, Carbohydrate: 37 g, Dietary Fiber: 2 g, Total Fat: 0 g, Saturated Fat: 0 g, Monounsaturated Fat: 0 g, Cholesterol: 0 mg, Sodium: 23 mg*

Apricot Orange

SERVES 2 | YIELDS ABOUT 3 CUPS
TIME: 5 TO 10 MINUTES

A good breakfast drink. Both oranges and apricots are packed with carotenoid antioxidants and vitamin C, and they taste great together.

1½ CUPS UNSWEETENED APRICOT JUICE

½ CUP ORANGE JUICE

¼ CUP MINCED UNSULFURED DRIED APRICOTS (ABOUT 5 WHOLE)

⅔ CUP COOKED OATMEAL

Whirl all of the ingredients in a blender until smooth.

APRICOT ORANGE SMOOTHIE—PER 1 SERVING (OF 2), 1½ CUPS *Calories: 206, Protein: 4 g, Carbohydrate: 48 g, Dietary Fiber: 4 g, Total Fat: 1 g, Saturated Fat: 0 g, Monounsaturated Fat: 0 g, Cholesterol: 0 mg, Sodium: 100 mg*

Ginger Orange Tea

SERVES 2 | YIELDS 2 CUPS | TIME: 10 MINUTES

We serve this very popular drink hot in winter and with ice in warm weather. Spicy, invigorating ginger is esteemed as an aid to good digestion, as an anti-inflammatory agent, and for its warming effect. We make Ginger Orange Tea with freshly squeezed orange and lemon juice.

1 ROUNDED TABLESPOON GRATED PEELED GINGER ROOT

1 CUP WATER

1 CUP ORANGE JUICE

1 TABLESPOON LEMON JUICE

1 TO 2 TABLESPOONS HONEY

1 In a small saucepan, bring the grated ginger and water to almost boiling, then cover and steep for at least 5 minutes. Use a fine-meshed strainer to strain the ginger tea, pressing the liquid out of the grated ginger with the back of a spoon.

2 Stir together the orange juice, lemon juice, honey, and ginger tea. Reheat for a hot beverage, or chill and add ice.

SERVING AND MENU IDEAS: Serve this gingery tea hot as a wake-up potion at breakfast or at any time of day. It can also be just right as a dessert beverage, perhaps with Fruit and Nut Truffles (page 314). Serve it iced for the perfect drink to offer with Curried Tofu and Mango Salad (page 88) or with Three-Soy Sauté with Soba (page 164).

GINGER ORANGE TEA—PER 1 SERVING (OF 2), 1 CUP
Calories: 92, Protein: 1 g, Carbohydrate: 23 g, Dietary Fiber: 0 g, Total Fat: 0 g, Saturated Fat: 0 g, Monounsaturated Fat: 0 g, Cholesterol: 0 mg, Sodium: 6 mg

Vegetable Cream Cheese

YIELDS ABOUT 2 CUPS | TIME: 15 MINUTES

More than half of the volume of this delightful spread is nutritious and tasty vegetables. Spread it on bagels, toast, or crackers any time of day.

8 OUNCES NEUFCHÂTEL CHEESE
½ CUP MINCED RED BELL PEPPERS
½ CUP MINCED CARROTS
½ CUP MINCED CELERY
¼ CUP MINCED CHIVES
GROUND BLACK PEPPER

In a bowl, mash the neufchâtel with a fork. Stir in the bell peppers, carrots, celery, and chives, and add black pepper to taste. Will keep for several days in a well-covered container in the refrigerator.

NOTE: The easiest way to mince chives is to hold them in a bunch and snip them with scissors.

VARIATIONS: For a vegan version, replace the neufchâtel with Tofutti, a dairy- and lactose-free "cream cheese." Tofutti is sweeter than neufchâtel, so we usually add a pinch of salt and a teaspoon of lemon juice.

Add chopped fresh dill.

SERVING AND MENU IDEAS: Spread this textured cream cheese on bagels and serve with Green Eggs, No Ham (page 58) or other scrambled eggs. Or spread it on rye bread and serve with Chilled Beet Borscht (page 135).

VEGETABLE CREAM CHEESE—PER 1 SERVING (OF 8), ¼ CUP *Calories: 80, Protein: 3 g, Carbohydrate: 2 g, Dietary Fiber: 1 g, Total Fat: 7 g, Saturated Fat: 4 g, Monounsaturated Fat: 2 g, Cholesterol: 22 mg, Sodium: 124 mg*

THE GLYCEMIC INDEX: BAD CARB, GOOD CARB, FAST CARB, SLOW CARB

Foods are made up of macronutrients: protein, carbohydrates, and fats. When foods are digested they are utilized by the body as energy or stored as fat cells. "High glycemic" foods elevate blood glucose and insulin levels and stimulate fat storage. "Low glycemic" foods do not overly elevate blood glucose and insulin and do not stimulate fat-storing mechanisms.*

The Glycemic Index (GI) is a measurement based on the amount of increase in blood glucose levels after eating a specific food. As our bodies digest food, carbohydrates are broken down into glucose. The GI rates carbohydrates from zero to 100, with 100 the rating for pure glucose. The lower the GI of the carbohydrate in a given food, the longer it takes for the body to break down that nutrient into glucose; the higher the GI, the more rapidly it will be turned to glucose. Carbohydrates with a very high GI cause extreme spikes in blood sugar level.† The impact of food on blood sugar levels is also influenced by other foods eaten at the same time; how and for how long it's cooked; the amount of protein, fiber, and fat it contains; and your body's own reaction to the food.

"Good carbohydrates" are generally the same as "slow carbs." They are digested more slowly and release glucose into the bloodstream at a slow and sustained pace, and they provide nutrients that the body needs: vitamins, minerals, fiber, and phytonutrients. "Bad carbohydrates" are generally "fast carbs," those with a high GI that are quickly digested and turned into glucose, and may also lack other valuable nutrients.

So-called bad carbs or fast carbs may fill the bill for a person doing strenuous, intense exercise for short periods, or one who needs a quick boost of energy or to raise low blood sugar. The downside of carbs with a high GI is that once they are turned to glucose and cause a blood sugar spike, the body then produces an increased amount of insulin to handle the elevated blood sugar. As the insulin works, blood sugar levels spiral downward, creating a noticeable decrease in energy and increased sensations of hunger. On the other hand, slow carbs, those with a low GI, turn into glucose over a longer period of time, raising blood sugar gradually and steadily. They increase energy in a more sustained way, without a spike in blood sugar, while maintaining a feeling of satiety.

When foods or meals that have a high Glycemic Index trigger the release of insulin into the blood, the elevated blood insulin levels stimulate the uptake of fat from the blood into fat cells and inhibit the breakdown and release of stored fat from fat cells. Some scientists believe that consuming a food high on the Glycemic Index can result in an increase in stored body fat.‡

How do we recognize and distinguish the good or slow carbs from the bad or fast carbs? The surest way is to consult a Glycemic Index chart or database. But in general, fast carbs are found in foods that are highly processed and loaded with white flour, starches, and refined sugars, while slower carbs are found in whole grains, nuts, seeds, dried beans, fruits, and vegetables.

* Source: Glycemic Solutions Clinic

† Source: Good Carbs, Bad Carbs, Johanna Burani, M.S., R.D., C.D.E.

‡Source: U.S. Food and Drug Administration: *Calories Count: Report of the Working Group on Obesity*

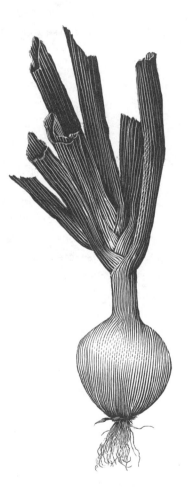

Sesame Flaxseed Cornbread

SERVES 9 | HANDS-ON TIME: 15 MINUTES | BAKING TIME: 20 MINUTES

A hearty, whole grain quick bread with a pleasantly nutty flavor. We prefer the flavor of this bread with the sweetener, but it's fine without.

---

3 TABLESPOONS BROWN SESAME SEEDS

3 TABLESPOONS WHOLE FLAXSEEDS (SEE NOTE)

1 CUP WHOLE WHEAT PASTRY FLOUR

½ TEASPOON SALT

½ TEASPOON BAKING SODA

2 TEASPOONS BAKING POWDER

1 CUP WHOLE GRAIN CORNMEAL (SEE PAGE 22)

2 LARGE EGGS

1 CUP PLAIN NONFAT YOGURT

¼ CUP OLIVE OIL

¼ CUP HONEY, PURE MAPLE SYRUP, OR AGAVE SYRUP (OPTIONAL)

NOTE: Flaxseeds can be purchased ground or whole. Flaxseeds must be ground for the nutrients to be fully available. We keep whole flaxseeds in the refrigerator or freezer, and grind them as needed.

1 Preheat the oven to 375°. Lightly oil a 9-inch square or 10-inch round baking pan. Sprinkle with 1 tablespoon of the sesame seeds and shake the pan to evenly coat the bottom.

2 In a spice grinder or blender, whirl the remaining sesame seeds and the flaxseeds until they reach a consistency like cornmeal.

3 In a mixing bowl, sift together the flour, salt, baking soda, and baking powder, and stir in the ground seeds and the cornmeal. In a separate bowl, beat together the eggs, yogurt, oil, and sweetener, if using. Make a well in the dry ingredients and stir in the wet ingredients until just blended; don't overmix.

4 Spread the batter evenly in the prepared pan. Bake for about 20 minutes, until golden brown and a knife inserted in the center comes out clean.

SERVING AND MENU IDEAS: For breakfast, serve hot cornbread with peach jam or apple butter. Or for an appealing brunch, bake some Sesame Flaxseed Cornbread while you make Southwestern Scramble (page 39). Serve it with Down-home Black-eyed Peas (page 221) and Maque Choux (page 309) for a homey Southern-style supper.

SESAME FLAXSEED CORNBREAD—PER 1 SERVING (OF 9) *Calories: 323, Protein: 10 g, Carbohydrate: 42 g, Dietary Fiber: 7 g, Total Fat: 14 g, Saturated Fat: 2 g, Monounsaturated Fat: 7 g, Cholesterol: 48 mg, Sodium: 350 mg*

Vegan Cornbread

SERVES 8 | HANDS-ON TIME: 20 MINUTES | BAKING TIME: 35 TO 40 MINUTES

This is a moist, slightly sweet yet savory cornbread that is chock-full of corn, bell peppers, and scallions. Use fresh corn kernels cut off of the cob for an especially delectable taste treat.

DRY INGREDIENTS

1 CUP WHOLE WHEAT FLOUR (SEE NOTE)

1 CUP WHOLE GRAIN CORNMEAL (SEE PAGE 22)

1 TABLESPOON BAKING POWDER

1 TEASPOON SALT

WET INGREDIENTS

1 TABLESPOON APPLE CIDER VINEGAR

1 TABLESPOON OLIVE OR VEGETABLE OIL

¼ CUP PACKED BROWN SUGAR OR MAPLE SYRUP

1½ CUPS SOYMILK

½ CUP FINELY CHOPPED SCALLIONS OR CHIVES

½ CUP FINELY CHOPPED RED BELL PEPPERS

½ CUP FRESH OR FROZEN CORN KERNELS

NOTE: King Arthur brand has white whole wheat flour that we especially like for baking.

1 Preheat the oven to 375°. Lightly oil an 8-inch square baking pan or a 9-inch pie plate.

2 Sift the dry ingredients into a mixing bowl. In a separate bowl, whisk together the wet ingredients. Make a well in the dry ingredients, pour in the wet ingredients, and add the scallions, peppers, and corn. Stir just until mixed.

3 Pour the batter into the prepared pan and bake until a toothpick inserted in the middle comes out clean and the bread pulls away from the sides of the pan, 35 to 40 minutes.

VARIATION: For a simple, plain cornbread, omit the corn, peppers, and scallions. The cornbread will bake faster, 20 to 25 minutes.

SERVING AND MENU IDEAS: Try some warm cornbread with Three Sisters at Four Corners Stew (page 258) or Sweet Potato, Apple, and Chipotle Soup (page 132). Or have it with Tropical Lime Tofu (page 179) and Roasted Sweet Potatoes (page 299) or Kale with Cranberries (page 298).

VEGAN CORNBREAD—PER 1 SERVING (OF 8)
Calories: 185, Protein: 6 g, Carbohydrate: 35 g, Dietary Fiber: 4 g, Total Fat: 4 g, Saturated Fat: 0 g, Monounsaturated Fat: 2 g, Cholesterol: 0 mg, Sodium: 509 mg

Gluten-free Currant Sweet Bread

SERVES 8 | HANDS-ON TIME: 15 MINUTES | BAKING TIME: 25 TO 30 MINUTES

We think this currant-rich sweet bread is as good as any made with wheat. It is excellent warm from the oven, or toast it and slather it with your favorite spread.

2 LARGE EGGS

1 CUP SOYMILK

¼ CUP OLIVE OR VEGETABLE OIL

¼ CUP PACKED BROWN SUGAR OR PURE MAPLE SYRUP

1 TEASPOON GRATED ORANGE OR LEMON ZEST

⅔ CUP CURRANTS

⅔ CUP GRATED CARROTS

1 CUP WHOLE GRAIN CORNMEAL (SEE PAGE 22)

1 CUP ALL-PURPOSE GLUTEN-FREE FLOUR (SEE NOTES)

1 TEASPOON XANTHAN GUM (OPTIONAL) (SEE NOTES)

1 TEASPOON GROUND CINNAMON

½ TEASPOON SALT

NOTES: All-purpose gluten-free flour is available in natural foods stores and well-stocked supermarkets. It usually has either rice flour or chickpea flour as the main ingredient. Bob's Red Mill and Arrowhead Mills are two widely available brands.

Xanthan gum is a thickening agent with the ability to hold small particles of food together, making it an excellent substitute for gluten in baking. It's rather expensive but it goes a long way and really does improve the texture of gluten-free baked goods. It is available where gluten-free flour is found.

1 Preheat the oven to 375°. Lightly oil an 8-inch square baking pan or a 9-inch pie plate.

2 In a mixing bowl, whisk together the eggs, soymilk, oil, and brown sugar. Stir in the orange zest, currants, and grated carrots. Place the cornmeal, gluten-free flour, xanthan gum if using, cinnamon, and salt in a sifter or fine mesh strainer and sift onto the egg and soymilk mixture. Stir until well combined. Pour the batter into the prepared pan and bake until puffed and golden brown, 25 to 30 minutes.

VARIATIONS: Try this quick bread with a mixture of chopped apricots and prunes instead of currants. We like the grated carrots but you can omit them if you prefer.

GLUTEN-FREE CURRANT SWEET BREAD—
PER 1 SERVING (OF 8) *Calories: 251, Protein: 5 g, Carbohydrate: 37 g, Dietary Fiber: 3 g, Total Fat: 9 g, Saturated Fat: 2 g, Monounsaturated Fat: 6 g, Cholesterol: 47 mg, Sodium: 186 mg*

Blueberry and Almond Quick Bread

SERVES 8 | HANDS-ON TIME: 30 MINUTES | BAKING TIME: 25 MINUTES

This is one sweet little quick bread: full of good-for-you stuff that can be varied according to the season or what you have on hand. Try it for breakfast, a snack, or even dessert.

¼ CUP OLIVE, VEGETABLE, OR NUT OIL

¼ CUP PACKED BROWN SUGAR

2 LARGE EGGS

¼ TEASPOON PURE ALMOND EXTRACT

1 CUP MASHED RIPE BANANAS
OR 1 CUP UNSWEETENED APPLESAUCE

1 CUP WHOLE WHEAT FLOUR

½ CUP COARSELY GROUND ROLLED OATS
(SEE NOTE)

¼ CUP GROUND FLAXSEEDS

1 TEASPOON BAKING POWDER

½ TEASPOON BAKING SODA

½ TEASPOON SALT

½ CUP COARSELY GROUND ALMONDS

½ CUP DRIED BLUEBERRIES
OR 1 CUP FRESH OR FROZEN BLUEBERRIES

NOTE: Whirl rolled oats in a blender or food processor until coarsely ground.

1 Preheat the oven to 365°. Oil an 8-inch square baking pan.

2 In a bowl, by hand, or with an electric mixer, whisk the oil and brown sugar until well blended. Add 1 egg and beat until the ingredients turn a creamy light caramel color. Beat in the second egg and the almond extract. Stir in the mashed bananas.

3 In a separate bowl, stir together the flour, oats, and ground flaxseeds. Sift in the baking powder, baking soda, and salt. Mix well.

4 Add the dry ingredients to the liquid ingredients and stir until well mixed. Stir in the almonds and blueberries. Pour the batter into the prepared pan and bake for 25 minutes, until a knife inserted in the middle comes out clean. Cool in the pan for at least 10 minutes before serving.

5 Serve warm or at room temperature. Well covered, this quick bread will keep for several days in the refrigerator or a couple of days at room temperature.

VARIATIONS: In place of dried blueberries, use dried cranberries (chopped) or other dried fruit.

Add ½ teaspoon vanilla in place of, or in addition to, the almond extract.

SERVING AND MENU IDEAS: This bread is lovely with tea or coffee, or try it with Apricot Orange Fruit Smoothie (page 43).

BLUEBERRY AND ALMOND QUICKBREAD—
PER 1 SERVING (OF 8) *Calories: 257, Protein: 7 g, Carbohydrate: 30 g, Dietary Fiber: 5 g, Total Fat: 14 g, Saturated Fat: 1 g, Monounsaturated Fat: 7 g, Cholesterol: 53 mg, Sodium: 308 mg*

Breakfast Muffins

Often the sugar- and fat-laden muffins you'll find at the corner coffee emporium are about half the size of a birthday cake and contain half a day's worth of calories. We think our breakfast muffins are a better choice. They're filled with whole grains and lots of real fruit, and they have no added fat. They're just sweet enough to be a tasty and satisfying breakfast.

Apple Muffins with Oat Bran and Dates

YIELDS 12 MUFFINS | HANDS-ON TIME: 25 MINUTES | BAKING TIME: 15 TO 20 MINUTES

These muffins are delectable and satisfying. We love them made with dates, but they're also good with chopped raisins or dried cranberries.

½ CUP PLAIN NONFAT YOGURT

2 LARGE EGGS, LIGHTLY BEATEN

1 TEASPOON PURE VANILLA EXTRACT

2 TABLESPOONS MOLASSES

¾ CUP FINELY CHOPPED DATES

1 CUP OAT BRAN

2 CUPS FINELY CHOPPED PEELED APPLES

½ CUP WHOLE WHEAT FLOUR

1½ TEASPOONS BAKING SODA

½ TEASPOON SALT

1 TEASPOON GROUND CINNAMON

¼ CUP ROLLED OATS
(NOT QUICK OR INSTANT)

2 TABLESPOONS GROUND FLAXSEEDS

½ CUP FINELY CHOPPED WALNUTS
(OPTIONAL)

1 Preheat the oven to 375°. Lightly oil a standard 12-cup muffin tin or line it with papers.

2 In a mixing bowl, stir together the yogurt, eggs, vanilla, and molasses. Stir in the dates, oat bran, and apples.

3 In a separate bowl, sift together the flour, baking soda, salt, and cinnamon and stir in the oats and ground flaxseeds. Fold the dry mixture into the wet mixture just until combined.

4 Spoon the batter into the prepared muffin tin; fill to the brims, about ⅓ cup of batter in each cup. Sprinkle each muffin with chopped walnuts, if desired. Bake for 15 to 20 minutes, until a toothpick inserted the center of a muffin comes out clean. Cool on a wire rack. Muffins will keep in a well-covered container for several days.

APPLE MUFFINS WITH OAT BRAN AND DATES—
PER 1 MUFFIN (OF 12) *Calories: 111, Protein: 4 g, Carbohydrate: 23 g, Dietary Fiber: 3 g, Total Fat: 2 g, Saturated Fat: 0 g, Monounsaturated Fat: 1 g, Cholesterol: 35 mg, Sodium: 276 mg*

Whole Wheat Banana Berry Muffins

YIELDS 12 MUFFINS | HANDS-ON TIME:
20 MINUTES | BAKING TIME: 25 TO 30 MINUTES

Overripe bananas are best for baking: sweeter and more flavorful. You can put unpeeled ripe bananas directly into the freezer without wrapping them. Thaw them for about 30 minutes before using in banana bread, muffins, or smoothies.

1½ CUPS MASHED RIPE BANANAS
(ABOUT 4 BANANAS)

½ CUP PLAIN NONFAT YOGURT

2 LARGE EGGS, LIGHTLY BEATEN

1 TEASPOON PURE VANILLA EXTRACT

2 TABLESPOONS HONEY

1¼ CUPS WHOLE WHEAT FLOUR

1½ TEASPOONS BAKING POWDER

1 TEASPOON BAKING SODA

½ TEASPOON SALT

¼ CUP WHEAT GERM

1 CUP FRESH OR FROZEN RASPBERRIES OR BLUEBERRIES

2 TEASPOONS WHOLE WHEAT FLOUR TO COAT BERRIES

1 Preheat the oven to 375°. Lightly oil a standard 12-cup muffin tin or line it with papers.

2 In a mixing bowl, stir together the mashed bananas, yogurt, eggs, vanilla, and honey. In a separate bowl, sift together the whole wheat flour, baking powder, baking soda, and salt and stir in the wheat germ. Fold the dry ingredients into the wet mixture just until combined. Toss the berries with 2 teaspoons of flour and gently fold into the batter.

3 Spoon the batter into the prepared muffin tin; fill to the brims, about ⅓ cup of batter in each cup. Bake for 25 to 30 minutes, until a toothpick inserted in the center of a muffin comes out clean. Cool on a wire rack. Muffins will keep in a well-covered container for several days.

SERVING AND MENU IDEAS: Serve Breakfast Muffins with a nice, hot cup of tea or with one of our Four Fruit Smoothies (pages 42–43).

**WHOLE WHEAT BANANA BERRY MUFFINS—
PER 1 MUFFIN (OF 12)** *Calories: 111, Protein: 4 g, Carbohydrate: 22 g, Dietary Fiber: 3 g, Total Fat: 1 g, Saturated Fat: 0 g, Monounsaturated Fat: 0 g, Cholesterol: 35 mg, Sodium: 283 mg*

EGGS

EGGS: BACK ON THE GOOD-FOR-YOU LIST

Over the years, many people in the extended Moosewood family have raised chickens, and when the eggs are bountiful, we enjoy the surplus at the restaurant. Well-taken-care-of free-range chickens lay the best-tasting, most deeply colored eggs. It's not just that chickens are happier when they have the freedom to roam a bit; eggs are more nutritious when the chickens eat a wide variety of green growing things and worms and bugs.

Eggs are an exceptionally nutritious food, which is not surprising when you consider that an egg contains everything needed for the nourishment of a developing chick. Eggs are a good source of protein and contain more than a dozen vitamins and minerals: the B vitamins, vitamins A, D, and E, folic acid, calcium, iron, zinc, iodine, phosphorous, selenium, choline, lutein, and tryptophan. The six grams of protein in an egg is second in quality only to the protein in human milk.

And the nutritional benefits of eggs seem to be greater than the sum of their parts. Take lutein, a carotenoid thought to prevent age-related macular degeneration and cataracts. Egg yolks contain less lutein than spinach, yet eating eggs increases lutein concentration in the blood more than eating spinach does. It is not yet known why the lutein in eggs is more available, but it is likely due to the fats (cholesterol and choline) in egg yolks; lutein is fat-soluble and so cannot be absorbed unless fat is also present. So to maximize lutein absorption, maybe we should combine eggs and spinach. This serves as a reminder that looking at nutrients in isolation cannot give the whole picture, and eating them in isolation (say, in supplements) probably won't give our bodies' integrated systems complete access. Yet another reason to eat whole foods.

During the last few decades, ever since cholesterol was associated with heart disease and stroke, many health experts advised people to avoid eggs. After reading a great deal of the information currently available, here is what we think: It is now generally agreed that eggs, rather than contributing to stroke and heart disease, may help lower your risk. In most people, the body's own production of cholesterol will decline when more cholesterol is absorbed through diet. However, there is a small proportion of people whose bodies are unable to maintain cholesterol homeostasis in this way, and they are termed "cholesterol sensitive," because their blood cholesterol levels rise when they eat foods high in cholesterol. Most people on a low-fat diet can eat one or two eggs a day without measurable changes in their blood cholesterol level. It now seems that saturated fat in the diet (as well as refined starches, trans fats, and sugars), not dietary cholesterol, influences blood cholesterol the most. In addition, the latest research suggests that eating whole eggs may, in fact, result in a significant improvement in the LDL (low-density lipoprotein, or "bad" cholesterol) to HDL (high density lipoprotein, or "good" cholesterol) ratio, even in those people whose blood cholesterol levels rise when they eat cholesterol-rich foods. Individual responses to eating foods that contain cholesterol vary enormously; genetic factors and total diet are essential pieces of the picture.

There are plenty of reasons to buy local eggs from cage-free chickens. No antibiotics or hormones, unadulterated feed, and access to outdoors and light means healthier chickens, healthier eggs for you, and a cleaner shared environment. Although not labeled "Certified Organic," eggs from small local farms may in fact be organic: USDA organic certification is a lengthy and costly process, and small farmers may not be able to afford it, yet may practice good organic methods. On conventional commercial farms and in egg factories, chicken feed may not be vegetarian and is made from grains treated with antibiotics and hormones. Conventional grain has been sprayed with pesticides and herbicides, and persistent toxic chemicals, which are stored in fat, may end up in the egg yolks. On certified organic egg cartons, you may also see a "Certified Humane" logo, which means that the hens are raised observing specific standards of care for farm animal treatment.

Omega-3s (essential fatty acids in the yolks that protect the heart and arteries) in wild grasses and weeds give free-range eggs more punch than the average eggs from confined hens and factory farms. Typically, the highest omega-3 chickens are fed meal that has algae added, the same stuff that gives wild fish a high nutritional rating. These enriched eggs provide the same amount of omega-3s as a three-ounce serving of oily fish such as salmon.

Refrigerated eggs will stay fresh for about a month. Store them in their original carton or in a covered container with the pointed ends facing down to prevent the air chamber and yolk from being displaced. Don't wash eggs, because it may remove their protective coating.

Eggs have been a symbol of fertility and a religious symbol throughout history. The association of eggs with the Easter holiday is rooted in both biology and culture. Before modern poultry-raising techniques, hens laid very few eggs during the winter, and so Easter, on the calendar near the beginning of spring, coincided with the hens' cycle of laying numerous eggs. Because eggs were considered a luxury food, they were forbidden during Lent, so Christians had to wait until Easter to eat eggs. The custom of painting eggshells has a long history and was popular in many ancient civilizations, including Chinese, Persian, Greek, and Egyptian.

Bacteria such as salmonella multiply in raw eggs, so follow these egg safety tips:

Before purchasing, examine the eggs for cracks. If any eggs are stuck to the bottom of the carton, suspect cracks.

Don't wash eggs before storing them. Washing may remove the invisible protective coating that surrounds the shell, allowing bacteria to enter.

Store eggs in the refrigerator in their original carton. This not only keeps the eggs from absorbing the aroma of other foods, it also keeps them out of those convenient little egg holders on some refrigerator doors, where they don't belong because door storage is too warm.

Wash your hands and utensils thoroughly after contact with raw eggs.

If you're mixing raw eggs into recipes, such as cookie dough, avoid the temptation to let your child (or you!) lick the bowl.

Cook eggs thoroughly, until the whites and the yolks are firm: five minutes for poached eggs and seven minutes for hard-boiled.

Commercial egg products, such as eggnog and mayonnaise, have been pasteurized. Don't use raw eggs in uncooked recipes made at home.

Green Eggs, No Ham

SERVES 2 OR 3 | TIME: 15 MINUTES

Listen, Dr. Seuss: "We like green eggs **no** ham! We do! We like them, Sam-I-am!" This vegetarian scrambled egg dish with arugula is a quick, green, any-day breakfast.

---

4 CUPS LIGHTLY PACKED BABY ARUGULA OR SPINACH (ABOUT 4 OUNCES)

4 LARGE EGGS

SALT AND GROUND BLACK PEPPER

2 TEASPOONS OLIVE OIL

2 TABLESPOONS CHOPPED SCALLIONS OR SNIPPED CHIVES

Rinse and drain the arugula and pat it dry, so that the eggs won't be too wet.

In a bowl, lightly beat the eggs with dashes of salt and pepper and set aside. Warm the oil in a skillet on medium-high heat, and then add the scallions and arugula. Sprinkle with salt and cook, stirring constantly, for about 2 minutes, until the arugula has just wilted. Add the eggs, lower the heat and cook, stirring to scramble, until the eggs are set.

SERVING AND MENU IDEAS: Some whole grain toast with marmalade and you're set for breakfast. Green Eggs, No Ham is also delicious served in pita, lavash, or a wrap, with tomatoes and cheese.

GREEN EGGS, NO HAM—PER 1 SERVING (OF 3)
Calories: 223, Protein: 9 g, Carbohydrate: 3 g, Dietary Fiber: 0 g, Total Fat: 19 g, Saturated Fat: 4 g, Monounsaturated Fat: 11 g, Cholesterol: 288 mg, Sodium: 236 mg

Migas

SERVES 4 | TIME: 20 MINUTES

A breakfast, brunch, or supper dish of Mexican origin now classic in the Southwestern United States, migas is spicy eggs scrambled with crumbled corn tortillas. It's a good choice for folks on a wheat-free diet.

1 TABLESPOON OLIVE OIL

¾ CUP DICED ONIONS

¼ TEASPOON DRIED OREGANO

¼ TEASPOON RED PEPPER FLAKES

3 LARGE EGGS

3 TABLESPOONS WATER

¼ TEASPOON SALT

GENEROUS DASH OF GROUND BLACK PEPPER

2 CUPS CRUSHED CORN TORTILLA CHIPS

1 CUP DICED FRESH TOMATOES

½ CUP GRATED CHEDDAR CHEESE

1 In a skillet on medium heat, warm the oil. Add the onions, oregano, and red pepper flakes and cook, stirring often, until the onions have begun to soften, 5 or 6 minutes.

2 Meanwhile, in a bowl, whisk together the eggs, water, salt, and black pepper. Stir in the tortilla chips and set aside.

3 Add the tomatoes to the onions and continue to cook for a couple of minutes. Pour the egg mixture into the skillet and stir well. Reduce the heat to low, cover, and cook until the eggs are mostly set, 3 or 4 minutes, and then stir again. Sprinkle the cheese on top, cover, and cook until the eggs are set, about 3 or 4 minutes.

VARIATIONS: You can use chopped scallions in place of the onions: cook a minute or two before adding the tomatoes.

Use ½ cup diced bell peppers and ½ cup diced tomatoes.

Use 2 whole eggs and 2 egg whites.

Use a minced fresh chile in place of the red pepper flakes.

Try flavored tortilla chips.

SERVING AND MENU IDEAS: Migas is nice topped with chopped Spanish olives and fresh cilantro. Serve with your favorite salsa and/or Simple Guacamole (page 69) or avocado slices. Make a feast of it with Roasted Sweet Potatoes (page 299) or Winter Squash "Rice Mexicali" (page 270).

MIGAS—PER 1 SERVING (OF 4) *Calories: 351, Protein: 12 g, Carbohydrate: 31 g, Dietary Fiber: 3 g, Total Fat: 21 g, Saturated Fat: 6 g, Monounsaturated Fat: 9 g, Cholesterol: 174 mg, Sodium: 454 mg*

Egg White Omelet with Herbs

SERVES 2 | TIME: 15 MINUTES

A trio of fresh herbs and a bit of garlic boost the flavor of this light egg white omelet. Substitute whatever fresh herbs you have on hand or in your garden.

4 LARGE EGG WHITES

2 TABLESPOONS MILK

1 TABLESPOON GRATED PECORINO ROMANO OR PARMESAN CHEESE

PINCH OF SALT

1 TEASPOON CHOPPED FRESH THYME

1 TABLESPOON CHOPPED FRESH BASIL

1 TABLESPOON CHOPPED FRESH PARSLEY

1 TABLESPOON OLIVE OIL

1 GARLIC CLOVE, MINCED OR PRESSED

GROUND BLACK PEPPER

1 Whisk together the egg whites, milk, cheese, salt, and fresh herbs. Set aside.

2 In a small skillet, warm the olive oil on medium heat. Add the garlic and cook for about a minute, until golden. Pour the egg mixture into the skillet and stir briefly. Cook until the edges begin to brown and the eggs are mostly set, about 3 minutes. Flip the omelet and cook the other side until it is lightly browned, a minute or less. Season with black pepper to taste.

SERVING AND MENU IDEAS: For breakfast, serve with bagels and Vegetable Cream Cheese (page 45) and fresh fruit. For dinner, think French. How about Mushroom-Walnut Spread (page 66) with a baguette to start and then a crisp salad, such as Celeriac Apple Slaw (page 94) or Arugula, Kumquat, Walnut, and Fig Salad (page 95)?

EGG WHITE OMELET WITH HERBS—PER 1 SERVING (OF 2) *Calories: 131, Protein: 10 g, Carbohydrate: 2 g, Dietary Fiber: 0 g, Total Fat: 9 g, Saturated Fat: 2 g, Monounsaturated Fat: 5 g, Cholesterol: 6 mg, Sodium: 229 mg*

Polenta with Greens and Eggs

SERVES 4 | TIME: 30 MINUTES

To start the day happy and fortified, eat this rustic Italian dish. It is also a comforting and satisfying dinner.

POLENTA

2½ CUPS WATER

½ TEASPOON SALT

¾ CUP WHOLE GRAIN CORNMEAL (SEE PAGE 22)

2 TEASPOONS EXTRA-VIRGIN OLIVE OIL

GREENS

1 BUNCH OF SWISS CHARD (14 TO 16 OUNCES)

2 TABLESPOONS OLIVE OIL

3 GARLIC CLOVES, MINCED OR PRESSED

⅛ TEASPOON RED PEPPER FLAKES

¼ TEASPOON SALT

2 TEASPOONS BALSAMIC VINEGAR

EGGS

1 TEASPOON OLIVE OIL

4 LARGE EGGS

1 TABLESPOON WATER

1 For the polenta, in a medium saucepan on high heat, bring the water and salt to a boil. Gradually pour in the cornmeal, whisking constantly to prevent lumps. Reduce the heat to low, cover, and cook, stirring often, until thick and creamy, about 10 minutes.

2 For the greens, rinse the Swiss chard and stack the stalks on a cutting board. Cut off the stems and coarsely chop them. Then chop the leaves. In a skillet on medium heat, warm the olive oil. Add the garlic, chopped chard stems, and red pepper flakes and cook for 3 minutes. Add the chopped leaves and the salt, cover, and cook until just wilted, about 5 minutes. Toss with the vinegar, transfer to a bowl, and set aside.

3 For the eggs, in the same skillet, warm the olive oil. Gently break the eggs into the skillet, drizzle in the water, cover, and cook on low heat until the egg whites are set, about 3 minutes.

4 Spoon the polenta onto four plates and top each with Swiss chard and an egg.

VARIATION: Replace the chard with an equal amount of kale, broccoli rabe, spinach, or escarole.

SERVING AND MENU IDEAS: Top with grated Cheddar or Parmesan cheese and/or your favorite salsa. Serve sliced tomatoes on the side.

POLENTA WITH GREENS & EGGS—PER 1 SERVING (OF 4) *Calories: 260, Protein: 9 g, Carbohydrate: 23 g, Dietary Fiber: 3 g, Total Fat: 16 g, Saturated Fat: 3 g, Monounsaturated Fat: 9 g, Cholesterol: 186 mg, Sodium: 718 mg*

Caramelized Onion Omelet

SERVES 2 | TIME: 35 MINUTES

It takes a while to caramelize onions, but it's the only way to get that flavor. We suggest that whenever you make some, you make extra. They're sweet and very flavorful and we're sure you'll find many uses for them. At Moosewood, we often serve vegetarian burgers (pages 150–156) with caramelized onions on top.

1 LARGE SPANISH ONION, HALVED AND THINLY SLICED (SEE NOTE)

½ TEASPOON SALT

1 TABLESPOON OLIVE OIL

2 TABLESPOONS CHOPPED FRESH BASIL OR ½ CUP CHOPPED ARUGULA

PINCH OF GRATED NUTMEG

GROUND BLACK PEPPER

3 LARGE EGGS

2 TABLESPOONS GRATED PARMESAN AND/OR SHREDDED MOZZARELLA CHEESE

NOTE: A large Spanish onion yields about 3 cups of raw onion slices, 1 cup caramelized.

1 In a large uncovered skillet on medium-high heat, cook the onions and ¼ teaspoon of the salt in the olive oil until soft and deep golden brown, about 25 minutes; stir often and reduce the heat if they start to brown too fast. Stir in the basil or arugula and nutmeg. Sprinkle with black pepper and set aside.

2 In a medium bowl, beat the eggs and remaining ¼ teaspoon of salt. Stir in the caramelized onions and the cheese.

3 To make the omelet, lightly oil a large skillet and warm it on medium-high heat. Pour in the egg and onion mixture and tilt the pan to evenly cover the bottom. Cook until the eggs are set and the bottom is golden brown, about 3 minutes. Flip the omelet and cook on the other side until browned, a minute or two.

SERVING AND MENU IDEAS: Serve with sliced tomatoes and whole grain toast for breakfast. At dinner, serve with Greek Tomato-Yogurt Soup (page 125) or with Curried Millet (page 286) and Our Favorite Raw Slaw (page 267).

CARAMELIZED ONION OMELET—PER 1 SERVING (OF 2) *Calories: 194, Protein: 13 g, Carbohydrate: 6 g, Dietary Fiber: 1 g, Total Fat: 13 g, Saturated Fat: 3 g, Monounsaturated Fat: 7 g, Cholesterol: 216 mg, Sodium: 785 mg*

Egg Foo Yung

SERVES 4 | TIME: 40 MINUTES

One bite and you'll feel like you're dining at your favorite Chinese restaurant instead of just having eggs for dinner. This tasty Chinese-style omelet is densely packed with vegetables, which gives it a wonderful texture.

GRAVY

1 CUP WATER

1 TABLESPOON SOY SAUCE

1 TABLESPOON CORNSTARCH

A FEW DROPS OF DARK SESAME OIL

OMELET

6 LARGE EGGS

2 TEASPOONS SOY SAUCE

DASH OF GROUND BLACK PEPPER

2 TEASPOONS VEGETABLE OIL

1 TEASPOON DARK SESAME OIL

¾ CUP THINLY SLICED ONIONS

½ RED BELL PEPPER, CUT INTO THIN SLICES

2 CUPS PREPARED BROCCOLI OR CABBAGE SLAW MIX (ABOUT 6 OUNCES)

2 CUPS BEAN SPROUTS (4 OUNCES)

VEGETABLE OIL

1 To make the gravy, in a small saucepan, stir together the water, soy sauce, cornstarch, and sesame oil until smooth. Bring to a boil on high heat, stirring often. Reduce the heat and simmer, stirring constantly, for a minute, until the gravy is clear and thickened. Set aside.

2 To make the omelet, in a bowl, beat together the eggs, soy sauce, and black pepper. Set aside.

3 In a large skillet on medium-high heat, warm the vegetable oil and sesame oil. Add the onions and bell peppers and stir-fry for a couple of minutes. Add the broccoli slaw and stir-fry for a minute. Add the bean sprouts and cook another minute until the vegetables are crisp-tender.

4 Pour the beaten eggs over the vegetables and cook on low heat until the eggs are set, 5 to 6 minutes.

5 Serve the omelet topped with the gravy.

VARIATIONS: Add or substitute other vegetables: thinly sliced bok choy or snow peas, sliced water chestnuts, corn kernels, peas—just not much more than 5 cups, or the eggs won't be able to hold them all together.

SERVING AND MENU IDEAS: Serve on brown rice or with Ginger Tofu Soup (page 121). Strong hot tea is an appropriate beverage; try Ginger Orange Tea (page 44). Cantaloupe with Fresh Raspberry Sauce (page 313) is a perfect dessert.

EGG FOO YUNG—PER 1 SERVING (OF 4)
Calories: 181, Protein: 12 g, Carbohydrate: 9 g, Dietary Fiber: 2 g, Total Fat: 11 g, Saturated Fat: 2 g, Monounsaturated Fat: 5 g, Cholesterol: 217 mg, Sodium: 585 mg

APPETIZERS, SAUCES & MORE

Mushroom-Walnut Spread

YIELDS ABOUT 3 CUPS | HANDS-ON TIME: 35 MINUTES | CHILLING TIME: AT LEAST 2 HOURS

To serve as an appetizer with crudités, crackers, or pita wedges, put this spread in a beautiful bowl and decorate it with colorful tomatoes, sprigs of green parsley, or edible flowers. It also makes a tasty sandwich spread.

2 TABLESPOONS OLIVE OIL

1 CUP CHOPPED ONIONS

3 GARLIC CLOVES, CHOPPED

3 CUPS SLICED OR CHOPPED CREMINI, PORTABELLA, OR OTHER MUSHROOMS

1 TEASPOON MINCED FRESH ROSEMARY

3 TABLESPOONS DRY SHERRY OR MARSALA

SALT

¾ CUP TOASTED WALNUTS

1 15-OUNCE CAN RED KIDNEY BEANS, DRAINED

2 TABLESPOONS LIGHT MISO

¼ CUP CHOPPED FRESH PARSLEY

¼ TEASPOON GROUND BLACK PEPPER

1 Warm the oil in a skillet or saucepan on medium-low heat. Cook the onions and garlic until softened, about 6 minutes. Add the mushrooms, rosemary, and sherry, and sprinkle lightly with salt. Cover and cook until the mushrooms are soft and juicy, 5 to 10 minutes (see Note).

2 In a food processor, whirl the walnuts until finely chopped. Add the beans and the mushroom mixture and process until smooth, stopping to scrape down the sides of the bowl (see Note). Add the miso, parsley, and black pepper and process briefly; it's nice to see little flecks of green parsley.

3 Chill well before serving.

NOTE: Different mushrooms cooked in different pans on different heat levels will produce different amounts of juice. If your mushrooms are very juicy when cooked, spoon them into the food processor and then add just enough juice to make a smooth, moist spread. If there isn't enough mushroom juice, add some water or some of the bean liquid.

VARIATIONS: Replace the rosemary with fresh thyme, or use both.

Add chives or scallions in place of or in addition to parsley.

Use pecans instead of walnuts.

SERVING AND MENU IDEAS: Serve as an appetizer before Greener Spanakopita (page 186) or Pasta with Ruby Chard and Cherries (page 235). Or serve as a spread on rye bread and pair with Chilled Beet Borscht (page 135) or Raw Broccoli Salad (page 97).

MUSHROOM-WALNUT SPREAD—PER ½ CUP
Calories: 218, Protein: 7 g, Carbohydrate: 18 g, Dietary Fiber: 5 g, Total Fat: 13 g, Saturated Fat: 2 g, Monounsaturated Fat: 5 g, Cholesterol: 0 mg, Sodium: 323 mg

Chinese Vegetable Garden Pickles

YIELDS 5 TO 6 CUPS | HANDS-ON TIME: 25 MINUTES | PRESSING TIME: 2 HOURS | PICKLING TIME: OVERNIGHT

Rice vinegar provides a mellow undertone for these crisp, bright, gingery pickled veggies with a hint of anise. Best of all, the technique is easy and these pickles are excellent keepers.

RAW VEGETABLES SUCH AS CARROTS, CAULIFLOWER, RED PEPPERS, DAIKON, GREEN CABBAGE, AND RED ONIONS

1 TABLESPOON PLUS 1 TEASPOON SALT

2 CUPS WATER

1 CUP RICE VINEGAR

2 TEASPOONS SUGAR

1 TABLESPOON DRIED PEPPERCORNS (RED, GREEN, WHITE, AND/OR BLACK)

1½ TABLESPOONS MINCED PEELED GINGER ROOT

¼ TO ½ TEASPOON RED PEPPER FLAKES

1 PIECE STAR ANISE

---

1 Wash, trim, peel, and chop the vegetables into bite-sized pieces, enough to make 6 cups. (It looks pretty when the vegetables have different shapes; for instance, angular carrot slices, cauliflower florets, round or half-moon daikon, and half circles of red onion.) Toss the vegetables with 1 tablespoon of the salt and place them in a colander over a bowl or in the sink. Cover the vegetables with a plate and weight with a heavy book or can for 2 hours.

2 While the vegetables are pressing, in a nonreactive saucepan, stir together the water, vinegar, sugar, 1 teaspoon of salt, peppercorns, ginger root, red pepper flakes, and star anise. Bring to a boil, and then reduce the heat and simmer for 5 minutes. Set aside to cool.

3 After 2 hours, the vegetables will be somewhat reduced in volume. Rinse well and drain thoroughly, pressing to remove most of the water. Place the vegetables in a bowl or large jar, pour the vinegar mixture over them, and stir or invert several times. Cover and refrigerate overnight.

4 Will keep refrigerated in a closed container for 3 weeks.

SERVING AND MENU IDEAS: Serve these as a colorful, zesty appetizer before Bok Choy and Country-style Soft Tofu (page 166), Orange-Glazed Tofu on Greens (page 180), or Cabbage with Fermented Black Beans (page 171). We also like to use them to garnish salads.

CHINESE VEGETABLE GARDEN PICKLES—PER 1 CUP
Calories: 84, Protein: 1 g, Carbohydrate: 9 g, Dietary Fiber: 2 g, Total Fat: 0 g, Saturated Fat: 0 g, Monounsaturated Fat: 0 g, Cholesterol: 0 mg, Sodium: 412 mg

Mango Pickles

YIELDS ABOUT 3 CUPS | HANDS-ON TIME: 20 MINUTES | SITTING TIME: AT LEAST A DAY

A perfect garnish for Indian, Southeast Asian, and Caribbean dishes, these unusual pickles are tart, with a little sweet, a little bite, and the delightful crunch of mustard seeds. Make them at least a day ahead so the flavors can develop.

1 UNRIPE MANGO
1 TEASPOON GRATED LIME ZEST
1 TABLESPOON LIME JUICE
1 TEASPOON GRATED PEELED GINGER ROOT
2 TEASPOONS MINCED FRESH CHILES
¼ TEASPOON SALT
2 TEASPOONS VEGETABLE OIL
1 TEASPOON BLACK OR YELLOW MUSTARD SEEDS

1   Peel and pit the mango, cut the flesh into bite-sized pieces, and place them in a small bowl. Add the lime zest, lime juice, ginger, chiles, and salt and mix well.

2   In a small skillet on medium-high heat, warm the oil and then add the mustard seeds, stirring until the seeds start to pop. Cover and cook for about a minute, until they stop popping, but take care that they don't scorch. Add the hot oil and mustard seeds to the bowl and stir well. Cover and refrigerate for a day or two to allow the flavors to meld. The pickles will be spicy hot at first, but will mellow with time. They will keep refrigerated in a closed container for a week.

SERVING AND MENU IDEAS: Mango Pickles add a fresh, piquant counterpoint served with Creamy Curried Pea Soup (page 126), Caribbean Stuffed Sweet Potatoes (page 195), Southeast Asian Tofu with Lemongrass (page 183), Tempeh-Quinoa Burgers (page 152), or Down-home Black-eyed Peas (page 221).

MANGO PICKLES—PER ¾ CUP *Calories: 60, Protein: 1 g, Carbohydrate: 10 g, Dietary Fiber: 1 g, Total Fat: 3 g, Saturated Fat: 0 g, Monounsaturated Fat: 2 g, Cholesterol: 0 mg, Sodium: 147 mg*

Simple Guacamole

YIELDS 1 GENEROUS CUP | TIME: 10 MINUTES

When the avocados are wonderful, a simple, straightforward guacamole is wonderful too.

2 LARGE RIPE HASS AVOCADOS
2 TABLESPOONS LEMON OR LIME JUICE
¼ TEASPOON SALT
1½ TABLESPOONS MINCED RED ONIONS (OPTIONAL)
PINCH OF CAYENNE OR DASH OF TABASCO OR OTHER HOT PEPPER SAUCE (OPTIONAL)

Slice lengthwise around each avocado down to the pit. Twist the halves apart, and remove the pit. Scoop out the flesh and mash it in a bowl. Stir in the lemon juice and salt, adding more to taste. Stir in the red onions and cayenne, if using. Serve immediately.

SERVING AND MENU IDEAS: Serve with tortilla chips, whole grain chips, crisp crackers, or whole wheat toast. Good with Migas (page 59) or Oaxacan Tlayuda (page 219), or on top of Southwestern Black Bean Burgers (page 154). Serve as a dip with crudités before New World Pizza (page 188) or as a sandwich spread topped with tomato slices to go with Latin Corn Soup (page 128).

SIMPLE GUACAMOLE—PER ¼ CUP *Calories: 163, Protein: 2 g, Carbohydrate: 9 g, Dietary Fiber: 7 g, Total Fat: 15 g, Saturated Fat: 2 g, Monounsaturated Fat: 10 g, Cholesterol: 0 mg, Sodium: 153 mg*

Toasted Pepitas and Cranberries

YIELDS 2 GENEROUS CUPS | HANDS-ON TIME: 5 MINUTES | BAKING TIME: 10 MINUTES

Pumpkin seeds (pepitas) are crisp, dried cranberries are chewy, and together in this recipe, they are deliciously sweet and a little salty. A wonderful garnish for salads and soups, but just as likely to disappear as an irresistible snack.

1½ CUPS SHELLED PUMPKIN SEEDS

1 TABLESPOON SOY SAUCE

1 TEASPOON OLIVE OIL

½ TEASPOON DRIED THYME (OPTIONAL) (SEE NOTE)

¾ CUP DRIED CRANBERRIES, CHOPPED

1 Spread the pumpkin seeds on a baking sheet and toast in a preheated 375° oven for 7 or 8 minutes, just until they begin to darken.

2 Meanwhile, in a small bowl, whisk together the soy sauce, olive oil, and thyme, if using.

3 Remove the toasted pumpkin seeds from the oven, and while still hot, drizzle them with the soy sauce mixture and stir to coat. Put them back in the oven for a couple of minutes, taking care not to let them burn. When they have cooled, stir in the cranberries. Store in a closed container at room temperature.

NOTE: Commercially packaged dried thyme varies in quality and strength. Fresh thyme dries in a day or two at room temperature, and then the leaves can be easily stripped from the stems and crumbled for a vibrant, fresh taste. Store in the pantry or freezer.

SERVING AND MENU IDEAS: These are great to nibble on while sipping one of the Four Fruit Smoothies (pages 42–43). Sprinkle as a garnish on Sweet Potato, Apple, and Chipotle Soup (page 132), Curried Yellow Pepper Soup (page 115), or Wild Rice Pilaf with Chestnuts (page 288).

TOASTED PEPITAS AND CRANBERRIES—PER ¼ CUP
Calories: 178, Protein: 6 g, Carbohydrate: 13 g, Dietary Fiber: 2 g, Total Fat: 13 g, Saturated Fat: 2 g, Monounsaturated Fat: 4 g, Cholesterol: 0 mg, Sodium: 118 mg

Yellow Split Pea Dip

YIELDS ABOUT 4 CUPS | TIME: ABOUT 1 HOUR

Serve Yellow Split Pea Dip to up the protein quotient of a meal, or simply because it's a delicious spread on bread or dip for vegetables.

1 CUP CHOPPED CARROTS

1 CELERY STALK, COARSELY CHOPPED

2 CUPS CHOPPED ONIONS

1 CUP YELLOW SPLIT PEAS

4 CUPS WATER

3 TABLESPOONS LEMON JUICE

3 TABLESPOONS OLIVE OIL

¼ CUP COARSELY CHOPPED FRESH PARSLEY

1 TEASPOON SALT

DASH OF GROUND PEPPER

1 Put the carrots, celery, onions, split peas, and water into a saucepan, cover, and bring to a boil. Reduce the heat and simmer uncovered until the split peas are very soft, about 45 minutes. Ideally, the water will be completely absorbed by the time the split peas are cooked. If needed, add water in small amounts during cooking; or if there is liquid left when the split peas are done, drain, reserving the liquid.

2 In a food processor, whirl the vegetable-pea mixture, lemon juice, olive oil, parsley, salt, and pepper until fairly smooth. If necessary to reach the consistency you prefer, add some water or reserved cooking liquid.

3 Serve warm or chilled. Will keep refrigerated in a covered container for a week.

SERVING AND MENU IDEAS: Serve with wedges of toasted whole wheat pita and a colorful array of crudités, such as radish halves, sugar snap peas, broccoli and cauliflower florets, carrot and celery sticks, and strips of bell peppers. It's good before Greek Tomato-Yogurt Soup (page 125), Greener Spanakopita (page 186), Quinoa and Collard Leaf Dolmas (page 200), or Pasta with Grape Tomatoes and Feta (page 237). For a salad plate, serve it with Cauliflower "Tabouli" (page 269) and pita bread.

YELLOW SPLIT PEA DIP—PER ½ CUP *Calories: 155, Protein: 7 g, Carbohydrate: 21 g, Dietary Fiber: 8 g, Total Fat: 5 g, Saturated Fat: 1 g, Monounsaturated Fat: 4 g, Cholesterol: 0 mg, Sodium: 318 mg*

Spicy Eggplant Spread

YIELDS ABOUT 3½ CUPS | TIME: ABOUT AN HOUR

This classic Indian dish, *Bhaigan Bhartha* (or *Baigan Bharta*), is spicy, smoky, and intense. It's versatile enough to be served with any Indian meal, as an appetizer, side dish, or even the main dish, but don't wait till you're cooking a theme dinner to try it. It can be eaten hot or cold and keeps well (for at least a week) in the refrigerator.

2 MEDIUM EGGPLANTS
(ABOUT 1 POUND EACH)

2 TABLESPOONS VEGETABLE OIL

1½ TEASPOONS CUMIN SEEDS

1½ CUPS CHOPPED ONIONS

1 TABLESPOON GRATED PEELED GINGER ROOT

3 OR 4 GARLIC CLOVES, MINCED OR PRESSED

1 OR 2 FRESH CHILES, FINELY CHOPPED

2 CUPS CHOPPED FRESH TOMATOES

1 TEASPOON SALT

¼ CUP CHOPPED FRESH CILANTRO

1 Prick the eggplants a few times with a fork, put them on a baking sheet, and roast in a preheated 425° oven until soft, 30 minutes or so. Remove from the oven and set aside to cool.

2 While the eggplants roast, heat the oil in a large skillet on medium-high heat, add the cumin seeds and let them sizzle for about 20 seconds, and then add the onions, ginger, and garlic. Lower the heat to medium-low and cook, stirring often, until the onions are translucent and starting to brown, about 12 minutes. Add the chiles, tomatoes, and salt and cook on low heat, stirring occasionally, until the tomatoes are soft and their juice has mostly evaporated, about 15 minutes.

3 When the eggplants have cooled enough to handle, cut them in half lengthwise, scoop out the flesh, coarsely chop it, and add it to the skillet. Stir in the cilantro and cook for about 5 minutes, until everything is heated through. Serve warm or chilled. For a smooth spread, whirl in a food processor.

VARIATIONS: For a more traditional smoked flavor, grill the eggplants. Or cook them directly on a gas flame, turning carefully with tongs, until all sides are charred and the eggplant is soft throughout, about 30 minutes. This will make something of a mess on your stove, and may set off your smoke detector, but imparts a lovely smoky flavor. When the eggplants have cooled enough to handle, remove as much of the charred peel as you can.

Substitute parsley or basil for the cilantro.

SERVING AND MENU IDEAS: Serve as an appetizer with Indian breads, or crackers, or pita. This makes a great dinner served on rice and topped with yogurt. And it's a delicious accompaniment to Chickpea Crêpes (page 73).

SPICY EGGPLANT SPREAD—PER ½ CUP *Calories: 97, Protein: 2 g, Carbohydrate: 14 g, Dietary Fiber: 6 g, Total Fat: 4 g, Saturated Fat: 0 g, Monounsaturated Fat: 2 g, Cholesterol: 0 mg, Sodium: 341 mg*

Chickpea Crêpes

YIELDS 5 OR 6 CREPES | TIME: 40 MINUTES

The nutty flavor of chickpea flour and golden spices of India make these thin, lacy, golden-brown crêpes perfect with any Indian meal. The batter can be refrigerated for a day or two; it separates, so whisk well before using. This recipe is gluten-free.

| 1 CUP CHICKPEA FLOUR (SEE NOTE) |
| 1 CUP WATER |
| ½ TEASPOON SALT |
| ¼ TEASPOON GROUND TURMERIC |
| ¼ TEASPOON CAYENNE |
| 2 TEASPOONS GRATED PEELED GINGER ROOT |
| VEGETABLE OIL |
| ½ TEASPOON BLACK MUSTARD SEEDS |
| ½ TEASPOON CUMIN SEEDS |
| 2 GARLIC CLOVES, MINCED (OPTIONAL) |
| 2 TABLESPOONS CHOPPED CILANTRO AND/OR SCALLIONS (OPTIONAL) |
| VEGETABLE OIL SPRAY (OPTIONAL) |

1 In a bowl, whisk together the chickpea flour (sifted if lumpy), water, salt, turmeric, cayenne, and ginger until smooth. Set aside.

2 In a small skillet on medium heat, warm 1 tablespoon oil. Add the mustard and cumin seeds, cover, and cook until the mustard seeds begin to pop. Remove from the heat and stir in the garlic, if using, and let it sizzle for a moment. Whisk the mixture into the batter. Stir in the cilantro, if using.

3 Warm a lightly oiled or sprayed 8- to 10-inch skillet on medium heat. (Use a crêpe pan or a skillet with sloping sides. A smaller pan is fine, but use less batter for each crêpe, because if the crêpe is too thick, it will be gummy in the middle.) Pour ⅓ cup of batter into the skillet and tilt the pan to spread the batter thinly over the bottom and up the sides. Cook covered for about 2 minutes, until firm and golden on the bottom. Drizzle a little oil around the edges of the crêpe and turn it over. Cook uncovered for a minute or two. Continue with the remaining batter, coating the pan with more oil as needed. The crêpes cool down quickly, so either serve each as it comes out of the pan, or stack them on a plate in a warm oven until all are cooked.

NOTE: Chickpea flour (also called garbanzo flour, *besan,* and gram flour) is a pale yellow, finely ground flour used in Indian cuisine. Look for it in the international sections of large supermarkets.

VARIATIONS: Use minced fresh chiles instead of cayenne.

If you make the crêpes without drizzling oil around the edges before you cook them on the second side, the outer edge will be soft rather than crisp.

SERVING AND MENU IDEAS: These crêpes are delicious all by themselves, or try them with Curried Yellow Pepper Soup (page 115), Spicy Eggplant Spread (page 72), or Pineapple and Tomato Salad (page 87).

CHICKPEA CRÊPES—PER 1 SERVING (OF 6), 1 CRÊPE *Calories: 83, Protein: 4 g, Carbohydrate: 9 g, Dietary Fiber: 2 g, Total Fat: 4 g, Saturated Fat: 0 g, Monounsaturated Fat: 2 g, Cholesterol: 0 mg, Sodium: 205 mg*

Romesco Sauce

YIELDS ABOUT 1¾ CUPS | TIME: 35 MINUTES

There are many variations on this slightly spicy, lightly smoky sauce from the Catalan region of Spain. All share the richness of nuts and the heat of chiles.

1 DRIED ANCHO CHILE (SEE NOTE)

⅓ CUP EXTRA-VIRGIN OLIVE OIL

2 GARLIC CLOVES, SLICED

¼ TEASPOON RED PEPPER FLAKES

1 SLICE WHOLE WHEAT BREAD, LIGHTLY TOASTED AND CRUMBLED

¾ CUP CHOPPED FRESH TOMATOES

⅓ CUP TOASTED HAZELNUTS OR ALMONDS

⅔ CUP DRAINED CANNED ROASTED RED PEPPERS

1 TABLESPOON RED WINE VINEGAR

¾ TEASPOON SALT

GROUND BLACK PEPPER

1 In a small bowl, pour boiling water over the ancho chile to cover and soak for about 15 minutes. Drain, remove the stem, chop, and set aside.

2 Meanwhile, warm the oil in a small skillet on medium-low heat and cook the garlic just until it begins to show color. Add the red pepper flakes, bread, and tomatoes. Cook for 3 minutes, stirring well to coat the bread with the garlicky oil and to soften the tomato a bit. Remove from the heat.

3 In a food processor, briefly whirl the nuts to chop coarsely. Add all the other ingredients including the soaked ancho and process until the sauce is fairly smooth. Add the salt and a dash of black pepper.

4 Romesco can be made ahead of time and refrigerated, but allow it to warm a bit at room temperature before serving. It will keep refrigerated in a covered container for a week.

NOTE: Dried ancho chiles, available at well-stocked supermarkets and specialty stores that carry Latin American foods, add a flavor that's more complex than simply spicy hot. If you can't find them, increase the red pepper flakes.

SERVING AND MENU IDEAS: Romesco Sauce makes a tasty dip for raw vegetables, spread for crusty bread, or sauce for grilled or steamed vegetables. Serve Spanish Stew (page 246) with a dollop of Romesco Sauce; add some to any simple omelet, soup, or stew that will benefit from a little kick or enrichment. Use it as the sauce on Vegetable Sauté Capriccio (page 170). Top baked sweet potatoes with Romesco, or put a spoonful in the center of a cooked artichoke.

ROMESCO SAUCE—PER ¼ CUP *Calories: 157, Protein: 1 g, Carbohydrate: 5 g, Dietary Fiber: 1 g, Total Fat: 15 g, Saturated Fat: 2 g, Monounsaturated Fat: 11 g, Cholesterol: 0 mg, Sodium: 510 mg*

Pineapple Salsa with Blueberries

YIELDS ABOUT 3 CUPS | HANDS-ON TIME: 20 MINUTES | SITTING TIME: BEST AFTER AN HOUR

In this festive-looking salsa, the sweet flavor of fruit is spiked with chiles, lemon, and garlic. It's a great way to get more good-for-you blueberries into your diet.

---

2 CUPS CHOPPED FRESH PINEAPPLE

1 SMALL FRESH CHILE, MINCED

¼ CUP CHOPPED FRESH PARSLEY

2 GARLIC CLOVES, PRESSED OR MINCED

2 TABLESPOONS LEMON JUICE

1 TABLESPOON OLIVE OIL OR EXTRA-VIRGIN OLIVE OIL

¼ TEASPOON SALT

½ CUP PEELED, SEEDED, AND DICED CUCUMBERS

½ CUP MINCED RED OR ORANGE BELL PEPPERS

¾ CUP FRESH BLUEBERRIES

1 TABLESPOON CHOPPED CHIVES OR SCALLIONS

---

1 In a food processor, pulse 1 cup of the pineapple and the chile, parsley, garlic, lemon juice, olive oil, and salt just until minced, not smoothly puréed. Transfer to a bowl and stir in the remaining pineapple and the cucumbers, bell peppers, blueberries, and chives.

2 If you have time to set the salsa aside for at least 30 minutes, the flavors will meld and mature; after an hour or two it will really come into its own.

3 Serve at room temperature. Covered and refrigerated, this salsa will keep for 3 days.

VARIATIONS: Instead of fresh pineapple, use an undrained 20-ounce can of pineapple in its own juice (crushed or small chunks).

Use frozen blueberries (we like the smaller wild blueberries in this salsa). Rinse briefly under tap water to remove any frost and add directly to the salsa; they'll thaw in a few minutes.

SERVING AND MENU IDEAS: Makes a delicious and unusual dip for tortilla chips. Serve as a topping for Southwestern Black Bean Burgers (page 154) or beside Oaxacan Tlayuda (page 219). Or use it as the salsa for Southwestern Scramble (page 39).

PINEAPPLE SALSA WITH BLUEBERRIES—PER ¼ CUP
Calories: 33, Protein: 0 g, Carbohydrate: 6 g, Dietary Fiber: 1 g, Total Fat: 1 g, Saturated Fat: 0 g, Monounsaturated Fat: 1 g, Cholesterol: 0 mg, Sodium: 50 mg

Egg-Lemon Sauce

YIELDS ABOUT 1¼ CUPS | TIME: 10 TO 15 MINUTES

This is a classic Greek sauce, but we recommend that you don't limit it to Greek meals. It's a fast and easy way to gild stuffed grape leaves or a variety of stuffed vegetables. Or use it to jazz up steamed vegetables and rice.

¾ CUP VEGETABLE BROTH (SEE PAGE 33)

¼ CUP LEMON JUICE

1 TEASPOON CORNSTARCH

2 LARGE EGGS

¼ TEASPOON SALT

GENEROUS DASH OF GROUND BLACK PEPPER

1 TEASPOON CHOPPED FRESH DILL (OPTIONAL)

1 In a small saucepan, bring ½ cup of the broth and the lemon juice to a boil on high heat.

2 Meanwhile, in a bowl, dissolve the cornstarch in the remaining ¼ cup of broth and then whisk in the eggs. When the lemon-broth boils, pour in the egg mixture in a thin steady stream, stirring constantly. Reduce the heat to low and cook, stirring constantly, until the sauce thickens, about a minute. Be careful not to let it boil or the eggs may curdle. Add the salt, black pepper, and dill if you wish.

SERVING AND MENU IDEAS: Especially good with steamed broccoli or asparagus spears, or as a dip for artichokes. Try some on Quinoa and Collard Leaf Dolmas (page 200).

EGG LEMON SAUCE—PER 1 TABLESPOON *Calories: 9, Protein: 1 g, Carbohydrate: 1 g, Dietary Fiber: 0 g, Total Fat: 0 g, Saturated Fat: 0 g, Monounsaturated Fat: 0 g, Cholesterol: 21 mg, Sodium: 41 mg*

Toasted Sesame Sauce

YIELDS ABOUT 1 ½ CUPS | TIME: 15 MINUTES

We've been making our always-popular version of Sichuan noodles, using peanut butter, since the 1970s. Toasted Sesame Sauce is a more recent variation, and it's especially appreciated by our customers who have allergies to nuts, but no problems eating seeds.

We call for a mild to moderate amount of hot chili paste in the recipe, but add more to taste. Some of us, who like it hot, make it *really* hot.

2 TABLESPOONS VEGETABLE OIL

1 CUP BROWN SESAME SEEDS

3 TABLESPOONS SOY SAUCE

3 TABLESPOONS RICE VINEGAR

1 ½ TABLESPOONS PURE MAPLE SYRUP, HONEY, OR BROWN SUGAR

1 TEASPOON CHINESE CHILI PASTE

½ TO 1 CUP WATER

1 In a small skillet on medium-low heat, warm the oil. Add the sesame seeds and cook, stirring constantly, until the seeds are fragrant and make a popping sound, 3 or 4 minutes.

2 In a blender, combine the toasted sesame seeds, soy sauce, vinegar, sweetener, Chinese chili paste, and ½ cup of the water and purée until the seeds are ground and the sauce is fairly smooth. Add more water to reach the consistency you prefer. The sauce sometimes thickens slightly as it sits. Add more soy sauce and/or Chinese chili paste to taste.

3 Covered and refrigerated, the sauce will keep for at least a week. If it separates, whisk until smooth.

VARIATIONS: If you don't have rice vinegar, use cider vinegar or white vinegar.

You can replace Chinese chili paste with minced fresh chiles and garlic to taste.

SERVING AND MENU IDEAS: Add more or less water to the sauce to create a pourable sauce for noodles, a spread for bread, or a thick dip for vegetable crudités and crackers. Use this sauce on linguine, udon or soba noodles, or steamed vegetables and rice. It makes a zesty salad dressing. Here's a great meal: Coat noodles with Toasted Sesame Sauce, and serve with steamed carrots and broccoli and An Easy Baked Tofu (page 177).

TOASTED SESAME SAUCE—PER 1 TABLESPOON
Calories: 53, Protein: 1 g, Carbohydrate: 3 g, Dietary Fiber: 1 g, Total Fat: 4 g, Saturated Fat: 1 g, Monounsaturated Fat: 2 g, Cholesterol: 0 mg, Sodium: 116 mg

Creamy Tomato Sauce

YIELDS 4 GENEROUS CUPS | TIME: 45 MINUTES

We've noticed that there are a number of popular cookbooks out there based on the assumption that good parents have to sneak vegetables into the diets of their unsuspecting children who otherwise would refuse to eat them. Well, whether the vegetables in this attractive, smooth sauce are stealth or not, it's a delicious and versatile topping for pasta, rice, polenta, or even other vegetables.

2 TABLESPOONS OLIVE OIL

1 CUP CHOPPED ONIONS

2 GARLIC CLOVES, MINCED OR PRESSED

½ CUP GRATED OR MINCED CARROTS

½ CUP DICED RED OR ORANGE BELL PEPPERS

¼ TEASPOON SALT

¼ TEASPOON GROUND BLACK PEPPER

½ TEASPOON DRIED OREGANO

½ TEASPOON GROUND FENNEL

2 TABLESPOONS RED WINE (OPTIONAL)

1 28-OUNCE CAN DICED TOMATOES

¼ CUP CHOPPED FRESH BASIL

⅓ CUP NEUFCHÂTEL CHEESE (ABOUT 2½ OUNCES)

1 Warm the oil in a saucepan on medium-low heat. Add the onions and garlic and cook for about 5 minutes until the onions begin to soften. Add the carrots, bell peppers, salt, black pepper, oregano, fennel, and wine, if using. Cover and cook, stirring occasionally, until the vegetables are quite soft, about 8 minutes.

2 Add the tomatoes and simmer for 10 to 15 minutes, stirring occasionally. Cook covered unless the sauce seems too thin. Stir in the basil and neufchâtel. In a blender or food processor, purée the sauce until smooth. Add more salt and pepper to taste.

VARIATIONS: Zucchini or yellow squash can be used instead of bell peppers, but will make a thinner sauce.

Grated sweet potatoes or winter squash can replace carrots.

Add some chopped fresh fennel.

The sauce can be made without the neufchâtel.

SERVING AND MENU IDEAS: Use any time a tomato sauce is needed; this is perfect for over ravioli or gnocchi or whole grain pasta. Use as the sauce on Polenta Domes with Garlicky Greens (page 282), to top Tofu, Leek, and Almond Stuffed Portabellas (page 193), or as the sauce on Vegetable Sauté Capriccio (page 170).

CREAMY TOMATO SAUCE—PER ¼ CUP *Calories: 48, Protein: 1 g, Carbohydrate: 4 g, Dietary Fiber: 1 g, Total Fat: 3 g, Saturated Fat: 1 g, Monounsaturated Fat: 2 g, Cholesterol: 5 mg, Sodium: 66 mg*

Two Nut-free Pestos

Both sunflower seeds and pumpkin seeds are an economical alternative to pine nuts in pesto, and with seeds you can create a tasty pesto for people who are allergic to nuts. Fresh basil is, of course, a must. The pepita pesto gets additional flavor from both fresh and sun-dried tomatoes. Each of these pestos makes a good spread, dip, or pasta topping. Make extra; they keep well in the freezer.

Sunflower Pesto

YIELDS ABOUT 1 CUP | TIME: 10 MINUTES

½ CUP TOASTED SUNFLOWER SEEDS

1 OR 2 GARLIC CLOVES, CHOPPED

⅓ CUP OLIVE OIL

¼ TEASPOON SALT

PINCH OF GROUND BLACK PEPPER

2 PACKED CUPS FRESH BASIL LEAVES

⅓ CUP GRATED PARMESAN CHEESE (OPTIONAL)

In a food processor, pulse the sunflower seeds and garlic until crumbly. Add the olive oil, salt, pepper, basil, and Parmesan, if using. Whirl until quite smooth.

NOTE: For a milder flavor, gently cook the garlic in a tablespoon of the olive oil for 1 minute in either a small saucepan or the microwave oven.

SERVING AND MENU IDEAS: Use as a spread for crackers, toast, or sandwiches. Toss with pasta, steamed green beans, and ripe tomatoes.

SUNFLOWER PESTO—PER 2 TABLESPOONS
Calories: 130, Protein: 2 g, Carbohydrate: 3 g, Dietary Fiber: 1 g, Total Fat: 13 g, Saturated Fat: 2 g, Monounsaturated Fat: 7 g, Cholesterol: 0 mg, Sodium: 74 mg

Pepita and Sun-dried Tomato Pesto

YIELDS ABOUT 1¾ CUPS | TIME: 20 MINUTES

½ CUP SUN-DRIED TOMATOES

½ CUP SHELLED PUMPKIN SEEDS (PEPITAS)

2 GARLIC CLOVES, CHOPPED

⅓ CUP OLIVE OIL OR EXTRA-VIRGIN OLIVE OIL

2 PACKED CUPS FRESH BASIL LEAVES

½ CUP CHOPPED FRESH TOMATOES

¼ TEASPOON SALT

GENEROUS DASH OF GROUND BLACK PEPPER

1 In a small pan on the stovetop or in a bowl in the microwave oven, bring to a boil the sun-dried tomatoes covered with water and then set aside until softened, at least 5 minutes. Drain and chop.

2 In a food processor, whirl the pumpkin seeds, garlic, oil, basil, fresh tomatoes, salt, pepper, and softened sun-dried tomatoes until smooth.

SERVING AND MENU IDEAS: Great as a dip for tortilla chips or crudités. Add a dollop to perk up your favorite bean soup or vegetable stew.

PEPITA AND SUN-DRIED TOMATO PESTO—
PER 2 TABLESPOONS *Calories: 81, Protein: 2 g, Carbohydrate: 3 g, Dietary Fiber: 1 g, Total Fat: 8 g, Saturated Fat: 1 g, Monounsaturated Fat: 4 g, Cholesterol: 0 mg, Sodium: 84 mg*

Three Herbed and Spiced Salts

Herbed and spiced salts are not new. Cooks have been making them for generations, and you can find them in supermarkets and health food stores. Making your own, however, is worth the time it takes, because the difference between a commercial seasoned salt and the ones you can make from scratch is fairly dramatic.

Freshly made seasoned salts are excellent enhancements for all kinds of dishes. They're a great way to cut down on salt intake, capitalizing on flavor instead of mere saltiness. We call for coarse sea salt, but finely ground sea salt may also be used.

Indian-Spiced Salt

YIELDS ABOUT ⅓ CUP | TIME: 15 MINUTES

Spice up your favorite salad, soup, rice, vegetable, or grain dishes with a little of this Indian-style seasoned salt. We love it sprinkled on a baked sweet potato.

3 TABLESPOONS BROWN SESAME SEEDS
1 TABLESPOON CORIANDER SEEDS
1 TABLESPOON CUMIN SEEDS
¼ TEASPOON RED PEPPER FLAKES
1½ TEASPOONS COARSE SEA SALT

1 In a heavy skillet on medium-low heat, toast all of the seeds for 3 to 4 minutes. Cool thoroughly. Place the seeds, red pepper flakes, and salt in a spice grinder and whirl for a few seconds.

2 Stored in a glass jar in the refrigerator, Indian-Spiced Salt will stay flavorful for about a month.

Aromatico

YIELDS ABOUT ⅓ CUP | TIME: 15 MINUTES

Aromatico is a Mediterranean-style seasoned salt with pungent and deeply scented flavors. The salt seems to preserve the intensity of the fresh herbs. Use on steamed vegetables, soup, pasta, eggs, and grain dishes calling for Mediterranean flavors. Sprinkle it on sliced fresh tomatoes drizzled with olive oil.

3 TABLESPOONS FENNEL SEEDS
1½ TEASPOONS COARSE SEA SALT
1½ TEASPOONS MINCED FRESH ROSEMARY
1 TABLESPOON MINCED FRESH THYME

1 In a heavy skillet on medium-low heat, toast the fennel seeds for 3 to 4 minutes, stirring or shaking the pan occasionally. Cool thoroughly. Place the fennel seeds and salt in a spice grinder and whirl for a few seconds. Stir in the minced fresh herbs.

2 Stored in a glass jar in the refrigerator, Aromatico will keep for about a month.

Gomasio

YIELDS ABOUT ⅓ CUP | TIME: 15 MINUTES

Gomasio is the Japanese name for a classic seasoning made of salt and sesame seeds. Store sesame seeds in a tightly sealed container in the freezer for up to six months to retain freshness. Maximize their flavor by toasting the seeds yourself. Try Gomasio on rice, hot cereal, vegetables, and tofu. It's especially good on steamed or sautéed broccoli or spinach.

3 TABLESPOONS BROWN SESAME SEEDS
1½ TEASPOONS COARSE SEA SALT

1 In a heavy skillet on medium-low heat, toast the sesame seeds for 4 to 5 minutes, until aromatic, stirring or shaking the pan occasionally. Let stand for a few minutes, until cool to the touch. Place the sesame seeds and salt in a spice grinder and whirl for a few seconds just to blend the ingredients. Gomasio should retain some of the texture of the seeds.

2 Stored in a glass jar in the refrigerator, Gomasio will stay flavorful for 3 to 4 weeks.

VARIATION: Replace ¼ teaspoon of the salt with nori flakes. Grind a sheet of toasted nori (see page 91) for a heaping tablespoon of small flakes.

SALADS

Spinach Salad with Chèvre and Walnuts

SERVES 4 | TIME: 20 MINUTES

Soft spinach leaves and creamy goat cheese contrast beautifully with crunchy walnuts and chewy kalamata olives.

DRESSING

½ TEASPOON GRATED LEMON ZEST

1 TABLESPOON LEMON JUICE

¼ TEASPOON SALT

⅛ TEASPOON RED AND BLACK PEPPER (SEE NOTES)

¼ CUP OLIVE OIL

2 TABLESPOONS MILK

SALAD

6 CUPS BABY SPINACH (ABOUT 8 OUNCES)

¼ CUP THINLY SLICED RED ONIONS

4 OUNCES CHÈVRE

12 KALAMATA OR OIL-CURED BLACK OLIVES, PITTED

½ CUP CHOPPED TOASTED WALNUTS

1 To make the dressing, put the lemon zest, lemon juice, salt, and red and black pepper in a serving bowl. Whisk in the olive oil, then the milk, until smooth.

2 Add the spinach and red onions to the serving bowl. Cut the chèvre into slices or small cubes, slice or chop the olives, and sprinkle both over the salad. Toss gently to distribute the dressing well (see Notes). Just before serving, sprinkle the walnuts on the salad.

NOTES: In a spice grinder or with a mortar and pestle, crush together equal parts of red pepper flakes and black peppercorns. Use some for this recipe and set aside the rest for other cooking. Or just use black or red pepper.

If the salad is going to sit for more than a few minutes after preparation, make the dressing in a separate bowl and toss it with the spinach just before serving.

SERVING AND MENU IDEAS: This salad goes well with Greek Tomato-Yogurt Soup (page 125), Greek Lentil Burgers (page 155), or Greek Pizza (page 190), as well as quite a few dishes that aren't Greek. Try it as a prelude to Ratatouille Rice (page 281), Pasta with Tomato-Peach Sauce (page 233), or Italian Sweet Potato Gratin (page 199).

SPINACH SALAD WITH CHÈVRE AND WALNUTS— PER 1 SERVING (OF 4), DRESSED *Calories: 226, Protein: 10 g, Carbohydrate: 6 g, Dietary Fiber: 2 g, Total Fat: 19 g, Saturated Fat: 7 g, Monounsaturated Fat: 4 g, Cholesterol: 21 mg, Sodium: 242 mg*

Curly Endive with Hazelnuts, Raspberries, and Manchego

SERVES 4 | TIME: 30 MINUTES

Any bitter green—frisée, curly endive, arugula—is good in this salad of complex flavors. The toasty hazelnuts, sweet-tart raspberries, salty Manchego, and bitter greens create a colorful and lively range of flavors.

RASPBERRY VINAIGRETTE

A FEW FRESH RED RASPBERRIES

1 TABLESPOON RASPBERRY, RED WINE, OR CIDER VINEGAR

1 TEASPOON BALSAMIC VINEGAR

PINCH OF SUGAR

¼ TEASPOON SALT

⅛ TEASPOON GROUND BLACK PEPPER

¼ CUP OLIVE OIL

SALAD

6 CUPS COARSELY CHOPPED CURLY ENDIVE

¼ CUP THINLY SLICED RED ONIONS

½ CUP FRESH RED RASPBERRIES

⅓ CUP COARSELY CHOPPED TOASTED HAZELNUTS

¾ CUP SHREDDED MANCHEGO CHEESE

1 Make the Raspberry Vinaigrette right in the salad bowl. With the back of a spoon, crush the raspberries into the vinegars, sugar, salt, and pepper. Whisk in the oil.

2 Add the greens, red onions, and raspberries to the salad bowl and toss with the dressing. Sprinkle the nuts and cheese on top of the salad, or pass them at the table.

VARIATIONS: Frozen raspberries work in the dressing, but not as an ingredient of the salad.

Replace all or part of the olive oil with walnut oil or hazelnut oil.

In place of hazelnuts, use any other toasted nut.

In place of Manchego, use crumbled feta cheese or chèvre, or shaved Parmesan cheese.

Omit the cheese and/or nuts, and the salad is still delicious.

SERVING AND MENU IDEAS: This crisp, light salad pairs well with Latin Corn Soup (page 128) or Roman Grain and Mushroom Soup (page 120). It would be welcome at any dinner party. Try it with Spanish Stew (page 246), Greener Spanakopita (page 186), or Savory Asparagus and Mushroom Bread Pudding (page 207).

CURLY ENDIVE WITH HAZELNUTS, RASPBERRIES, AND MANCHEGO—PER 1 SERVING (OF 4), DRESSED *Calories: 304, Protein: 9 g, Carbohydrate: 8 g, Dietary Fiber: 5 g, Total Fat: 27 g, Saturated Fat: 8 g, Monounsaturated Fat: 16 g, Cholesterol: 22 mg, Sodium: 237 mg*

Red and Green Pasta Salad

SERVES 4 | YIELDS 3 CUPS SAUCE | TIME: 45 MINUTES

This is a quintessential summer pasta salad. Raw vegetables and arugula pair well with nutty whole grain pasta.

¾ POUND CHUNKY WHOLE GRAIN PASTA

1 TABLESPOON EXTRA-VIRGIN OLIVE OIL

1 TABLESPOON BALSAMIC VINEGAR

½ TEASPOON SALT

¼ CUP CHOPPED FRESH BASIL (PACKED)

VEGETABLES

½ CUP SUN-DRIED TOMATOES

2 CUPS DICED FRESH TOMATOES

½ CUP DICED BELL PEPPERS

½ CUP DICED FRESH FENNEL BULB

¼ CUP MINCED RED ONIONS

¼ CUP CHOPPED FRESH BASIL (PACKED)

1 TABLESPOON EXTRA-VIRGIN OLIVE OIL

2 TABLESPOONS LEMON JUICE

½ TEASPOON SALT

¼ TEASPOON GROUND BLACK PEPPER

2 TO 3 OUNCES ARUGULA (ABOUT 4 CUPS)

CUBED FRESH MOZZARELLA CHEESE (OPTIONAL)

1 Bring a large covered pot of salted water to a boil. Add the pasta and cook until al dente. Rinse with cool water and drain well. Transfer the pasta to a bowl and toss with the oil, vinegar, salt, and basil.

2 Meanwhile, in a small pan on the stovetop or in a bowl in the microwave oven, bring to a boil the sun-dried tomatoes covered with water, and then remove from the heat and let sit until softened, at least 5 minutes. Drain the softened sun-dried tomatoes, finely chop them, and set aside.

3 While the pasta cooks and the sun-dried tomatoes soak, prepare the vegetables: Combine the fresh tomatoes, bell peppers, fennel, red onions, and basil in a bowl. Stir in the chopped sun-dried tomatoes, olive oil, lemon juice, salt, and pepper.

4 To serve, arrange the arugula on individual plates, top with pasta and then vegetables. Dot with cubes of fresh mozzarella, if desired.

VARIATIONS: Replace the fresh mozzarella with grated Parmesan.

Top with toasted pine nuts.

SERVING AND MENU IDEAS: Start with Green Soup (page 266). Fill a big platter with melon wedges. Open a bottle of good red wine. Arrange the pasta salad on plates, and you're set. Or this pasta salad can be part of a backyard picnic with Simple Guacamole (page 69), Raw Broccoli Salad (page 97), and Greek Lentil Burgers (page 155), followed by Ice Pops (page 322).

RED AND GREEN PASTA SALAD (PASTA ONLY)—
PER 1 SERVING (OF 4), 1½ CUPS *Calories: 298,
Protein: 13 g, Carbohydrate: 64 g, Dietary Fiber: 0 g,
Total Fat: 1 g, Saturated Fat: 0 g, Monounsaturated
Fat: 0 g, Cholesterol: 0 mg, Sodium: 7 mg*

VEGETABLES—PER ¾ CUP *Calories: 79, Protein: 2 g,
Carbohydrate: 11 g, Dietary Fiber: 3 g, Total Fat: 4 g,
Saturated Fat: 1 g, Monounsaturated Fat: 3 g,
Cholesterol: 0 mg, Sodium: 444 mg*

ARUGULA—PER 1 SERVING (OF 4), 1 CUP
*Calories: 38, Protein: 0 g, Carbohydrate: 1 g,
Dietary Fiber: 0 g, Total Fat: 3 g, Saturated Fat: 0 g,
Monounsaturated Fat: 2 g, Cholesterol: 0 mg,
Sodium: 296 mg*

Pineapple and Tomato Salad

SERVES 4 | YIELDS ABOUT 4 CUPS | HANDS-ON TIME: 20 MINUTES | MARINATING TIME: 10 MINUTES

Brighten curries and other spicy dishes with this colorful and refreshing salad.

2 CUPS FRESH PINEAPPLE CHUNKS

2 CUPS CHOPPED TOMATOES

2 TABLESPOONS OLIVE OIL OR EXTRA-VIRGIN OLIVE OIL

1 TABLESPOON RED WINE VINEGAR, OR MORE TO TASTE

2 TABLESPOONS FINELY CHOPPED FRESH MINT

⅓ CUP FINELY CHOPPED SCALLIONS

¼ TEASPOON SALT

GROUND BLACK PEPPER

In a bowl, toss together all of the ingredients. Set aside for about 10 minutes before serving so the flavors will meld.

VARIATIONS: Other fresh fruit can be used. Go for whatever is in season and is sweet and juicy: mango, cantaloupe, a blend of peaches and apricots.

In place of mint, use cilantro or Thai basil.

SERVING AND MENU IDEAS: This is really pretty served on red lettuce leaves or a bed of arugula. It is especially good with Curried Red Lentil Burgers (page 151), Indian Stuffed Sweet Potatoes (page 196), Curried Millet (page 286), or Cabbage with Fermented Black Beans (page 171) on rice. Or serve it with Creamy Curried Pea Soup (page 126).

PINEAPPLE AND TOMATO SALAD—PER 1 SERVING
(OF 4), 1 CUP *Calories: 116, Protein: 1 g,
Carbohydrate: 14 g, Dietary Fiber: 2 g, Total Fat: 7 g,
Saturated Fat: 1 g, Monounsaturated Fat: 5 g,
Cholesterol: 0 mg, Sodium: 15 mg*

Curried Tofu and Mango Salad

SERVES 4 | YIELDS ABOUT 6 CUPS | TIME: 35 MINUTES

Tofu becomes firmer when crumbled and cooked briefly in a skillet, making a nice, chewy base for this creamy salad. The creaminess comes from yogurt and a touch of mayonnaise. Miso and soy sauce contribute a subtle savory richness, perfectly balanced by the sweet lusciousness of mango.

2 TEASPOONS SOY SAUCE

2 TEASPOONS CIDER VINEGAR OR RED WINE VINEGAR

2 TABLESPOONS LIGHT MISO

1 CAKE OF FIRM TOFU (ABOUT 16 OUNCES)

1 TABLESPOON VEGETABLE OIL

⅔ CUP DICED CELERY

⅔ CUP DICED RED BELL PEPPERS

⅓ CUP MINCED SCALLIONS

1 LARGE RIPE MANGO

2 TABLESPOONS MAYONNAISE

3 TABLESPOONS PLAIN NONFAT YOGURT

1 TEASPOON CURRY POWDER

¼ TEASPOON GROUND CUMIN

¼ TEASPOON SALT

⅛ TEASPOON GROUND BLACK PEPPER

1 In a small bowl, mix together the soy sauce, vinegar, and miso and set aside.

2 Crumble the tofu into bite-sized pieces. Heat the oil in a skillet on medium-high heat. Add the tofu and cook, stirring often, until the tofu becomes drier and shrinks slightly, about 5 minutes. Add the miso mixture to the tofu, stir to coat and cook for a minute. Remove from the heat and set aside to cool.

3 Place the celery, bell peppers, and scallions in a serving bowl. Peel and pit the mango and cut the flesh into bite-sized pieces. Add to the serving bowl.

4 In a small bowl, mix together the mayonnaise, yogurt, curry powder, cumin, salt, and pepper. Stir this dressing into the vegetables and mango. Add the cooled tofu and mix well.

SERVING AND MENU IDEAS: Serve this as a fruity mock chicken salad on a bed of greens (we especially like Boston lettuce, baby spinach, or watercress) and garnish with toasted cashews or pecans. Or use as a sandwich filling in whole wheat pita bread. Serve it to follow a soup, such as Mellow Gazpacho (page 127) or Watercress and Cauliflower Soup (page 116). It makes a lovely, light meal with a vegetable on the side, perhaps Green Beans with Ginger and Garlic (page 303) or Roasted Sweet Potatoes (page 299).

CURRIED TOFU AND MANGO SALAD—PER 1 SERVING (OF 4), 1½ CUPS *Calories: 265, Protein: 18 g, Carbohydrate: 29 g, Dietary Fiber: 2 g, Total Fat: 9 g, Saturated Fat: 1 g, Monounsaturated Fat: 3 g, Cholesterol: 5 mg, Sodium: 580 mg*

Sweet Potato–Walnut Salad on Arugula

SERVES 4 TO 6 | YIELDS ABOUT ¾ CUP DRESSING | TIME: 35 MINUTES

This delectable salad combines four nutritional powerhouses. Sweet potatoes were named the most nutritious vegetable in a 2006 listing by the Center for Science in the Public Interest. In the world of nuts, walnuts are high in antioxidants and the richest source of omega-3s. Arugula, with its distinctive flavor, is a great source of important nutrients including beta-carotene, vitamin C, calcium, and vitamin K. Parsley contributes iron, potassium, and vitamin C.

TANGY YOGURT DRESSING

½ CUP PLAIN NONFAT YOGURT

2 TABLESPOONS WHITE VINEGAR

2 TABLESPOONS CHOPPED SUN-DRIED TOMATOES (PACKED IN OLIVE OIL)

1 TEASPOON DIJON MUSTARD

½ TEASPOON SALT

¼ TEASPOON GROUND BLACK PEPPER

3 LARGE SWEET POTATOES (ABOUT 2 POUNDS)

2 CUPS TRIMMED AND HALVED GREEN BEANS

1 CUP COARSELY CHOPPED TOASTED WALNUTS

¼ CUP MINCED FRESH PARSLEY

4 OUNCES ARUGULA (ABOUT 8 CUPS)

SALT AND GROUND BLACK PEPPER

1   Whirl the dressing ingredients in a blender until smooth. Set aside.

2   Peel the sweet potatoes and cut into ¾-inch cubes (about 6 cups). Steam until just tender. Steam the green beans until tender.

3   In a bowl, toss the sweet potatoes and green beans with the dressing, walnuts, and parsley.

4   Arrange the arugula on a serving platter, spoon on the sweet potato salad, and sprinkle with salt and pepper to taste. Serve warm, at room temperature, or chilled.

VARIATION: Replace the green beans with sugar snap peas.

SERVING AND MENU IDEAS: Serve this tasty, big salad chilled at a summer al fresco meal alongside Watermelon Salad (page 99) and Southwestern Black Bean Burgers (page 154) or Broccoli-Cheese Wrap (page 138). Serve it warm with Down-home Black-eyed Peas (page 221), or with Curried Millet (page 286) and Kale with Cranberries (page 298). It can even be a novel incarnation for sweet potatoes at the holiday table.

SWEET POTATO-WALNUT SALAD ON ARUGULA— PER 1 SERVING (OF 6), DRESSED *Calories: 281, Protein: 8 g, Carbohydrate: 36 g, Dietary Fiber: 7 g, Total Fat: 14 g, Saturated Fat: 1 g, Monounsaturated Fat: 2 g, Cholesterol: <1 mg, Sodium: 298 mg*

Quinoa Tabouli

SERVES 4 TO 6 | YIELDS ABOUT 4 CUPS | TIME: 30 MINUTES

We've replaced the usual cracked wheat with quinoa, considered to be the most nutritious of grains, in this tabouli. It's classically seasoned with lemon and garlic, and green with lots of vitamin-rich parsley.

1 CUP RAW QUINOA

2 CUPS WATER

¼ TEASPOON SALT

1 TEASPOON DRIED MINT OR 1 TABLESPOON CHOPPED FRESH MINT

1 RED, GREEN, OR YELLOW BELL PEPPER

4 SCALLIONS

2 GARLIC CLOVES

1½ CUPS LIGHTLY PACKED FRESH PARSLEY LEAVES

2 TABLESPOONS LEMON JUICE

1½ TABLESPOONS OLIVE OIL

SALT AND GROUND BLACK PEPPER

1 Rinse and drain the quinoa in a fine-meshed strainer to remove any residue of the grain's bitter coating. In a covered saucepan on high heat, bring the quinoa, water, salt, and mint (if using dried) to a boil. Reduce the heat to low, cover, and simmer until the water has been absorbed and the quinoa is tender, about 15 minutes. Fluff with a fork and place in a serving bowl.

2 While the quinoa cooks, finely chop the bell pepper, mince the scallions and garlic, and finely chop the parsley and mint (if using fresh). Add them to the serving bowl with the cooked quinoa. Pour on the lemon juice and olive oil and mix well. Add salt and pepper to taste.

3 Serve warm, at room temperature, or chilled.

SERVING AND MENU IDEAS: Garnish with cherry tomatoes, sliced cucumbers, chopped toasted almonds, grated feta, and/or kalamata olives. This tabouli goes well with all things Greek. Try it with Greek Tomato-Yogurt Soup (page 125), Greek Lentil Burgers (page 155), Greek Black-eyed Peas (page 218), or Seitan Gyro (page 142). It makes a great salad plate, with Yellow Split Pea Dip (page 71), with crudités, or Watermelon Salad (page 99) with feta cheese, and Mellow Gazpacho (page 127). Or serve it warm with Pomegranate-glazed Tofu (page 179), Herbed Vegetable Packets (page 197), or Broccoli-Feta Stuffed Sweet Potatoes (page 194).

QUINOA TABOULI—PER 1 SERVING (OF 6), ¾ CUP
Calories: 153, Protein: 5 g, Carbohydrate: 23 g, Dietary Fiber: 3 g, Total Fat: 5 g, Saturated Fat: 1 g, Monounsaturated Fat: 3 g, Cholesterol: 0 mg, Sodium: 116 mg

Scattered Sushi Salad

SERVES 4 | TIME: 50 MINUTES

Deconstruct a sushi roll and you have sushi salad: a one-dish meal for lunch or a light supper. Instead of white sushi rice, we've used short-grain brown rice, which has a chewy texture and more complex flavor, as well as greater nutritional benefits.

2 CUPS SHORT-GRAIN BROWN RICE
3½ CUPS WATER
3 TABLESPOONS RICE VINEGAR
3 TABLESPOONS SOY SAUCE
2 CUPS BITE-SIZED PIECES OF BROCCOLI
4 LARGE EGGS
½ TEASPOON SALT
2 TABLESPOONS WATER
1 CUP GRATED PEELED CARROTS
4 SCALLIONS, SLICED ON THE DIAGONAL
1 SHEET OF NORI (SEE PAGE 162)
2 TABLESPOONS TOASTED BROWN SESAME SEEDS

1 Rinse and drain the rice and place it in a small covered saucepan with the water. Bring to a boil, reduce the heat to low, and simmer covered until the rice is tender but still chewy and the water has been absorbed, about 40 minutes.

2 Meanwhile, combine the rice vinegar and soy sauce in small bowl and set aside.

3 Steam the broccoli until tender and set aside to cool.

4 In a small bowl, beat the eggs with the salt and water. Lightly oil or spray a 10-inch skillet, warm on medium-high heat, and then add about half of the egg mixture. Tilt the skillet so the eggs cover the bottom and cook like a crêpe. When it's almost cooked through, flip the eggs and cook for a few seconds on the other side. Place the cooked eggs on a plate and cook the remaining eggs the same way. When the eggs have cooled, cut into strips and set aside.

5 Using tongs, toast the nori briefly over an open flame (or an electric burner on high) and then crumble and set aside.

6 When the rice is done, toss it with the steamed broccoli, grated carrots, sliced scallions, and dressing. Garnish with the egg strips, crumbled nori, and sesame seeds.

VARIATION: Use seasoned nori, such as teriyaki-flavored. Look for it in Asian markets, natural foods stores, and larger supermarkets.

SERVING AND MENU IDEAS: Augment Scattered Sushi Salad with Basic Miso Soup (page 133) or Orange-Glazed Tofu on Greens (page 180).

SCATTERED SUSHI SALAD—PER 1 SERVING (OF 4)
Calories: 422, Protein: 11 g, Carbohydrate: 82 g, Dietary Fiber: 7 g, Total Fat: 6 g, Saturated Fat: 1 g, Monounsaturated Fat: 2 g, Cholesterol: 0 mg, Sodium: 780 mg

Roasted Beet Salad

SERVES 6 | YIELDS ABOUT ¾ CUP DRESSING, ABOUT 4 CUPS ROASTED BEETS | TIME: 40 MINUTES

This dish celebrates the earthy essence of beets. Roasted beets are sweet and dark and vitamin-rich. You can roast them ahead of time, cool and dress them, and assemble the salad later.

4 MEDIUM BEETS (4 TO 5 OUNCES EACH)

1 TABLESPOON OLIVE OIL

¼ TEASPOON SALT

DASH OF GROUND BLACK PEPPER

CITRUS DRESSING

½ CUP OLIVE OIL

2 TABLESPOONS LEMON JUICE

2 TABLESPOONS ORANGE JUICE

½ TEASPOON SALT

1 GARLIC CLOVE, MINCED OR PRESSED OR 2 MINCED SHALLOTS (OPTIONAL)

8 CUPS SALAD GREENS

½ CUP CRUMBLED CHÈVRE, FETA, RICOTTA SALATA, OR BLUE CHEESE

½ CUP CHOPPED TOASTED PECANS

1 Peel and cut the beets into ½- to 1-inch cubes. Toss them with the oil, salt, and pepper and spread them in a single layer on a lightly oiled baking sheet. Roast in a 400° oven for 15 minutes, stir, and return to the oven until tender, about 10 minutes.

2 While the beets are roasting, whisk together the dressing ingredients and set aside.

3 When the beets are tender, toss them with about 2 tablespoons of the dressing. Arrange the salad greens on individual plates and mound the beets on top. Top each salad with about a tablespoon of the cheese and pecans. Pass the remaining dressing at the table.

VARIATION: You can bake the beets whole, wrapped in aluminum foil. Rinse the beets, cut off the tops and most of the taproot, and wrap them individually in aluminum foil. Bake in a 375° oven until tender, about an hour. Unwrap the beets, rub them to remove their peels, and cut the beets into cubes. Toss with some of the dressing.

SERVING AND MENU IDEAS: This salad is a flavorful, light meal on its own, perhaps with rye bread on the side. It's excellent paired with Roman Grain and Mushroom Soup (page 120), Mushroom-Barley "Risotto" (page 280), or Italian Lentils (page 217). It adds color and sweetness served beside Kasha-stuffed Peppers (page 191), Vegetable Tofu Scramble (page 181), or Greek Vegetable Pie (page 204).

ROASTED BEET SALAD—PER 1 SERVING (OF 6), ⅔ CUP *Calories: 84, Protein: 3 g, Carbohydrate: 11 g, Dietary Fiber: 4 g, Total Fat: 4 g, Saturated Fat: 4 g, Monounsaturated Fat: 2 g, Cholesterol: 0 mg, Sodium: 237 mg*

CITRUS DRESSING—PER 2 TABLESPOONS *Calories: 164, Protein: 0 g, Carbohydrate: 1 g, Dietary Fiber: 0 g, Total Fat: 18 g, Saturated Fat: 2 g, Monounsaturated Fat: 13 g, Cholesterol: 0 mg, Sodium: 194 mg*

Mango Slaw

SERVES 4 TO 6 | YIELDS ABOUT 4 CUPS | HANDS-ON TIME: 40 MINUTES | MARINATING TIME: 20 MINUTES

The interplay of sweet, spicy, salty, and tart flavors in each bite of this very pretty slaw is especially appealing. It makes a good side dish for any Southeast Asian or Indian meal that isn't too spicy. Mango Slaw will keep nicely for 2 or 3 days; it becomes less crisp, but more flavorful.

1 FIRM SLIGHTLY UNDERRIPE MANGO

1½ CUPS SHREDDED RED OR GREEN CABBAGE

1 CUP SHREDDED CARROTS

¼ CUP THINLY SLICED FRESH MINT LEAVES

DRESSING

¼ CUP LIME JUICE

2 TABLESPOONS BROWN SUGAR, MAPLE SYRUP, OR OTHER SWEETENER

½ TEASPOON SALT

1 TABLESPOON OLIVE OIL OR VEGETABLE OIL

2 GARLIC CLOVES, MINCED OR PRESSED

1 SMALL FRESH CHILE, MINCED

1 TABLESPOON GRATED PEELED GINGER ROOT

1 Peel the mango with a sharp paring knife or vegetable peeler. Cut the peeled mango lengthwise into halves, slicing as close to the pit as possible. Slice off any flesh that remains attached to the pit. Cut the mango flesh into thin strips and place in a serving bowl. Add the cabbage, carrots, and mint.

2 In a separate small bowl, whisk together the lime juice, sugar, and salt. In a small skillet on medium-high heat, warm the oil and cook the garlic, chiles, and ginger until sizzling and fragrant, about a minute, and whisk into the lime juice mixture.

3 Pour the dressing over the slaw and toss until well coated. Let sit for about 20 minutes, so the flavors have time to marry.

NOTE: Cooking the garlic, chiles, and ginger isn't essential, but makes for a mellower flavor. You can also heat them in the oil in a microwave oven for about 30 seconds.

VARIATIONS: Add ¼ cup chopped cilantro, basil, or Thai basil.

Add ½ cup thinly sliced onions or scallions.

Replace the chile with hot sauce or cayenne to taste.

SERVING AND MENU IDEAS: This salad is nice topped with chopped peanuts and good with Chickpea Crêpes (page 73). It makes a zesty topping for Tempeh-Quinoa Burgers (page 152) or Curried Red Lentil Burgers (page 151). Try it with Curried Millet (page 286) or Indian Stuffed Sweet Potatoes (page 196). We like it with Tropical Lime Tofu (page 179) and Roasted Sweet Potatoes (page 299) for a great Caribbean meal.

MANGO SLAW—PER 1 SERVING (OF 6), ⅔ CUP, DRESSED *Calories: 80, Protein: 1 g, Carbohydrate: 15 g, Dietary Fiber: 2 g, Total Fat: 2 g, Saturated Fat: 0 g, Monounsaturated Fat: 2 g, Cholesterol: 0 mg, Sodium: 218 mg*

Celeriac Apple Slaw

SERVES 4 TO 6 | YIELDS ABOUT 6 CUPS | TIME: 35 MINUTES

Crisp, sweet, and refreshing, this is an elegant slaw. Speckled with green, red, and black, it is a colorful side dish, ideal with grilled or spicy fare. We suggest a sweet apple with a crunchy texture for the best slaw.

1 LEMON

3 CUPS PEELED AND GRATED SWEET, FIRM APPLES

2 TABLESPOONS ORANGE JUICE

2½ CUPS PEELED AND GRATED CELERIAC

1 TABLESPOON EXTRA-VIRGIN OLIVE OIL

½ CUP CURRANTS OR CHOPPED RAISINS

⅓ CUP CHOPPED FRESH BASIL

¼ CUP MINCED RED ONIONS

¼ TEASPOON SALT

PINCH OF CAYENNE

Into a serving bowl, grate the lemon peel, for about 2 teaspoons of zest. Juice the lemon and add 3 tablespoons of lemon juice to the bowl. Add the grated apples and stir well: the lemon juice will prevent discoloration. Add all of the remaining ingredients and toss well. Serve at room temperature or chilled.

SERVING AND MENU IDEAS: This slaw works well as a fresh counterpoint to Bulgarian Lentil and Vegetable Stew (page 257), Winter Squash Stuffed with Two-Rice Pilaf (page 198), or Tofu, Leek, and Almond Stuffed Portabellas (page 193). Or think French and serve it with Caramelized Onion Omelet (page 62) or Tempeh Bourgignon (page 250).

CELERIAC APPLE SLAW—PER 1 SERVING (OF 6), 1 CUP *Calories: 96, Protein: 1 g, Carbohydrate: 19 g, Dietary Fiber: 3 g, Total Fat: 3 g, Saturated Fat: 0 g, Monounsaturated Fat: 2 g, Cholesterol: 0 mg, Sodium: 163 mg*

Arugula, Kumquat, Walnut, and Fig Salad

SERVES 4 | YIELDS ABOUT 8 CUPS | TIME: 20 MINUTES

Spicy, sweet, and citrusy flavors mingle in every bite of this simple salad. If kumquats are hard to come by, try orange sections and a little orange zest.

DRESSING

1 TABLESPOON RED WINE VINEGAR

1 TABLESPOON BALSAMIC VINEGAR

2 TEASPOONS DIJON MUSTARD

⅓ CUP OLIVE OIL

SALT AND GROUND BLACK PEPPER

SALAD

8 DRIED FIGS

12 KUMQUATS

6 CUPS ARUGULA

½ CUP CHOPPED TOASTED WALNUTS

1 To make the dressing, place the vinegars and mustard in a salad bowl. Drizzle in the olive oil while whisking constantly. The dressing should be thick and creamy. Add salt and pepper to taste.

2 Slice the figs. Thinly slice the unpeeled kumquats crosswise. Add the arugula, kumquats, and figs to the salad bowl and gently toss with the dressing. Serve the salad topped with the walnuts.

VARIATION: Balsamic and red wine vinegar give this dressing a wonderful flavor, but the dressing is fine made with lemon juice, mild cider vinegar, or white vinegar.

SERVING AND MENU IDEAS: Sprinkle with pecorino Romano or Parmesan cheese. This salad is a fresh and bright companion for heartier fare, such as Roman Grain and Mushroom Soup (page 120), Mediterranean Eggplant Casserole (page 205), or Italian Stew with Winter Squash and Chickpeas (page 247). It has an affinity with most Mediterranean-style dishes. Try it beside Mellow Gazpacho (page 127) or Rice Salad with Herbs (page 100).

ARUGULA, KUMQUAT, WALNUT, AND FIG SALAD— PER 1 SERVING (OF 4), DRESSED *Calories: 426, Protein: 6 g, Carbohydrate: 37 g, Dietary Fiber: 9 g, Total Fat: 31 g, Saturated Fat: 4 g, Monounsaturated Fat: 16 g, Cholesterol: 0 mg, Sodium: 52 mg*

Bulghur and Fruit Salad

SERVES 6 TO 8 | YIELDS ABOUT 8 CUPS | TIME: 35 MINUTES

Nutty, chewy bulghur is the perfect companion for sweet, crunchy apples, toasted pecans, and the rich scent of cardamom and cinnamon.

2 CUPS BOILING WATER

2 CUPS BULGHUR (SEE NOTE)

½ TEASPOON SALT

¼ CUP MINCED RED ONIONS

¼ CUP MINCED RED BELL PEPPERS

¼ CUP CHOPPED FRESH PARSLEY

1 ORANGE

2 TABLESPOONS LEMON JUICE

1 APPLE

⅓ CUP OLIVE OIL

¼ CUP DRIED CRANBERRIES OR DRIED CHERRIES, CHOPPED

½ TEASPOON GROUND BLACK PEPPER

¼ TEASPOON GROUND CARDAMOM

¼ TEASPOON GROUND CINNAMON

½ CUP TOASTED PECANS, CHOPPED

NOTE: There are several different grades of bulghur, some more refined than others. The amount of time it takes for the bulghur to soften corresponds to the grade. At Moosewood, we usually use coarse bulghur.

1 In a bowl, pour the boiling water over the bulghur and salt. Cover and set aside.

2 Meanwhile, place the onions, peppers, and parsley in a serving bowl. If you like orange zest, grate about a teaspoon into the bowl. Juice the orange. Add the orange and lemon juices. Dice the apple, add it to the serving bowl, and toss well. Add the olive oil, dried cranberries, black pepper, cardamom, and cinnamon and mix well.

3 When the bulghur is tender, fluff it with a fork and add it to the serving bowl, stirring well. Serve at room temperature or chilled. Sprinkle the pecans on top just before serving.

SERVING AND MENU IDEAS: This makes a great combo plate with Watercress and Cauliflower Soup (page 116) or Creamy Curried Pea Soup (page 126). It's a perfect side dish for Greener Spanakopita (page 186) or Spinach-Tofu Burgers (page 153).

BULGHUR & FRUIT SALAD—PER 1 SERVING (OF 8), 1 CUP *Calories: 330, Protein: 6 g, Carbohydrate: 38 g, Dietary Fiber: 9 g, Total Fat: 19 g, Saturated Fat: 2 g, Monounsaturated Fat: 12 g, Cholesterol: 0 mg, Sodium: 155 mg*

Raw Broccoli Salad

SERVES 4 | YIELDS ABOUT 4 CUPS | HANDS-ON TIME: 15 MINUTES | SITTING TIME: AT LEAST 30 MINUTES

This sweet and tangy salad is good for a picnic or a buffet. It's great to make ahead because it's even better the next day (or the day after that).

1 LARGE HEAD BROCCOLI (ABOUT 1 POUND)
½ CUP MAYONNAISE
2 TEASPOONS MAPLE SYRUP OR OTHER SWEETENER
4 TEASPOONS CIDER VINEGAR
¼ TEASPOON SALT
⅛ TEASPOON GROUND BLACK PEPPER
¼ CUP CURRANTS OR RAISINS
1 MEDIUM TOMATO, DICED

1 Slice off the tough bottom of the broccoli and peel any tough skin from the stems. Finely chop the florets and smaller stems. Cut large stems lengthwise into halves or quarters and thinly slice. You should have about 4 cups of chopped broccoli. Set aside.

2 In a serving bowl, whisk together the mayonnaise, maple syrup, vinegar, salt, and pepper. Fold in the broccoli, currants, and tomatoes. Set aside for the flavors to meld, at least 30 minutes, or even better, for a day in the refrigerator.

VARIATIONS: Add 2 tablespoons sliced scallions.

Add a tablespoon of prepared white horseradish to the dressing.

SERVING AND MENU IDEAS: This salad is deliciously crunchy served next to Mushroom-Barley "Risotto" (page 280), Tempeh-Quinoa Burgers (page 152), or Skillet Barbecue Tofu in a Pita (page 139). It pairs well with spicy Sweet Potato, Apple, and Chipotle Soup (page 132). For a picnic, include Mellow Gazpacho (page 127), Sweet Potato–Walnut Salad on Arugula (page 89), and some deviled eggs.

RAW BROCCOLI SALAD—PER 1 SERVING (OF 4), 1 CUP *Calories: 271, Protein: 5 g, Carbohydrate: 16 g, Dietary Fiber: 5 g, Total Fat: 22 g, Saturated Fat: 3 g, Monounsaturated Fat: 5 g, Cholesterol: 10 mg, Sodium: 355 mg*

Seaweed Salad

SERVES 6 | YIELDS ABOUT 3 CUPS | TIME: 15 MINUTES

The wakame is green, the arame is a rich brown, the dulse is reddish brown, and the bits of cucumber are, well, cucumber green. This simple salad looks good, tastes great, and is exceptionally nourishing. Add any or all of the extras we list under Variations. It's also fine made with all seaweed, no cucumber. Or substitute other seaweeds, dried or fresh.

½ OUNCE DRIED WAKAME (ABOUT ½ CUP)

½ OUNCE DRIED ARAME (ABOUT ½ CUP)

2 TABLESPOONS RICE VINEGAR OR LEMON JUICE

2 TABLESPOONS SOY SAUCE

1 TABLESPOON DARK SESAME OIL

1 TEASPOON FRUIT PRESERVES (PEACH, PLUM, APRICOT) OR SUGAR

1 MEDIUM CUCUMBER

2 TABLESPOONS DULSE FLAKES

1 In separate bowls, soak the wakame and arame in warm water for 5 to 10 minutes.

2 Meanwhile, in a serving bowl, mix together the vinegar, soy sauce, sesame oil, and preserves. Peel the cucumber, cut it in half lengthwise, scoop out the seeds, and dice. Add to the serving bowl.

3 Drain the wakame and arame and squeeze out excess water. If uncut, cut into ¼-inch-wide strips. Add to the serving bowl. Add the dulse flakes and stir well. Serve at room temperature or chilled.

NOTE: See pages 161–63 for an overview of many different seaweeds.

VARIATIONS: Add as many of the following as you like:

2 TABLESPOONS THINLY SLICED SCALLIONS

2 TABLESPOONS CHOPPED CILANTRO

1 TABLESPOON TOASTED SESAME SEEDS

½ TEASPOON GRATED PEELED GINGER ROOT

½ TEASPOON RED PEPPER FLAKES

½ CUP MUNG BEAN SPROUTS

SERVING AND MENU IDEAS: Serve as a side with Three-Soy Sauté with Soba (page 164), Saucy Miso Tofu (page 178) on brown rice, or Japanese Noodles with Tomatoes (page 230).

SEAWEED SALAD—PER 1 SERVING (OF 6), ½ CUP
Calories: 40, Protein: 1 g, Carbohydrate: 4 g, Dietary Fiber: 1 g, Total Fat: 2 g, Saturated Fat: 0 g, Monounsaturated Fat: 1 g, Cholesterol: 0 mg, Sodium: 272 mg

Watermelon Salad

SERVES 4 | YIELDS ABOUT 4 CUPS | TIME: 10 MINUTES

Watermelon is thirst quenching, cooling, sweet, high in vitamin C, and the very essence of summer. Here's a refreshing watermelon salad that complements Mexican, Caribbean, and Mediterranean dishes and is a nice addition to almost any summer menu.

4 CUPS CUBED SEEDLESS WATERMELON

4 TEASPOONS OLIVE OIL

1½ TEASPOONS BALSAMIC VINEGAR

2 TABLESPOONS MINCED FRESH MINT

¼ CUP MINCED RED ONIONS

PINCH OF SALT

In a serving bowl, mix together the watermelon, olive oil, vinegar, mint, red onions, and salt.

VARIATION: Add ¼ cup diced feta cheese.

SERVING AND MENU IDEAS: Serve on a bed of your favorite greens; include some sharp tasting greens for a nice contrast to the sweetness of the watermelon. Try it beside Oaxacan Tlayuda (page 219), Down-home Black-eyed Peas (page 221), Ratatouille Rice (page 281), or Latin Corn Soup (page 128). It provides a nice balance with a grain salad such as Quinoa Tabouli (page 90) or Rice Salad with Herbs (page 100).

WATERMELON SALAD—PER 1 SERVING (OF 4), 1 CUP
Calories: 92, Protein: 1 g, Carbohydrate: 13 g, Dietary Fiber: 1 g, Total Fat: 5 g, Saturated Fat: 1 g, Monounsaturated Fat: 3 g, Cholesterol: 0 mg, Sodium: 3 mg

Rice Salad with Herbs

SERVES 4 AS A MAIN DISH, 8 AS A SIDE | YIELDS ABOUT 7 CUPS | TIME: ABOUT 1 HOUR

This fresh, vibrant salad is attractive and keeps well. Include the optional bell peppers and celery for color and crunch and for a more substantial dish. It looks great topped with tomato wedges.

1 ½ CUPS RINSED AND DRAINED RAW BROWN RICE

2 TEASPOONS OLIVE OIL

2 ½ CUPS WATER

½ TEASPOON SALT

DRESSING

¼ CUP EXTRA-VIRGIN OLIVE OIL

2 TABLESPOONS WHITE BALSAMIC VINEGAR, RED WINE VINEGAR, OR CIDER VINEGAR

2 TABLESPOONS LEMON JUICE

2 GARLIC CLOVES, MINCED OR PRESSED

1 ½ TEASPOONS DIJON MUSTARD

¼ TEASPOON SALT

GROUND BLACK PEPPER

¾ CUP MINCED SCALLIONS

¾ CUP MINCED FRESH PARSLEY

½ CUP MINCED FRESH DILL OR BASIL

3 TABLESPOONS TOASTED PINE NUTS

½ CUP DICED CELERY OR FRESH FENNEL (OPTIONAL)

½ CUP DICED RED, ORANGE, OR YELLOW BELL PEPPERS (OPTIONAL)

1   In a saucepan with a tight-fitting lid on high heat, stir the rice and oil for a minute. Add the water and salt, cover, bring to a boil. Then reduce the heat and simmer gently until the water has been absorbed and the rice is tender, about 45 minutes.

2   Meanwhile, whisk together all of the dressing ingredients in a small bowl and set aside.

3   When the rice is ready, transfer it to a large bowl, toss thoroughly with the dressing, and set aside to cool for 10 to 15 minutes. Stir in the scallions, parsley, dill, pine nuts, and celery and bell peppers, if using. If you have time, set the salad aside at room temperature for a bit so that the flavors will blend.

4   Serve warm, at room temperature, or chilled.

VARIATION: Add some minced fresh mint, tarragon, and/or oregano.

SERVING AND MENU IDEAS: Get out a colorful platter, arrange a bed of fresh greens, mound on the salad, and decorate with sprigs of fresh herbs, lemon wedges, and a few juicy black olives. Add some crumbled feta cheese or chèvre, or cubes of fresh mozzarella or Tropical Lime Tofu (page 179). Serve it after Chilled Beet Borscht (page 135) or Green Soup (page 266), or with Roasted Beet Salad (page 92).

RICE SALAD WITH HERBS—PER 1 SERVING (OF 8)
Calories: 270, Protein: 4 g, Carbohydrate: 31 g, Dietary Fiber: 2 g, Total Fat: 15 g, Saturated Fat: 2 g, Monounsaturated Fat: 9 g, Cholesterol: 0 mg, Sodium: 243 mg.

Japanese Lunchbox Salad

SERVES 4 | YIELDS ABOUT ½ CUP DRESSING | TIME: 20 MINUTES

This may be the quickest, simplest way to enjoy many of the flavors you might find in a Japanese bento box, put together here not in separate small compartments but in an all-in-one salad. We've chosen the salad items with an eye toward color, texture, and ease of preparation. The dish is tied together with a light but intense lemon and ginger dressing. For a carry-along lunch, pack the dressing separately.

LEMON GINGER DRESSING

2 TABLESPOONS PEANUT OIL OR VEGETABLE OIL

2 TABLESPOONS LEMON JUICE

1 TABLESPOON SOY SAUCE

1 TABLESPOON DRY SHERRY

1 TABLESPOON GRATED PEELED GINGER ROOT

1 GARLIC CLOVE, MINCED

SALAD

4 CUPS LOOSELY PACKED SALAD GREENS, BABY SPINACH, OR FRISÉE

2 CUPS COOKED BROWN RICE

16 OUNCES SEASONED TOFU, SLICED OR CUBED (SEE NOTE)

1 CUP CARROT MATCHSTICKS

1 CUP CHERRY TOMATOES, HALVED

1 RIPE HASS AVOCADO

2 TEASPOONS TOASTED SESAME SEEDS OR GROUND FLAXSEEDS

1 In a blender, whirl all of the dressing ingredients until smooth.

2 On a large platter or on individual serving plates, spread out the greens and mound the rice in the center. Arrange the tofu, carrots, and tomatoes on the greens and rice.

3 Just before serving, slice around the avocado lengthwise, twist the halves apart, and remove the pit. Cut the flesh into thin slices right in the skin, scoop the slices out with a serving spoon, and place them on the salad. Drizzle the dressing on the salad. Sprinkle with sesame seeds and serve.

NOTE: Seasoned tofu (smooth, dense tofu that has been baked or simmered in a variety of spices) is a ready-to-eat product found in the refrigerator case of many supermarkets. Or use one of our Four Stovetop Tofus (pages 178–180) or An Easy Baked Tofu (page 177).

SERVING AND MENU IDEAS: A light but satisfying meal on its own, or start with Azuki Bean and Spinach Soup (page 124), or put Quick-braised Snow Peas and Radishes (page 308) on the side.

JAPANESE LUNCHBOX SALAD—PER 1 SERVING (OF 4), DRESSED *Calories: 343, Protein: 12 g, Carbohydrate: 33 g, Dietary Fiber: 7 g, Total Fat: 20 g, Saturated Fat: 3 g, Monounsaturated Fat: 9 g, Cholesterol: 0 mg, Sodium: 480 mg*

Greens with Roasted Vegetables Salad

SERVES 4 | HANDS-ON TIME: 15 MINUTES | BAKING TIME: 20 TO 25 MINUTES

We serve some variation of this luscious main dish salad every week at Moosewood. We like the combination of crisp fresh salad greens and moist and deeply flavorful roasted vegetables. Here we give you a basic recipe and suggestions for variations; the possibilities are endless. Experiment with different kinds of greens, various flavorful cheeses, other roasted vegetables, dried fruit, toasted or spiced nuts, croutons, baked tofu, various dressings. . . .

Leftover roasted vegetables will keep for 3 or 4 days when covered and refrigerated.

---

1 LARGE SPANISH ONION

2 MEDIUM BELL PEPPERS (RED, YELLOW, OR ORANGE)

1 MEDIUM ZUCCHINI

1 LARGE FENNEL BULB

2 TABLESPOONS OLIVE OIL

½ TEASPOON SALT

¼ TEASPOON GROUND BLACK PEPPER

2 GARLIC CLOVES, MINCED OR PRESSED

1 TEASPOON DRIED OREGANO OR MARJORAM, OR CRUMBLED DRIED ROSEMARY

---

8 CUPS SALAD GREENS (7 OR 8 OUNCES)

SHALLOT VINAIGRETTE (PAGE 111) OR YOUR FAVORITE VINAIGRETTE (OPTIONAL)

CRUMBLED FETA, CHÈVRE, OR BLUE CHEESE, OR SHREDDED PARMESAN OR SHARP PROVOLONE CHEESE (OPTIONAL)

---

1 Cut the onion in half and slice into wedges. Cut the peppers into 1- to 1½-inch chunks. Cut the zucchini in half lengthwise and slice on the diagonal. Cut the fennel bulb in half, core, and trim the tough outer layer. Cut into 1-inch chunks. (You can change the proportion of vegetables, as long as you end up with about 8 cups total.) Place all of the vegetables in a bowl and add the olive oil, salt, pepper, garlic, and herbs. Mix well. Place on a lightly oiled baking sheet large enough to hold all of the vegetables in a single layer. Roast in a preheated 400° oven for about 15 minutes and then stir the vegetables. Bake for another 5 to 10 minutes until the vegetables are tender and beginning to brown. Set aside to cool.

2 While the vegetables are roasting, rinse and dry the salad greens.

3 To serve, arrange the salad greens on plates or large salad bowls and drizzle with dressing. Top with the roasted vegetables and the cheese, if using.

VARIATIONS: Add roasted mushrooms and/or winter squash. These should be roasted separately from the other vegetables.

To roast portabella mushrooms: Choose 3 large portabellas (about 5 inches in diameter), remove the stems and discard or save for another dish, and rinse the caps. Whisk together 1 tablespoon olive oil, 1 tablespoon soy sauce, 1 garlic clove, minced or pressed, ¼ teaspoon dried oregano, and 1 teaspoon balsamic vinegar if you wish. Brush both sides of the caps with this mixture and place the portabellas gill side down in a lightly oiled baking dish. Drizzle on any extra olive oil mixture. Roast in a 400° oven for about 25 minutes until tender and juicy. Flip over the caps and cool. Slice or chop.

To roast butternut squash: Peel and seed a medium butternut squash (about 2½ pounds). Cut into 1- to 1½-inch chunks and toss with 1 tablespoon olive oil, ½ teaspoon salt, and ¼ teaspoon dried thyme. Place on a lightly oiled baking sheet and roast in a 400° oven for 20 to 25 minutes until tender.

SERVING AND MENU IDEAS: Serve this main dish salad with a cup of Chilled Beet Borscht (page 135) or Creamy Curried Pea Soup (page 126). Or for a nice fall or winter meal, serve with An Easy Baked Tofu (page 177) and Wild Rice Pilaf with Chestnuts (page 288). Have Apple-Blueberry Crumble (page 316) for dessert.

GREENS WITH ROASTED VEGETABLES SALAD— PER 1 SERVING (OF 4), NOT DRESSED *Calories: 129, Protein: 3 g, Carbohydrate: 15 g, Dietary Fiber: 4 g, Total Fat: 7 g, Saturated Fat: 1 g, Monounsaturated Fat: 5 g, Cholesterol: 0 mg, Sodium: 363 mg*

FATS AND OILS

Part of the appeal of most food is mouth feel, a term that is literally descriptive of the sensual element that makes us love smooth guacamole, creamy chocolate mousse, warm croissants, poached eggs on buttery toast, a crisp and juicy apple, chewy baked tofu, fresh and tender corn on the cob, warm polenta topped with beans and greens, sorbet both melting and with sharp shards of ice—we could go on for pages, but back to the topic at hand. Fat creates a significant amount of that alluring mouth feel: think of olive oil drizzled on steamed vegetables. Fat is also a medium for carrying the fragrance and flavor of a complex medley of spices, herbs, and seasonings. One of its practical uses is preventing food from sticking to pots and pans, but it causes distress when it sticks to our waists or the inside of our arteries.

Concern about fat in our bodies and in our diets has become an obsession for many people. But all fats are not created equal when it comes to health, and with an understanding of the difference between the better fats and the bad fats, you can enjoy that delicious mouth feel without worrying about what it might be doing to your body. Dietary fat is essential to good nutrition; oils help the body absorb nutrients like lutein from green vegetables and lycopene from tomatoes. But how much and what kinds of fats to use? The answers are not simple and involve consideration of cholesterol, calories, and omega fatty acids, among others . . . and new elements continually enter the discussion as we understand more about how fats affect our health.

In terms of blood cholesterol, at the simplest level the currently accepted rule boils down to: as much as possible, limit your fat intake to monounsaturated oils; second-best are polyunsaturated oils; avoid trans fats, hydrogenated fats, and most saturated fats. Naturally occurring fats are described primarily as monounsaturated, polyunsaturated, or saturated. Animal products are high in saturated fats and unsaturated fats are mostly from plant-based sources. Cooking oils contain some of each type, but are classified according to the highest percentage. For example, olive oil is defined as a monounsaturated fat because on average it contains 74 percent monounsaturated, 14 percent saturated, and 8 percent polyunsaturated fats.

Monounsaturated fats help the body reduce total serum cholesterol by reducing LDL, or "bad" cholesterol, while increasing HDL, or "good" cholesterol. Monounsaturated fats can be protective against conditions like cardiovascular disease associated with high levels of undesirable LDL. Plant oils like olive oil, canola, peanut, and avocado oils are high in monounsaturated fat.

Polyunsaturated fats reduce LDLs, but there is some discussion about whether or not they have any positive effect on HDLs. Polyunsaturated oils include corn, flaxseed, grapeseed, soybean, safflower, sunflower, and sesame.

Animal products like butter, cream, rich cheeses, and meat are highest in saturated fats. There is quite a debate over "good" versus "bad" saturated fats, with a few respectable sources pointing out that our bodies seem to respond differently to the saturated fats in tropical oils, such as coconut oil and possibly palm oil, than to saturated animal fats. Coconut oil has gotten a lot of bad press in recent years, but it looks to us as if ideas about the healthfulness of coconut oil may turn around soon, much like ideas about avocados and eggs.

Fats that are produced by the partial hydrogenation of liquid vegetable oils are called trans-unsaturated or just trans fats. Margarine and solid vegetable shortening made as hydrogenated fats have gotten very bad press and even been banned in some localities because they raise LDL and reduce HDL. Trans fats are easy to avoid if you read labels: Stay away from anything "hydrogenated."

Enjoying beneficial fats with appealing flavors, like avocados, olive oil, and nuts and seeds, can make it easier to follow a healthful diet because then we don't feel that our food choices are overly spartan. Some nutritionists think we can consume up to 35 percent of a day's calories in unsaturated fat without negative effect.

Another important dietary issue concerns our intake of omega-3 and omega-6 fatty acids, a subject that has generated enormous attention among nutritionists. The discussion has centered on the best proportion of omega-3s to omega-6s in our diet. While both help protect against heart disease, an imbalance of the two, with a significantly higher amount of omega-6s, will negate the beneficial effects of the omega-3s. The ideal ratio is about 6 (for omega-6s) to 1 (for omega-3s). The following chart shows percentages in cooking and salad oils.

	OMEGA-6	OMEGA-3	PROPORTION OF OMEGA-6 TO OMEGA-3
Canola	20%	9%	2 to 1
Soy	51%	7%	7 to 1
Olive	9%	1%	9 to 1
Corn	54%	1%	54 to 1
Safflower	75%	1%	75 to 1

Flaxseeds are the richest vegetarian source of omega-3s and are excellent in baked goods and other foods, but the oil must be refrigerated or it quickly turns rancid. For information about the nutrient value and dietary use of nuts and seeds, see pages 156–157. Omega-3 fatty acids are also found in leafy vegetables—another good reason to eat your greens! Our discussion has centered on, and is limited to, vegetable fats, but omega fatty acids are a significant nutritional element in fish and fish oils, also.

It is important to make sure that the total calories you consume stay at a reasonable level. Interestingly, all oils—no matter what the source—contain 120 calories per tablespoon. The best way to avoid unwanted weight gain or an unhealthy diet is to think about everything you're eating, not just the fat. For example, refined carbohydrates like white rice and sugary desserts may be low in fat, but they are high in calories and are high on the Glycemic Index (see pages 46–47).

When we examine traditional diets around the world, we see fascinating differences in fat intake. Diets in Mediterranean locales like Crete showed fat constituting 40 percent of the calories in the diet, while in Japan, fat made up only 10 percent of the calories. Yet, the rate of heart disease was lower in Crete for those whose diet was close to traditional than for the similar group in Japan. Was it the amount of olive oil and wild greens, or exercise, climbing up and down the very hilly terrain? Was the Japanese diet too high in sodium? Just one more example of the complexity of the dietary, lifestyle, and genetic factors that affect our health.

COOKING AND SALAD OILS

In general, oils that are cold- or expeller-pressed, GMO-free, and from organically grown sources are healthier for both you and the environment. Many oils are extracted in denaturing processes that rely upon bleaching, heat, and chemicals that negate positive nutritional value.

OLIVE OIL
Americans consume more than twice as much olive oil as they did ten years ago. The popularity of Italian and other Mediterranean cuisines, olive oil's well-publicized healthful

benefits, and its wonderful flavor have all contributed to our new love affair. The color, flavor, and fragrance of olive oils grown and pressed in different regions vary considerably. Images of hillside olive groves and upright screw presses give us romantic associations with olive oil, although today most large-scale, commercial "pressing" is done with centrifuges.

Extra-virgin olive oil is the highest grade and is mechanically—never chemically—produced. To be labeled "extra-virgin," milling and extraction must occur within twenty-four hours of olive harvest and the oil must contain less than 1 percent acidity. Extra-virgin is the most flavorful grade of olive oil, and depending on the olive varieties and growing region, its flavor is variously described as fruity, nutty, peppery, or sweet. In order to enjoy its health and flavor attributes fully, avoid heating extra-virgin olive oil beyond 325 degrees.

Pure olive oil, usually called simply "olive oil," has an acidity of 1 to 3 percent and a less distinctive flavor and fragrance, and it has undergone more processing, such as filtering and refining. It is an all-purpose olive oil with a higher smoking point that makes it good for cooking.

Light, "lite," and extra-light olive oils were developed for American consumers as a marketing concept. All olive oil has 120 calories and 14 grams of fat per tablespoon, including those labeled light. "Light" refers to the color and flavor, which are pale and bland, not the calorie content. Light olive oil has undergone considerable processing, often chemical refining, to remove the olive flavor. We don't recommend light olive oil.

Olive pomace oil is considered an inferior grade, and is mostly used for soap-making and industrial purposes. Pomace is the pulverized skins and pits left after pressing; olive pomace oil is obtained by processing pomace with solvents, heat, or other physical treatments to extract more oil. Avoid any olive oil whose label mentions pomace. It often also says "contains extra-virgin olive oil." It is usually significantly less expensive, but it is not as healthful and it has an unappealing flavor.

NUT OILS

Flavorful walnut and hazelnut oils are delicious in dressings for salads. Both are highly perishable and should be stored in the refrigerator. Considering their expense, it's good to know that a little goes a long way.

CANOLA OIL

Canola oil is the marketing alias of the unfortunately named rapeseed oil. Canola's mild, unobtrusive flavor makes it a versatile oil that can be used for all kinds of cooking and dressings.

SOY OIL

Most oils that are simply called "vegetable oil" are made from soybeans. Soy oil has a neutral flavor and is very versatile. Soy oil is one of the most common oils available.

Umeboshi Dressing

YIELDS ABOUT ¾ CUP | TIME: 5 MINUTES

Pickled salted plums, or *umeboshi,* are a popular Japanese condiment prized for centuries for their strong, piquant flavor and as an aid to digestion (see page 33). We've used them here to make a delicious, mauve-colored, no-fat dressing. The dressing is intensely flavored, so don't overwhelm salad or cooked vegetables by using too much. A little goes a long way.

---

4 OR 5 1-INCH UMEBOSHI (SEE NOTE)

2 TABLESPOONS SAKE

2 TABLESPOONS SUGAR

⅓ CUP WATER

NOTE: Umeboshi are available packaged and jarred in Asian markets and in many health food stores and supermarkets. Look for packaged varieties in the refrigerator case. Eden brand makes a jarred umeboshi paste, or *bainiku,* that can be used in place of the fresh plum flesh in this recipe.

1 Squeeze each plum by hand to pop out the pit, then discard the pit and chop the flesh. You will need about ¼ cup, lightly packed.

2 In a blender, purée the umeboshi, sake, sugar, and water to reach a smooth consistency. Add more sugar and/or water to taste.

3 Umeboshi Dressing will keep for three weeks in the refrigerator.

SERVING AND MENU IDEAS: This dressing is delicious on steamed broccoli, salad greens, and cooked greens such as kale, Swiss chard, and baby bok choy. It complements beets, and is excellent spread on corn on the cob. It also makes an interesting dipping sauce for sushi or crudités. Try it on shredded carrots for a bright little side salad to accompany Azuki Bean and Spinach Soup (page 124).

UMEBOSHI DRESSING—PER 1½ TABLESPOONS
Calories: 20, Protein: 0, Carbohydrate: 4 g, Dietary Fiber: 0 g, Total Fat: 0 g, Saturated Fat: 0 g, Monounsaturated Fat: 0 g, Cholesterol: 0 mg, Sodium: 355 mg

Avocado Citrus Dressing

YIELDS ABOUT 2 CUPS | TIME: 15 MINUTES

When this dressing is on the menu at Moosewood, it is very popular with both our customers and our staff. We almost always use cilantro in the dressing, but basil is a fine alternative.

> 1 LARGE RIPE HASS AVOCADO, PITTED AND PEELED
>
> ⅓ CUP ORANGE JUICE
>
> 5 TABLESPOONS LIME OR LEMON JUICE
>
> ¼ CUP CHOPPED FRESH CILANTRO OR BASIL
>
> 1 GARLIC CLOVE, CHOPPED
>
> ¼ TEASPOON SALT
>
> DASH OF CAYENNE OR GROUND BLACK PEPPER
>
> 1 TO 2 TABLESPOONS OLIVE OIL (OPTIONAL)

Place all of the ingredients in a blender and purée until smooth and creamy. If the dressing is too thick, add a little water. Add more salt to taste. Let the dressing sit for several minutes for the flavors to marry. Will keep for a week in the refrigerator. If the chilled dressing congeals, bring it to room temperature before serving.

VARIATIONS: If you're making the cilantro version, add ½ teaspoon ground cumin or coriander.

Add ¼ cup chopped scallions.

SERVING AND MENU IDEAS: Use this dressing on salad greens to go with New World Pizza (page 188), Oaxacan Green Mole Stew (page 251), or Tex-Mex Stuffed Portabellas (page 192). Drizzle it on a plate of sliced fresh tomatoes to serve with Southwestern Black Bean Burgers (page 154) or Latin Corn Soup (page 128).

AVOCADO CITRUS DRESSING—PER 1 TABLESPOON
Calories: 11, Protein: 0 g, Carbohydrate: 1 g, Dietary Fiber: 0 g, Total Fat: 1 g, Saturated Fat: 0 g, Monounsaturated Fat: 1 g, Cholesterol: 0 mg, Sodium: 18 mg

Pear and Thyme Vinaigrette

YIELDS 1 GENEROUS CUP | TIME: 10 MINUTES

This sweet, creamy dressing is great on zesty greens like arugula topped with some toasted or spiced nuts and a sprinkling of crumbled blue cheese, feta cheese, or chèvre. A pear that is still sweet and juicy, but a bit too soft for eating out of hand, will work fine here.

1 RIPE PEAR, CORED AND CHOPPED

⅓ CUP OLIVE OIL

2 TABLESPOONS CIDER VINEGAR

2 TABLESPOONS WATER OR UNSWEETENED APPLE OR PEAR JUICE

1 TEASPOON DIJON MUSTARD

1 TEASPOON FRESH THYME LEAVES

¼ TEASPOON SALT

GENEROUS DASH OF GROUND BLACK PEPPER

1 SMALL GARLIC CLOVE, PRESSED OR MINCED (OPTIONAL)

MAPLE SYRUP (OPTIONAL)

1 Combine all of the ingredients in a blender and purée until smooth and creamy. If the dressing is too thick, add a little more water or juice. Add some maple syrup if you want it a touch sweeter.

2 This dressing will keep in the refrigerator for 3 or 4 days. If the chilled dressing congeals, bring it to room temperature before serving.

SERVING AND MENU IDEAS: On frisée or other sharp-tasting greens, this makes a perfect autumn or winter salad to accompany Tuscan Harvest Soup (page 123), Root Vegetable Hash (page 165), or Winter Squash Stuffed with Two-Rice Pilaf (page 198). On milder greens, its sweetness balances dishes with a bitter edge, such as Pasta with Broccoli Rabe and Beans (page 229).

PEAR AND THYME VINAIGRETTE—PER 1 TABLESPOON
Calories: 116, Protein: 1 g, Carbohydrate: 14 g, Dietary Fiber: 2 g, Total Fat: 7 g, Saturated Fat: 1 g, Monounsaturated Fat: 5 g, Cholesterol: 0 mg, Sodium: 151 mg

Shallot Vinaigrette

YIELDS ABOUT 1 CUP | TIME: 10 MINUTES

This vinaigrette infused with the flavors of shallots and herbs can transform the simplest roasted vegetables or green salad.

½ CUP MINCED SHALLOTS

¼ CUP OLIVE OIL

¼ CUP EXTRA-VIRGIN OLIVE OIL

¼ CUP CIDER VINEGAR OR RED WINE VINEGAR

½ TEASPOON SALT

¼ TEASPOON GROUND BLACK PEPPER

2 TABLESPOONS CHOPPED FRESH BASIL OR 1 TABLESPOON CHOPPED FRESH TARRAGON (OPTIONAL)

2 TABLESPOONS WATER

1 Cook the shallots in the olive oil until soft, either in a small skillet on medium-high heat for 2 or 3 minutes, or in a microwave for about a minute.

2 In a small bowl, whisk the warm shallots and olive oil with the extra-virgin olive oil, vinegar, salt, pepper, basil if using, and water. Or put everything except for the water in a blender and whirl, adding the water as it blends. Add more vinegar, salt, and/or pepper to taste.

3 Shallot Vinaigrette will keep in the refrigerator for about a week. If the chilled dressing congeals, bring it to room temperature before serving.

SERVING AND MENU IDEAS: This is perfect as the dressing for Greens with Roasted Vegetables Salad (page 102). This subtle dressing can make steamed green beans or asparagus compelling dishes. It's also good on sliced fresh tomatoes, avocados, or shredded carrots. Use it to dress salad greens to go with Mock Risotto Primavera (page 279) or Tempeh Bourguignon (page 250).

SHALLOT VINAIGRETTE—PER 1 TABLESPOON
Calories: 61, Protein: 0 g, Carbohydrate: 0 g, Dietary Fiber: 0 g, Total Fat: 7 g, Saturated Fat: 1 g, Monounsaturated Fat: 5 g, Cholesterol: 0 mg, Sodium: 73 mg

SOUPS

Stracciatella

YIELDS ABOUT 6 CUPS | TIME: 20 MINUTES

*S*tracciatella means "torn to rags or tatters," which describes the egg and cheese mixture cooked in this classic Italian soup. We've added greens to create a filling and healthful dish. This quick and simple soup, best eaten as soon as it comes off the stove, is one of our favorite at-home suppers.

2 LARGE EGGS

2 TABLESPOONS GRATED PARMESAN CHEESE

PINCH OF GRATED NUTMEG (OPTIONAL)

SPRINKLING OF SALT AND GROUND BLACK PEPPER

2 TABLESPOONS EXTRA-VIRGIN OLIVE OIL

3 GARLIC CLOVES, MINCED OR PRESSED

PINCH OF RED PEPPER FLAKES

2 CUPS LIGHTLY PACKED CHOPPED FRESH SPINACH

¼ CUP CHOPPED FRESH BASIL

2 CUPS VEGETABLE BROTH (SEE PAGE 33)

2 CUPS WATER

1 TABLESPOON LEMON JUICE

1 In a bowl, beat the eggs with the Parmesan, nutmeg, salt, and pepper. Set aside.

2 In a soup pot on low heat, warm the oil. Cook the garlic and red pepper flakes for 30 seconds. Add the spinach and basil and stir until the spinach has just wilted. Add the broth and water and bring to a boil. Then reduce to a low simmer and drizzle the egg mixture into the center of the pot in a thin stream while stirring gently. The egg mixture will form "tatters" as it hits the hot liquid. Be careful not to overstir. Stir in the lemon juice and add salt to taste. Serve right away, while the spinach is bright green.

VARIATION: Replace the spinach with other greens such as escarole, mizuna, chard, arugula, or watercress.

SERVING AND MENU IDEAS: Serve with Shredded Zucchini and Carrots Open-faced Sandwiches (page 141), or with crudités and whole grain bread.

STRACCIATELLA—PER 1 CUP *Calories: 83, Protein: 3 g, Carbohydrate: 2 g, Dietary Fiber: 0 g, Total Fat: 6 g, Saturated Fat: 1 g, Monounsaturated Fat: 4 g, Cholesterol: 72 mg, Sodium: 107 mg*

Curried Yellow Pepper Soup

YIELDS ABOUT 7 CUPS | TIME: 55 MINUTES

This very pretty golden soup is enhanced by fragrant curry spices.

1 CUP CHOPPED ONIONS

2 TABLESPOONS VEGETABLE OIL

1 CUP FINELY CHOPPED CARROTS OR PEELED SWEET POTATOES

1 APPLE, PEELED AND CHOPPED

3 YELLOW OR ORANGE BELL PEPPERS, CHOPPED (4 TO 5 CUPS)

1 TABLESPOON GRATED PEELED GINGER ROOT

½ TEASPOON GROUND TURMERIC

½ TEASPOON GROUND CARDAMOM

¼ TEASPOON GROUND CINNAMON

⅛ TEASPOON CAYENNE

2 CUPS WATER OR VEGETABLE BROTH (SEE PAGE 33)

1 CUP COCONUT MILK

1 TABLESPOON LIME OR LEMON JUICE

½ TEASPOON SALT

1 In a soup pot on medium heat, cook the onions in the oil until softened, about 5 minutes. Add the carrots and apples and continue to cook, stirring often, for about 10 minutes. Stir in the bell peppers, salt, ginger, turmeric, cardamom, cinnamon, and cayenne, and cook for a minute, stirring constantly. Add the water or broth and stir well. Cover and bring to a boil. Reduce to a simmer and cook until the vegetables are tender, about 10 minutes.

2 Stir in the coconut milk and lime juice. In a blender, purée in batches until silky smooth. Add salt to taste.

VARIATIONS: Replace the apple with 1 cup of apple juice.

Substitute unsweetened soymilk or almond milk for the coconut milk.

SERVING AND MENU IDEAS: Garnish each serving with a dollop of yogurt, a sprig of mint or cilantro, and/or a thin slice of lime. Excellent with Chickpea Crêpes (page 73), or Bulghur and Fruit Salad (page 96).

CURRIED YELLOW PEPPER SOUP—PER 1 CUP
Calories: 168, Protein: 2 g, Carbohydrate: 15 g, Dietary Fiber: 4 g, Total Fat: 13 g, Saturated Fat: 8 g, Monounsaturated Fat: 3 g, Cholesterol: 0 mg, Sodium: 191 mg

Watercress and Cauliflower Soup

YIELDS ABOUT 8 CUPS | TIME: 40 MINUTES

Lightly stepping in for the more usual potato in our puréed soups, cauliflower provides a thick, smooth, mildly flavored base for the sharp brightness of watercress in this beautiful emerald green soup. You might never guess there's cauliflower in there.

---

2 TABLESPOONS EXTRA-VIRGIN OLIVE OIL

1 CUP CHOPPED ONIONS

1 QUART (4 CUPS) VEGETABLE BROTH
(SEE NOTE)

6 CUPS COARSELY CHOPPED CAULIFLOWER

1 TEASPOON SALT

6 CUPS CHOPPED WATERCRESS, THICK STEM
ENDS REMOVED

GROUND BLACK PEPPER

NOTE: Our favorite broth for this soup is Imagine brand No-Chicken Broth.

1 In a soup pot on low heat, warm the olive oil. Add the onions and cook, stirring occasionally, until softened but not browned, 5 to 10 minutes. Add the broth, cauliflower, and salt and bring to a boil. Reduce the heat and simmer covered until the cauliflower is tender, about 15 minutes.

2 Remove the pot from the heat and stir in the watercress. In a blender, purée the soup in batches until smooth and uniformly bright green. Season with black pepper to taste.

SERVING AND MENU IDEAS: Top with croutons, a dollop of sour cream, chopped fresh tomatoes, or all three. We like this soup with Rice Salad with Herbs (page 100), Couscous with Pistachios and Apricots (page 287), or Curried Tofu and Mango Salad (page 88).

WATERCRESS & CAULIFLOWER SOUP—PER 1 CUP
Calories: 59, Protein: 2 g, Carbohydrate: 6 g, Dietary Fiber: 2 g, Total Fat: 3 g, Saturated Fat: .5 g, Monounsaturated Fat: 2 g, Cholesterol: 0 mg, Sodium: 325 mg

PHYTONUTRIENTS

The plant pigments that give fruits and vegetables their beautiful colors are actually disease-fighting phytonutrients. Each color supplies different phytochemicals, and deeply saturated colors have higher levels of phytonutrients than pale colors. Because many fruits and vegetables contain more than one pigment, you can't always see which phytonutrients are present. For example, beta-carotene, an orange pigment, is obvious in carrots, cantaloupe, and sweet potatoes, but it is also present in dark green leafy vegetables such as kale and spinach, which have large amounts of green chlorophyll in their leaves. The more colors you eat, the greater the variety of phytonutrients you take in and the greater chance that you are getting the chemical compounds your body needs for optimal health. The more different colors you eat at once, the better, because of a synergistic effect: Each phytochemical may work alone but more often works in combination with other nutrients.

At Moosewood Restaurant, we've long given out a bumper sticker that says "Eat Your Greens." Maybe we should print up a new one that will stretch across the whole back of the car and read "Eat Your Greens, Reds, Blues, Purples, Yellows, Oranges, Whites, and Browns."

Phytonutrients, or phytochemicals, are naturally occurring chemicals in plants that protect them from diseases, pollution, and overexposure to the sun. When we eat the plants, the phytonutrients protect us, too. There are thousands of phytochemicals that are beneficial to humans, almost all found in vegetables and fruits and in foods made from plants, such as coffee, tea, wine, and chocolate. Phytonutrients boost the immune system, fight cancer, build bones, protect the heart, slow the effects of aging and environmental pollution, help repair DNA, increase HDL, or "good" cholesterol, decrease inflammation, improve vision, eliminate toxins, enhance communication among cells . . . the list goes on and on. Each fruit and vegetable family has its own unique health-protecting benefits. And all this is in addition to the vitamins, minerals, fiber, and great flavor that plant foods provide.

Phytonutrient research began fairly recently. The USDA opened a phytonutrient laboratory in 1997. There's a tremendous amount yet to be learned about phytonutrients, but so far, researchers have identified a few hundred protective phytochemicals out of what will likely be thousands. With names like anthocyanin, lycopene, beta-carotene, chlorogenic acid, phenethyl, isothiocyanate, monoterpene, and zeaxanthin, they don't sound too tasty. The exact chemistry involved in nutrition is probably more than the average diner wants to learn, but how wonderful to know that the delicious bright red cherries you're eating will go to work to protect your health. The best way to get the full benefit of phytonutrients is to eat a variety of colorful fruits and vegetables. As we say again and again in this cookbook—eat more plant foods!

PHYTONUTRIENTS: A GUIDE TO PRODUCE BY COLOR

BLUE/PURPLE

Fruits: blackberries, fresh and dried black currants, fresh and dried blueberries, elderberries, fresh and dried plums, purple figs, purple grapes, raisins

Vegetables: purple asparagus, purple bell peppers, purple cabbage, purple eggplants, purple potatoes

PHYTOCHEMICALS/BENEFITS
Contain anthocyanins and phenolics that lower the risk of some cancers; promote urinary tract health; help memory function; promote healthy aging

GREEN

Fruits: avocados, green apples, green grapes, green pears, honeydew melon, kiwi, limes

Vegetables: artichokes, asparagus, bok choy, broccoli, broccoli rabe, Brussels sprouts, celery, collard greens, cucumbers (with skin), curly endive, green beans, green bell peppers, green cabbage, kale, leeks, lettuces, mustard greens, napa cabbage, okra, peas, scallions, spinach, turnip greens, zucchini

PHYTOCHEMICALS/BENEFITS
Contain indoles, lutein, monoterpenes, phenethyl isothiocyanate, sulforaphane, and zeaxanthin that lower the risk of breast, prostate, lung, and other cancers; promote eye health; help build strong bones and teeth; boost immunity

WHITE/TAN/BROWN

Fruits: bananas, Bosc pears, dates, tan figs, white nectarines, white peaches

Vegetables: cauliflower, garlic, ginger, jicama, mushrooms, onions, parsnips, shallots, soybeans, turnips, white potatoes

PHYTOCHEMICALS/BENEFITS
Contain allicin, genistein, phenethyl isothiocyanate, and phytosterols that promote heart health; help maintain healthful cholesterol level; lower the risk of breast, lung, and other cancers; slow cholesterol absorption

YELLOW/ORANGE

Fruits: apricots, cantaloupe, golden apples, grapefruit, lemons, mangoes, oranges, papayas, persimmons, tangerines, yellow nectarines, yellow peaches, yellow pears

Vegetables: acorn squash, butternut squash, carrots, pumpkins, rutabaga, sweet corn, sweet potatoes, yellow beets, yellow bell peppers, yellow potatoes, yellow summer squash, yellow tomatoes

PHYTOCHEMICALS/BENEFITS
Contain bioflavonoids, carotenoids, and limonoids that promote heart health; promote eye health; lower the risk of some cancers; boost immunity

RED

Fruits: blood oranges, cherries, cranberries, pomegranates, pink/red grapefruit, raspberries, red apples, red grapes, red pears (with skin), strawberries, watermelon

Vegetables: radicchio, radishes, red beets, red bell peppers, red onions, red potatoes, red tomatoes, rhubarb

PHYTOCHEMICALS/BENEFITS
Contain anthocyanins, catechins, cholorgenic acid, and lycopene that promote heart health; help memory function; lower the risk of some cancers; promote urinary tract health; boost immunity

Adapted from educational materials of the Produce for Better Health Foundation.

Roman Grain and Mushroom Soup

YIELDS ABOUT 8½ CUPS | SOAKING TIME: AT LEAST 6 HOURS | COOKING TIME: 1 HOUR

This hearty fall and winter soup is substantial and very satisfying. In Italy, a soup like this might be made with farro, an ancient relative of wheat that, legend has it, fed the armies of Rome. Although farro is hard to find in North America, its relative, spelt, is not so difficult to track down and shares its nutty flavor and ancient history. Look for spelt berries in natural food stores or well-stocked supermarkets.

We prefer this soup with aromatic dried porcini mushrooms, but if you don't have them, try the variation.

---

1 CUP SPELT BERRIES

3 BAY LEAVES

¼ CUP LIGHTLY PACKED DRIED PORCINI MUSHROOMS

1 CUP HOT WATER

2 TABLESPOONS OLIVE OIL

1 CUP DICED ONIONS

1 CUP DICED CARROTS

1 CUP DICED CELERY

1½ TEASPOONS SALT

2 TEASPOONS MINCED FRESH ROSEMARY OR 1 TEASPOON DRIED ROSEMARY, CRUMBLED OR GROUND

5 OR 6 SPRIGS FRESH THYME OR 1 TEASPOON DRIED THYME

1½ TEASPOONS MINCED FRESH SAGE OR ¾ TEASPOON RUBBED SAGE

⅓ CUP WHITE WINE

3 CUPS CHOPPED PORTABELLA MUSHROOMS

⅓ CUP CHOPPED FRESH PARSLEY

GROUND BLACK PEPPER

---

1 Soak the spelt berries in water to cover overnight or for at least 6 hours. Drain, discard the liquid, and place the spelt berries and bay leaves in a saucepan with fresh water to cover plus a couple of inches. Bring to a boil and then reduce the heat and simmer covered for 45 to 50 minutes, until tender. Drain, reserving the cooking liquid.

2 While the spelt berries cook, soak the dried porcini in the hot water in a bowl, and start to cook the vegetables. Warm the oil in a soup pot on medium-high heat and add the onions. Cook for 3 or 4 minutes before adding the carrots, celery, and salt, and if you are using dried, the rosemary, thyme, and sage. Cook, stirring often, for about 5 minutes. Add the wine and stir well. Remove the softened porcini mushrooms from the soaking liquid. Strain the liquid through a coffee filter or very fine strainer and add to the pot. Dice the porcini and add to the soup.

3 Add enough water to the reserved spelt cooking liquid to yield 3 cups, and add it to the soup pot. Add the cooked spelt, the portabella mushrooms, and the herbs if you are using fresh, and simmer covered for 15 minutes.

4 Before serving, remove the thyme sprigs and the bay leaves. Stir in the parsley and add black pepper to taste.

VARIATIONS: Replace the dried porcini mushrooms with an additional cup of chopped portabella mushrooms, and in place of the porcini soaking liquid, spelt cooking liquid, and water, add 1 quart of mushroom broth or vegetable broth (see page 33).

Substitute an equal amount of barley for the spelt berries. See page 19 for cooking directions. Reserve the cooking liquid and follow the recipe directions.

SERVING AND MENU IDEAS: Pass grated Parmesan cheese or pecorino Romano cheese at the table. A good partner for this soup might be a green salad with Pear and Thyme Vinaigrette (page 110), or a side dish of Cabbage Braised in Red Wine (page 306), or bread with Figs and Chèvre Sandwich Spread (page 145).

ROMAN GRAIN AND MUSHROOM SOUP—PER 1 CUP *Calories: 122, Protein: 5 g, Carbohydrate: 21 g, Dietary Fiber: 5 g, Total Fat: 4 g, Saturated Fat: 4 g, Monounsaturated Fat: 0 g, Cholesterol: 0 mg, Sodium: 437 mg*

Ginger Tofu Soup

YIELDS ABOUT 7 CUPS | TIME: 20 MINUTES (WITH LEFTOVER RICE)

This light soup is quick and easy to make. Feeling under the weather? This warming soup infused with ginger may be just the thing.

1 QUART (4 CUPS) VEGETABLE BROTH (SEE NOTE)

1 CUP THINLY SLICED CELERY

2 GARLIC CLOVES, MINCED OR PRESSED

¼ CUP PEELED GINGER ROOT MATCHSTICKS (2-INCH PIECES)

2 TABLESPOONS SOY SAUCE

1 CAKE OF FIRM TOFU (ABOUT 16 OUNCES)

1 CUP COOKED BROWN RICE

4 SCALLIONS, CUT ON THE DIAGONAL

NOTE: The better the broth, the better this soup. We like Imagine or Pacific brands: our favorite for this soup is a mock chicken broth.

1 Place the vegetable broth in a soup pot and bring to almost boiling. Add the celery, garlic, ginger, and soy sauce. Reduce the heat and simmer for 5 minutes.

2 Cut the tofu into small cubes and add to the pot. Gently stir in the rice. Return to a simmer and cook for 5 minutes. Add the scallions and serve.

SERVING AND MENU IDEAS: Have a bowl of this soup before Hijiki and Vegetable Sauté (page 160) or Egg Foo Yung (page 63), or serve Roasted Sweet Potatoes (page 299) on the side.

GINGER TOFU SOUP—PER 1 CUP *Calories: 69, Protein: 5 g, Carbohydrate: 9 g, Dietary Fiber: 1 g, Total Fat: 1 g, Saturated Fat: 0 g, Monounsaturated Fat: 0 g, Cholesterol: 0 mg, Sodium: 273 mg*

Eastern European "Minestrone"

YIELDS ABOUT 10 CUPS | TIME: 45 MINUTES

Teeming with colorful vegetables and the characteristic flavors of Hungarian, Romanian, and Bulgarian cuisines, this thick, hearty soup makes us think of an Italian minestrone that swapped its Mediterranean herbs for the earthy, rich spices of Eastern Europe.

1 ½ CUPS CHOPPED ONIONS

2 GARLIC CLOVES, MINCED OR PRESSED

½ CUP THINLY SLICED CELERY

2 TABLESPOONS OLIVE OIL

2 ½ TABLESPOONS SWEET PAPRIKA (SEE NOTE)

2 BAY LEAVES

1 TEASPOON GROUND CARAWAY SEEDS

1 CUP DICED CARROTS

¾ CUP GREEN BEANS CUT INTO ½-INCH PIECES

½ CUP DICED PEELED BEETS, TURNIPS, OR PARSNIPS

¾ CUP DICED RED OR YELLOW BELL PEPPERS

1 15-OUNCE CAN WHITE BEANS, DRAINED

1 28-OUNCE CAN DICED TOMATOES

1 QUART (4 CUPS) WATER OR VEGETABLE BROTH (SEE PAGE 33)

1 TABLESPOON LEMON JUICE

1 TEASPOON SALT

1 TEASPOON GROUND BLACK PEPPER

2 OUNCES WHOLE GRAIN LINGUINE OR SPAGHETTI, BROKEN INTO 1-INCH-LONG PIECES

2 TABLESPOONS CHOPPED FRESH DILL

In a large soup pot on medium heat, cook the onions, garlic, and celery in the olive oil for 8 minutes, stirring occasionally. Add the paprika, bay leaves, and caraway and stir for a minute. Add the carrots, green beans, beets, and bell peppers, cover, and cook for 5 minutes, stirring occasionally. Add the white beans, tomatoes, water, lemon juice, salt, and pepper and bring to a boil. Stir in the pasta pieces, cover, and simmer on medium heat until the pasta is al dente, 10 to 15 minutes. Stir in the dill. Remove the bay leaves before serving.

NOTE: Good paprika is highly aromatic. The Hungarian brand Pride of Szeged is particularly flavorful.

SERVING AND MENU IDEAS: Serve topped with plain nonfat yogurt or low-fat sour cream. We like this big soup accompanied by some radishes with coarse salt, hard-boiled eggs, and bread. Or pair it with a salad such as Celeriac Apple Slaw (page 94) or Roasted Beet Salad (page 92). It's good with a Cabbage and Mushrooms Open-faced Sandwich (page 141). Apple and Dried Fruit Strudel (page 327) is the perfect dessert.

EASTERN EUROPEAN "MINESTRONE"—PER 1 CUP
Calories: 142, Protein: 6 g, Carbohydrate: 24 g, Dietary Fiber: 6 g, Total Fat: 4 g, Saturated Fat: 1 g, Monounsaturated Fat: 2 g, Cholesterol: 0 mg, Sodium: 464 mg

Tuscan Harvest Soup

YIELDS ABOUT 10 CUPS | TIME: 1 HOUR AND 10 MINUTES

In Tuscany, this soup is traditionally made in early winter just after the olives have been pressed. Fresh olive oil is usually peppery, so for the best results, use the most flavorful, assertive olive oil you can find.

2 CUPS CHOPPED ONIONS

1 TEASPOON SALT

2 TABLESPOONS OLIVE OIL

4 GARLIC CLOVES, COARSELY CHOPPED

2 TEASPOONS GROUND FENNEL SEEDS

1 CUP CHOPPED CELERY

1½ CUPS CHOPPED CARROTS

1 CUP CHOPPED FENNEL BULB

2 CUPS CHOPPED GREEN CABBAGE

2 CUPS PEELED AND CUBED BUTTERNUT SQUASH

1 QUART (4 CUPS) VEGETABLE BROTH (SEE PAGE 33)

1 CUP WATER

1 15-OUNCE CAN CANNELLINI BEANS, DRAINED

¼ TEASPOON GROUND BLACK PEPPER

2 TABLESPOONS MINCED FRESH THYME

¼ CUP FINELY CHOPPED FENNEL LEAVES OR PARSLEY

3 TABLESPOONS LEMON JUICE

1 SLICE WHOLE GRAIN BREAD FOR EACH SERVING

EXTRA-VIRGIN OLIVE OIL

1 In a covered soup pot on medium-low heat, cook the onions and salt in the olive oil for about 5 minutes. Add the garlic, ground fennel, and celery and cook for about 3 minutes. Stir in the carrots and cook for about 3 minutes. Add the chopped fennel bulb and cabbage, and cook for about 5 minutes. Add the squash, vegetable broth, and water. Bring to a boil. Then reduce the heat, cover, and simmer until the squash softens but does not fall apart, 5 to 10 minutes.

2 In a blender, purée 1 cup of the beans with 1 cup of the soup. Stir the purée into the soup pot. Add the remaining beans and the black pepper, thyme, and fennel leaves. Simmer covered for at least 10 minutes until all of the vegetables are tender and the flavors have melded.

3 Just before serving, stir in the lemon juice and toast the bread. To serve, place a slice of bread in each soup bowl and drizzle with a little extra-virgin olive oil. Ladle the soup over the bread and drizzle a little extra-virgin olive oil on top.

SERVING AND MENU IDEAS: Top each bowl of soup with chopped fresh tomatoes and/or shredded Parmesan cheese. This soup is substantial, but a few olives, a wedge of cheese, some pears or grapes, and a glass of red wine wouldn't be unwelcome.

TUSCAN HARVEST SOUP—PER 1 CUP *Calories: 152, Protein: 5 g, Carbohydrate: 26 g, Dietary Fiber: 6 g, Total Fat: 4 g, Saturated Fat: 1 g, Monounsaturated Fat: 2 g, Cholesterol: 0 mg, Sodium: 536 mg*

Azuki Bean and Spinach Soup

YIELDS ABOUT 10 CUPS | TIME: 1 HOUR

Here is a wholesome, mild-tasting soup in which each flavor—azuki, spinach, and scallions—shines through. Azuki are small red beans with a thin white keel. They are high in protein and easily digested. Originally from China and Japan, they are now cultivated in the United States and are available organically grown.

1½ CUPS DRIED AZUKI BEANS

1 QUART (4 CUPS) VEGETABLE BROTH (SEE PAGE 33)

4 CUPS WATER

5 CUPS CHOPPED FRESH SPINACH (ABOUT 10 OUNCES)

½ CUP DIAGONALLY SLICED SCALLIONS

2½ TABLESPOONS SOY SAUCE

2 TABLESPOONS RICE VINEGAR

1 In a soup pot, bring the beans, broth, and water to a boil. Lower the heat and simmer with the pot lid slightly ajar for about 50 minutes.

2 When the beans are soft and tender but not falling apart, stir in the spinach, scallions, soy sauce, and rice vinegar. Add more water or broth for the consistency you like. For the best color and freshest flavor, serve the soup as soon as the spinach has wilted.

SERVING AND MENU IDEAS: Top each bowl of soup with grated daikon, carrots, or radishes and/or more scallions. Serve as a prelude to Scattered Sushi Salad (page 91) or Japanese Noodles with Tomatoes (page 230).

AZUKI BEAN AND SPINACH SOUP—PER 1 CUP
Calories: 118, Protein: 9 g, Carbohydrate: 22 g, Dietary Fiber: 4 g, Total Fat: 0 g, Saturated Fat: 0 g, Monounsaturated Fat: 0 g, Cholesterol: 0 mg, Sodium: 325 mg

Greek Tomato-Yogurt Soup

YIELDS ABOUT 6 CUPS | TIME: 30 MINUTES

A good start for any Greek or Mediterranean meal, this soup can also make a complete meal with pita bread and a Greek salad.

2 TABLESPOONS OLIVE OIL

1 CUP CHOPPED ONIONS

2 GARLIC CLOVES, MINCED OR CHOPPED

1 BAY LEAF

½ TEASPOON SALT

½ TEASPOON DRIED OREGANO
OR 1½ TEASPOONS FRESH

¼ TEASPOON DRIED THYME
OR 1 TEASPOON FRESH

4 CUPS CHOPPED FRESH TOMATOES
OR 1 28-OUNCE CAN DICED TOMATOES

2 SUN-DRIED TOMATOES

GENEROUS DASH OF GROUND BLACK
PEPPER

1½ CUPS VEGETABLE BROTH
(SEE PAGE 33)

1 CUP PLAIN NONFAT YOGURT

1 In a covered soup pot on low heat, warm the olive oil and cook the onions, garlic, bay leaf, salt, and herbs, if using dried, until the onions are very soft, about 12 minutes.

2 Add the tomatoes, sun-dried tomatoes, black pepper, and herbs, if using fresh. Simmer covered, stirring occasionally, until the tomatoes are very soft and juicy, about 10 minutes.

3 Remove the bay leaf. Add the vegetable broth and yogurt. Purée in batches in a blender until smooth and creamy. Reheat gently or refrigerate to serve chilled.

NOTE: We add the vegetable broth and yogurt at the end to cool down the soup for a safer puréeing process, but if the tomatoes and onions begin to stick or if you'll use an immersion blender, add the broth earlier.

VARIATION: This soup can be made without yogurt.

SERVING AND MENU IDEAS: Nice garnishes for this soup include finely chopped toasted walnuts and chopped mint, scallions, and/or parsley. This soup is good with almost any meal. Try it with Spinach-Tofu Burgers (page 153), Greener Spanakopita (page 186), or Curried Millet (page 286).

GREEK TOMATO-YOGURT SOUP—PER 1 CUP
Calories: 107, Protein: 4 g, Carbohydrate: 12 g, Dietary Fiber: 2 g, Total Fat: 5 g, Saturated Fat: 1 g, Monosaturated Fat: 4 g, Cholesterol: 2 mg, Sodium: 279 mg

Creamy Curried Pea Soup

YIELDS ABOUT 6 CUPS | TIME: 45 MINUTES

This is a smooth, beautiful chartreuse-colored soup flavored with curry spices and cilantro. We make it greener and more healthful with the addition of spinach.

2 TABLESPOONS OLIVE OIL

1 ½ CUPS CHOPPED ONIONS

2 GARLIC CLOVES, CHOPPED

½ TEASPOON SALT

1 CUP CHOPPED CARROTS

1 TABLESPOON CURRY POWDER

½ TEASPOON GROUND TURMERIC

1 QUART (4 CUPS) VEGETABLE BROTH (SEE PAGE 33)

2 CUPS FRESH OR FROZEN GREEN PEAS

3 CUPS FRESH SPINACH (ABOUT 5 OUNCES)

⅓ CUP PACKED FRESH CILANTRO, LARGE STEMS REMOVED

⅛ TEASPOON GROUND BLACK PEPPER

4 OUNCES NEUFCHÂTEL CHEESE

1 In a soup pot on medium-high heat, warm the oil. Add the onions, garlic, and salt and cook, stirring frequently, until the onions soften, about 5 minutes. Add the carrots and cook for another 3 minutes. Stir in the curry powder and turmeric. Add the broth and 1 cup of the peas, cover, and bring to a boil. Reduce the heat and simmer until all of the vegetables are very soft, about 15 minutes.

2 Remove from the heat and stir in the spinach, cilantro, black pepper, and neufchâtel. In a blender in batches, purée the soup until very smooth. Stir in the remaining cup of peas and add salt to taste. Reheat gently on low heat—don't let it boil.

SERVING AND MENU IDEAS: Serve this soup with a light, fruity salad, such as Mango Slaw (page 93) or Bulghur and Fruit Salad (page 96).

CREAMY CURRIED PEA SOUP—PER 1 CUP
Calories: 176, Protein: 6 g, Carbohydrate: 17 g, Dietary Fiber: 6 g, Total Fat: 9 g, Saturated Fat: 4 g, Monounsaturated Fat: 5 g, Cholesterol: 14 mg, Sodium: 395 mg

Mellow Gazpacho

YIELDS ABOUT 6 CUPS | TIME: 30 MINUTES

In this smooth, refreshing gazpacho, the addition of whole wheat bread puréed with the other ingredients mellows the acidity of the tomatoes.

3 TO 4 CUPS CHOPPED FRESH TOMATOES

2 TABLESPOONS EXTRA-VIRGIN OLIVE OIL

1½ CUPS PEELED, SEEDED, AND CHOPPED CUCUMBERS

2 CUPS CHOPPED RED BELL PEPPERS

2 GARLIC CLOVES, MINCED OR PRESSED

2 SLICES WHOLE WHEAT BREAD (ABOUT 2 CUPS CUBED)

2 TABLESPOONS LEMON JUICE OR CIDER VINEGAR

2 TO 3 CUPS TOMATO JUICE

1 TEASPOON SALT

½ TEASPOON GROUND BLACK PEPPER

½ TEASPOON TABASCO SAUCE OR A TOUCH OF CAYENNE

¼ CUP MINCED FRESH PARSLEY, LARGE STEMS REMOVED

¼ CUP MINCED SCALLIONS

In a blender in batches, purée the tomatoes, olive oil, cucumbers, bell peppers, garlic, bread, lemon juice, tomato juice, salt, black pepper, and Tabasco. Start with the smaller amount of tomato juice and add more until the gazpacho is the consistency you like. Stir in the parsley and scallions. Chill until cold.

SERVING AND MENU IDEAS: Serve this soup as a starter for Migas (page 59) or Spinach Quesadillas (page 187). Or pair it with something green, like Raw Broccoli Salad (page 97) or salad greens with Avocado Citrus Dressing (page 109).

MELLOW GAZPACHO—PER 1 CUP *Calories: 114, Protein: 3 g, Carbohydrate: 16 g, Dietary Fiber: 4 g, Total Fat: 5 g, Saturated Fat: 1 g, Monounsaturated Fat: 3 g, Cholesterol: 0 mg, Sodium: 662 mg*

Latin Corn Soup

YIELDS ABOUT 9 CUPS | TIME: 45 MINUTES

The purée of coconut milk and white hominy creates a lusciously thick, mild base for this colorful, nutritious soup. You might be surprised by how much you like the radishes. Finishing touches of cilantro and fresh avocado add a richness of flavor and texture that we really like.

2 CUPS THINLY SLICED ONIONS

2 TEASPOONS OLIVE OIL

3 GARLIC CLOVES, MINCED OR PRESSED

1 FRESH CHILE, MINCED

2 TEASPOONS GROUND CORIANDER

1½ TEASPOONS DRIED OREGANO

1 TEASPOON SALT

2 CUPS WATER OR VEGETABLE BROTH (SEE PAGE 33)

¼ CUP THINLY SLICED RADISHES

2 CUPS PEELED AND DICED SWEET POTATOES

1 CUP DICED RED BELL PEPPERS

1 15-OUNCE CAN WHITE HOMINY, DRAINED (SEE NOTE)

1 14-OUNCE CAN COCONUT MILK (SEE NOTE)

1 14-OUNCE CAN DICED TOMATOES

1½ CUPS FRESH OR FROZEN CORN KERNELS

2 TABLESPOONS LIME JUICE

2 TABLESPOONS CHOPPED FRESH CILANTRO

AVOCADO CUBES (OPTIONAL)

1 In a soup pot on medium-high heat, cook the onions in the oil for about 5 minutes, until just beginning to soften. Add the garlic, chiles, coriander, oregano, and salt and stir constantly for a minute. Stir in 1 cup of the water and the radishes, sweet potatoes, and bell peppers. Cover and simmer, stirring occasionally, until the vegetables are tender, about 10 minutes.

2 While the vegetables simmer, in a blender, purée the hominy with the remaining water and the coconut milk until smooth. When the vegetables are tender, add the purée and the tomatoes and corn and bring back to a simmer, stirring occasionally.

3 Stir in the lime juice and cilantro. Top each serving with ripe avocado cubes, if you wish.

NOTE: Look for brands of coconut milk and of hominy without preservatives.

VARIATION: For a lighter soup, you can omit the hominy and forget the blender.

SERVING AND MENU IDEAS: If you'd like to serve a little side dish with the soup, try crisp corn tortilla chips and Simple Guacamole (page 69). Pair Latin Corn Soup with Oaxacan Tlayuda (page 219) for a feast.

LATIN CORN SOUP—PER 1 CUP *Calories: 354, Protein: 7 g, Carbohydrate: 58 g, Dietary Fiber: 7 g, Total Fat: 13 g, Saturated Fat: 10 g, Monounsaturated Fat: 1 g, Cholesterol: 0 mg, Sodium: 294 mg*

Zuppa Verde

YIELDS ABOUT 11 CUPS | TIME: 35 MINUTES

In Italy, this light, nourishing soup would be called *Zuppa della Buona Salute* (Soup of Good Health) because of its restorative qualities. We serve it ladled over toasted slices of whole wheat bread, but if you want to avoid wheat or extra carbohydrates, the soup is fine without the toast.

2 TABLESPOONS OLIVE OIL

2½ CUPS FINELY CHOPPED ONIONS

1 CUP FINELY CHOPPED CARROTS

2 GARLIC CLOVES, MINCED OR PRESSED

1 HEAD OF CURLY ENDIVE (ABOUT 12 OUNCES), CHOPPED (ABOUT 6 CUPS)

1 HEAD OF ESCAROLE (ABOUT 10 OUNCES), CHOPPED (ABOUT 4 CUPS)

½ TEASPOON RED PEPPER FLAKES

½ TEASPOON DRIED OREGANO

1 28-OUNCE CAN DICED TOMATOES

½ TEASPOON SALT

4 CUPS WATER

½ CUP FINELY CHOPPED FRESH PARSLEY

GROUND BLACK PEPPER

1 SLICE OF WHOLE WHEAT BREAD FOR EACH SERVING (OPTIONAL)

GRATED PECORINO ROMANO OR PARMESAN CHEESE

OLIVE OIL

1 In a soup pot on medium heat, warm the oil. Add the onions, carrots, and garlic and cook, stirring frequently, for about 8 minutes, until the onions have softened. Add the endive, escarole, red pepper flakes, and oregano and stir for a minute or two until the greens have wilted. Add the tomatoes, salt, and water, cover, and bring to a simmer. Reduce the heat to medium-low and cook for about 5 minutes, until the vegetables are tender. Add the parsley, black pepper, and more salt to taste.

2 Toast a piece of bread for each serving. Place the toast in wide, shallow bowls and ladle hot soup on top. Sprinkle with grated cheese and drizzle with a little olive oil.

VARIATIONS: Endive has a bracing, bitter edge that many people love but others find harsh. For a milder soup, use 2 heads of escarole.

Add a 15-ounce can of small red beans or cannellini, rinsed and drained, or a cup of frozen or fresh peas with the parsley.

SERVING AND MENU IDEAS: Start with Mushroom-Walnut Spread (page 66) as a dip with crudités and end with Fruit and Nut Truffles (page 314). Or, for a great cross-cultural combo, follow the soup with Sweet Potato Pie with Pecan-Oat Crust (page 326).

ZUPPA VERDE—PER 1 CUP *Calories: 75, Protein: 2 g, Carbohydrate: 12 g, Dietary Fiber: 4 g, Total Fat: 3 g, Saturated Fat: 0 g, Monounsaturated Fat: 2 g, Cholesterol: 0 mg, Sodium: 296 mg*

Chinese Ten-Vegetable Hot and Sour Soup

YIELDS ABOUT 16 CUPS | TIME: 70 MINUTES

We know that our soup has more than the ten vegetables in the title but we love them all. It is a big soup, in both quantity and flavor. It keeps and reheats well.

3 TABLESPOONS VEGETABLE OIL

1 CUP THINLY SLICED ONIONS

1 TABLESPOON GRATED PEELED GINGER ROOT

2 FRESH CHILES, MINCED

1 CUP DICED CELERY

1 CUP DICED CELERIAC (CELERY ROOT)

1 CUP DICED PEELED SWEET POTATOES

1 CUP DICED CARROTS

1½ CUPS CHOPPED GREEN CABBAGE

2½ QUARTS (10 CUPS) WATER OR VEGETABLE BROTH (SEE PAGE 33)

½ CUP SOY SAUCE

⅓ CUP RICE VINEGAR

2 TEASPOONS SALT

2 TEASPOONS GROUND BLACK PEPPER

½ CUP COLD WATER

¼ CUP CORNSTARCH

5 OUNCES SLICED FRESH SHIITAKE MUSHROOMS

1 CUP DICED ZUCCHINI OR YELLOW SQUASH

1 SMALL RED BELL PEPPER, DICED

8 OUNCES FIRM TOFU, CUT INTO ½-INCH CUBES

1½ CUPS SLICED BOK CHOY (SPLIT STALKS LENGTHWISE, THEN CUT INTO ¼-INCH-THICK DIAGONAL SLICES)

1 CUP DICED FRESH TOMATOES

2 TEASPOONS DARK SESAME OIL

THINLY SLICED SCALLIONS

1 Heat the vegetable oil in a soup pot on medium heat. Cook the onions, ginger, and chiles for a minute or two. Stir in the celery, celeriac, sweet potatoes, carrots, and cabbage, cover, and cook for couple of minutes. Add the water and bring to a boil. Reduce the heat and simmer for about 5 minutes.

2 While the soup simmers, in a bowl, combine the soy sauce, vinegar, salt, pepper, cold water, and cornstarch. Stir well and set aside.

3 Stir the shiitake mushrooms, zucchini, bell peppers, and tofu into the soup pot. Simmer until all of the vegetables are tender, 5 to 8 minutes. Add the soy sauce–cornstarch mixture and stir until the soup thickens. Add the bok choy and tomatoes and bring the soup back to a simmer. Add the sesame oil. Garnish with scallions.

NOTE: Because the vegetables in this soup are added in pretty rapid succession, it's best to have most of them prepped before you start to cook.

VARIATIONS: In place of fresh shiitakes, use cremini, oyster mushrooms, or dried shiitakes.

Rather than using both, use either carrots or sweet potatoes, either cabbage or bok choy, and either celery or celeriac.

SERVING AND MENU IDEAS: You might like to have some plain rice on the side, or some whole grain bread. For a sweet ending, try Pineapple Ice Pops (page 322).

CHINESE TEN-VEGETABLE HOT AND SOUR SOUP— PER 1 CUP *Calories: 92, Protein: 3 g, Carbohydrate: 12 g, Dietary Fiber: 2 g, Total Fat: 4 g, Saturated Fat: 0 g, Monounsaturated Fat: 2 g, Cholesterol: 0 mg, Sodium: 785 mg*

Sweet Potato, Apple, and Chipotle Soup

YIELDS ABOUT 12 CUPS | TIME: 1 HOUR

Hearty in flavor, creamy in texture, and lovely to look at, this vegan soup is both sweet and spicy hot.

2 TABLESPOONS VEGETABLE OIL

2½ CUPS CHOPPED ONIONS

2 GARLIC CLOVES, MINCED OR PRESSED

1 CUP THINLY SLICED CELERY

5 CUPS THINLY SLICED PEELED SWEET POTATOES

2 CUPS CHOPPED APPLES

1 TABLESPOON MINCED CANNED CHIPOTLE PEPPERS IN ADOBO SAUCE

1 QUART (4 CUPS) VEGETABLE BROTH (SEE PAGE 33)

1 CUP WATER

1½ TEASPOONS SALT

½ TEASPOON GROUND CINNAMON

¼ TEASPOON GROUND BLACK PEPPER

1 CUP UNSWEETENED APPLE JUICE

1 Warm the oil in a soup pot on high heat. Add the onions and garlic and cook, stirring continually, until the onions begin to soften, about 3 minutes. Add the celery, sweet potatoes, apples, chipotle peppers in adobo sauce, vegetable broth, water, salt, cinnamon, and black pepper. Cover and bring to a boil. Then lower the heat, and simmer gently until the sweet potatoes and apples are soft, about 20 minutes.

2 Add the apple juice to the pot. Purée the soup in a blender in batches until smooth and creamy. Blend in more chipotle peppers, adobo sauce, and/or black pepper to suit your taste.

SERVING AND MENU IDEAS: To add a little crunch, serve the soup topped with croutons, crumbled tortilla chips, toasted chopped pecans, or best of all, Toasted Pepitas and Cranberries (page 70). Also good topped with a dollop of yogurt and some chopped fresh cilantro. For a flavorful meal, serve with Raw Broccoli Salad (page 97) and Southwestern Black Bean Burgers (page 154) or with Curly Endive with Hazelnuts, Raspberries, and Manchego (page 85) and Sesame Flaxseed Cornbread (page 48).

SWEET POTATO, APPLE, AND CHIPOTLE SOUP—
PER 1 CUP *Calories: 109, Protein: 1 g, Carbohydrate: 21 g, Dietary Fiber: 3 g, Total Fat: 3 g, Saturated Fat: 0 g, Monounsaturated Fat: 1 g, Cholesterol: 0 mg, Sodium: 377 mg*

Basic Miso Soup

YIELDS ABOUT 8 CUPS | TIME: 25 MINUTES

For centuries, there have been health claims for miso too numerous to list. We've published plenty of different recipes for miso soup in our previous cookbooks and we couldn't imagine doing this book without one. In Japan, miso soup can be served at any meal, including breakfast, which is when some of us appreciate it most. It is nourishing and both soothing and energizing.

8 CUPS WATER

¼ OUNCE KOMBU
(TWO 6-INCH-LONG PIECES)

1 MEDIUM YELLOW ONION
(ABOUT 1 CUP SLICED)

1 CAKE OF FIRM OR SOFT TOFU
(ABOUT 16 OUNCES)

¼ TO ½ CUP MISO

2 CUPS LIGHTLY PACKED BABY SPINACH

NOTE: Hundreds of different misos, varying greatly in flavor and richness, are made in Japan. White and yellow misos are usually milder and less salty than stronger-tasting red, brown, and black misos. If you are going to buy just one miso, we recommend it be a milder, medium-colored one.

1 In a covered soup pot, bring the water and kombu to a boil; lower the heat and simmer. Meanwhile, thinly slice the onion and cut the tofu into small cubes, adding them to the pot as you prepare them.

2 In a small bowl, stir together ¼ cup of miso and 1 cup of the hot broth to make a smooth sauce. Set aside.

3 When the onions are soft, remove the kombu pieces. Stir in the miso and spinach. Taste the broth and if you'd like more miso flavor, add more until you're satisfied. Be sure to stir some hot broth into the miso before adding. After you've added the miso, don't let the soup boil: miso's healthful enzymes are destroyed by high temperatures.

SERVING AND MENU IDEAS: Embellish with chopped scallions, mung sprouts, dark sesame oil, and/or sesame seeds. Basic Miso Soup is good with sandwiches and salads and makes a great first course. We like it with Greens with Roasted Vegetables Salad (page 102) and before Hijiki and Vegetable Sauté (page 160).

BASIC MISO SOUP—PER 1 CUP *Calories: 80, Protein: 6 g, Carbohydrate: 9 g, Dietary Fiber: 2 g, Total Fat: 2 g, Saturated Fat: 0 g, Monounsaturated Fat: 1 g, Cholesterol: 0 mg, Sodium: 682 mg*

Heavenly Dulse Soup

YIELDS ABOUT 5 GENEROUS CUPS | TIME: 30 MINUTES

This brothy soup has a delicate balance of flavors: the mildly briny dulse makes it deliciously earthy and the soy sauce adds depth.

1 TABLESPOON VEGETABLE OIL

1½ CUPS FINELY CHOPPED CELERY

DASH OF SALT

2 TABLESPOONS GRATED PEELED GINGER ROOT

½ CUP MINCED SCALLIONS

3 CUPS WATER

½ CAKE OF SOFT TOFU (ABOUT 8 OUNCES)

3 TABLESPOONS SOY SAUCE

2 TABLESPOONS DULSE FLAKES (SEE PAGES 162–163)

3 CUPS THINLY SLICED MUSTARD GREENS, SPINACH, OR BOK CHOY

2 TABLESPOONS LIME JUICE

1 In a soup pot on medium heat, warm the oil. Add the celery, salt, ginger, and scallions, cover, and cook until the celery is soft, about 10 minutes. Add the water, cover, and bring to a boil.

2 Meanwhile, cut the tofu into ¼-inch cubes. When the soup boils, add the tofu, soy sauce, and dulse flakes. Simmer uncovered for at least 5 minutes. Stir in the greens and cook until wilted, about 3 minutes. Just before serving, add the lime juice. Add more salt to taste.

SERVING AND MENU IDEAS: Try this with Roasted Sweet Potatoes (page 299) or a side of beets with Umeboshi Dressing (page 108).

HEAVENLY DULSE SOUP—PER 1 CUP *Calories: 71, Protein: 4 g, Carbohydrate: 6 g, Dietary Fiber: 2 g, Total Fat: 4 g, Saturated Fat: 0 g, Monounsaturated Fat: 2 g, Cholesterol: 0 mg, Sodium: 581 mg*

Chilled Beet Borscht

YIELDS 9 CUPS | HANDS-ON TIME: 45 MINUTES | CHILLING TIME: AT LEAST 2 HOURS

This gorgeous magenta-colored soup is both sweet and sour. If you like beets, it'll soon be one of your favorite recipes. At Moosewood, the night before we want to serve this soup, we cook the beets, peel them, and return them to the pot of cooking liquid, which we put into the refrigerator to chill. Then in the morning, we finish the recipe and have a refreshing, cold soup in time for lunch on a hot summer day.

---

2 POUNDS BEETS

1 MEDIUM ONION

1 TEASPOON SALT

6 CUPS WATER

6 TABLESPOONS LEMON JUICE

2 TABLESPOONS SUGAR

2 CUPS TOMATO JUICE

---

1 Wash the beets and trim the tops and bottoms. If the beets are small, leave them whole; if they're large, cut into halves or quarters. Peel the onion and cut it into large chunks. Place the beets, onions, and salt into a soup pot. Add the water, cover the pot, and bring to a boil. Reduce the heat and simmer until the beets are easily pierced with a fork, about 35 minutes.

2 When the beets are tender, remove them from the cooking liquid. Peel the beets under cold running water. Strain the beet stock and discard the onions. (There should be 3 to 5 cups of stock remaining.) In a blender in batches, purée half of the peeled beets with 3 cups of the beet stock and the lemon juice, sugar, and tomato juice. Grate or dice the remaining cooked beets and stir into the purée. Refrigerate until thoroughly chilled, at least 2 hours.

VARIATION: For a sugarless borscht, omit the sugar, reduce the tomato juice to 1 cup, and add either 1 cup apple juice or 1 cup orange juice. Start with just 3 tablespoons of lemon juice and add more to taste.

SERVING AND MENU IDEAS: Top with chopped scallions, fresh dill, or hard-boiled eggs, or a dollop of sour cream or plain yogurt. Good served with Rice Salad with Herbs (page 100) or Seitan Gyro (page 142).

CHILLED BEET BORSCHT—PER 1 CUP *Calories: 78, Protein: 2 g, Carbohydrate: 18 g, Dietary Fiber: 3 g, Total Fat: 0 g, Saturated Fat: 0 g, Monounsaturated Fat: 0 g, Cholesterol: 0 mg, Sodium: 486 mg*

SANDWICHES

Broccoli-Cheese Wrap

SERVES 4 | YIELDS ABOUT 4 CUPS FILLING | TIME: 20 MINUTES

This creamy, broccoli-cheese filling has a little spark from red pepper flakes and is nicely flavored with basil. It's so good straight out of the pot that it may never make it into the wrap!

1 TABLESPOON OLIVE OIL

1 CUP CHOPPED ONIONS

½ TEASPOON SALT

3 CUPS CHOPPED BROCCOLI

4 GARLIC CLOVES, MINCED OR PRESSED

2 TEASPOONS DRIED OREGANO

¼ TO ½ TEASPOON RED PEPPER FLAKES (OPTIONAL)

1 CUP LOW-FAT RICOTTA CHEESE

½ CUP GRATED PART-SKIM MOZZARELLA CHEESE

½ CUP GRATED FETA CHEESE OR CHÈVRE

2 TABLESPOONS CHOPPED FRESH BASIL

SALT AND GROUND BLACK PEPPER

4 LARGE OR 8 SMALL WHOLE WHEAT TORTILLAS

1 Warm the oil in a skillet on medium heat. Add the onions and salt and cook until softened, stirring occasionally, 5 to 7 minutes. Stir in the broccoli, garlic, oregano, and red pepper flakes, if using, and cook until the broccoli is bright green and tender, 7 to 10 minutes. Remove from the heat and stir in the ricotta, mozzarella, and feta cheeses and the basil. Season to taste with salt and pepper.

2 To make wraps: In an unoiled skillet or griddle on medium heat, warm each tortilla for about 30 seconds on each side, until softened, or warm the stack of tortillas in a microwave oven for about 20 seconds. Roll the filling in smaller tortillas like an enchilada. For larger tortillas, place filling in the center, fold one side and then the other up and over the filling, and then tuck the open ends under. Eat as is, or brown lightly in an oiled skillet on medium heat.

VARIATIONS: Use lavash or other flat bread in place of tortillas.

The filling is really good tossed with pasta.

SERVING AND MENU IDEAS: Cold fresh orange wedges or fresh tomato slices are just perfect alongside. Serve with Mellow Gazpacho (page 127).

BROCCOLI-CHEESE WRAP—PER 1 SERVING (OF 4), 1 TORTILLA FILLED WITH 1 CUP OF FILLING
Calories: 337, Protein: 20 g, Carbohydrate: 37 g, Dietary Fiber: 7 g, Total Fat: 16 g, Saturated Fat: 8 g, Monounsaturated Fat: 6 g, Cholesterol: 43 mg, Sodium: 847 mg

Skillet Barbecue Tofu in a Pita

SERVES 2 TO 4 | YIELDS 2 WHOLE PITA SANDWICHES | TIME: 25 MINUTES

Tofu with Worcestershire sauce—who would have thought it could be so delicious? It gives the sandwich a bit of a backyard barbecue flavor, and sweet onions are the perfect complement. This sandwich is saucy and satisfying.

1 TABLESPOON OLIVE OIL

2 CUPS THINLY SLICED ONIONS

½ TEASPOON SALT

¼ TEASPOON DRIED THYME

⅛ TEASPOON GROUND BLACK PEPPER

2 TABLESPOONS VEGETARIAN WORCESTERSHIRE SAUCE

2 TEASPOONS SOY SAUCE

2 TEASPOONS DIJON MUSTARD

1 TEASPOON BALSAMIC VINEGAR

8 OUNCES OF FIRM TOFU, CUT INTO ½-INCH CUBES

2 6-INCH WHOLE WHEAT PITA BREADS

1 TOMATO, SLICED

LETTUCE LEAVES

1 In a skillet, warm the oil until a piece of onion sizzles when added. Stir in the onions, salt, thyme, and black pepper. Cook on medium-high heat, stirring often, until the onions have softened and browned, about 10 minutes.

2 While the onions cook, in a bowl, whisk together the Worcestershire sauce, soy sauce, mustard, and vinegar. Add the tofu cubes and toss to coat with sauce.

3 When the onions are done, stir in the tofu and marinade. Cover and cook on low heat until the tofu is hot, about 5 minutes.

4 Toast the pitas. Cut in half and line each pocket with tomato slices and lettuce. Fill with the tofu and onions.

SERVING AND MENU IDEAS: Have a picnic, even if you're at the kitchen table: serve with Sweet Potato–Walnut Salad on Arugula (page 89) or Our Favorite Raw Slaw (page 267).

SKILLET BARBECUE TOFU IN A PITA—PER 1 SERVING (OF 4), ½ PITA SANDWICH
Calories: 195, Protein: 9 g, Carbohydrate: 30 g, Dietary Fiber: 4 g, Total Fat: 6 g, Saturated Fat: 1 g, Monounsaturated Fat: 3 g, Cholesterol: 0 mg, Sodium: 766 mg

Three Open-faced Vegetable and Cheese Sandwiches

These sandwiches take cheese toast to a healthier place: whole grain bread is toasted with a modest amount of cheese and then smothered with a generous amount of vegetables, making a quick and healthful lunch or light supper. In the recipes we call for particular cheeses, but use whatever cheese you like best.

For inspiration for other delicious open-faced sandwiches, think about one of our Two Nut-free Pestos (page 79) and some roasted vegetables from Greens with Roasted Vegetables Salad (page 102).

Broccoli and Red Peppers

YIELDS 4 OPEN-FACED SANDWICHES, ABOUT 3 CUPS TOPPING | TIME: 20 MINUTES

We expect that you'll eat this sandwich with a fork and knife. If you want to eat it with your hands, slice the bell peppers and broccoli, instead of chopping, so they'll lie flat on the bread.

1 TABLESPOON OLIVE OIL

1 GARLIC CLOVE, MINCED OR PRESSED

3 CUPS CHOPPED BROCCOLI
(BITE-SIZED PIECES)

1 CUP CHOPPED RED BELL PEPPERS

½ TEASPOON SALT

GENEROUS DASH OF RED PEPPER FLAKES
OR GROUND BLACK PEPPER

1 TEASPOON MINCED FRESH ROSEMARY
OR 1 TABLESPOON CHOPPED FRESH BASIL

2 TABLESPOONS WATER

¾ CUP GRATED MILD PROVOLONE CHEESE

4 SLICES WHOLE GRAIN BREAD

1 In a skillet on medium-high heat, warm the olive oil. Add the garlic, broccoli, bell peppers, salt, red pepper flakes, and rosemary and cook, stirring constantly, for about 2 minutes. Add the water, cover, and cook, stirring occasionally, until the vegetables are tender, about 7 minutes. Uncover and remove from the heat.

2 Meanwhile, sprinkle the grated cheese on the bread. In an oven or toaster oven, melt the cheese. Top with the cooked vegetables.

SERVING AND MENU IDEAS: Serve this as an accompaniment to Roman Grain and Mushroom Soup (page 120).

BROCCOLI AND RED PEPPERS—PER 1 SERVING (OF 4)
Calories: 216, Protein: 11 g, Carbohydrate: 20 g, Dietary Fiber: 4 g, Total Fat: 11 g, Saturated Fat: 5 g, Monounsaturated Fat: 5 g, Cholesterol: 17 mg, Sodium: 658 mg

Shredded Zucchini and Carrots

YIELDS 2 OPEN-FACED SANDWICHES,
ABOUT 1½ CUPS TOPPING | TIME: 20 MINUTES

A favorite straight-out-of-the-garden meal.

1 TABLESPOON OLIVE OIL

½ CUP FINELY CHOPPED ONIONS

2 GARLIC CLOVES, MINCED OR PRESSED

PINCH OF RED PEPPER FLAKES

½ CUP GRATED CARROTS

1 CUP GRATED ZUCCHINI

¼ TEASPOON SALT

1 TABLESPOON CHOPPED FRESH BASIL

½ CUP GRATED GRUYÈRE CHEESE

2 SLICES WHOLE GRAIN BREAD

GROUND BLACK PEPPER

1 In a skillet on medium heat, warm the oil. Add the onions, garlic, and red pepper flakes and cook for 5 minutes, stirring often. Stir in the carrots and cook for a minute. Add the zucchini and salt, cover, and cook until the vegetables are tender, about 5 minutes. Uncover, stir in the basil, and remove from the heat.

2 Meanwhile, sprinkle the grated cheese on the bread. In an oven or toaster oven, melt the cheese. Mound the vegetables on top and sprinkle with black pepper.

SERVING AND MENU IDEAS: This is delicious with Sweet Potato, Apple, and Chipotle Soup (page 132).

SHREDDED ZUCCHINI AND CARROTS—
PER 1 SERVING (OF 2) *Calories: 279, Protein: 12 g, Carbohydrate: 22 g, Dietary Fiber: 4 g, Total Fat: 17 g, Saturated Fat: 6 g, Monounsaturated Fat: 8 g, Cholesterol: 30 mg, Sodium: 538 mg*

Cabbage and Mushrooms

YIELDS 2 OPEN-FACED SANDWICHES,
ABOUT 1⅔ CUPS TOPPING | TIME: 25 MINUTES

1 TABLESPOON OLIVE OIL

½ CUP FINELY CHOPPED ONIONS

2 CUPS FINELY CHOPPED GREEN CABBAGE

½ TEASPOON SALT

½ TEASPOON DRIED THYME

2 TABLESPOONS WATER

2 CUPS SLICED MUSHROOMS

1 TABLESPOON CHOPPED FRESH DILL

2 TABLESPOONS NEUFCHÂTEL CHEESE
OR ½ CUP GRATED DILLED HAVARTI CHEESE

2 SLICES RYE, PUMPERNICKEL, OR WHOLE WHEAT BREAD

1 In a skillet on medium-high heat, warm the olive oil. Add the onions and stir-fry for about 3 minutes. Add the cabbage, salt, and thyme, and stir-fry for about 3 minutes. Add the water, cover, and cook, stirring occasionally, for about 5 minutes. Add the mushrooms and cook uncovered, stirring occasionally, until the vegetables are tender, about 7 minutes. Remove from the heat and stir in the dill.

2 Meanwhile, if using neufchâtel, toast the bread and then spread on the neufchâtel. If using dilled Havarti, sprinkle the grated cheese on the bread, and in an oven or toaster oven, melt the cheese. Serve topped with the cooked vegetables.

CABBAGE AND MUSHROOMS—PER 1 SERVING (OF 2), ABOUT ⅔ CUP TOPPING *Calories: 216, Protein: 8 g, Carbohydrate: 24 g, Dietary Fiber: 5 g, Total Fat: 12 g, Saturated Fat: 3 g, Monounsaturated Fat: 6 g, Cholesterol: 11 mg, Sodium: 786 mg*

Seitan Gyro

SERVES 4 TO 8 | YIELDS ABOUT 4 CUPS OF FILLING | TIME: 30 MINUTES

At Moosewood, we serve pita sandwiches for lunch most days of the week. Even though sometimes they are a bit messy to eat, they are always popular with our customers and staff.

For this pita filling, we toss vegetables, seitan, and feta cheese in a simple dressing. Seitan is made from wheat gluten; it is low in fat and is a good source of protein. It can be found in the refrigerated section of supermarkets.

1 CUP DICED FRESH TOMATOES

1 CUP DICED CUCUMBERS

1 CUP DICED SEITAN (ABOUT 4 OUNCES)

½ CUP CUBED FETA CHEESE

½ CUP DICED AVOCADO

2 TABLESPOONS DICED RED ONIONS (OPTIONAL)

YOGURT TAHINI DRESSING

2 TABLESPOONS PLAIN NONFAT YOGURT

2 TABLESPOONS TAHINI

2 TABLESPOONS RED WINE VINEGAR

½ TEASPOON SALT

1 TEASPOON DRIED OREGANO (OPTIONAL)

GROUND BLACK PEPPER

4 WHOLE WHEAT PITA BREADS

LETTUCE LEAVES

1 In a bowl, combine the tomatoes, cucumbers, seitan, feta, avocado, and red onions, if using. In a separate bowl, whisk together the dressing ingredients. Pour the dressing over the vegetables and mix well. Add pepper to taste.

2 Cut the pitas in half and lightly toast them. Place a lettuce leaf in each half and fill with about ½ cup of the vegetable mixture.

VARIATION: Sometimes we make this pita filling with a vinaigrette dressing. Whisk together ¼ cup olive oil, 2 tablespoons red wine vinegar, ½ teaspoon salt, 1 teaspoon dried oregano (optional), and a dash of black pepper.

SERVING AND MENU IDEAS: Greek Tomato-Yogurt Soup (page 125) and Cauliflower "Tabouli" (page 269) are both good partners for Seitan Gyro.

SEITAN GYRO—PER 1 SERVING (OF 8), ½ PITA SANDWICH *Calories: 144, Protein: 5 g, Carbohydrate: 22 g, Dietary Fiber: 4 g, Total Fat: 5 g, Saturated Fat: 2 g, Monounsaturated Fat: 2 g, Cholesterol: 8 mg, Sodium: 234 mg*

YOGURT TAHINI DRESSING—PER 1 TABLESPOON *Calories: 24, Protein: 1 g, Carbohydrate: 1 g, Dietary Fiber: 1 g, Total Fat: 2 g, Saturated Fat: 0 g, Monounsaturated Fat: 1 g, Cholesterol: 0 mg, Sodium: 151 mg*

Chunky Guacamole Sandwich

SERVES 4 | YIELDS 2½ CUPS GUACAMOLE | TIME: 15 MINUTES

We take every opportunity we can to include avocados in our meals, not just because they are good for us but because we love them. Avocado salsa with our breakfast scramble, sliced avocados on our salad, avocado in dressings, soups, and stews, and as a dip for appetizers. We even make a smooth, lime-green avocado dessert shake. Here is one of our all-time favorite sandwiches with creamy, delectable avocados. For good measure we add some vegetables, cilantro, and lime.

---

2 LARGE HASS AVOCADOS

1 MEDIUM TOMATO, DICED (ABOUT ¾ CUP)

½ CUCUMBER, PEELED, SEEDED, AND DICED (ABOUT ¾ CUP)

2 TABLESPOONS LIME OR LEMON JUICE

1 GARLIC CLOVE, MINCED OR PRESSED

2 TABLESPOONS FINELY CHOPPED SCALLIONS OR SNIPPED CHIVES

2 TABLESPOONS FINELY CHOPPED FRESH CILANTRO

½ TEASPOON SALT

4 SLICES OF WHOLE WHEAT BREAD

---

1 Slice lengthwise around each avocado down to the pit. Twist the halves apart and remove the pit. Hold an avocado half in the palm of your hand and score the flesh into cubes. Use a spoon to scoop the cubes into a bowl. Repeat with the other halves. Stir in the tomatoes, cucumbers, lime juice, garlic, scallions, cilantro, and salt. Add more salt and/or lime juice to taste.

2 Toast the bread and spread each piece with a generous ½ cup of chunky guacamole.

SERVING AND MENU IDEAS: Top the sandwiches with grated cheddar or Monterey Jack cheese. Serve Chunky Guacamole in pita instead of on toast.

CHUNKY GUACAMOLE SANDWICH—PER 1 SERVING (OF 4), *Calories: 237, Protein: 5 g, Carbohydrate: 23 g, Dietary Fiber: 9 g, Total Fat: 16 g, Saturated Fat: 2 g, Monounsaturated Fat: 10 g, Cholesterol: 0 mg, Sodium: 434 mg*

Spinach, Beans, and Tomatoes on Cheese Toast

SERVES 4 | TIME: 35 MINUTES

This is a filling sandwich, a meal in itself. The flavor of the oven-roasted tomatoes is deep and sweet. The fresh spinach and basil are barely wilted right in the baking pan with the tomatoes and beans, so they remain bright green and full of flavor.

---

3 CUPS LARGE CHUNKS FRESH PLUM TOMATOES

1 TABLESPOON OLIVE OIL

4 GARLIC CLOVES, MINCED OR PRESSED

PINCH OF SALT

¼ TEASPOON GROUND BLACK PEPPER

1 15-OUNCE CAN PINTO, RED, OR WHITE BEANS, RINSED AND DRAINED

4 CUPS PACKED BABY SPINACH (ABOUT 6 OUNCES)

2 TABLESPOONS CHOPPED FRESH BASIL

4 SLICES WHOLE GRAIN BREAD

½ CUP GRATED PARMESAN CHEESE

---

1 Lightly oil a 9 × 13-inch baking pan.

2 Toss together the tomatoes, oil, garlic, salt, and pepper in the prepared pan. Bake uncovered in a 400° oven for 20 minutes. Stir in the beans and return to the oven until hot, about 5 minutes. Add the spinach and basil and stir everything together to moisten the spinach. Return to the oven until the spinach is beginning to wilt, 4 or 5 minutes.

3 Remove from the oven and use a potato masher to mash the ingredients together, until the spinach has wilted and most of the beans are mashed. Cover to keep warm and set aside.

4 Arrange the bread on an unoiled baking sheet and sprinkle each slice with a couple of tablespoons of grated cheese. Put the bread into the oven for about 5 minutes, until the bread is crisp and the cheese has melted.

5 To serve, top each slice of cheese toast with a generous half-cup of the bean mixture.

VARIATION: Instead of sliced bread, use 2 pitas to make 4 little "pita pizzas": At the outer edge of each pita, slip the point of a sharp knife in toward the center between the upper and lower sides, and cut around the outer edge. Separate into two thin circles. Sprinkle the Parmesan on the rough inner sides and proceed as with bread slices.

SERVING AND MENU IDEAS: This casual (okay, maybe we really mean messy) sandwich has a Mediterranean profile, so enjoy it with a glass of red wine and top it off with Fig and Pecan Baked Apples (page 318)—they can share the oven with the sandwich topping.

SPINACH, BEANS, AND TOMATOES ON CHEESE TOAST—PER 1 SERVING (OF 6) *Calories: 288, Protein: 16 g, Carbohydrate: 38 g, Dietary Fiber: 10 g, Total Fat: 9 g, Saturated Fat: 3 g, Monounsaturated Fat: 4 g, Cholesterol: 11 mg, Sodium: 702 mg*

Figs and Chèvre Sandwich Spread

YIELDS 1½ CUPS OF SPREAD | TIME: 20 MINUTES

This delightful goat cheese spread, filled with little nuggets of toasted walnuts and chewy sweet figs, is particularly delicious on rye or pumpernickel bread. Toast the bread, or not, cover each slice with the spread, and top with fresh apple slices.

- ¾ CUP CHÈVRE
- ⅓ CUP NEUFCHÂTEL CHEESE
- ½ CUP MINCED DRIED FIGS
- ½ CUP FINELY CHOPPED TOASTED WALNUTS
- ¼ CUP FINELY CHOPPED SCALLIONS OR SNIPPED CHIVES
- ¼ TEASPOON SALT
- GROUND BLACK PEPPER
- WATER OR MILK (OPTIONAL)

In a bowl, mash together the chèvre and neufchâtel. Stir in the figs, walnuts, scallions, and salt. Add pepper to taste. Stir in a tablespoon or so of water or milk if the mixture is too thick to spread.

SERVING AND MENU IDEAS: This is also great as a snack or appetizer with whole grain crackers and/ or pear or apple slices.

FIGS AND CHÈVRE SANDWICH SPREAD— PER 1 SERVING (OF 6) *Calories: 180, Protein: 7 g, Carbohydrate: 10 g, Dietary Fiber: 2 g, Total Fat: 13 g, Saturated Fat: 5 g, Monounsaturated Fat: 3 g, Cholesterol: 21 mg, Sodium: 210 mg*

FOOD SENSITIVITIES

During the last few years, the number of our customers requesting modifications and alternatives to our menu items because of food intolerances has increased considerably. We do the best we can to accommodate these needs, and in the process we've learned quite a bit about food allergies and sensitivities.

Food allergies are serious business. True food allergies occur in about 2 to 5 percent of the population. An allergic reaction to a specific food or food group is often relatively mild but can also be injurious or life-threatening. A person can be allergic to any food, and allergies can develop at any age. The food allergies most frequently seen in this country are to peanuts, tree nuts, seafood, fish, and gluten. In children, the most common allergies are to milk and eggs.

Allergies arise when the body misidentifies a food as harmful and creates a specific antibody to that food. The next time that food is eaten, it is recognized as dangerous, and the immune system releases a barrage of chemicals that trigger allergy symptoms. Some better known symptoms are hives and asthma, but in addition to the skin and respiratory system, allergens can also compromise the gastrointestinal tract, the cardiovascular system, and the nervous system.

At Moosewood, we've become skilled at reading labels of any prepared foods we use and at recognizing hidden allergens. We take care to meticulously report to our servers all of the ingredients in all of our dishes so they can pass this information on to our diners.

More commonly, our customers' restrictions are based on intolerances and sensitivities. Intolerances are not considered allergies because symptomatic reactions are not a consequence of an immune system reaction. Though not allergies, intolerances can still cause serious discomfort that may involve multiple body systems. Intolerance to milk is a good example; it is caused by the absence of an enzyme needed to digest lactose.

People can also have adverse reactions to food additives that are used as preservatives or for color, texture, and flavor enhancement, such as sulfites, dyes, and MSG. Sulfites are also naturally occurring substances in wine fermentation; some people react adversely to all wines and other people can tolerate wines without synthetic sulfites. Histamines can occur naturally and reach quite high levels in cheese, wine, and some fish. Since histamines are one of the chemicals released by the immune system involved in an allergic reaction, ingestion of these foods can cause "histamine toxicity" and the occurrence of allergy-like symptoms.

Food sensitivities might cause the least dramatic symptoms in an eater but can still be quite uncomfortable. We have customers who have trouble digesting garlic and onions, and others who do not do well with tomatoes or peppers. Some sensitivities, allergists warn, can be harbingers of a more serious allergic reaction down the road, so it is important to heed the reaction and avoid that food. These warnings can be as benign as a tingling on the roof of the mouth after eating a certain nut, or mild joint pain or congestion following the ingestion of wheat or another grain, or as discomforting as dizziness, excessive perspiration, or painful cramping.

The good news for those of us with food allergies and intolerances is that there are now many products on the market that are gluten-free, wheat-free, dairy-free, and certified to be prepared under conditions that assure no contamination by nuts, gluten, or eggs. This bounty of alternatives makes it possible to prepare delicious meals and enjoyable snacks. For the lactose intolerant, there is soymilk, and for those allergic to soy, there are almond, rice, and oat milks. Folks allergic to wheat can often enjoy other varieties of flour, such as spelt, kamut, and amaranth, that are available in breads crackers and cookies. Those with gluten allergies can find pasta, cereals, and baked goods made with corn, rice, millet, and quinoa.

Among researchers, there is mostly speculation about why it appears that we as a population are becoming more sensitive to the available food supply. Heredity appears to be involved. Many people with food allergies have parents with allergies, though not necessarily to food—it might be to ragweed, dust, or cats. And it has been established that significant segments of certain cultures are lactose intolerant. In addition, there is speculation that an overconsumption or dependence on a particular food can lead to an allergy or intolerance. In the United States, we see higher incidences of problems with wheat, gluten, and corn than elsewhere; in Japan this is true of rice; and in Scandinavia of codfish. Another viewpoint is that because of diminishing agricultural diversity we consume less variety within food groups, and so people vulnerable to developing allergies or intolerances are more likely to be overexposed to substances that may cause them problems.

We are at a juncture in history when there is an urgent need for sustainability, a lessening of dependence on energy-intensive modes of food distribution and on the fossil fuel needed for pesticides and fertilizers. It will be interesting to see if there is a significant shift to locally produced foods grown with organic methods, and if so, if this promotes greater diversity in the varieties of foods grown, and whether increases in food sensitivities and allergies slow down or reverse.

BURGERS

Moosewood Veggie Burgers

At Moosewood, we make burgers for lunch at least a couple of times a week. We make lots of different burgers and are always ready to try a new one, much to the delight of our regulars. We top them with salsa, or caramelized onions, or guacamole, or cheese, or a dressing. We serve them on rice, bulghur pilaf, or toast. Whatever way we end up serving them in the restaurant and at home, we think that our recipes make burgers that taste much better than the frozen veggie burgers you can buy in the store. The ingredients are better, the flavor is better, and the texture is better. All of the veggie burger recipes in this book have beans, or tofu, or tempeh, plus plenty of vegetables. All but Greek Lentil Burgers are wheat-free, and all but Southwestern Black Bean Burgers are vegan. Yet they're very different from each other.

Burgers take some time to make, but they freeze well, so at home we usually make a double or triple batch so we can stockpile them in the freezer. To freeze: Bake the burgers as instructed. Allow them to cool to room temperature, and then stack them in freezer bags, separating the burgers with squares of parchment paper or waxed paper. Reheat the burgers in the oven or microwave, or on the stovetop in an oiled skillet. Any of our veggie burgers can be grilled outside or tabletop, but bake them first because if you try to grill them unbaked they'll probably fall apart. You can put warm, room-temperature, or cold burgers on the grill, just brush both sides with oil first.

Any of the burger mixtures can be baked as a loaf: Pat the mixture into a lightly oiled 8-inch square baking pan, and bake for about ten minutes longer than the time given for the burgers.

Curried Red Lentil Burgers

YIELDS 6 BURGERS | HANDS-ON TIME: 1 HOUR | BAKING TIME: 20 MINUTES

These attractive golden burgers are fragrant with aromatic spices. Notice that this recipe calls for cooked rice, so if you don't have any left over, start it first.

1 CUP DRIED RED LENTILS

2 CUPS WATER

½ TEASPOON GROUND TURMERIC

1 TEASPOON SALT

1½ CUPS CHOPPED ONIONS

3 GARLIC CLOVES, MINCED OR PRESSED

2 TABLESPOONS OLIVE OIL

½ CUP DICED CELERY

1 CUP DICED RED BELL PEPPERS

1 TABLESPOON GRATED PEELED GINGER ROOT

1 TABLESPOON CURRY POWDER

½ TEASPOON GROUND CINNAMON

2 CUPS COOKED BROWN RICE (BASMATI IS NICE)

¾ CUP FINELY CHOPPED TOASTED CASHEWS OR PEANUTS

1 TABLESPOON LEMON JUICE

¼ CUP FINELY CHOPPED FRESH CILANTRO

1 Rinse and drain the lentils. Put them in a small saucepan with the water and bring to a boil, stirring often. Add the turmeric and ½ teaspoon of the salt, reduce the heat to low, cover, and simmer until the lentils are very soft and the water has been absorbed, about 20 minutes. (Red lentils are starchy and can sink to the bottom of the pan and burn in a heartbeat, so keep the heat very low and stir occasionally.) If there is liquid left, drain the lentils before adding them to the burger mixture.

2 Meanwhile, in a skillet or saucepan on medium heat, cook the onions and garlic in the oil until softened, about 6 minutes. Stir in the celery and bell peppers and continue to cook for about 7 minutes; if needed to prevent sticking, reduce the heat and cover the pan, or add a splash of water. Add the ginger, curry powder, cinnamon, and remaining salt and cook for a minute, stirring constantly. Remove from the heat, add the rice, nuts, lemon juice, cilantro, and lentils and mix well.

3 When the burger mixture is cool enough to handle, shape it into 6 patties using a heaping ½ cup for each, and place on an oiled baking sheet. Bake in a preheated 400° oven for about 20 minutes.

SERVING AND MENU IDEAS: Serve topped with yogurt and fruit chutney. Especially nice with Pineapple and Tomato Salad (page 87) or spicy Mango Slaw (page 93).

CURRIED RED LENTIL BURGERS—PER 1 BURGER (OF 6) *Calories: 357, Protein: 14 g, Carbohydrate: 48 g, Dietary Fiber: 13 g, Total Fat: 13 g, Saturated Fat: 2 g, Monounsaturated Fat: 8 g, Cholesterol: 0 mg, Sodium: 588 mg*

Tempeh-Quinoa Burgers

YIELDS 6 BURGERS | HANDS-ON TIME: 40 MINUTES | BAKING TIME: 35 MINUTES

These burgers are vegan, wheat-free, and low in fat. Pretty high in protein, too, thanks to the quinoa and tempeh.

½ CUP QUINOA

2 CUPS THINLY SLICED PEELED SWEET POTATOES

1 CUP WATER

½ TEASPOON SALT

1 TABLESPOON OLIVE OIL

1 CUP DICED ONIONS

1 CUP MINCED BELL PEPPERS

2 GARLIC CLOVES, MINCED OR PRESSED

8 OUNCES TEMPEH, DICED

1 TEASPOON DRIED OREGANO

¼ TEASPOON GROUND BLACK PEPPER

4 TEASPOONS SOY SAUCE

2 TABLESPOONS TOMATO PASTE, KETCHUP, OR TOMATO SALSA

1 TABLESPOON DARK SESAME OIL (OPTIONAL)

2 TEASPOONS DIJON MUSTARD

⅓ CUP CHOPPED FRESH CILANTRO

¼ CUP BROWN SESAME SEEDS

1 Rinse the quinoa in a fine-meshed strainer to remove any residue of the grain's bitter coating. In a saucepan, combine the rinsed quinoa, sweet potatoes, water, and ¼ teaspoon of the salt. Cover and bring to a boil; reduce the heat to low and simmer until the sweet potatoes are tender and the quinoa is soft and translucent, about 15 minutes.

2 Meanwhile, heat the olive oil in a skillet on medium heat. Add the onions and the remaining ¼ teaspoon of salt and cook until the onions begin to soften, 5 minutes. Stir in the bell peppers and garlic, cover, and cook for about 3 minutes. Add the tempeh, oregano, black pepper, and soy sauce, cover, and cook for 7 or 8 minutes, stirring occasionally. Transfer to a bowl and set aside.

3 When the sweet potatoes and quinoa are cooked, mash them in the saucepan and add to the bowl with the vegetables. Thoroughly mix in the tomato paste, sesame oil, mustard, and parsley, and refrigerate until cool enough to handle.

4 Shape the mixture into burgers, using a heaping ½ cup for each (wet hands help) and sprinkle each side with sesame seeds. Place on a lightly oiled baking sheet and bake in a preheated 375° oven until firm and golden, about 35 minutes.

VARIATION: For appetizers, shape the mixture into balls using ¼- to ⅓-cup of the mixture for each ball, roll in cornmeal (omit the sesame seeds), and bake for about 25 minutes.

SERVING AND MENU IDEAS: Serve in pita, or on whole grain toast, rice, or salad greens. Accompany with Simple Guacamole (page 69) or sliced avocados and tomatoes.

TEMPEH-QUINOA BURGERS—PER 1 BURGER (OF 6)
Calories: 268, Protein: 12 g, Carbohydrate: 30 g, Dietary Fiber: 5 g, Total Fat: 13 g, Saturated Fat: 2 g, Monounsaturated Fat: 5 g, Cholesterol: 0 mg, Sodium: 454 mg

Spinach-Tofu Burgers

YIELDS 6 BURGERS | HANDS-ON TIME: 35 MINUTES | BAKING TIME: 35 MINUTES

The mild and nutty flavor of these burgers makes them a good vehicle for "all the fixin's."

10 OUNCES FRESH SPINACH
1 TABLESPOON OLIVE OIL
1 CUP CHOPPED SCALLIONS
½ CUP GRATED CARROTS
½ TEASPOON DRIED OREGANO OR 1 ½ TEASPOONS FRESH
1 OR 2 GARLIC CLOVES, PRESSED OR MINCED
½ CUP WALNUTS
½ CUP COOKED BROWN RICE
1 CAKE OF FIRM TOFU (ABOUT 16 OUNCES)
1 ROUNDED TEASPOON DIJON MUSTARD
2 TABLESPOONS LIGHT MISO
GENEROUS DASH OF GROUND BLACK PEPPER
2 TABLESPOONS CHOPPED FRESH DILL OR BASIL

1 Steam the spinach and drain it well. You should end up with about ¾ cup, packed.

2 Warm the olive oil in a saucepan on medium-high heat and cook the scallions, carrots, oregano, and garlic until soft, 3 to 4 minutes.

3 In a food processor, pulse the walnuts and rice until crumbly, then transfer to a mixing bowl. Pulse half of the tofu and half of the drained spinach just until combined and uniformly colored but not gummy, and add to the mixing bowl. Pulse the rest of the spinach and tofu with the mustard, miso, black pepper, and dill just until well blended and add to the mixing bowl. Add the cooked scallions and carrots, and mix well. Add more miso, or some salt or soy sauce to taste.

4 Shape the mixture into 6 burgers (about ⅔ cup for each), and place on a lightly oiled baking sheet. In a preheated 350° oven, bake the burgers for about 35 minutes, until puffed and browned.

VARIATIONS: In place of fresh spinach, use a 10-ounce package of frozen chopped spinach, thawed and drained well.

Use ½ cup of whole wheat bread crumbs in place of rice.

For appetizers, shape into small balls and bake for 15 to 20 minutes, until browned; serve with lemon-tahini dressing.

SERVING AND MENU IDEAS: These burgers are particularly good on whole wheat buns with mustard, tomato slices, red onions, and shredded crunchy greens, such as romaine, or with melted cheese or lemon-tahini dressing. Or serve the patties on rice or bulghur and top with Creamy Tomato Sauce (page 78). Try them with Roasted Sweet Potatoes (page 299) and a tomato salad.

SPINACH-TOFU BURGERS—PER 1 BURGER (OF 6)
Calories: 199, Protein: 18 g, Carbohydrate: 11 g, Dietary Fiber: 3 g, Total Fat: 10 g, Saturated Fat: 1 g, Monounsaturated Fat: 3 g, Cholesterol: 0 mg, Sodium: 299 mg

Southwestern Black Bean Burgers

YIELDS 6 BURGERS | HANDS-ON TIME: 30 MINUTES | BAKING TIME: 25 MINUTES

Tortilla chips and black beans flavored with cumin and coriander give these burgers a Southwestern flavor, and the mushrooms give them "meatiness." They're tender and chewy on the inside and lightly crusted on the outside.

---

2 TEASPOONS OLIVE OIL

1 CUP CHOPPED ONIONS

2 TEASPOONS GROUND CUMIN

1 TEASPOON GROUND CORIANDER

¼ TEASPOON SALT

DASH OF GROUND BLACK PEPPER

1 CUP FINELY CHOPPED MUSHROOMS

1 CUP GRATED CARROTS

1 FRESH CHILE, MINCED
OR ¼ TEASPOON CAYENNE

¼ CUP ORANGE JUICE

1 CUP GROUND CORN TORTILLA CHIPS
(SEE NOTE)

2 15-OUNCE CANS BLACK BEANS,
RINSED AND DRAINED

1 LARGE EGG, LIGHTLY BEATEN

---

1 Warm the oil in a skillet on medium-high heat. Add the onions and cook for 5 minutes, stirring often. Stir in the cumin, coriander, salt, and pepper and cook until the onions soften, a couple of minutes. Add the mushrooms, carrots, chiles, and orange juice, lower the heat to medium, cover, and cook, stirring occasionally, until tender, about 8 minutes.

2 While the vegetables cook, combine the ground tortilla chips, beans, and egg in a large bowl and mash well with a potato masher, or pulse in a food processor and then transfer to a bowl. When the vegetables are tender, drain, and stir into the bean mixture.

3 Form the burger mixture into six patties (a heaping ½ cup per burger) and place on a lightly oiled baking sheet. Bake in a preheated 375° oven for 25 minutes, until firm and lightly crusted.

NOTE: Whirl tortilla chips in a food processor until they reach the consistency of coarse meal.

SERVING AND MENU IDEAS: Serve the burger on romaine, topped with salsa. Make an open-faced sandwich on whole wheat or rye toast and top with fresh tomato slices and alfalfa sprouts, or go conventional with ketchup and pickles. Put it on a whole wheat bun with tomato and avocado slices and Monterey Jack cheese. Serve with one or more: Sweet Potato, Apple, and Chipotle Soup (page 132), Green Soup (page 266), Quinoa and Sweet Potatoes (page 284), Winter Squash "Rice Mexicali" (page 270), a green salad with Avocado Citrus Dressing (page 109).

SOUTHWESTERN BLACK BEAN BURGERS—
PER 1 BURGER (OF 6) *Calories: 252, Protein: 13 g, Carbohydrate: 41 g, Dietary Fiber: 13 g, Total Fat: 5 g, Saturated Fat: 1 g, Monounsaturated Fat: 2 g, Cholesterol: 36 mg, Sodium: 847 mg*

Greek Lentil Burgers

YIELDS 4 TO 6 BURGERS | HANDS-ON TIME: 45 MINUTES | BAKING TIME: 25 TO 30 MINUTES

Tasty, sturdy, and "meaty," these burgers are infused with the flavors of the Greek islands.

½ CUP DRIED BROWN LENTILS

2 CUPS WATER

2 TABLESPOONS OLIVE OIL

1 CUP CHOPPED ONIONS

½ TEASPOON SALT

4 GARLIC CLOVES, MINCED OR PRESSED

½ CUP DICED RED BELL PEPPERS

2 TEASPOONS GROUND CUMIN

1 TEASPOON GROUND CORIANDER

½ TEASPOON GROUND BLACK PEPPER

1 TEASPOON DRIED OREGANO
OR 1 TABLESPOON FRESH

1 TEASPOON DRIED DILL
OR 1 TABLESPOON FRESH

1 15-OUNCE CAN CHICKPEAS, DRAINED

2 LARGE EGGS

2 CUPS TOASTED WHOLE WHEAT BREAD CRUMBS

1 Place the lentils and water in a small saucepan and bring to a boil; then lower the heat to medium and cook uncovered until tender, 30 to 40 minutes. Drain and set aside.

2 Meanwhile, warm the oil in a skillet on medium-high heat. Add the onions and salt and cook until softened, about 7 minutes. Add the garlic, bell peppers, cumin, coriander, and black pepper and cook for 5 minutes more. Stir in the oregano and dill and set aside.

3 In a food processor, pulse the chickpeas and eggs until smooth. Transfer to a large bowl. When the lentils are ready, add the cooked vegetables, lentils, and 1 cup of the bread crumbs to the bowl and mix well. Set aside until cool enough to handle.

4 Form the mixture into four 1-cup balls or six ⅔-cup balls. Roll them in the remaining cup of breadcrumbs to coat evenly and then flatten into patties. Place on a lightly oiled baking sheet. Bake in a preheated 350° oven until golden brown and firm, 25 to 30 minutes.

SERVING AND MENU IDEAS: Serve in a pita pocket with feta cheese, shredded greens, and lemon-tahini dressing, or on rice next to a crisp cucumber-tomato salad dressed with olive oil and red wine vinegar. It also works on a whole wheat bun with all the traditional toppings. Greek Tomato-Yogurt Soup (page 125) and/or Herbed Vegetable Packets (page 197) go well with this burger. Make the burgers the centerpiece of a Mediterranean meal with Couscous with Pistachios and Apricots (page 287), Pomegranate Carrots (page 302), and Filo Nut Cigars (page 330).

GREEK LENTIL BURGERS—PER 1 BURGER (OF 6)
Calories: 372, Protein: 17 g, Carbohydrate: 55 g, Dietary Fiber: 12 g, Total Fat: 10 g, Saturated Fat: 2 g, Monounsaturated Fat: 5 g, Cholesterol: 71 mg, Sodium: 604 mg

NUTS AND SEEDS

Harvard Medical School has declared nuts and seeds "nutritional powerhouses." They are one of the most nutrient-dense foods around: a potent mix of protein, monounsaturated fats, fiber, essential fatty acids, and vitamin E. Walnuts and flaxseeds are especially rich repositories of cholesterol-lowering omega-3 fatty acids. Nuts and seeds are also significant sources of antioxidants (see pages 202–203), vitamins, and minerals. A few nuts a day may well keep the doctor away.

Nuts and seeds have made headlines for their promising contribution to heart health. Over thirty studies, both clinical trials and studies following participants over time, have shown that serum cholesterol and triglyceride levels are favorably reduced with the introduction of nuts and seeds into the diet, and that the incidence of coronary heart disease and heart attacks is significantly less in people who eat nuts or nut butter multiple times a week. Men, women, vegetarians, meat-eaters, people who exercise a lot and those who get little exercise, both thin and overweight people, and the old and the young—all were found to benefit from eating nuts. Guess that covers us all! Among people who substituted fats from nuts for a portion of the saturated fats (mostly from meat and dairy) in their previous

diet, a greater risk reduction was seen. Based on the available data, the United States Food and Drug Administration (FDA) has released a qualified endorsement of nuts and seeds for their possible positive effects on cardiac health. FDA guidelines recommend eating a quarter-cup of nuts or two tablespoons of nut butter or seeds four or five times weekly.

Nuts and seeds appear to be so important to blood pressure stabilization that they have become an integral part of the highly effective DASH Diet for controlling hypertension. (The DASH Diet is the outcome of a large, multiple medical center study of diet and hypertension sponsored by the National Institutes of Health.) Nuts, in their variety, are good to very good sources of calcium, magnesium, and potassium—all minerals known to reduce hypertension. As part of the DASH Diet, participants are instructed to consume nuts and seeds in quantities that closely resemble the FDA's guidelines.

Researchers are investigating early findings that the inclusion of nuts in a meal may lower the Glycemic Index of the meal, or the rate at which blood sugar levels rise after eating. A daily dose of nuts may be good for people diagnosed with diabetes or prediabetes. Studies also indicate that eating nuts may lower the risk of developing dementia, macular degeneration, and gallstones.

Nuts are calorie dense, a factor that has worried those concerned about obesity; however, studies are showing that including a moderate amount of nuts in your diet may help expedite weight loss. Weight-loss study participants on low-fat diets that included nuts regularly commented that they "did not feel like they were on diet." Snacking on nuts instead of celery sticks may be the difference between serial dieting and discovering a way of eating you can live with.

Do all nuts and seeds have the same nutritional profile? Well, yes and no, and that's a good thing. All nuts and seeds, including peanuts (which are botanically not nuts but legumes) appear to lower lipid levels, potentially offering protection against heart disease. Many types of nuts are rich in particular nutrients. Brazil nuts are exceptionally rich in selenium; sunflower seeds and almonds are excellent sources of vitamin E; sesame seeds and cashews are rich in copper and manganese; pumpkin seeds are rich in magnesium; walnuts have high levels of linoleic acid; and chestnuts are low in fat.

There are countless delectable ways to include nuts and seeds in your diet. They can be snacked on raw, toasted, or spiced. They're a good appetizer and companion to beverages:

check out Toasted Pepitas and Cranberries (page 70). Nuts can be chopped and folded into pilafs, muffins, and quick breads, or ground and incorporated in breads, cookies, and pastry shells. Nut butters serve not only as sandwich spreads, but also as bases for dips, soups, and stews. Nut butters are a delicious ingredient in smoothies. And then, of course, you can sprinkle nuts on green salads, fruit salads, or pasta salads.

Because each type of nut and seed has its unique nutritional profile, we think it would be a mistake to consider any one type a magic bullet. Once again, variety may be the key. What is certain is that nuts and seeds are a healthful addition to any diet.

TOASTING NUTS

In the oven or toaster oven, bake nuts in a single layer on a dry baking sheet at 350° for about 5 minutes, stirring a couple of times, until aromatic and becoming crisp and brown. Or spread the nuts in a single layer in a dry heavy skillet on medium heat, and stir often, especially as they become aromatic and brown. You can even toast nuts in a microwave oven; they will become crisp with a toasted flavor, but not browned. Nuts become more crisp as they cool; don't chop them until they've cooled to close to room temperature.

STIR-FRYS & SAUTÉS

Hijiki and Vegetable Sauté

SERVES 4 AS A MAIN DISH, 6 TO 8 AS A SIDE DISH | TIME: 35 MINUTES

In this handsome sauté, glistening black hatch marks of hijiki are punctuated with bright spots of green, orange, and red. Every element provides a different mouth feel and unique flavor.

Hijiki, readily available dried and packaged in most supermarkets, is the most mineral-rich of all seaweeds and tastes unmistakably of the sea. Shelled edamame, green soy beans, usually found in the frozen vegetable section of supermarkets, have a mild, nutty, almost sweet flavor.

1 GENEROUS CUP FROZEN SHELLED EDAMAME (ABOUT 5 OUNCES)

1 OUNCE DRIED HIJIKI (SEE PAGE 162)

1 TABLESPOON OLIVE OIL OR VEGETABLE OIL

1½ CUPS THINLY SLICED ONIONS

1 CUP CARROT MATCHSTICKS

1 CUP DICED RED BELL PEPPERS

2½ TABLESPOONS SOY SAUCE

1 TABLESPOON MIRIN (SEE PAGE 27)

1½ TEASPOONS DARK SESAME OIL

⅛ TEASPOON GROUND BLACK PEPPER

1 Bring a pot of water (about 6 cups) to a boil. Add the frozen edamame and return to a boil; cover and simmer on low heat until tender, 3 to 4 minutes. Scoop out the edamame and set aside. Add the hijiki to the pot, return to a boil, cover, and simmer on low heat until softened, about 8 minutes. Drain and set aside.

2 Meanwhile, warm the oil in a large skillet on medium heat. Add the onions, cover, and cook until the onions begin to soften, about 5 minutes. Add the carrots, bell peppers, and 1 tablespoon of the soy sauce. Increase the heat to medium-high and stir continuously until the carrots are crisp-tender, about 5 more minutes. Lower the heat to medium, stir in the drained hijiki and edamame, the remaining soy sauce, and the mirin, sesame oil, and black pepper. Mix well, cover, and cook for another minute or two, until everything is hot.

VARIATIONS: In place of edamame, use snow peas cut crosswise into strips, or green peas, or baby lima beans.

SERVING AND MENU IDEAS: Serve plain as a side dish, or as a main dish on rice or on soba, udon, or other noodles. Good as is, or served with lemon wedges or rice vinegar. Roasted Sweet Potatoes (page 299) are an excellent complement.

HIJIKI AND VEGETABLE SAUTÉ—PER 1 SERVING (OF 8)
Calories: 76, Protein: 3 g, Carbohydrate: 8 g, Dietary Fiber: 2 g, Total Fat: 4 g, Saturated Fat: 1 g, Monounsaturated Fat: 2 g, Cholesterol: 0 mg, Sodium: 233 mg

SEAWEED

Seaweed is one of the earth's most abundant foods and also one of the most underutilized. Seaweed is prized by coastal dwellers throughout the world; its use in cooking is especially widespread along the Asian seacoast and in Ireland, Iceland, and Inuit-inhabited regions. The Japanese incorporated sea greens into their cooking at least 10,000 years ago. In northwestern Europe, where it has been harvested and dried for more than 1,000 years, seaweed dishes are not uncommon. At our stores here in Ithaca, we find both imported seaweed and seaweed from the Maine coast.

Seaweed is perhaps the most nutritious single food; certainly, ounce for ounce, it is higher in vitamins and minerals than any food. Seaweeds are continuously bathed in mineral-rich seawater, and their mineral content is from 7 to 38 percent of their dry weight. Seaweed supplies all the minerals needed for human health in proportions very similar to those in human blood. The most significant elements are calcium, iodine, phosphorous, sodium, and iron. It's a rich protein source and a good source of vitamins A, B, C, and E. All seaweeds are quite low in calories and high in fiber.

Commonly ascribed health benefits are wide ranging and numerous, and include reducing blood cholesterol, supporting thyroid function, nerve transmission, and digestion, and strengthening bones and teeth. Seaweed has antibiotic properties known to be effective against penicillin-resistant bacteria. Seaweed nourishes the skin and hair and is reputed to have anti-aging properties.

Seaweeds range in size from minuscule plankton to gigantic kelp, and its colors cover a spectrum from yellow-green, deep kelly green, and blue-green to red and brown and black. The leaves of various seaweeds are strands or strings, broad bands or sheets, flat or curly, and even grain-like. We've heard the flavors of different seaweeds described as briny, sweet, nutty, anise-like, mild, and stimulating.

We probably all know people who swear they'll never eat seaweed, but they probably already do. It's a common ingredient in baked goods, toothpaste, jelly, ice cream, chocolate milk, wine, and beer.

As the oceans become more polluted, some people worry that seaweed is contaminated, but laboratory analyses have shown that pollutants aren't concentrated in seaweed.

In this book, we use seaweed in stocks, soups, stews, salads, and stir-fries. You can also steep it for tea and wrap rice in it for sushi. Some of the most popular sea greens are wakame, kelp, dulse, kombu, nori, hijiki, arame, agar, and alaria.

Wakame has a lovely ocean taste. Its leaves are 13 percent protein, and deliver substantial amounts of calcium. Dried wakame is green when reconstituted and swells to about triple its dry volume. Some people describe its texture as pleasingly slippery, but when it soaks too long, we would call it rather slimy, so don't let it sit too long in the soaking water; often five minutes is enough. In soup, the sliminess—which is actually a form of fiber—melts into the liquid and is not noticeable. Also, mixing wakame with an acid like vinegar or briefly cooking it in a little oil counteracts the texture. It often appears in salads, as a garnish for sashimi, and in soups. It's our favorite for Seaweed Salad (page 98).

Kombu, also called konbu and laminaria, is the best-known type of kelp. Kombu's broad leaves grow up to thirty-three feet long. It has a sweet (for seaweed) flavor and a leathery texture, and is most commonly used to make dashi stock, but it is also eaten finely chopped. You can also find *kombu-cha*, kombu tea: dried, flavored pieces of kombu to steep in water.

Nori may be the most familiar seaweed in the United States, since it's used as a wrapper for sushi. In Japan, more than 300,000 metric tons of fresh nori are harvested annually. It comes in iridescent black, dark green, or purplish sheets about eight inches square. Wrap unused nori in plastic and keep it in a cool, dark place. It's usually not cooked, though there are traditional recipes calling for softened nori. You may be able to find a soft nori paste to eat with rice, sort of like a Japanese version of Marmite.

Hijiki may be the most versatile seaweed of all. It is a black seaweed with more texture than other seaweeds; its surface is less viscous and more porous. Its flavor is fairly neutral. Hijiki is very high in fiber— in its dried form about 40 percent of it is fiber—and a good source of calcium and iron. Hijiki is not commonly seen on Japanese restaurant menus because in Japan it's used mostly for home cooking. It comes in dried form and is usually soaked in cold water for about an hour and then rinsed before use. If you're in a hurry, you can blanch it for a couple of minutes in boiling water, which hydrates it quickly. In our recipes, we specify weight rather than volume for hijiki because it comes in two forms: regular hijiki, which is twig-like in dried form, and *me hijiki,* small buds of hijiki that look like black tea. An ounce of regular hijiki fills about a cup, and an ounce of *me hijiki,* because it is more densely packed, about one-half cup. When reconstituted, hijiki swells to about five times its dried weight.

Dulse grows in smooth, hand-shaped fronds, and you can buy it dried whole or in flakes. It has a pleasing tangy and salty flavor. It is a superior source of iron and iodine, and although it tastes salty, it contains less sodium than many other seaweeds. You can toast dulse in the oven, about two minutes at 350° until crisp and somewhat greenish in color, then sprinkle it on salads, nut mixes, and popcorn, or add it to salad dressings, soups, and stir-fries.

Arame is a species of kelp. After harvesting it is steamed, shredded, and air-dried. It is mild-tasting, firm-textured, easy to prepare, and versatile. Cooked, it resembles hijiki but is more delicate and milder in flavor. Rinse dried arame briefly and soak in cold water for a few minutes. It doubles in size after rehydration. Arame is good in salads, steamed or sautéed, and added to soups, stir-frys, stuffings, and other dishes.

Alaria is an olive-brown alga whose fronds have golden midribs and grow up to twelve feet long. It turns a delicate green when cooked.

Perfect for stocks and soups, it is similar to wakame, with the same nutritional value, but it takes longer to cook (20 minutes) and is less expensive.

Agar seaweed is most familiar in the United States as agar agar, a gelling agent, available as powder or flakes. (See page 18 for cooking information.) The name "agar agar" is Malaysian in origin, and the long red and purple fronds of agar seaweed have been harvested there for hundreds of years. Long strands of agar seaweed are one of the ingredients in the seaweed salad served at many Japanese restaurants. Agar agar is produced by a traditional method of cooking and pressing the seaweed and then naturally freeze-drying the residue. It is a good source of iodine and trace minerals as well as some calcium and iron, and it has mild laxative properties. It has no calories. It is a high-protein food and should be refrigerated for storage.

Three-Soy Sauté with Soba

SERVES 4 | TIME: 30 MINUTES

This attractive sauté is a study in contrasting textures and tastes: savory mushrooms, earthy soba, tender tofu, and pale green edamame.

---

6 OUNCES FROZEN SHELLED EDAMAME (ABOUT 1¼ CUPS)

12 OUNCES SOBA NOODLES OR WHOLE WHEAT SPAGHETTI

¼ CUP SOY SAUCE

½ CUP WATER, APPLE JUICE, OR ORANGE JUICE

1 TABLESPOON RICE VINEGAR

1 TEASPOON DARK SESAME OIL

½ TEASPOON CHINESE CHILI PASTE, MORE TO TASTE

1 ROUNDED TEASPOON GRATED PEELED GINGER ROOT

8 OUNCES TOFU, CUT INTO SMALL CUBES (WE LIKE SOFT TOFU IN THIS DISH)

1 TABLESPOON VEGETABLE OIL

8 OUNCES FRESH SHIITAKES, STEMMED AND SLICED

1 LARGE RED BELL PEPPER, CUT INTO THIN 2-INCH-LONG STRIPS

6 SCALLIONS, CUT INTO 2-INCH-LONG PIECES

2 TEASPOONS CORNSTARCH DISSOLVED IN 2 TABLESPOONS COLD WATER

---

1 Bring a large pot of salted water to a boil. Add the edamame and cook until tender, about 4 minutes. With a large slotted spoon or a sieve, scoop out the edamame and set aside. Return the water to a rolling boil and cook the pasta until al dente. Drain.

2 While the water heats and the edamame and then the pasta cook, make the sauté. In a bowl, whisk together the soy sauce, water, rice vinegar, sesame oil, chili paste, and grated ginger. Add the tofu cubes and stir gently. Set aside to marinate.

3 In a skillet or wok on medium-high heat, warm the vegetable oil. Add the shiitakes and bell peppers and cook until barely tender, about 3 minutes. Stir in the scallions and cooked edamame and cook until heated through. Pour in the tofu cubes and marinade and the dissolved cornstarch and cook, stirring gently, until hot and bubbling.

4 Serve the sauté over the pasta.

VARIATIONS: Also good on brown rice pasta, udon noodles, kamut or spelt pasta, or brown rice.

SERVING AND MENU IDEAS: Start with something piquant such as Chinese Vegetable Garden Pickles (page 67). End with something sweet and fruity, such as Pomegranate Gel with Fruit (page 312), or Pineapple-Cinnamon Popsicles (page 321).

THREE-SOY SAUTÉ WITH SOBA—PER 1 SERVING (OF 4) *Calories: 455, Protein: 23 g, Carbohydrate: 78 g, Dietary Fiber: 4 g, Total Fat: 9 g, Saturated Fat: 1 g, Monounsaturated Fat: 4 g, Cholesterol: 0 mg, Sodium: 1,289 mg*

Root Vegetable Hash

SERVES 6 | HANDS-ON TIME: 30 MINUTES | COOKING TIME: 30 MINUTES

Good for breakfast, brunch, lunch, or dinner, this beautiful magenta hash includes a variety of root vegetables. Use a total of eight cups of diced root vegetables in any proportion you like. Just be sure to include beets to get the magenta color.

SEASONING MIXTURE

2 TEASPOONS DRIED MARJORAM

2 TEASPOONS DRIED OREGANO

½ TEASPOON DRIED THYME

1½ TEASPOONS SALT

½ TEASPOON GROUND BLACK PEPPER

HASH

3 TABLESPOONS OLIVE OIL

2½ CUPS CHOPPED ONIONS

4 GARLIC CLOVES, MINCED OR PRESSED

2 CUPS CARROTS CUT INTO ½-INCH DICE

2 CUPS SWEET POTATOES PEELED AND CUT INTO ½-INCH DICE

2 CUPS BEETS PEELED AND CUT INTO ½-INCH DICE

2 CUPS TURNIPS AND/OR RUTABAGA PEELED AND CUT INTO ½-INCH DICE

3 TABLESPOONS WATER

1 Stir together all of the seasoning ingredients in a small bowl and set aside.

2 In a 10-inch or larger skillet on medium-high heat, warm the oil. Cook the onions and garlic for about 5 minutes. Add all of the vegetables and stir well. Sprinkle with the seasoning mixture and water and stir well. Reduce the heat to medium-low, cover, and cook, stirring every 10 minutes or so, until the vegetables are tender, about 30 minutes.

VARIATIONS: Sometimes we add ½ cup peeled and diced burdock root or Jerusalem artichoke.

Add sherry in place of water.

SERVING AND MENU IDEAS: Serve as the traditional bed of hash with a poached egg on top or serve next to Green Eggs, No Ham (page 58). Also good with bagels with Vegetable Cream Cheese (page 45) and Cantaloupe with Fresh Raspberry Sauce (page 313). For a simple supper, serve with a green salad with Pear and Thyme Vinaigrette (page 110).

ROOT VEGETABLE HASH—PER 1 SERVING (OF 6)
Calories: 175, Protein: 3 g, Carbohydrate: 22 g, Dietary Fiber: 5 g, Total Fat: 7 g, Saturated Fat: 1 g, Monounsaturated Fat: 5 g, Cholesterol: 0 mg, Sodium: 119 mg

Bok Choy and Country-style Soft Tofu

SERVES 4 | TIME: 50 MINUTES

Three easy components add up to one of our favorite at-home comfort meals. Country-style Soft Tofu is smooth and custardy. The cubes of soft tofu cooked in a flavorful gravy can be made ahead, refrigerated, and re-warmed. Its soft consistency goes best with the firm, chewy texture of short grain brown rice. Bok choy, delicately flavored and nutrient-packed, should be stir-fried for just a couple of minutes; the green leaves become wilted and tender and the succulent stems retain a juicy crunch. On its own, Bok Choy with Garlic is a quick side dish.

RICE

2 CUPS BROWN RICE

3 CUPS WATER

COUNTRY-STYLE SOFT TOFU

1 CAKE OF SOFT TOFU (ABOUT 16 OUNCES)

1 CUP WATER

1 TABLESPOON SOY SAUCE

2 TEASPOONS DARK SESAME OIL

1/2 TEASPOON RICE VINEGAR, CIDER VINEGAR, OR WHITE VINEGAR

2 TABLESPOONS CORNSTARCH

BOK CHOY WITH GARLIC

1 POUND BABY BOK CHOY (ABOUT 12 SMALL HEADS, ABOUT 7 INCHES LONG)

1/2 CUP WATER

3 TABLESPOONS SOY SAUCE

1 TEASPOON DARK SESAME OIL (OPTIONAL)

1 TABLESPOON VEGETABLE OIL

8 GARLIC CLOVES, MINCED OR PRESSED

1 Cook the rice. In a saucepan with a tight-fitting lid, bring the rice and water to a boil. As soon as it boils, lower the heat and simmer, covered, until the water has been absorbed and the rice is tender, about 45 minutes.

2 To make Country-style Soft Tofu: Cut the tofu into 1-inch cubes and set aside. In a saucepan, whisk together the water, soy sauce, sesame oil, vinegar, and cornstarch. Bring to a low boil on medium-high heat and then reduce the heat and simmer, stirring constantly until thickened. Gently stir in the tofu cubes; the cubes of tofu are delicate and break easily, so use a wooden spoon or rubber spatula. Cook until heated through. Cover and keep warm until ready to serve.

3 To make Bok Choy with Garlic: Rinse the baby bok choy. If the heads of bok choy are small, cut each head lengthwise into quarters leaving the stems attached at the root end. If larger, cut lengthwise into quarters and then crosswise into 1-inch slices. Place the bok choy next to the stovetop. In a bowl, whisk together the water, soy sauce, and sesame oil, and place next to the stovetop. About 10 minutes before the rice is done, in a wok or large skillet, heat the oil until shimmering hot. Add the garlic and sizzle very briefly, just until it begins to color; take care not to let it burn. Immediately add the bok choy and stir-fry for a couple of minutes, until bright green and just crisp-tender. Pour the soy sauce mixture into the wok and stir well to coat the greens. Keep warm until the rice is done and you're ready to serve the meal.

4 Serve Country-style Soft Tofu on the rice, with Bok Choy with Garlic on the side.

SERVING AND MENU IDEAS: Top with any or all: chopped scallions, toasted sesame seeds, chopped toasted peanuts or almonds, a few drops of hot chili oil. A complete meal, we think, but if you'd like something extra, try sliced ripe tomatoes, or hot and sour Mango Pickles (page 68), or Roasted Sweet Potatoes (page 299).

COUNTRY-STYLE SOFT TOFU—PER 1 SERVING (OF 4)
Calories: 100, Protein: 6 g, Carbohydrate: 7 g, Dietary Fiber: 0 g, Total Fat: 5 g, Saturated Fat: 1 g, Monounsaturated Fat: 1 g, Cholesterol: 0 mg, Sodium: 139 mg

BOK CHOY WITH GARLIC—PER 1 SERVING (OF 4)
Calories: 71, Protein: 3 g, Carbohydrate: 5 g, Dietary Fiber: 1 g, Total Fat: 5 g, Saturated Fat: 0 g, Monounsaturated Fat: 3 g, Cholesterol: 0 mg, Sodium: 751 mg

BROWN RICE—PER 1 SERVING (OF 4), 1 CUP
Calories: 232, Protein: 5 g, Carbohydrate: 50 g, Dietary Fiber: 3 g, Total Fat: 1 g, Saturated Fat: 0 g, Monounsaturated Fat: 0 g, Cholesterol: 0 mg, Sodium: 549 mg

Vegetables in Spicy Lemongrass-Tamarind Sauce

SERVES 4 | TIME: 45 MINUTES

Indian and Southeast Asian cuisines use tamarind, the fruit of a native tree, to add a smooth texture and body to sauces as well as a rich, tart flavor. Here, tamarind is combined with other popular Asian ingredients—lemongrass, chiles, coconut, ginger, and garlic—to create an intriguing flavor.

A lot of vegetables work well in this stir-fry: broccoli, zucchini, bell peppers, summer squash, bok choy, other Asian greens. A total of six cups of raw vegetables will do it.

2 TABLESPOONS CHOPPED FRESH LEMONGRASS (SEE NOTE)

1 COARSELY CHOPPED FRESH CHILE

3 TABLESPOONS CHOPPED RED ONIONS

1 TABLESPOON GRATED PEELED GINGER ROOT

2 GARLIC CLOVES, MINCED OR PRESSED

1 CUP COCONUT MILK

2 TABLESPOONS SOY SAUCE

2 TABLESPOONS TAMARIND CONCENTRATE (SEE PAGE 32)

⅓ CUP HOT WATER

2 TEASPOONS CORNSTARCH

2 CUPS STEMMED SNOW PEAS CUT IN HALF

1 TABLESPOON VEGETABLE OIL

2 CUPS SHREDDED GREEN CABBAGE

2 CUPS CARROTS CUT INTO MATCHSTICKS OR THIN HALF-MOONS

4 SCALLIONS, SLICED ON THE DIAGONAL

NOTE: You'll need several stalks of lemongrass. Peel away the tough outer layers and use only the tender inside of the thicker root end section of the stalk. Use the upper, more fibrous part of the stalk for Southeast Asian Tofu with Lemongrass (page 183).

1   In a food processor or blender, purée the lemongrass, chiles, red onions, ginger, and garlic with ½ cup of the coconut milk, until it forms a fairly smooth paste. Add the remainder of the coconut milk and the soy sauce, tamarind, and hot water, and whirl to make a smooth sauce. In a small bowl, stir the cornstarch into about 2 tablespoons of this sauce until smooth. Set aside both the remaining tamarind sauce and the cornstarch mixture.

2   Steam the snow peas for about a minute, until bright green and still crisp. Set aside.

3   In a large skillet or wok, heat the oil for a moment, and then add the cabbage. Stir-fry for a couple of minutes before adding the carrots. Continue to stir-fry until the vegetables have softened, about 3 minutes. Add the tamarind sauce and cook for a couple of minutes, until the vegetables are just crisp-tender and the sauce is hot. Add the cornstarch mixture and the scallions and stir-fry for about 2 minutes, until the sauce has thickened. Serve topped with the steamed snow peas.

SERVING AND MENU IDEAS: Serve with a flavorful rice like brown basmati or with whole grain noodles. For side dishes, try Pineapple and Tomato Salad (page 87) and/or Tropical Lime Tofu (page 179). For dessert, have Honeydew and Basil Popsicles (page 320).

VEGETABLES IN SPICY LEMONGRASS-TAMARIND SAUCE—PER 1 SERVING (OF 4) *Calories: 146, Protein: 4 g, Carbohydrate: 17 g, Dietary Fiber: 4 g, Total Fat: 8 g, Saturated Fat: 3 g, Monounsaturated Fat: 3 g, Cholesterol: 0 mg, Sodium: 378 mg*

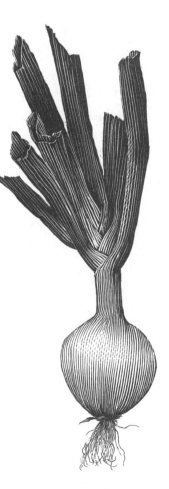

Vegetable Sauté Capriccio

SERVES 6 TO 8 | TIME: 40 MINUTES

This fresh-tasting, beautiful-looking sauté requires a large skillet (12-inch) or a wok to hold its wealth of colorful vegetables. The vegetables look attractive and cook uniformly when cut into slender sticks and stalks. The light Raw Tomato Sauce can be made in a blender in minutes and is delicious with other dishes as well.

RAW TOMATO SAUCE

2 CUPS CHOPPED FRESH TOMATOES

3 TABLESPOONS EXTRA-VIRGIN OLIVE OIL

¼ TEASPOON SALT

⅛ TEASPOON GROUND BLACK PEPPER

SEVERAL SPRIGS OF FRESH PARSLEY (OPTIONAL)

3 FRESH BASIL LEAVES (OPTIONAL)

1 GARLIC CLOVE, PRESSED (OPTIONAL)

SAUTÉ

1 LARGE SPANISH ONION

1 LARGE CARROT

1 RED BELL PEPPER

¼ CUP EXTRA-VIRGIN OLIVE OIL

1 MEDIUM HEAD OF BROCCOLI (ABOUT 12 OUNCES)

1 MEDIUM ZUCCHINI

8 OUNCES SHUCKED FRESH BABY CORN OR 1 MEDIUM YELLOW SUMMER SQUASH

SALT AND GROUND BLACK PEPPER

1 To prepare the Raw Tomato Sauce: In a blender, whirl all of the ingredients until smooth. Set aside.

2 To prepare the sauté: Cut off the ends of the onion, cut it in half, and peel. Slice each half from end to end into slender strips. Cut the carrot into matchsticks 2 to 3 inches long. Cut the pepper into thin strips.

3 Warm the olive oil in a large skillet or wok on medium-high heat and add the onions, carrots, and peppers. Stir occasionally while you prepare the other vegetables, adding each as it is cut. Cut off about ½ inch of the stem end of the broccoli, peel the stem if it seems tough, and cut the stem into thin sticks, each tipped with a floret (for about 4 cups). Stir into the skillet. Seed the zucchini if needed and cut into 3-inch-long matchsticks. Stir into the skillet and reduce the heat to medium. Cut each baby corn in half lengthwise or cut the yellow squash into matchsticks and add to the pan. Cook for a couple of minutes until all of the vegetables are crisp-tender. Season with salt and black pepper.

4 Top each serving of vegetables with a ladleful of Raw Tomato Sauce.

SERVING AND MENU IDEAS: We like Vegetable Sauté Capriccio on short-grain brown rice, accompanied by cubed fresh mozzarella or An Easy Baked Tofu (page 177).

VEGETABLE SAUTÉ CAPRICCIO—PER 1 SERVING (OF 8) *Calories: 182, Protein: 3 g, Carbohydrate: 18 g, Dietary Fiber: 4 g, Total Fat: 12 g, Saturated Fat: 1 g, Monounsaturated Fat: 9 g, Cholesterol: 0 mg, Sodium: 102 mg*

Cabbage with Fermented Black Beans

SERVES 4 | TIME: 35 MINUTES

Cabbage is good for you. It is rich in vitamin C, fiber, and phytonutrients. The pungent sauce is great with both red and green cabbage or with bok choy, broccoli, cauliflower, or kale.

FERMENTED BLACK BEAN SAUCE

2 TABLESPOONS FERMENTED BLACK BEANS (SEE NOTE)

¼ CUP HOT WATER

2 TABLESPOONS DRY SHERRY OR RICE WINE

½ TEASPOON DARK SESAME OIL

1 TABLESPOON LEMON JUICE OR VINEGAR

½ TEASPOON CHINESE CHILI PASTE (OPTIONAL)

STIR-FRIED CABBAGE

1 TABLESPOON VEGETABLE OIL

4 CUPS THINLY SLICED RED OR GREEN CABBAGE

½ CUP THINLY SLICED ONIONS

1 TABLESPOON MINCED OR PRESSED GARLIC

2 TEASPOONS GRATED PEELED GINGER ROOT

½ TEASPOON SALT

NOTE: Fermented black beans are pungent and salty, and add a complex flavor to sauces or stir-fries. They are available in Asian markets and well-stocked groceries. They come in 8- to 16-ounce packs, usually seasoned with ginger and orange peel, and can be stored in a glass jar in the refrigerator for about a year. Rinse them to remove excess salt.

1 To make the Fermented Black Bean Sauce: In a small bowl, stir together the black beans, hot water, sherry, sesame oil, lemon juice, and chili paste and set aside.

2 For the cabbage: In a large skillet or wok on high heat, warm the vegetable oil. Add the cabbage, onions, garlic, ginger, and salt. Stir fry until the cabbage is crisp-tender, about 10 minutes.

3 Mash the softened black beans with a fork, pour the sauce into the skillet, and cook for a couple of minutes. Add more salt to taste.

SERVING AND MENU IDEAS: Serve with lemon wedges or a cruet of vinegar, because a little extra tartness brightens the flavor of this classic Chinese side dish. Good with brown rice or soba or udon noodles. Add An Easy Baked Tofu (page 177) or Orange-glazed Tofu on Greens (page 180) to make it a meal.

CABBAGE WITH FERMENTED BLACK BEANS—PER 1 SERVING (OF 4) *Calories: 98, Protein: 2 g, Carbohydrate: 10 g, Dietary Fiber: 2 g, Total Fat: 6 g, Saturated Fat: 1 g, Monounsaturated Fat: 2 g, Cholesterol: 0 mg, Sodium: 510 mg*

TOFU

SOY

For almost 5,000 years, soy has been a staple food in China. During recent years in the United States, soy products including tofu, soymilk, soy yogurt, edamame, soy sauce, soybean pastes, and tempeh have exploded onto the market. Despite this impressive list of foods, most of the U.S. soybean crop is still grown for animal feed and biofuels. Soy is high in protein and low in saturated fat. Acre for acre, soy produces twenty times more protein that beef, and it's much less expensive to grow.

Regular consumption of soy contributes to a healthy, balanced diet. The discovery of a much lower breast cancer rate, fewer menopausal symptoms, and less osteoporosis among Asian women has generated a lot of speculation about the benefits of a soy-based diet. The role of soy in the prevention or reduction of breast cancer is under careful study. So far, research by the National Cancer Institute is inconclusive. Many women have taken high-dose soy supplements both for prevention and treatment, but now it is believed that intensive soy therapy may not be healthy. Current research is also exploring the benefits of soy in preventing diseases of the cardiovascular system, bones, kidneys, and prostate gland.

Soy foods include:

Edamame are young, tender green soybeans, available in the pod or shelled, and found in the store fresh or frozen. In the pod, they can be quickly steamed to a bright green, salted, and popped out of their cases to make an instant snack or appetizer. Shelled edamame are delicious and nutritious in stews, salads, and sautés. Edamame are very low in sodium, a good source of dietary fiber, protein, thiamine, iron, magnesium, phosphorus, and copper, and a very good source of vitamin K, folate, and manganese.

Tofu was made first in ancient China, and has been a staple in Asian cuisines for hundreds of years. Today, throughout Asia, it is made fresh daily in thousands of tofu shops and sold on the street. Tofu, also known as soybean curd, is made by curdling fresh hot soymilk with a coagulant and then pressing the curds into a cake. Traditionally, the curdling agent used to make tofu is *nigari,* a compound found in natural ocean water, or calcium sulfate, a naturally occurring mineral. In recipes, tofu acts like a sponge, soaking up flavor. Crumble it into a pot of spicy chili sauce and it tastes like chili. Blend it with cocoa and sweetener and it becomes chocolate cream pie filling.

At Moosewood, we use tofu every day in appetizers, soups, main courses, sandwiches, and salads. Tofu has a rich and varied place in Asian cuisines, and it is also an excellent alternative in dishes that traditionally call for meat. We use it in many different guises in dishes inspired by almost any cuisine. We love and respect this age-old vegetarian food, and are grateful that in Ithaca we have Ithaca Soy, our own local producer of tofu.

Tofu is rich in high-quality protein. It is also a good source of B vitamins and iron. When the curdling agent used to make tofu is a calcium salt, the tofu is an excellent source of calcium. It is low in saturated fat and contains no cholesterol. Generally, the softer the tofu, the lower the fat, protein, and calcium content. Tofu is also very low in sodium. Three and a half ounces of tofu has 145 calories and only 9 grams of fat; the same amount of whole milk cheese has 265 calories and 20 grams of fat.

The three main types of tofu available in American grocery stores (look in the Asian aisle for aseptic packages or in the refrigerated dairy section) are firm, soft, and silken.

Firm tofu is dense and solid and holds up well in soups, when stir-fried and baked, and on the grill. Use it when you want the tofu to maintain its shape. Also good crumbled into soups and stews, and grated for "burgers." Firm tofu is higher in protein, fat, and calcium than other forms of tofu.

Soft tofu is a good choice for egg-like scrambles, Asian soups, and purées.

Silken tofu is made by a slightly different process that results in a creamy, custard-like product. Silken tofu works well for smoothies, tofu mayonnaise, and other puréed dishes. In Japan, silken tofu is enjoyed as is, with a touch of soy sauce and topped with chopped scallions.

Tempeh has been a favorite food and staple source of protein in Indonesia for several hundred years. Tempeh is made by the controlled fermentation of cooked soybeans with a *Rhizopus* mold. The fermentation binds the soybeans into a compact cake with a firm texture and a nutty mushroom flavor. Often tempeh is sliced and fried until the surface is crisp and golden brown. It can be used in soups, spreads, salads, and sandwiches. Tempeh retains all the fiber of the beans with some added digestive benefits from the enzymes created during the fermentation process, which produce natural antibiotic agents but leave the desirable soy isoflavones and most of the saponins intact. Tempeh is a complete protein food that contains all the essential amino acids.

Soy sauce has been enhancing savory dishes for at least 2,500 years. Soy sauce, first brewed in China and then in Japan, varies from subtle to assertive. Soy sauce is a salty, earthy-tasting brown liquid brewed from soy beans and a roasted grain, usually wheat, and then inoculated with the *Aspergillus soyae* mold. Mixed with a little salt and yeast and fermented for as long as four years, each soy sauce is unique. The longer the fermentation, the more distinguished the flavor. Even climate and water may affect the final result. It is common in the United States to find Chinese, Japanese, Malaysian, Indonesian, Korean, Taiwanese, Vietnamese, Hawaiian, and Philippine soy sauces.

Connoisseurs consider different types of soy sauce to be as varied and complex as different wines or olive oils. In January 2007, *Cook's Illustrated* ran a taste test on a dozen tamari and soy sauces from China, Japan, and the United States. The winners were Ohsawa Nama Shoyu, a traditionally brewed soy sauce from Japan, and Lee Kum Kee Tabletop Soy Sauce from China. The first is sweet and delicate, and the second is more malty and savory.

"Light" soy sauce is milder and lower in sodium. Tamari has very little or no wheat, making it a more pungent sauce. Wheat-free soy sauce is available. Look for naturally fermented soy sauces, and avoid soy sauces that contain additions of other vegetable proteins, corn syrup, and caramel coloring.

Miso, another fermented product used for flavoring dishes, is usually made from soybeans, or from rice, barley, or wheat, and a yeast mold (known as *koji.*) The fermentation time, ranging from weeks to years, depends upon the specific type of miso being produced. Once this process is complete, the fermented ingredients are ground into a paste similar in texture to nut butter. Miso ranges in color from white to dark brown. The lighter varieties are mellower and less salty, and the darker ones are saltier and have a more intense flavor. Some misos are pasteurized, while others are not.

Because it is fermented with a B_{12}-synthesizing bacteria, miso is commonly recommended as a B_{12} source for vegans. Miso is quite high in sodium, but a little miso goes a long way toward providing your daily needs for the trace minerals zinc, manganese, and copper. In addition, a single tablespoon of miso contains two grams of protein but just twenty-five calories. An impressive nutrient profile for a flavoring agent! Use miso in your cooking instead of salt for nutritional benefits in addition to enhanced flavor.

Miso makes delicious broth and soup stock, sauces, dressings, and gravies. Add it at the end of cooking; boiling or overheating destroys the beneficial enzymes. Miso will keep up to two years in a covered jar in the refrigerator. A good rule of thumb is that one tablespoon of miso or two tablespoons of soy sauce add the "saltiness" of one teaspoon of salt.

Soy yogurt and soymilk are good lactose-free substitutes for their dairy counterparts. Soymilk has about the same amount of protein as cow's milk, with one-third the fat, fewer calories, no cholesterol, and fifteen times the iron. Soymilk comes plain or flavored and sweetened or unsweetened, and often it is fortified with calcium. Plain soymilk can be substituted for cow's milk in most recipes.

Unfortunately, our food chain has been permeated with bioengineered soy used to make soy oil, meat extenders, infant formula, and processed foods. Buying certified organic soy foods is the best bet for getting the healthiest product.

An Easy Baked Tofu

SERVES 4 | HANDS-ON TIME: 10 MINUTES | BAKING TIME: 30 TO 40 MINUTES

Baked tofu is quick, versatile, protein-rich, and flavorful. It can make any meal more complete, and it makes a great snack, too.

1 CAKE OF EXTRA-FIRM OR FIRM TOFU (ABOUT 16 OUNCES)

2 TABLESPOONS DARK SESAME OIL

2 TABLESPOONS SOY SAUCE

2 TABLESPOONS KETCHUP

Cut the tofu into bite-sized cubes and place in an unoiled baking dish large enough to hold a single layer. Stir together the sesame oil, soy sauce, and ketchup and drizzle over the tofu. With a rubber spatula, gently turn to coat thoroughly. In a 400° oven, bake uncovered for 30 to 40 minutes, stirring once or twice, until the tofu is browned, firm, and chewy. Serve hot, at room temperature, or chilled.

SERVING AND MENU IDEAS: This tofu goes well with Japanese Noodles with Tomatoes (page 230). For a simple meal, serve it with a side vegetable or two, such as Mashed Cauliflower with Shallots (page 304) or Green Beans with Ginger and Garlic (page 303).

AN EASY BAKED TOFU—PER 1 SERVING (OF 4)
Calories: 134, Protein: 9 g, Carbohydrate: 5 g, Dietary Fiber: 0 g, Total Fat: 9 g, Saturated Fat: 1 g, Monounsaturated Fat: 3 g, Cholesterol: 0 mg, Sodium: 606 mg

Four Stovetop Tofus

At Moosewood, we have a long history of baking tofu with many different flavorful seasonings. During warm weather, or when we don't need or want to heat the oven, we turn to these stovetop tofus for quick and delicious meals.

Saucy Miso Tofu

SERVES 4 | TIME: 30 MINUTES

Sweet and sour, this tofu can be spicy hot if you like. Miso and plenty of onions add depth of flavor.

> 2 TABLESPOONS VEGETABLE OIL OR OLIVE OIL
>
> 1 LARGE ONION, THINLY SLICED (ABOUT 1½ CUPS)
>
> 1 CAKE OF FIRM TOFU (ABOUT 16 OUNCES)
>
> 2 TABLESPOONS RICE VINEGAR OR CIDER VINEGAR
>
> 2 TABLESPOONS MIRIN OR SHERRY
>
> 1 TABLESPOON GRATED PEELED GINGER ROOT
>
> 4 TEASPOONS SOY SAUCE
>
> ½ TEASPOON CHINESE CHILI PASTE (OPTIONAL)
>
> ¼ CUP LIGHT MISO
>
> ½ CUP WARM WATER

1 Warm the oil in a large skillet on medium heat. Add the onions and cook covered, stirring frequently, until softened, about 5 minutes.

2 Cut the tofu into bite-sized cubes or triangles and add them to the skillet. Cook uncovered, stirring frequently, for about 4 minutes. Then stir in the vinegar, mirin, ginger, soy sauce, and chili paste, if using. Cook until the liquid has been absorbed, 2 or 3 minutes.

3 Meanwhile, whisk together the miso and water. Add to the skillet and cook until bubbly. (Longer cooking destroys some of the healthful benefits of the miso.)

VARIATION: If you don't have mirin or sherry, use a tablespoon of peach or apricot jam and a tablespoon of water, or 2 teaspoons white or brown sugar and 1 tablespoon of water.

SERVING AND MENU IDEAS: Serve on a bed of rice, soba, or udon noodles topped with scallions, and with thinly sliced, steamed Chinese cabbage on the side. This tofu also goes well with Seaweed Salad (page 98), Roasted Sweet Potatoes (page 299), Mashed Cauliflower with Shallots (page 304), and Herbed Vegetable Packets (page 197).

SAUCY MISO TOFU—PER 1 SERVING (OF 4)
Calories: 208, Protein: 11 g, Carbohydrate: 13 g, Dietary Fiber: 2 g, Total Fat: 11 g, Saturated Fat: 1 g, Monounsaturated Fat: 5 g, Cholesterol: 0 mg, Sodium: 883 mg

Pomegranate-glazed Tofu

SERVES 4 | TIME: 20 MINUTES

This tofu is imbued with the tart flavor of antioxidant-rich pomegranate juice and enhanced with rosemary and orange.

1 CAKE OF FIRM TOFU (ABOUT 16 OUNCES), CUT INTO 1-INCH CUBES

2 TABLESPOONS OLIVE OIL

1 CUP PURE POMEGRANATE JUICE

2 GARLIC CLOVES, MINCED OR PRESSED

1 TABLESPOON SOY SAUCE

2 TEASPOONS DIJON MUSTARD

1 TEASPOON GRATED ORANGE ZEST

1 TEASPOON MINCED FRESH ROSEMARY

1 In a large skillet on medium-high heat, warm the olive oil. Add the tofu cubes and cook for about 3 minutes per side until lightly golden.

2 Whisk together the pomegranate juice, garlic, soy sauce, mustard, orange zest, and rosemary. When the tofu pieces are golden, pour the sauce over the tofu and simmer on medium heat for about 5 minutes. Turn over the tofu and continue to simmer for 3 to 5 minutes until the tofu has absorbed some of the sauce and the rest has reduced to a glaze.

SERVING AND MENU IDEAS: Serve with Mediterranean or Middle Eastern dishes.

POMEGRANATE-GLAZED TOFU—PER 1 SERVING (OF 4)
Calories: 173, Protein: 8 g, Carbohydrate: 13 g, Dietary Fiber: 0 g, Total Fat: 10 g, Saturated Fat: 1 g, Monounsaturated Fat: 6 g, Cholesterol: 0 mg, Sodium: 44 mg

Tropical Lime Tofu

SERVES 4 | TIME: 25 MINUTES

This tangy and flavorful tofu goes well with dishes from the Caribbean, Southeast Asia, and Latin America.

2 TABLESPOONS OLIVE OIL

3 GARLIC CLOVES, MINCED OR PRESSED

½ TEASPOON CUMIN SEEDS (OPTIONAL)

1 CAKE OF FIRM TOFU (ABOUT 16 OUNCES), CUT INTO 1-INCH CUBES

½ TEASPOON GROUND CUMIN

⅓ CUP LIME JUICE

2 TABLESPOONS SOY SAUCE

¼ TEASPOON GROUND BLACK PEPPER OR RED PEPPER FLAKES

1 In a large skillet on medium-high heat, warm the olive oil. Add the garlic and cumin seeds, if using, and cook for a minute. Add the tofu cubes and cook, stirring occasionally, until lightly golden, about 8 minutes.

2 Meanwhile, whisk together the ground cumin, lime juice, soy sauce, and pepper. When the tofu is golden, pour the lime juice mixture over it and cook, stirring occasionally, until the liquid has been absorbed, about 6 minutes.

SERVING AND MENU IDEAS: Serve with Quinoa and Sweet Potatoes (page 284), or on a bed of rice. Delicious with a Mango Slaw (page 93) or Kale with Sweet Potatoes (page 305).

TROPICAL LIME TOFU—PER 1 SERVING (OF 4)
Calories: 144, Protein: 9 g, Carbohydrate: 6 g, Dietary Fiber: 0 g, Total Fat: 10 g, Saturated Fat: 1 g, Monounsaturated Fat: 6 g, Cholesterol: 0 mg, Sodium: 342 mg

Orange-glazed Tofu on Greens

SERVES 4 | TIME: 35 MINUTES

This tofu, made simply with just a few ingredients, has a subtle and sophisticated combination of tastes—great on a bed of lightly stir-fried greens.

TOFU

2 TABLESPOONS VEGETABLE OIL

2 GARLIC CLOVES, MINCED OR PRESSED

1 CAKE OF FIRM TOFU (ABOUT 16 OUNCES), CUT INTO 1-INCH CUBES

ORANGE SAUCE

1 LARGE ORANGE

2 TABLESPOONS SOY SAUCE

¼ CUP MINCED SCALLIONS

GREENS

1 TEASPOON VEGETABLE OIL

8 TO 10 CUPS COARSELY CHOPPED GREENS, RINSED (SEE NOTE)

¼ TEASPOON SALT

1 TABLESPOON TOASTED SESAME SEEDS

NOTE: Orange-glazed Tofu is good on almost any kind of greens; try Swiss chard, watercress, spinach, bok choy, or arugula.

1 For the tofu, warm the vegetable oil in a large skillet on medium heat. Add the garlic and cook for a few seconds. Add the tofu cubes and cook, stirring occasionally, until lightly golden, about 8 minutes.

2 While the tofu is cooking, prepare the sauce. Grate the orange peel to yield 1 teaspoon of zest, then juice the orange. You need 6 tablespoons of liquid; if you don't have enough orange juice, add water or sake. In a small bowl or cup, mix together the zest, juice, soy sauce, and scallions.

3 When the tofu is golden, pour in the sauce and continue to cook on medium heat, stirring occasionally, until the sauce has been absorbed, about 5 minutes. Transfer to a bowl and set aside.

4 For the greens, warm the oil in the skillet and add the still-damp greens. Sprinkle with the salt and stir-fry until just wilted. Spoon the greens onto a serving platter, top with the tofu, and sprinkle on the sesame seeds.

SERVING AND MENU IDEAS: This is a lovely light meal simply with the addition of brown rice.

ORANGE-GLAZED TOFU ON GREENS—PER 1 SERVING (OF 4) *Calories: 178, Protein: 10 g, Carbohydrate: 8 g, Dietary Fiber: 1 g, Total Fat: 12 g, Saturated Fat: 1 g, Monounsaturated Fat: 6 g, Cholesterol: 0 mg, Sodium: 502 mg*

Vegetable Tofu Scramble

SERVES 4 | TIME: 40 MINUTES

Tofu scrambles are a favorite everyday vegan brunch, lunch, or dinner. In this scramble, tofu is the perfect foil for the assertive flavors of smoky paprika and oregano, with a sprinkling—or more—of spicy red pepper flakes.

1 TABLESPOON OLIVE OIL

1½ CUPS CHOPPED ONIONS

¼ TEASPOON SALT

¼ TEASPOON RED PEPPER FLAKES OR MORE TO TASTE

½ TEASPOON SMOKED PAPRIKA

1 TABLESPOON CHOPPED FRESH OREGANO OR 1 TEASPOON DRIED

3 CUPS CHOPPED FRESH MUSHROOMS

1½ CUPS CHOPPED RED BELL PEPPERS

1 CAKE OF FIRM TOFU (ABOUT 16 OUNCES)

2 TABLESPOONS SOY SAUCE

CHOPPED SCALLIONS OR SNIPPED CHIVES, OR CHOPPED FRESH PARSLEY

In a skillet on medium-high heat, warm the olive oil and cook the onions with the salt, stirring frequently, for a couple of minutes. Stir in the red pepper flakes, smoked paprika, and the oregano if using dried, and continue to cook for 3 or 4 minutes, until the onions have softened. Add the mushrooms and bell peppers and cook for about 5 minutes, until the mushrooms begin to release juice. Crumble the tofu into the vegetables, and cook, stirring often, for 8 to 10 minutes until heated through. Stir in the soy sauce and the oregano if using fresh, and cook for about 2 minutes longer. Serve topped with scallions.

VARIATIONS: Sweet paprika is a fine substitute for smoked paprika in this recipe.

If you like their smoky flavor and spiciness, add minced canned chipotles in adobo sauce with the soy sauce, and omit the paprika and red pepper flakes.

SERVING AND MENU IDEAS: Serve with toast or on rice or polenta. Fresh fruit is welcome with this mildly spicy, slightly salty dish. Or serve a fruity dessert, such as Pomegranate Gel with Fruit (page 312) or Cantaloupe with Fresh Raspberry Sauce (page 313).

VEGETABLE TOFU SCRAMBLE—PER 1 SERVING (OF 4)
Calories: 159, Protein: 11 g, Carbohydrate: 15 g, Dietary Fiber: 4 g, Total Fat: 7 g, Saturated Fat: 1 g, Monounsaturated Fat: 3 g, Cholesterol: 0 mg, Sodium: 644 mg

Tofu Mole

SERVES 4 TO 6 | TIME: 50 MINUTES

Mole is a distinctive earthy sauce used in Mexican cooking. Different regions of Mexico—in fact, different families—take pride in their unique mole sauces, which may take all day to make. Our chunky, mole-inspired sauce for tofu is much more quickly prepared, and includes flavors common in Mexican cuisine: cinnamon, chocolate, tomatoes, and chiles.

---

1 DRIED ANCHO CHILE (SEE NOTE)

½ CUP BOILING WATER

2 TABLESPOONS OLIVE OIL

1¼ CUPS CHOPPED ONIONS

2 GARLIC CLOVES, MINCED OR PRESSED

1 TEASPOON SALT

¼ TEASPOON DRIED THYME

⅛ TEASPOON GROUND CINNAMON

3 CUPS CHOPPED BELL PEPPERS

2 CUPS CHOPPED FRESH TOMATOES
OR 1 15-OUNCE CAN DICED TOMATOES

1 TABLESPOON UNSWEETENED COCOA
POWDER

1 CAKE OF FIRM TOFU (ABOUT 16 OUNCES),
CUT INTO 1-INCH CUBES

NOTE: Dried ancho chiles add a flavor that's more complex than simply spicy-hot. In this recipe, dried ancho chiles can be replaced by your favorite dried chiles.

1 Place the dried ancho in a small bowl, cover with the boiling water, and set aside to steep.

2 Meanwhile, in a saucepan on medium heat, warm the olive oil. Add the onions, garlic, and salt and cook, stirring now and then, until the onions are translucent, about 8 minutes. Stir in the thyme and cinnamon. Add the bell peppers and continue to cook until softened, about 5 minutes.

3 When the bell peppers are tender, finely chop the softened ancho and add to the saucepan with the soaking liquid, tomatoes, and cocoa. Bring to a boil, reduce the heat to low, cover, and simmer for about 5 minutes, stirring occasionally. Add the tofu cubes, cover, and simmer for about 20 minutes, stirring occasionally. Add more salt to taste.

VARIATION: For a spicier mole sauce, add minced canned chipotles in adobo sauce to taste. Omit the dried ancho chile and add water as needed for a saucy consistency.

SERVING AND MENU IDEAS: Try this Mexican-style tofu on rice or polenta. Serve it with Roasted Sweet Potatoes (page 299) or Sesame Flaxseed Cornbread (page 48). Include salad greens garnished with orange or grapefruit sections and drizzled with Avocado Citrus Dressing (page 109).

TOFU MOLE—PER 1 SERVING (OF 4) *Calories: 214, Protein: 11 g, Carbohydrate: 21 g, Dietary Fiber: 6 g, Total Fat: 11 g, Saturated Fat: 2 g, Monounsaturated Fat: 6 g, Cholesterol: 0 mg, Sodium: 345 mg*

Southeast Asian Tofu with Lemongrass

SERVES 4 | TIME: 40 MINUTES

Lemongrass has a citrusy fragrance and distinctive flavor and is a basic ingredient in the cooking of Southeast Asia. Here it provides a background note for other flavors in an aromatic sauce for tofu.

---

2 CUPS VEGETABLE BROTH (SEE PAGE 33)

2 LEMONGRASS STALKS

4 GARLIC CLOVES, SLICED

1 FRESH CHILE, DICED

½ CUP SLICED RED ONIONS

1 CUP DICED FRESH TOMATOES

1 CUP CARROTS CUT INTO MATCHSTICKS

2 TABLESPOONS SOY SAUCE

2 CUPS CHOPPED GREENS SUCH AS BABY BOK CHOY, SPINACH, OR TATSOI

1 CAKE OF SOFT TOFU (ABOUT 16 OUNCES), CUT INTO 1-INCH CUBES

1 TABLESPOON CORNSTARCH DISSOLVED IN ¼ CUP COLD WATER

¼ CUP CHOPPED FRESH CILANTRO, THAI BASIL, OR ITALIAN BASIL

2 TABLESPOONS LIME JUICE

---

1 In a covered soup pot on medium heat, bring the vegetable broth to a simmer.

2 Meanwhile, remove any dry outer leaves from the lemongrass stalks and trim the root ends. Slice about 2 inches of the root end of each stalk in half lengthwise, taking care not to separate it from the rest of the stalk. Tie the lemongrass stalks together with kitchen twine to make it easier to remove later. Add the lemongrass, garlic, chiles, and red onions to the broth, cover, and bring to a simmer.

3 After the broth has simmered for 15 minutes, add the tomatoes and carrots, increase the heat, and bring back to a simmer. Reduce the heat and simmer, covered, for 10 minutes. Remove the lemongrass stalks and add the soy sauce. Add the greens and tofu and increase the heat. When the broth returns to a boil, add the dissolved cornstarch in a steady stream, stirring constantly until thickened. Stir in the cilantro and lime juice. Add more soy sauce and/or lime juice to taste.

VARIATIONS: You can make this dish with water instead of vegetable broth; add ½ teaspoon salt to the water.

If you can't find lemongrass, add 1 teaspoon of grated lime zest when you add the greens and tofu.

Whole or sliced snow peas can replace the greens, and cook just as quickly.

SERVING AND MENU IDEAS: Serve on brown rice, soba noodles, or whole grain linguini and garnish with lime wedges. On the side, try Mango Slaw (page 93) or Mango Pickles (page 68). Herbed and Spiced Fresh Fruit Popsicles (pages 320–21) are a refreshing dessert.

SOUTHEAST ASIAN TOFU WITH LEMONGRASS— PER 1 SERVING (OF 4) *Calories: 134, Protein: 8 g, Carbohydrate: 19 g, Dietary Fiber: 3 g, Total Fat: 3 g, Saturated Fat: 0 g, Monounsaturated Fat: 1 g, Cholesterol: 0 mg, Sodium: 426 mg*

SAVORY PASTRIES, STUFFED VEGETABLES, CASSEROLES & MORE

Greener Spanakopita

SERVES 6 | YIELDS 6 TURNOVERS | HANDS-ON TIME: 35 MINUTES | BAKING TIME: 15 MINUTES

This greener-than-traditional version of spanakopita is lighter on the cheese, uses olive oil rather than butter, is loaded with masses of healthful greens, and is still a crowd-pleaser. Whole wheat filo is more flavorful than white flour filo and is easy to work with.

8 CUPS CHOPPED STURDY GREENS SUCH AS KALE OR COLLARDS (SEE NOTE)

8 CUPS CHOPPED DELICATE GREENS, SUCH AS SPINACH, CHARD, OR MUSTARD GREENS (SEE NOTE)

4 OUNCES NEUFCHÂTEL CHEESE, AT ROOM TEMPERATURE

¾ CUP GRATED FETA CHEESE

2 TABLESPOONS CHOPPED FRESH DILL

½ TEASPOON DRIED OREGANO

⅛ TEASPOON GROUND BLACK PEPPER

½ CUP OLIVE OIL

4 GARLIC CLOVES, MINCED OR PRESSED

16-OUNCE PACKAGE WHOLE WHEAT FILO DOUGH, THAWED (SEE PAGE 23)

2 TEASPOONS SESAME SEEDS

NOTE: Kale and collards vary noticeably from bunch to bunch, with more or fewer yellowing or wilted leaves and larger center stems. To get 8 packed cups of sorted, stemmed, and chopped sturdy greens you'll need about 1½ pounds. As for the delicate greens that are sold in bunches, our guess is 2 to 3 pounds (bunch weight). About 12 ounces of baby spinach gives you 8 cups.

1 Steam the sturdy greens until tender, about 10 minutes. Place them in a colander to drain. Steam the delicate greens until just wilted and add them to the colander. Press out as much water as possible. Place the drained greens in a mixing bowl. Add the neufchâtel, feta, dill, oregano, and pepper and mix well.

2 In a microwave oven or in a small pan on the stovetop, heat the oil and garlic just until the garlic sizzles and becomes golden but not browned. Pour the warm oil through a strainer and set aside. Stir the garlic into the greens and cheese mixture.

3 Place the bowl of filling, the reserved garlic oil, and a pastry brush near a dry flat work surface. Unfold the stack of filo sheets and place 2 sheets on the work surface with a short side facing you. Lightly brush the top with garlic oil. Keeping the 2 sheets together, fold in half lengthwise. Place a scant ½ cup of filling near the bottom and fold the lower left corner diagonally up and over the filling until the bottom edge meets the right side, forming a triangle. Fold the triangle straight up along its top edge, then fold along the diagonal. Continue to fold as you would a flag, alternating straight up and diagonally, until you reach the far end. Brush the top with oil and place on a lightly oiled baking sheet. Assemble the rest of the pastries, working down the stack two sheets at a time. Sprinkle the tops with sesame seeds. In a preheated 375° oven, bake for about 15 minutes, until puffed and golden.

SERVING AND MENU IDEAS: This popular pastry is nicely paired with soup, such as Greek Tomato-Yogurt Soup (page 125), Chilled Beet Borscht (page 135), or for a more substantial meal, Roman Grain and Mushroom Soup (page 120). Try Figs Baked with Chèvre and Pistachios (page 315) for a sweet ending.

GREENER SPANAKOPITA—PER 1 SERVING (OF 6), 1 PASTRY *Calories: 503, Protein: 13 g, Carbohydrate: 57 g, Dietary Fiber: 6 g, Total Fat: 26 g, Saturated Fat: 6 g Monosaturated Fat: 15 g, Cholesterol: 18 mg, Sodium: 486 mg*

Spinach Quesadillas

SERVES 4 | YIELDS 4 QUESADILLAS | TIME: 25 MINUTES

Whole grain, less cheese, lots of nutrient-rich spinach—and it's still a quesadilla. Kids gobble these down. Dip the triangles in your favorite salsa.

---

1 TABLESPOON OLIVE OIL

2 CUPS FINELY CHOPPED ONIONS

1 FRESH CHILE, MINCED

5 CUPS CHOPPED FRESH SPINACH, LARGE STEMS REMOVED (ABOUT 10 OUNCES)

PINCH OF DRIED OREGANO

¼ TEASPOON SALT

¼ TEASPOON GROUND BLACK PEPPER

4 8- OR 10-INCH WHOLE WHEAT FLOUR TORTILLAS

1 CUP GRATED MONTEREY JACK CHEESE

---

1 In a large saucepan on medium-high heat, warm the oil and cook the onions and chiles for 4 or 5 minutes, until softened. Add the spinach, oregano, salt, and pepper. Stir until the spinach has wilted, a minute or two. Remove from the heat and drain.

2 Place one of the tortillas in a dry skillet on medium heat (for a crisper quesadilla, lightly oil the skillet). Sprinkle on ¼ cup of the grated cheese. After about a minute, when the cheese has begun to melt, spread ¼ of the drained spinach mixture over half of the tortilla. Fold the tortilla over the spinach and cheese to make a half-circle and cook for a minute. Turn the quesadilla over and cook until the cheese is thoroughly melted and the bottom of the tortilla is speckled brown, about a minute.

3 Remove the quesadilla and slice it into wedges. Repeat with the remaining tortillas.

SERVING AND MENU IDEAS: Serve with your favorite salsa. Spinach Quesadillas are a great first course for Chili Fest Chili (page 222). Alongside a bowl of soup, such as Mellow Gazpacho (page 127) or Latin Corn Soup (page 128), they make a satisfying meal.

SPINACH QUESADILLAS—PER 1 SERVING (OF 4), 1 QUESADILLA *Calories: 245, Protein: 14 g, Carbohydrate: 31 g, Dietary Fiber: 5 g, Total Fat: 10 g, Saturated Fat: 5 g, Monounsaturated Fat: 4 g, Cholesterol: 18 mg, Sodium: 536 mg*

New World Pizza

SERVES 4 TO 6 | HANDS-ON TIME: 1 HOUR | BAKING TIME: 15 TO 20 MINUTES

It's hard to imagine, but until the Americas were "discovered" the rest of the world did without any corn, sweet and hot peppers, and tomatoes. Here's a delicious, spicy way to employ these gifts from the New World. Our whole wheat pizza dough is simple and uses a no-knead technique.

DOUGH

2¼ TEASPOONS ACTIVE DRY YEAST (¼-OUNCE PACKET)

1 TEASPOON SUGAR

1 CUP WARM WATER

⅓ CUP SOY FLOUR

1¾ CUPS WHOLE WHEAT BREAD FLOUR

1 TEASPOON OLIVE OIL

1 TEASPOON SALT

TOPPING

2 BELL PEPPERS

4 FRESH CHILES (2 MILD CHILES, SUCH AS ANCHO OR POBLANO, AND 2 HOT CHILES, SUCH AS JALAPEÑOS)

1½ CUPS ONION SLICES

4 GARLIC CLOVES, MINCED OR PRESSED

2 TABLESPOONS OLIVE OIL

1 TEASPOON SALT

1 TABLESPOON GROUND CUMIN

2 TEASPOONS DRIED OREGANO

1 15-OUNCE CAN DICED TOMATOES, WELL DRAINED, OR 1½ CUPS DICED FRESH PLUM TOMATOES

1 CUP FRESH OR FROZEN CORN KERNELS

1 CUP LIGHTLY PACKED GRATED MONTEREY JACK CHEESE

1 To make the dough: In a bowl, stir the yeast and sugar into the warm water and set aside until the yeast has dissolved and is bubbly. Stir in the soy flour, whole wheat flour, olive oil, and salt. Cover and place in a warm spot to rise for 45 minutes.

2 While the dough is rising, prepare the topping. Cut the bell peppers into lengthwise strips about ½-inch wide. Seed the chiles for a milder "hot," if you wish, and mince them. Toss the bell peppers and chiles with the onions, garlic, oil, salt, cumin, and oregano and spread in a single layer on a baking sheet. In a preheated 425° oven, roast for 20 minutes. Stir in the tomatoes and corn and continue to roast until the vegetables are tender and somewhat browned, about 10 minutes. Set aside.

3 Generously brush a 14- or 15-inch pizza pan with olive oil. When the dough has risen, use a spatula to scrape it onto the pizza pan. With floured hands, push and pat the sticky dough to evenly cover the pan, forming a rim at the edges.

4 Spread the vegetable mixture evenly over the dough and sprinkle with the cheese. In a preheated 450° oven, bake for about 15 minutes, until the topping is golden and bubbly and the bottom of the crust has browned.

VARIATION: If you want an even faster crust, the topping is the right amount to cover four whole wheat pita breads. Bake for 10 to 15 minutes at 400° until the topping is heated through and the cheese has melted.

SERVING AND MENU IDEAS: While you wait for the pizza to come out of the oven, dip tortilla chips in Simple Guacamole (page 69) or serve a soup like Green Soup (page 266) or Sweet Potato, Apple, and Chipotle Soup (page 132). Good side salads for this pizza are Our Favorite Raw Slaw (page 267), Raw Broccoli Salad (page 97), and Spinach Salad with Chèvre and Walnuts (page 84). Another New World gift, Hot Chocolate (page 337), is an easy, delicious dessert.

NEW WORLD PIZZA—PER 1 SERVING (OF 6)
Calories: 332, Protein: 16 g, Carbohydrate: 47 g, Dietary Fiber: 9 g, Total Fat: 11 g, Saturated Fat: 4 g, Monounsaturated Fat: 5 g, Cholesterol: 12 mg, Sodium: 978 mg

Greek Pizza

SERVES 4 TO 6 | HANDS-ON TIME: 1 HOUR | BAKING TIME: 15 TO 20 MINUTES

We love this unconventional pizza with its layer of lemony puréed chickpeas topped with traditional Greek pizza toppings.

DOUGH

SEE PAGE 188

TOPPING

1 15-OUNCE CAN CHICKPEAS, DRAINED

3 TABLESPOONS WATER

4 TEASPOONS LEMON JUICE, OR MORE TO TASTE

2 TABLESPOONS OLIVE OIL

¼ TEASPOON SALT

2 GARLIC CLOVES, MINCED OR PRESSED

5 CUPS CHOPPED FRESH SPINACH, LARGE STEMS REMOVED (ABOUT 10 OUNCES)

2 CUPS CHOPPED TOMATOES

1 14-OUNCE CAN ARTICHOKE HEARTS, WELL DRAINED AND CHOPPED

1 TEASPOON DRIED OREGANO

GROUND BLACK PEPPER

¾ CUP GRATED KASSERI, FETA, OR ASIAGO CHEESE (SEE NOTE)

NOTE: Kasseri is a flavorful goat and sheep milk cheese from Greece.

1 Prepare the dough. Cover and place in a warm spot to rise for 45 minutes.

2 While the dough is rising, prepare the topping. In a food processor, purée the chickpeas, water, lemon juice, 1 tablespoon of the olive oil, and the salt. Add more lemon juice or salt to taste. Set aside.

3 In a skillet on medium-high heat, cook the garlic in 1 tablespoon olive oil for just a moment before adding the spinach. Cook for a minute or two, until the spinach has just wilted and is still bright green. Place in a colander to drain.

4 Generously brush a 14- or 15-inch pizza pan with olive oil. When the dough has risen, use a spatula to scrape it onto the pizza pan. With floured hands, push and pat the sticky dough to evenly cover the pan, forming a rim at the edges.

5 Spread the chickpea purée over the dough and top with the spinach, tomatoes, and artichoke hearts. Sprinkle with the oregano, pepper, and cheese. Bake in a preheated 425° oven for 15 to 20 minutes, until the cheese has melted and the crust bottom has browned.

SERVING AND MENU IDEAS: Try Watermelon Salad (page 99) or Arugula, Kumquat, Walnut, and Fig Salad (page 95) on the side.

GREEK PIZZA—PER 1 SERVING (OF 6) *Calories: 551, Protein: 28 g, Carbohydrate: 83 g, Dietary Fiber: 22 g, Total Fat: 15 g, Saturated Fat: 4 g, Monounsaturated Fat: 6 g, Cholesterol: 17 mg, Sodium: 932 mg*

Kasha-stuffed Peppers

SERVES 4 TO 6 | YIELDS ABOUT 4 CUPS FILLING | TIME: 50 TO 60 MINUTES

Buckwheat groats, also called kasha, are hearty and earthy and one of those foods people either love or hate. They are high in fiber, lysine-rich, and gluten-free. In this recipe, we simmer kasha with mushrooms and cauliflower, fresh herbs, and wine to make a flavorful pilaf for stuffing peppers.

4 LARGE, 5 MEDIUM, OR 6 SMALLER RED, ORANGE, OR YELLOW BELL PEPPERS

OLIVE OIL FOR BRUSHING THE PEPPERS

KASHA PILAF

1 TABLESPOON OLIVE OIL

1 CUP DICED ONIONS

½ CUP DICED CELERY

2 GARLIC CLOVES, MINCED OR PRESSED

¾ CUP KASHA

1¼ CUPS WATER OR VEGETABLE BROTH (SEE PAGE 33)

2 TABLESPOONS RED WINE OR SHERRY

1 TABLESPOON SOY SAUCE

2 CUPS SLICED MUSHROOMS

2 CUPS CHOPPED CAULIFLOWER

1 TEASPOON MINCED FRESH ROSEMARY OR THYME (OPTIONAL)

½ TEASPOON SALT

GENEROUS DASH OF GROUND BLACK PEPPER

½ CUP CHOPPED FRESH PARSLEY

2 TABLESPOONS CHOPPED FRESH DILL

1 Slice the bell peppers in half lengthwise and remove the seeds, leaving the stem intact. Place the halves cut side down on a lightly oiled baking sheet and brush with olive oil. In a preheated 400° oven, bake for 15 to 20 minutes, until just tender and still retaining their shape. Remove from the oven, flip over the pepper halves on the baking sheet so they won't continue to cook, and set aside.

2 While the peppers bake, in a skillet on medium heat, warm the oil. Add the onions, celery, and garlic and cook until beginning to soften, about 5 minutes. Stir in the kasha and continue to cook for about 2 minutes, stirring constantly. Add the water, wine, soy sauce, mushrooms, cauliflower, rosemary if using, salt, and pepper, and bring to a boil. Reduce the heat to low, cover, and simmer, stirring occasionally, until the liquid has been absorbed and the vegetables are tender, about 20 minutes. Remove from the heat and stir in the parsley and dill.

3 Mound pilaf into each of the roasted pepper halves.

SERVING AND MENU IDEAS: Try topped with plain yogurt. Good starters are Chilled Beet Borscht (page 135) or Yellow Split Pea Dip (page 71) with crisp vegetable sticks. Side dishes that complement the peppers are Roasted Beet Salad (page 92) and Cabbage Braised in Red Wine (page 306).

KASHA-STUFFED PEPPERS—PER 1 SERVING (OF 6)
Calories: 270, Protein: 10 g, Carbohydrate: 53 g, Dietary Fiber: 9 g, Total Fat: 4 g, Saturated Fat: 1 g, Monounsaturated Fat: 2 g, Cholesterol: 0 mg, Sodium: 377 mg

Tex-Mex Stuffed Portabellas

SERVES 4 | YIELDS 4 CUPS FILLING | HANDS-ON TIME: 45 MINUTES | BAKING TIME: 40 TO 45 MINUTES

These portabellas are stuffed with red and yellow bell peppers seasoned with spicy chipotles and other Tex-Mex aromatic favorites. Smooth, creamy Monterey Jack cheese ties it all together.

1 ½ CUPS CHOPPED ONIONS

2 GARLIC CLOVES, MINCED OR PRESSED

2 TABLESPOONS OLIVE OIL

1 CANNED CHIPOTLE IN ADOBO SAUCE, MINCED

1 YELLOW AND 1 RED BELL PEPPER, FINELY CHOPPED (2 TO 2½ CUPS)

1 TEASPOON GROUND CORIANDER

1 TEASPOON GROUND CUMIN

½ TEASPOON PAPRIKA

½ TEASPOON SALT

¼ TEASPOON GROUND BLACK PEPPER

¼ CUP CHOPPED FRESH CILANTRO

3 FRESH PLUM TOMATOES, SEEDED AND FINELY DICED (ABOUT 1 CUP)

6 OUNCES MONTEREY JACK CHEESE, GRATED (ABOUT 2 CUPS)

4 LARGE PORTABELLA MUSHROOMS (4 TO 5 INCHES IN DIAMETER)

MINCED SCALLIONS

1   In a skillet on medium-high heat, cook the onions and garlic in the olive oil for a couple of minutes. Add the chipotles and bell peppers and cook for 2 minutes. Add the coriander, cumin, paprika, salt, and pepper and cook, stirring often, until the peppers are tender but still firm. Remove from the heat. Stir in the cilantro and tomatoes and two-thirds of the cheese.

2   Break off the stems of the portabellas and save them for another use or discard. Rinse the caps (gently, so they don't break), and place smooth side down in a lightly oiled baking dish large enough to hold them in a single layer. Mound each mushroom with about a cup of the filling. Sprinkle the remaining cheese on top. Cover the baking dish with foil folded lengthwise to form a little tent so that the foil won't stick to the cheese.

3   Bake in a preheated 350° oven for 30 minutes. Remove the foil and bake until the cheese browns, 10 to 15 minutes. Serve topped with scallions.

SERVING AND MENU IDEAS: Serve on a bed of rice or Quinoa and Sweet Potatoes (page 284). Green Soup (page 266) or Latin Corn Soup (page 128) is a good appetizer. Try Lemony Zucchini with a Bread Crumb Topping (page 301) or a green salad with Avocado Citrus Dressing (page 109) on the side. Ice Pops (page 322) are fun for dessert.

TEX-MEX STUFFED PORTABELLAS—PER 1 SERVING (OF 4) *Calories: 276, Protein: 16 g, Carbohydrate: 18 g, Dietary Fiber: 4 g, Total Fat: 17 g, Saturated Fat: 7 g, Monounsaturated Fat: 8 g, Cholesterol: 28 mg, Sodium: 546 mg*

Tofu, Leek, and Almond Stuffed Portabellas

SERVES 6 | YIELDS ABOUT 6 CUPS FILLING | HANDS-ON TIME: 35 MINUTES | BAKING TIME: 35 TO 40 MINUTES

Portabellas are perfect for filling with this savory herbed tofu. Each mushroom is a complete, juicy, and delicious serving.

---

3 TABLESPOONS OLIVE OIL

4 CUPS SLICED LEEKS (WHITE AND TENDER GREEN PARTS), THOROUGHLY RINSED

1 MEDIUM FENNEL BULB, CHOPPED (ABOUT 2 CUPS)

2 TEASPOONS GROUND FENNEL SEEDS

1 TEASPOON DRIED THYME

½ TEASPOON SALT

¼ TEASPOON GROUND BLACK PEPPER

1 CAKE OF FIRM TOFU (ABOUT 16 OUNCES), GRATED (SEE NOTE)

3 TABLESPOONS SOY SAUCE

½ CUP CHOPPED TOASTED ALMONDS

6 LARGE PORTABELLA MUSHROOMS (4 TO 5 INCHES IN DIAMETER)

NOTE: Grated tofu acts as the filling's binder. Grate tofu in a food processor using the grater blade, or whirl it in the bowl of a food processor. You can also use a hand grater. The point is to have very small pieces of tofu and no lumps.

1 Warm 2 tablespoons of the olive oil in a skillet on medium-low heat and cook the leeks and fennel for 5 minutes, stirring occasionally. Add the ground fennel, thyme, salt, and pepper and cook covered on low heat, stirring occasionally, until the vegetables are tender, about 10 minutes.

2 In a bowl, combine the cooked leeks and fennel with the grated tofu, soy sauce, and almonds and mix well.

3 Break off the stems of the portabellas and save them for another use or discard. Rinse the caps (gently, so they don't break), brush lightly with the remaining olive oil, and place smooth side down in a lightly oiled baking dish large enough to hold them in one layer. Mound each mushroom with about a cup of the tofu mixture and press down gently. In a preheated 350° oven, bake uncovered until the mushrooms are tender, 35 to 40 minutes.

VARIATION: Bake this filling in smaller mushrooms for a delicious appetizer.

SERVING AND MENU IDEAS: Serve on brown basmati rice with steamed asparagus on the side. Reserve the pan juice from the mushrooms to drizzle on the rice. Other good dishes to pair with these stuffed mushrooms are Chilled Beet Borscht (page 135), Mashed Cauliflower with Shallots (page 304), and Pomegranate Carrots (page 302).

TOFU, LEEK, AND ALMOND STUFFED PORTABELLAS— PER 1 SERVING (OF 6) *Calories: 234, Protein: 12 g, Carbohydrate: 21 g, Dietary Fiber: 5 g, Total Fat: 13 g, Saturated Fat: 1 g, Monounsaturated Fat: 8 g, Cholesterol: 0 mg, Sodium: 713 mg*

Baked Sweet Potatoes Stuffed Three Ways

SERVES 4 | SWEET POTATO BAKING TIME: 25 TO 50 MINUTES | STUFFING PREPARATION TIME: 20 MINUTES

Here we give you two methods for cooking sweet potatoes and three choices of stuffings, each one filled with good things and ready by the time the potatoes are cooked.

Baked Sweet Potatoes

4 MEDIUM-LARGE SWEET POTATOES

OLIVE OIL

1 Pierce the sweet potatoes in several places with a fork, and rub with olive oil. In a 450° oven, bake until soft enough that a fork inserted into the middle of the potatoes meets little resistance, about 45 minutes. Or in a microwave oven, place the sweet potatoes about an inch apart and cook for 6 minutes, then turn them over, reorienting their direction, and cook for 6 minutes more. Rearrange the sweet potatoes and cook for 2 minutes, and then test for doneness. If needed, cook in 2-minute increments, until a fork inserted into the middle of the potatoes meets little resistance.

2 While the sweet potatoes bake, prepare one of the stuffings.

PER SWEET POTATO, PLAIN *Calories: 112, Protein: 2 g, Carbohydrate: 26 g, Dietary Fiber: 4 g, Total Fat: 0 g, Saturated Fat: 0 g, Monounsaturated Fat: 0 g, Cholesterol: 0 mg, Sodium: 72 mg*

Broccoli-Feta Stuffing

1 TABLESPOON OLIVE OIL

4 GARLIC CLOVES, MINCED OR PRESSED

1/8 TEASPOON RED PEPPER FLAKES

4 CUPS FINELY CHOPPED BROCCOLI

1 CUP WATER

1/2 TEASPOON SALT

1/4 TEASPOON GROUND BLACK PEPPER

1/2 CUP CRUMBLED FETA CHEESE

1 In a large skillet on high heat, warm the olive oil. Add the garlic and red pepper flakes and cook until the garlic is golden, about a minute. Add the broccoli and stir-fry for a couple of minutes. Add the water and bring to a boil, then reduce the heat and simmer uncovered until most of the water has evaporated and the broccoli is tender, 8 to 10 minutes. Add the salt and pepper and set aside until the sweet potatoes are baked.

2 When the sweet potatoes have baked, cut them in half lengthwise and scoop out the pulp, leaving a shell at least 1/4 inch thick. Set the shells aside. Mash the pulp a bit and stir it into the broccoli mixture, along with the feta cheese. If the stuffing has cooled, turn on the heat under the skillet and rewarm. If the stuffing seems too crumbly, add a little water to hold it together.

3 Fill the baked sweet potato shells with stuffing. Serve each separately, or push the halves of each sweet potato together, with stuffing showing between the two shells.

SERVING AND MENU IDEAS: Serve with assorted olives or Greek Tomato-Yogurt Soup (page 125) or best of all, with a platter of sliced heirloom tomatoes drizzled with olive oil and sprinkled with Aromatico Salt (page 80).

BROCCOLI-FETA STUFFING—PER 1 SERVING (OF 4)
Calories: 114, Protein: 5 g, Carbohydrate: 8 g, Dietary Fiber: 2 g, Total Fat: 8 g, Saturated Fat: 3 g, Monounsaturated Fat: 3 g, Cholesterol: 17 mg, Sodium: 531 mg

Caribbean Stuffing

1 TABLESPOON OLIVE OIL
1½ CUPS MINCED ONIONS
3 CUPS RINSED, STEMMED, AND FINELY CHOPPED KALE (SEE NOTE)
3 TABLESPOONS WATER
1 15-OUNCE CAN UNDRAINED FIELD PEAS OR BLACK-EYED PEAS
3 TABLESPOONS LIME JUICE
1 TEASPOON ADOBO SAUCE, OR MORE TO TASTE (FROM A CAN OF CHIPOTLE PEPPERS IN ADOBO SAUCE)
SALT AND GROUND BLACK PEPPER
SOUR CREAM (OPTIONAL)

NOTE: In the market, bunches of kale vary considerably in weight, and have more or fewer large central stems and more or less waste because of yellowed or wilted leaves. In our experience, you'll need a ½- to 1-pound bunch of kale to get 3 cups after sorting, stemming, and chopping.

1 In a large skillet on medium heat, warm the olive oil. Add the onions and cook, stirring often, until softened, about 7 minutes. Stir in the kale and cook for a minute or two, until the kale is somewhat wilted and bright green. Add the water, cover, and steam on low heat until the kale is tender, about 3 minutes. Stir in the peas, lime juice, and adobo sauce. Cover and cook until hot, about 3 minutes. Set aside until the sweet potatoes are baked.

2 When the sweet potatoes have baked, cut them in half lengthwise and scoop out the pulp, leaving a shell at least ¼ inch thick. Set the shells aside. Mash the pulp a bit and stir it into the kale mixture. Add salt and pepper to taste. If the stuffing has cooled, turn on the heat under the skillet and rewarm. If the stuffing seems too crumbly, add a little water to hold it together.

3 Fill the baked sweet potato shells with stuffing. Serve each separately, or push the halves of each sweet potato together, with stuffing showing between the two shells.

4 Offer sour cream at the table.

SERVING AND MENU IDEAS: Serve with Mango Pickles (page 68), Pineapple and Tomato Salad (page 87), or a crisp romaine salad with Avocado Citrus Dressing (page 109). Serve the sweet potatoes on a bed of Curried Millet (page 286) with a side of Maque Choux (page 309).

CARIBBEAN STUFFING—PER 1 SERVING (OF 4)
Calories: 184, Protein: 6 g, Carbohydrate: 33 g, Dietary Fiber: 7 g, Total Fat: 4 g, Saturated Fat: 0 g, Monounsaturated Fat: 3 g, Cholesterol: 0 mg, Sodium: 274 mg

Indian Stuffing

1 TABLESPOON VEGETABLE OIL OR OLIVE OIL
1 CUP DICED ONIONS
1 CUP DICED RED BELL PEPPERS
4 GARLIC CLOVES, MINCED OR PRESSED
1 TABLESPOON GRATED PEELED GINGER ROOT
1 TABLESPOON CURRY POWDER
½ TEASPOON GROUND TURMERIC
¼ TEASPOON CAYENNE
½ TEASPOON SALT
1 15-OUNCE CAN CHICKPEAS, DRAINED
PLAIN NONFAT YOGURT (OPTIONAL)

1 In a large skillet, warm the oil on medium heat. Add the onions, bell peppers, and garlic and cook, stirring frequently, until the onions have softened, about 7 minutes. Stir in the ginger, curry powder, turmeric, cayenne, and salt. Add the chickpeas and heat thoroughly. Set aside until the sweet potatoes are baked.

2 When the sweet potatoes have baked, cut them in half lengthwise and scoop out the pulp, leaving a shell at least ¼ inch thick. Set the shells aside. Mash the pulp a bit and stir it into the skillet. If the stuffing has cooled, turn on the heat under the skillet and rewarm. If the stuffing seems too crumbly, add a little water to hold it together.

3 Fill the baked sweet potato shells with stuffing. Serve each separately, or push the halves of each sweet potato together, with stuffing showing between the two shells.

4 Offer yogurt at the table.

SERVING AND MENU IDEAS: Serve with Mango Slaw (page 93) or Kale with Cranberries (page 298). For dessert, have refreshing Pineapple-Cinnamon Popsicles (page 322).

INDIAN STUFFING—PER 1 SERVING (OF 4)
Calories: 194, Protein: 7 g, Carbohydrate: 32 g, Dietary Fiber: 7 g, Total Fat: 5 g, Saturated Fat: 1 g, Monounsaturated Fat: 3 g, Cholesterol: 0 mg, Sodium: 613 mg

Herbed Vegetable Packets

SERVES 8 | YIELDS ABOUT 8 CUPS FILLING | HANDS-ON TIME: 35 MINUTES | BAKING TIME: 25 TO 30 MINUTES

These packets are made by folding parchment paper. Inside, colorful vegetables are infused with fresh herbs, lemon, and olive oil. Part of their appeal is the fragrant aroma that is released when the packets are opened. You can vary the vegetables from season to season. Unopened packets are easily reheated.

---

2 CUPS DICED PEELED SWEET POTATOES

2 CUPS DICED BELL PEPPERS

1 CUP GREEN BEANS CUT INTO 1-INCH LENGTHS

1 CUP DICED ONIONS

2 CUPS ASPARAGUS CUT INTO 1-INCH LENGTHS

2 TABLESPOONS CHOPPED FRESH TARRAGON

2 TABLESPOONS CHOPPED FRESH BASIL

2 TABLESPOONS EXTRA-VIRGIN OLIVE OIL

¼ CUP LEMON JUICE

4 GARLIC CLOVES, MINCED OR PRESSED

1 TEASPOON SALT

⅛ TEASPOON GROUND BLACK PEPPER

8 SHEETS PARCHMENT PAPER, 12 × 15 INCHES EACH

---

1 In a large bowl, mix together the vegetables and herbs. (You can vary the proportion of different kinds of vegetables; just be sure you have about 8 cups altogether.) In a small cup or bowl, whisk together the oil, lemon juice, garlic, salt, and pepper; pour over the vegetables and herbs and mix well.

2 To make the packets, fold a sheet of parchment paper in half to form a 12 × 7½-inch rectangle. With a short side of the rectangle nearest you, place a cup of the vegetables in the center. Bring the two short sides up like a tent, fold them together, and roll down to the vegetables. Then, fold over and crimp the open sides to form a neat packet to seal in the vegetables. Place the packet on an unoiled baking sheet. Repeat with the remaining sheets of parchment paper.

3 In a preheated 375° oven, bake for 25 minutes. Remove a packet and carefully unfold it to test the tenderness of the vegetables. If the vegetables are not quite done, bake for an additional 5 minutes or so.

VARIATIONS: Use other vegetables such as butternut squash, zucchini, mushrooms, and carrots. We always include some red and orange vegetables in our packets.

Use 2 tablespoons each of chopped fresh dill and thyme instead of basil and tarragon.

SERVING AND MENU IDEAS: Herbed Vegetable Packets are a useful and versatile component of a healthful cooking repertoire. They can serve as a vegetable side dish for burgers, stovetop or baked tofu, or simple bean or pasta dishes. For a delightful entree, put the vegetables on a bed of rice, bulghur, polenta, couscous, quinoa, or a simple pilaf, and top with grated Parmesan, feta, or cheddar cheese.

HERBED VEGETABLE PACKETS—PER 1 SERVING (OF 8) *Calories: 94, Protein: 2 g, Carbohydrate: 15 g, Dietary Fiber: 3 g, Total Fat: 4 g, Saturated Fat: 1 g, Monounsaturated Fat: 2 g, Cholesterol: 0 mg, Sodium: 314 mg*

Winter Squash Stuffed with Two-Rice Pilaf

SERVES 4 | YIELDS ABOUT 4 CUPS PILAF FILLING | TIME: ABOUT AN HOUR

Thai black rice is also known as purple sticky rice and Chinese forbidden rice. Its color ranges from nutty dark brown to deep purple to black and it has a fruity aroma as it cooks. In Southeast Asia, it is used mostly in desserts.

1 TEASPOON VEGETABLE OIL

⅔ CUP BROWN RICE, RINSED

⅓ CUP THAI BLACK RICE, RINSED

1¾ CUPS WATER

1 GARLIC CLOVE, MINCED OR PRESSED

1 TEASPOON SALT

4 SMALL OR 2 LARGE DELICATA, ACORN, BUTTERNUT, OR BUTTERCUP SQUASH

1 TABLESPOON OLIVE OIL, PLUS SOME FOR BRUSHING

1 CUP DICED ONIONS

¾ CUP THINLY SLICED CELERY

¾ CUP MINCED RED OR YELLOW BELL PEPPERS

2 TEASPOONS MINCED FRESH THYME OR 1 TEASPOON DRIED

GENEROUS PINCH OF GROUND BLACK PEPPER

⅓ CUP CHOPPED FRESH PARSLEY

GRATED SHARP CHEDDAR OR PARMESAN CHEESE (OPTIONAL)

1 Warm the vegetable oil in a saucepan with a tight-fitting lid on medium heat. Add both types of rice and stir well. Add the water and garlic, sprinkle with salt, cover, and bring to a boil. Reduce the heat and simmer until the water has been absorbed and the rice is tender, 45 to 50 minutes.

2 Meanwhile, cut the squash in half lengthwise and remove the seeds. Brush the cut sides with olive oil and place facedown on a lightly oiled baking sheet. In a preheated 400° oven, bake until tender, 20 to 40 minutes depending on the size and variety of squash. When you remove the squash from the oven, flip them over on the baking sheet so they won't continue to cook.

3 While the rice and squash cook, warm the olive oil in a skillet on medium heat. Add the onions and celery and cook until the onions are translucent, about 8 minutes. Stir in the bell peppers, thyme, black pepper, and salt, cover, and cook until the vegetables are tender, 6 or 7 minutes. Remove from the heat and stir in the parsley.

4 When the rice is ready, combine it with the vegetables to make the pilaf filling. Mound the baked squash halves with filling and sprinkle with grated cheese, if you wish.

SERVING AND MENU IDEAS: A perfect autumn holiday dish. The pilaf filling is also good on its own.

WINTER SQUASH STUFFED WITH TWO-RICE PILAF— PER 1 SERVING (OF 4) *Calories: 328, Protein: 6 g, Carbohydrate: 65 g, Dietary Fiber: 7 g, Total Fat: 6 g, Saturated Fat: 1 g, Monounsaturated Fat: 4 g, Cholesterol: 0 mg, Sodium: 611 mg*

Italian Sweet Potato Gratin

SERVES 6 TO 8 | HANDS-ON TIME: 25 MINUTES | BAKING TIME: ABOUT 1 HOUR

Packed with flavor, sweetness, and vitamin A, sweet potatoes are making appearances on menus everywhere, in every course. This gratin, made with sweet potatoes with an Italian twist, is a hit at Moosewood.

¼ CUP OLIVE OIL

1 TEASPOON DRIED OREGANO

3 GARLIC CLOVES, MINCED OR PRESSED

2 TABLESPOONS CHOPPED FRESH BASIL

½ TEASPOON RED PEPPER FLAKES

¼ TEASPOON SALT

⅛ TEASPOON GROUND BLACK PEPPER

4 CUPS VERY THINLY SLICED PEELED SWEET POTATOES

4 CUPS VERY THINLY SLICED ONIONS

3 CUPS OF YOUR FAVORITE TOMATO SAUCE

1½ CUPS GRATED MOZZARELLA

½ CUP WHOLE WHEAT BREAD CRUMBS

¼ CUP GRATED PARMESAN CHEESE

1 In a bowl, mix together the olive oil, oregano, garlic, basil, red pepper flakes, salt, and black pepper. Set aside.

2 Evenly spread 1 cup of the sweet potatoes in a lightly oiled 9 × 13-inch baking pan (they won't completely cover the bottom of the pan). Spread 1 cup of the onions over the potatoes. Drizzle with about one-quarter of the oil-herb mixture, and top with a generous ½ cup of the tomato sauce. Sprinkle with about ⅓ cup of mozzarella and then about 2 tablespoons of the bread crumbs. Repeat this layering three more times, using up any extra tomato sauce or mozzarella on the top layer. Finish by sprinkling the Parmesan on top.

3 Cover and bake in a preheated 400° oven until the sweet potatoes are tender, about 45 minutes. Uncover and continue to bake until the gratin is bubbling and lightly browned, about 15 minutes. Remove from the oven and let stand for 5 minutes before serving.

SERVING AND MENU IDEAS: Serve this bright, sunny dish with a green salad with Shallot Vinaigrette (page 111), or try it with Our Favorite Raw Slaw (page 267) or Spinach Salad with Chèvre and Walnuts (page 84). How about a bowl of fresh grapes for dessert?

ITALIAN SWEET POTATO GRATIN—PER 1 SERVING (OF 8) *Calories: 351, Protein: 12 g, Carbohydrate: 42 g, Dietary Fiber: 7 g, Total Fat: 16 g, Saturated Fat: 5 g, Monounsaturated Fat: 9 g, Cholesterol: 14 mg, Sodium: 349 mg*

Quinoa and Collard Leaf Dolmas

SERVES 4 | YIELDS 8 STUFFED DOLMAS | HANDS-ON TIME: 45 MINUTES | BAKING TIME: 15 TO 20 MINUTES

These little packages of tasty quinoa pilaf wrapped in vitamin-rich collard leaves make a lovely centerpiece for lunch or dinner. The pilaf can be served as a side dish in its own right.

PILAF

1 CUP QUINOA

2 CUPS WATER

½ TEASPOON SALT

2 TABLESPOONS OLIVE OIL

1 CUP DICED ONIONS

2 OR 3 GARLIC CLOVES, MINCED

1 CUP MINCED RED AND/OR YELLOW BELL PEPPERS

1 CUP MINCED CELERY

1½ CUPS DICED ZUCCHINI

1 TEASPOON DRIED OREGANO OR 2 TEASPOONS FRESH

3 TABLESPOONS CHOPPED FRESH MINT LEAVES OR 1 TEASPOON DRIED

½ TEASPOON GROUND BLACK PEPPER

3 TABLESPOONS LEMON JUICE

8 LARGE COLLARD LEAVES

2 TOMATOES, SLICED

1 Thoroughly rinse and drain the quinoa in a fine-meshed strainer to remove any residue of the bitter coating. In a saucepan, combine the quinoa, water, and salt. Cover and bring to a simmer; then cook on low heat for 15 minutes. Remove from the heat, let sit for 5 minutes, and fluff with a fork.

2 While the quinoa cooks, warm the oil in a skillet or saucepan on medium heat. Add the onions and cook, stirring often, until translucent, about 8 minutes. Stir in the garlic, bell peppers, celery, zucchini, oregano, mint, and black pepper. Cover and cook, stirring a few times, until the vegetables are juicy and just tender, about 10 minutes. Add the lemon juice and cooked quinoa, and salt and pepper to taste.

3 Cut the large part of the main stem out of each collard leaf. Steam or boil the collard leaves until they begin to soften and are bright green. Spread the leaves on a plate to cool. When cool enough to handle, place a leaf on the countertop with the leaf tip away from you. Slightly overlap the center edges where the stem was cut away. Mound ½ cup of the quinoa filling in the center of the leaf near the bottom. Fold the sides of the leaf over the filling and then roll it up from stem end to tip end to form a neat package. Place the dolma seam side down in a lightly oiled 8-inch square baking pan.

4 Repeat with the rest of the collard leaves. The eight dolmas should fit snugly into the baking pan. Top with the tomato slices. Cover and bake in a preheated 375° oven for 15 to 20 minutes, until hot.

VARIATION: Replace the sliced tomatoes in the recipe with your favorite tomato sauce or our Creamy Tomato Sauce (page 78).

SERVING AND MENU IDEAS: Serve with lemon wedges and sprinkled with chopped fresh mint leaves. Serve with a crisp cucumber salad or a classic Greek salad, Greek Tomato-Yogurt Soup (page 125), Cauliflower "Tabouli" (page 269), Pomegranate Carrots (page 302), or Greek Black-eyed Peas (page 218). Don't forget Filo Nut Cigars (page 330) for dessert.

QUINOA AND COLLARD LEAF DOLMAS—
PER 1 SERVING (OF 4), 2 DOLMAS *Calories: 270, Protein: 10 g, Carbohydrate: 53 g, Dietary Fiber: 9 g, Total Fat: 4 g, Saturated Fat: 1 g, Monounsaturated Fat: 2 g, Cholesterol: 0 mg, Sodium: 377 mg*

ANTIOXIDANTS

At the very end of the twentieth century, nutrition researchers discovered that certain chemical substances, dubbed "antioxidants," are able to safeguard the body's cells by effectively mopping up or disposing of free radicals, the cell-damaging by-products of the body's normal oxidation process. It turns out that antioxidants come in many forms, including enzymes, vitamins, carotenoids, and minerals.

This research was heralded as a major breakthrough in furthering our understanding of how our bodies use the components of the foods we eat to sustain us and keep us healthy. The simplified equation goes something like this: More antioxidants means fewer damaging free radicals, which equals healthier cells. As specific antioxidants were identified, early observational research began to link them with potential health-promoting or disease-fighting properties. Charts showing the antioxidant levels of various fruits, vegetables, whole grains, nuts, and teas appeared in many magazines and nutrition newsletters.

In short order, there followed a surge of ads and claims for supplements that would boost your intake of antioxidants and help solve your health problems: "Get your beta-carotene and lycopene in one easy capsule." The mass marketing of antioxidant supplements was closely followed by the food industry's development of products that claimed to be health enhancing because of the addition of dietary supplements.

There's a lot about how antioxidants work that scientists do not yet understand, and as more research is done, conflicting results and inconclusive evidence are a big part of the picture. Promising early results pointed to potentially simple one-to-one correlations between particular antioxidants and certain disease-fighting properties. Subsequent research has disproven some of these findings and called others into question. It is clear that what the body does with antioxidants in order to protect and heal us is very complex.

To understand how antioxidant supplements could be such a hot item one year and then not-so-hot the next, it helps to take a look at the nature of nutritional research and the ways it's reported. Studies that use laboratory animals or test tubes can be strictly controlled, making it possible to isolate a single element, say a specific antioxidant, in order to determine its direct effect. However, the results of these studies may not be applicable to humans. Scientists may present their findings as possible indicators that are not yet conclusive, but headline news frequently reports it as a breakthrough and omits essential details. The general public then jumps to the conclusion that a certain prevention or cure has been established for a human ailment, when further research may prove that this is not the case at all, or that it's true only under certain limited conditions.

But current research does strongly support some broad-based facts: The compounds in the foods we eat are used by our bodies in an intricate balance dictated by our individual innate ability to heal naturally. And fresh produce, whole grains, and nuts are our most reliable sources of antioxidants.

Average U.S. life expectancy increased by twenty-five to thirty years during the period from 1900 to 2000. As we grow older and live longer, the incidence of cancer, heart-related malfunctions, osteoporosis, and diabetes also grows. Long-term exposure to air, water, and chemical pollution creates constant production of free radicals that attack healthy cells. Because antioxidants from food can help lower the chances of developing diseases commonly associated with aging, and almost surely ameliorate some of the negative effects of pollution, eating well is likely to be the very best prescription for health.

So how do we eat well? An easy strategy to insure we're getting our fair share of antioxidants is to regularly eat plenty of fresh fruits and vegetables, nuts, legumes, and whole grains. In the fruit category, choose fresh, frozen, and dried fruit over fruit jams, jellies, or juices. Foods with high antioxidant potential include prunes, plums, raisins, berries, kale, spinach, Brussels sprouts, broccoli, beets, red bell peppers, red grapes, oranges, cherries, yellow corn, and carrots. Prevailing evidence encourages using the whole rainbow in your diet. The more saturated the color of the food, the more antioxidants it has. So go for deep purple berries, red tomatoes, brilliant orange carrots, and dark green broccoli and kale.

As of 2008, the U.S. Dietary Guidelines recommended that Americans eat five to thirteen one-half to one-cup servings of fruits and vegetables every day. Walter Willett, nutrition department chair at Harvard School of Public Health, said in 2007, "I would . . . strongly promote generous consumption of fruits and vegetables." The Nutrition Action Newsletter for December 2007 warned, "Don't rely on juices or foods with added vegetable or fruit purées or powders for your daily servings. Eat your fruits and vegetables fresh or frozen, if you can." Dr. Nagi Kumar, director of nutrition research at Moffitt Cancer Center in Tampa, Florida, recommends, "a diet high in fiber and nutrients and low in fat with 8 to 10 servings of fruits and vegetables each day." Susan Mayne, an epidemiologist who served on a recent national panel on dietary antioxidants, says, "It may be that the way nature delivers these things is the best option people have. And, so far, that's what the research tells us."

Greek Vegetable Pie

SERVES 6 | YIELDS ONE 9-INCH PIE | HANDS-ON TIME: 50 MINUTES | BAKING TIME: 35 MINUTES

This delicious pie is made with an unusual brown rice, walnut, and olive crust and filled with leeks, red bell peppers, asparagus, tangy feta, and smooth cream cheese. Keep this recipe in mind when you have leftover brown rice.

CRUST

2 CUPS COOKED BROWN RICE

½ CUP WALNUTS

¼ CUP PITTED KALAMATA OLIVES

FILLING

2 TABLESPOONS OLIVE OIL

3 CUPS ASPARAGUS, 1-INCH PIECES

¼ TEASPOON SALT

3 CUPS THINLY SLICED LEEKS
(WHITE AND TENDER GREEN PARTS),
THOROUGHLY RINSED

1 CUP DICED RED BELL PEPPERS

3 OUNCES NEUFCHÂTEL CHEESE

1 CUP GRATED OR CRUMBLED FETA CHEESE

3 LARGE EGGS, LIGHTLY BEATEN

⅓ CUP CHOPPED FRESH DILL

PINCH OF GROUND BLACK PEPPER

1 In a food processor, pulse the crust ingredients until crumbly. Set aside.

2 Warm the oil in a skillet or saucepan on medium heat. Add the asparagus and salt and cook for 5 minutes, stirring occasionally. Stir in the leeks and cook for 3 minutes. Add the bell peppers, cover, and continue to cook, stirring occasionally, until all of the vegetables are tender, 5 or 6 minutes. Place the neufchâtel on top of the vegetables, cover, turn off the heat, and let sit for several minutes to soften.

3 Meanwhile, press the crust mixture into a lightly oiled 9-inch pie plate.

4 Stir the neufchâtel throughout the vegetables. Add ¾ cup of the feta cheese and the eggs, dill, and black pepper to the skillet and mix well. Spread the filling in the piecrust and top with the remaining feta.

5 Bake in a preheated 350° oven until the filling is set and golden, about 35 minutes.

VARIATIONS: Use 2 or 3 chopped softened sun-dried tomatoes in place of the olives in the crust.

Use broccoli instead of asparagus in the filling.

SERVING AND MENU IDEAS: Serve with a tossed green salad with Pear and Thyme Vinaigrette (page 110) or with a classic Greek salad. For an excellent first course, serve Greek Tomato-Yogurt Soup (page 125). A fine dessert is a big bowl of fresh strawberries or cherries, which could be accompanied by Filo Nut Cigars (page 330).

GREEK VEGETABLE PIE—PER 1 SERVING (OF 6)
Calories: 364, Protein: 14 g, Carbohydrate: 30 g, Dietary Fiber: 5 g, Total Fat: 22 g, Saturated Fat: 8 g, Monounsaturated Fat: 8 g, Cholesterol: 139 mg, Sodium: 716 mg

Mediterranean Eggplant Casserole

SERVES 6 TO 8 | HANDS-ON TIME: ABOUT AN HOUR | BAKING TIME: ABOUT 55 MINUTES

This attractive, hearty casserole is always popular at Moosewood. Lemony herbed bulgur pilaf, full of walnuts and sweet currants, is layered with roasted eggplant and fresh tomatoes and topped with a hearty feta and cottage cheese custard.

---

1 MEDIUM EGGPLANT (ABOUT 1¼ POUNDS)

SALT

2 TEASPOONS DRIED MARJORAM

1 CUP BULGHUR

1 CUP BOILING WATER

2 TABLESPOONS OLIVE OIL

2 CUPS CHOPPED ONIONS

4 GARLIC CLOVES, PRESSED

1 TEASPOON DRIED OREGANO

½ TEASPOON SALT

¼ CUP CURRANTS

3 LARGE EGGS, BEATEN

1½ CUPS CRUMBLED OR GRATED FETA CHEESE

2 CUPS SMALL CURD LOW-FAT COTTAGE CHEESE

¾ CUP GRATED PARMESAN CHEESE

¾ CUP CHOPPED FRESH BASIL OR PARSLEY

1 CUP CHOPPED TOASTED WALNUTS

1 TABLESPOON LEMON JUICE

GROUND BLACK PEPPER

2 LARGE RIPE TOMATOES, SLICED

---

1 Slice the eggplant into ½-inch-thick rounds and arrange them in a single layer on a lightly oiled baking sheet. Brush or spray the slices with olive oil and sprinkle with salt and 1 teaspoon of the marjoram. Bake uncovered in a preheated 400° oven until tender and lightly browned, about 20 minutes.

2 While the eggplant is baking, put the bulghur and boiling water into a heatproof bowl. Cover and set aside until the water has been absorbed and the bulghur is tender, about 15 minutes.

3 Meanwhile, warm the olive oil in a skillet on medium heat. Add the onions, garlic, oregano, salt, and the remaining marjoram, and cook, stirring occasionally, until the onions are soft, about 10 minutes. Stir in the currants and remove from the heat.

4 In a separate bowl, stir together the eggs, feta, cottage cheese, ½ cup of the Parmesan, and ¼ cup of the basil. Set aside.

5 Fluff the bulghur and stir in the onions and currants, the remaining ½ cup of the basil, and the toasted walnuts and lemon juice. Add more salt and pepper to taste.

6 To assemble the casserole, spread the bulghur pilaf evenly in a lightly oiled 9 × 13-inch baking pan. Layer the baked eggplant slices and then the tomato slices. Spoon on the egg and cheese mixture and spread it evenly over the top. Sprinkle on the rest of the Parmesan.

7 Cover the baking pan with foil, rounding it so the foil won't stick to the custard. Bake in a preheated 350° oven for 40 minutes, until the casserole is mostly set. Uncover and bake until the top is golden and the custard is firm, about 15 minutes.

SERVING AND MENU IDEAS: With this substantial casserole, serve a tangy salad such as Celeriac Apple Slaw (page 94).

MEDITERRANEAN EGGPLANT CASSEROLE—PER 1 SERVING (OF 8) *Calories: 417, Protein: 23 g, Carbohydrate: 30 g, Dietary Fiber: 8 g, Total Fat: 25 g, Saturated Fat: 8 g, Monounsaturated Fat: 7 g, Cholesterol: 115 mg, Sodium: 868 mg*

Savory Asparagus and Mushroom Bread Pudding

SERVES 6 | HANDS-ON TIME: 40 MINUTES | BAKING TIME: 40 MINUTES

This bread pudding is more healthful and lower in fat than most. We pack it with asparagus and mushrooms, and use whole wheat bread and a modest amount of cheese, milk, and eggs.

3 CUPS WHOLE GRAIN BREAD CUBES

1 LARGE ONION (ABOUT 1½ CUPS CHOPPED)

1 BUNCH OF ASPARAGUS (ABOUT 1 POUND)

½ TEASPOON SALT

4 CUPS SLICED MUSHROOMS

1 TABLESPOON VEGETABLE OIL

⅛ TEASPOON GROUND BLACK PEPPER

1 CUP MILK

4 LARGE EGGS

½ CUP CHÈVRE OR CRUMBLED FETA

2 TABLESPOONS CHOPPED FRESH DILL

3 TABLESPOONS GRATED PARMESAN CHEESE

1 Toast the bread cubes on an unoiled baking sheet in a 350° oven for about 15 minutes. Set aside.

2 Meanwhile, chop the onion. Snap off and discard the tough stem ends of the asparagus and cut the spears into 1-inch-long pieces (2 to 3 cups).

3 In a large skillet, warm the oil on medium-high heat. Add the onions and sprinkle with the salt. Cook, stirring often, until softened, about 8 minutes. Add the asparagus, lower the heat to medium, cover, and cook for 5 minutes, stirring once or twice. Add the mushrooms and pepper, cover, and cook until the asparagus is tender, about 5 minutes.

4 Spread the toasted bread cubes in a lightly oiled 9-inch square or 7 × 11-inch baking dish. Top with the cooked mushrooms and asparagus and the pan juice. In a blender, purée the milk, eggs, chèvre, and dill. Pour evenly over the vegetables in the baking dish and top with the Parmesan cheese.

5 Bake uncovered in a preheated 350° oven until the eggs are set, about 40 minutes. Let sit for 5 minutes before serving.

SERVING AND MENU IDEAS: This puffy bread pudding can be the centerpiece of a brunch, lunch, or supper, accompanied by a light salad, such as fruit salad, tomato salad, or Celeriac Apple Slaw (page 94).

SAVORY ASPARAGUS AND MUSHROOM BREAD PUDDING—PER 1 SERVING (OF 6) *Calories: 222, Protein: 14 g, Carbohydrate: 19 g, Dietary Fiber: 4 g, Total Fat: 11 g, Saturated Fat: 4 g, Monounsaturated Fat: 4 g, Cholesterol: 119 mg, Sodium: 454 mg*

Polenta Casserole with Winter Squash and Greens

SERVES 4 TO 6 | HANDS-ON TIME: 50 TO 55 MINUTES | BAKING TIME: 50 TO 60 MINUTES

A lovely, hearty, chilly-weather dish. The greens sandwiched between the golden layers look fabulous.

POLENTA LAYER

2⅓ CUPS WATER

⅔ CUP WHOLE GRAIN CORNMEAL (NOT QUICK-COOKING POLENTA; SEE PAGE 22)

2 SUN-DRIED TOMATOES, CHOPPED

¼ TEASPOON SALT

¼ TEASPOON DRIED THYME

½ CUP GRATED SHARP CHEDDAR CHEESE

GREENS LAYER

2 TABLESPOONS OLIVE OIL

3 GARLIC CLOVES, MINCED OR PRESSED

8 TO 10 PACKED CUPS STEMMED AND CHOPPED KALE OR COLLARDS (SEE NOTES)

¼ CUP WATER

¼ TEASPOON SALT

SQUASH LAYER

1½ CUPS MASHED OR PURÉED WINTER SQUASH (SEE NOTES)

1 LARGE EGG, BEATEN

¼ TEASPOON SALT

GENEROUS PINCH OF GROUND BLACK PEPPER

⅔ CUP GRATED SHARP CHEDDAR CHEESE

1 For the polenta layer: Bring the water to a boil in a heavy saucepan and whisk in the cornmeal. Add the sun-dried tomatoes, salt, and thyme and cook on low heat, stirring often, until the polenta is thick and creamy, about 10 minutes. Stir in the cheese. Pour into a lightly oiled 8-inch square baking pan and set aside.

2 For the greens layer: In a soup pot on medium heat, warm the oil. Add the garlic and cook briefly, stirring constantly. Add the chopped greens, water, and salt. Cover and cook, stirring occasionally, until the greens are tender but still bright green, about 10 minutes. Drain and add more salt to taste. Spread the greens over the polenta.

3 For the squash layer: In a bowl, stir together the squash, egg, salt, pepper, and half of the cheese. Spread the squash mixture over the greens and sprinkle the rest of the cheese on top.

4 In a preheated 350° oven, bake covered for 35 minutes. Uncover and bake for 10 to 15 minutes more, until golden and set. The casserole will be easier to serve if you let it sit for 5 or 10 minutes before cutting.

NOTES: Kale and collards vary noticeably from bunch to bunch, with larger or smaller bunches, more or fewer yellowing or wilted leaves and large center stems, so it's hard sometimes to guess how much you need to buy; it may be from 1½ to 2 pounds of kale or collards to get 8 to 10 packed cups of sorted, stemmed, and chopped greens.

Five to 6 cups of cubed peeled raw winter squash yields about 1½ cups puréed. Steam the squash cubes until tender, then mash well with a potato masher or purée in a food processor until smooth. We like to save the steaming water and use it to cook the polenta. A 12-ounce package of frozen squash yields about 1¼ cups and will work in this recipe. Thaw before using.

VARIATIONS: In place of cheddar, use provolone, feta, or fontina.

Use rosemary or sage instead of thyme.

Cook a small bulb of fresh fennel, sliced, with the garlic for a couple of minutes before adding the greens.

Add ½ teaspoon of ground fennel seeds to the polenta.

SERVING AND MENU IDEAS: Start with toasted baguette slices spread with Pepita and Sun-Dried Tomato Pesto (page 79). Serve the casserole with Roasted Beet Salad (page 92) or Roasted Brussels Sprouts and Pecans (page 300). Simply Baked Fruit (page 319) is an ideal dessert.

POLENTA CASSEROLE WITH WINTER SQUASH AND GREENS—PER 1 SERVING (OF 6) *Calories: 224, Protein: 12 g, Carbohydrate: 28 g, Dietary Fiber: 5 g, Total Fat: 9 g, Saturated Fat: 2 g, Monounsaturated Fat: 4 g, Cholesterol: 43 mg, Sodium: 779 mg*

BEANS

THE LEGUMES: BEANS, PEAS, AND LENTILS

Beans, peas, and lentils are delicious, hearty, nutritious, rich in protein, inexpensive, and versatile. They are an important part of a healthy diet, and an essential traditional element of vegetarian diets.

Legumes, also known as pulses, are one of the oldest cultivated crops; evidence of their cultivation goes back more than 7,000 years in some parts of the world. The lineage of most dried beans popular in the United States today can be traced back to Central and South America. Lentils and dried peas originated in central Asia, chickpeas in the Middle East, black-eyed peas in Africa, and azuki in Japan. Legumes are valued by farmers because they enhance nitrogen in the soil where they are grown, playing a valuable role in crop rotation.

Legumes are a major source of complex carbohydrates, fiber, protein, vitamins, and minerals such as potassium, magnesium, and zinc. They have no cholesterol, and little fats and saturated fats. In addition, they are very affordable. The U.S. Department of Agriculture Food Guide places dried beans both with the vegetable group and with the group of high-protein foods such as fish, eggs, meat, and nuts.

Bean protein is sometimes referred to as "incomplete" because it doesn't provide one of the essential amino acids needed from food for building protein in the body. In practice, though, this isn't a concern, because grains (which lack a different essential amino acid) provide the amino acid missing from dried beans and vice versa. Their proteins complement each other, so eat beans and rice, beans in a tortilla, beans and corn, or beans and bread. But it should also be noted that it is no longer considered necessary to eat complementary proteins at the same time, only to consume them over the course of a day.

Of the hundreds of varieties of dried beans in existence, only about two dozen are widely available throughout the United States, but there are also heirloom varieties grown locally or regionally with intriguing names such as Eye of Goat, Tongues of Fire, and Lazy Housewife. Beans have a delightful range of flavors. They blend well with many foods and spices, and they absorb flavors from other ingredients, making them well suited to an array of recipes and tastes.

Compared to dried beans, lentils are relatively quick to prepare; like beans, they absorb flavors from other foods and seasonings. They're also a very good source of cholesterol-lowering fiber, and their high fiber content prevents blood sugar levels from rising rapidly after a meal. Lentils provide good to excellent amounts of six important minerals, two B vitamins, and protein—all with virtually no fat.

BEANS AND PEAS

Azuki or *Adzuki beans,* originally from Asia, are small, with a vivid red color and solid flavor and texture. The name means "little bean" in Japanese.

Black beans are medium-sized, oval, and a matte black color. They have a soft, floury texture, and their flavor is almost sweet and somewhat mushroom-like.

Black-eyed peas have a creamy texture and distinctive flavor and aroma. They have white skin, a small black eye, and very fine wrinkles. Although used like beans, they are really peas. They cook quickly without presoaking. Originally from Africa, black-eyed peas are one of the most widely dispersed legumes in the world.

Butter beans are large and flat with a yellowish white color. They have a buttery flavor and silken, creamy texture.

Baby lima beans are medium-sized flat beans with a greenish white color, buttery flavor, and creamy texture.

Kidney beans are large and kidney-shaped. Some are a deep, glossy red, and some, called "light red," are pinkish. They have a solid flavor and texture.

Small red beans are dark red in color, and smaller and smoother in taste and texture than kidney beans.

Pink beans are medium-sized and a beautiful pink color, with a refined texture and delicate flavor.

Pinto beans contain the most fiber of all beans. Medium-sized and oval in shape, they are speckled reddish brown on a beige background, with solid texture and flavor.

Great Northern beans and cannellini beans are flat, kidney-shaped, largish or medium-sized white beans with a delicate flavor and thin skin.

Navy and pea beans are small, white, and oval, and have a delicate flavor. Their skin and fine texture do not break up during cooking.

Chickpeas, also called "garbanzo beans," are the most widely consumed legume in the world. Their texture is firm, and their flavor is distinctive and nutty. They are usually pale yellow, but in India there are red, black, and brown chickpeas.

LENTILS

Brown lentils are the standard lentils found in grocery stores everywhere. Brown lentils are most familiar in the United States in lentil soup. India is the world's biggest producer and consumer of lentils; they're eaten in some form every day in most Indian households.

French green lentils hold their shape better than brown lentils and have a deeper, richer flavor, which makes them excellent for salads. They take longer to cook than other lentils.

Golden lentils are small, firm, and rounder than most other lentils, with a mild, earthy flavor and soft texture.

Red lentils, the most widely cultivated variety in the world, are not really red, but a soft salmon-pink that turns golden when cooked. They cook faster than most lentils and don't hold their shape as well, so are best in soups or purées.

A note about the digestibility of beans, peas, and lentils: There are a number of common suggestions for ways to reduce gas after eating beans, but what we've noticed is that it isn't a problem for most people who eat beans regularly.

PRESOAKING AND COOKING DRIED BEANS AND PEAS

Before cooking beans, be sure to sort them. Spread the beans on a baking sheet or a flat, light-colored plate. Pick out and throw away the stones, and shriveled, broken, or badly colored beans. Jiggling the plate can help you see little rocks: the beans roll a bit, but the rocks, which are angular, usually don't. Rinse the beans thoroughly.

Soaking dried beans reduces the cooking time and returns moisture to the beans slowly, which helps to soften both the skins and the inside evenly, and produces beautiful beans with good flavor. Beans can rehydrate to triple their dried size, so be sure to use a big enough pot and plenty of water. But don't soak beans for too long, or they'll lose flavor and shape. If you've soaked beans and then can't cook them when you expected to, drain them and keep them in the refrigerator for up to a couple of days, until you can cook them. There are two popular methods for soaking beans.

Traditional overnight soak: For each pound (2 cups) of beans, add about 10 cups water and set aside to soak at room temperature if it's cool, or in the refrigerator if not, for 4 to 10 hours.

Quick soak: For each pound (2 cups) of beans, add about 10 cups water; heat to boiling and let boil for 2 to 3 minutes. Remove from heat, cover, and set aside for 1 to 4 hours.

STOVETOP COOKING

Drain off and discard the soaking water (this does not affect the nutritive value of the beans). Add fresh water to the beans. Cover the pot, bring to a boil, and then reduce the heat and simmer gently (too high a boil can split the beans) until done. The water should always cover the beans; you may need to add some water while the beans are cooking.

The cooking time of dried beans and peas can vary from 30 minutes to 2 or more hours, and in cookbooks and on the Web, recommended cooking times vary significantly. In our experience, the simmering time needed for any particular type of dried legume can vary broadly, even from batch to batch. We suspect that this has to do with how fresh the beans or peas are, but there could be other factors, too. We start testing them for doneness at the lower end of the range, either by mashing with a fork, squeezing between thumb and finger, or simply by tasting. If they're too firm or the skin isn't tender, we give them more time.

SLOW COOKER COOKING

Cook as on the stovetop, but soak and cook the beans in the slow cooker. Slow cookers vary in their heat output, so some experimentation may be necessary to find the cooking time that suits your cooker and tastes. See the instruction manual of your slow cooker for more guidance.

PRESSURE COOKER COOKING

A pressure cooker can cook presoaked beans in as little as 5 to 10 minutes. See the instruction manual for exact cooking times, which will depend on the type of bean.

BEAN COOKING TIMES

Presoaked, unless specified "no presoak"

Azuki beans: 40 to 90 minutes

Black beans: 60 to 90 minutes

Black-eyed peas: 30 to 60 minutes, no presoak

Butter beans: 60 to 90 minutes

Cannellini beans: 60 to 75 minutes

Chickpeas: 1 to 2 hours

Great Northern beans: 60 to 90 minutes

Kidney beans: 60 to 90 minutes

Lima beans: 45 to 90 minutes

Mung beans: 45 to 75 minutes

Pea beans: 50 to 90 minutes

Pinto beans: 60 to 90 minutes

Red beans, small: 60 minutes

Soybeans: 1 to 3 hours

Split peas, green: 30 to 60 minutes, no presoak

White beans, small: 60 minutes

North-South Chili

SERVES 4 TO 6 | YIELDS ABOUT 8 CUPS | TIME: 45 MINUTES

New England meets Tex Mex meets Creole in a warming, colorful dish chock-full of beans and vegetables.

2 TABLESPOONS OLIVE OIL

3 CUPS CHOPPED ONIONS

¼ TEASPOON SALT

5 GARLIC CLOVES, MINCED OR PRESSED

¼ TEASPOON RED PEPPER FLAKES

1 TEASPOON DRIED OREGANO

1 TEASPOON GROUND CUMIN

1 TEASPOON GROUND CORIANDER

1 TEASPOON PAPRIKA

1 TEASPOON CHILI POWDER

2 CUPS DICED PEELED WINTER SQUASH OR SWEET POTATOES

2 CUPS DICED GREEN OR YELLOW BELL PEPPERS

1 CUP WATER

1 15-OUNCE CAN RED KIDNEY BEANS, DRAINED

1 15-OUNCE CAN DICED TOMATOES

1 10-OUNCE PACKAGE FROZEN CUT OKRA

GROUND BLACK PEPPER

CHOPPED SCALLIONS AND/OR CILANTRO (OPTIONAL)

1 Warm the oil in a soup pot on medium-high heat. Add the onions and salt and cook until the onions are translucent, about 10 minutes.

2 Stir in the garlic, red pepper flakes, oregano, cumin, coriander, paprika, chili powder, squash, bell peppers, and water. Cook, stirring often, for 10 minutes.

3 Add the beans and tomatoes, cover, and simmer for 10 minutes, stirring occasionally to prevent sticking.

4 Add the okra and simmer for about 10 minutes. Add black pepper to taste.

5 Serve topped with scallions and/or cilantro, if you wish.

SERVING AND MENU IDEAS: This chili is delicious topped with grated pepper Jack or cheddar cheese, or with sour cream. Serve it with Sesame Flaxseed Cornbread (page 48) or tortilla chips, or on rice. Have something fruity and refreshing for dessert such as Pomegranate Gel with Fruit (page 312) or Herbed and Spiced Fresh Fruit Popsicles (page 320).

NORTH-SOUTH CHILI—PER 1 SERVING (OF 6), 1⅓ CUPS
Calories: 145, Protein: 5 g, Carbohydrate: 24 g, Dietary Fiber: 7 g, Total Fat: 4 g, Saturated Fat: 1 g, Monounsaturated Fat: 3 g, Cholesterol: 0 mg, Sodium: 268 mg

Italian Lentils

SERVES 6 | TIME: 45 MINUTES

Rich with the aromas and flavors of fennel and garlic, a classic sausage and lentil dish goes vegan. Soy sausage replaces conventional sausage, but the flavors familiar to this dish still remain.

1½ CUPS DRIED BROWN LENTILS

5 GARLIC CLOVES

1 BAY LEAF

5 CUPS WATER

1 RED OR YELLOW BELL PEPPER

1 MEDIUM FENNEL BULB

2 TABLESPOONS OLIVE OIL

2 CUPS CHOPPED ONIONS

½ TEASPOON GROUND FENNEL SEEDS

½ TEASPOON SALT

½ TEASPOON GROUND BLACK PEPPER

1 TABLESPOON SOY SAUCE

1 TABLESPOON RED WINE VINEGAR

8 TO 11 OUNCES ITALIAN-STYLE SOY SAUSAGE

1   In a covered saucepan, bring the lentils, 2 of the garlic cloves, the bay leaf, and the water to a boil. Reduce the heat and simmer for about 30 minutes, until the lentils are tender. Drain, remove the bay leaf, and set aside.

2   Meanwhile, dice the bell pepper. Prepare the fennel bulb: remove the outer layers if bruised or soft, cut in half lengthwise, remove the hard core, and dice. Press or mince the remaining garlic cloves.

3   In a soup pot on medium heat, warm 1 tablespoon of the olive oil and cook the onions, stirring frequently, until soft, about 10 minutes. Add the bell peppers, fresh fennel, garlic, ground fennel, salt, and pepper. Cook covered on low heat until the vegetables are tender, about 7 minutes. Add the soy sauce, vinegar, and cooked lentils. Cook, stirring often, for a few minutes, until hot.

4   Meanwhile, cut the soy sausage into bite-sized chunks. In a skillet on medium heat, warm the remaining tablespoon of olive oil. Cook the soy sausage for about 5 minutes, stirring often, until browned and crisp.

5   Serve the lentils topped with the soy sausage.

SERVING AND MENU IDEAS: Garnish this hearty dish with a drizzle of extra-virgin olive oil and chopped fresh parsley. Serve it on rice or with bread, and with a crisp green salad and sliced ripe tomatoes. Or try it with Roasted Beet Salad (page 92). Follow with Fig and Pecan Baked Apples (page 318).

ITALIAN LENTILS—PER 1 SERVING (OF 6)
Calories: 290, Protein: 19 g, Carbohydrate: 42 g, Dietary Fiber: 17 g, Total Fat: 5 g, Saturated Fat: 1 g, Monounsaturated Fat: 3 g, Cholesterol: 0 mg, Sodium: 641 mg

Greek Black-eyed Peas

SERVES 4 | HANDS-ON TIME: 35 MINUTES

At Moosewood, and in our homes, we make many different variations of greens and beans. You can make this dish with almost any kind of beans, but we think the distinctive flavor of black-eyed peas complements the flavors of fennel and endive.

2 TABLESPOONS OLIVE OIL

1 CUP CHOPPED ONIONS

½ TEASPOON SALT

3 GARLIC CLOVES, MINCED OR PRESSED

½ TEASPOON GROUND FENNEL SEEDS

2 TEASPOONS DRIED OREGANO

1½ CUPS DICED FENNEL BULB

4 CUPS CHOPPED CURLY ENDIVE
(ABOUT 8 OUNCES)

1 TABLESPOON SOY SAUCE

1 CUP CHOPPED FRESH TOMATOES

2 15-OUNCE CANS BLACK-EYED PEAS,
DRAINED (SEE NOTE)

GROUND BLACK PEPPER

NOTE: To make your black-eyed peas from scratch: Sort and rinse 1¼ cups (½ pound) dried black-eyed peas. Place them in a soup pot with 6 cups of water, bring to a boil, reduce the heat to a simmer, and cook until the peas are tender, about 45 minutes. For more tender skins, presoak in water overnight or all day, or cover with boiling water and soak for several hours.

1 In a large saucepan or skillet on medium heat, warm the oil. Add the onions, salt, garlic, ground fennel, and oregano. Cook, stirring often, until the onions are soft, about 10 minutes. Add the fresh fennel and cook until tender, 8 to 10 minutes.

2 Stir in the endive and cook covered until the greens are tender, about 5 minutes. Add the soy sauce, tomatoes, and black-eyed peas. Simmer for 5 minutes. Add salt and pepper to taste.

3 You can serve Greek Black-eyed Peas right away, but the flavor develops beautifully if the dish sits for at least half an hour.

SERVING AND MENU IDEAS: Serve Greek Black-eyed Peas topped with chopped scallions or chives and/or crumbled feta, or garnish with lemon wedges and black olives. They're delicious served over rice or couscous. Have Cauliflower "Tabouli" (page 269) on the side and Figs Baked with Chèvre and Pistachios (page 315) for dessert.

GREEK BLACK-EYED PEAS—PER 1 SERVING (OF 4)
Calories: 356, Protein: 9 g, Carbohydrate: 53 g, Dietary Fiber: 14 g, Total Fat: 13 g, Saturated Fat: 2 g, Monounsaturated Fat: 7 g, Cholesterol: 0 mg, Sodium: 445 mg

Oaxacan Tlayuda

SERVES 2 TO 4 | TIME: 35 MINUTES

Flatbreads with savory toppings are enjoyed worldwide. Tlayudas, tortillas baked or grilled with all sorts of toppings—sort of like Mexican pizza—are found throughout the Oaxacan region of Mexico. Pile on any extras you like, such as olives, avocado, corn, pineapple, or mango.

1 TABLESPOON VEGETABLE OIL

3 GARLIC CLOVES, MINCED OR PRESSED

½ CUP DICED ONIONS

¾ CUP DICED BELL PEPPERS

⅛ TEASPOON SALT

1 TEASPOON GROUND CUMIN

¼ TEASPOON CAYENNE

1 15-OUNCE CAN OF PINTO BEANS

2 WHOLE GRAIN TORTILLAS (9- TO 10-INCH)

1 CUP GRATED SHARP CHEDDAR CHEESE

1 CUP SHREDDED GREEN CABBAGE OR SLAW MIX

1 CUP DICED FRESH TOMATOES

2 TABLESPOONS CHOPPED FRESH CILANTRO

1 Warm the oil in a skillet on medium heat. Add the garlic, onions, bell peppers, salt, cumin, and cayenne and cook, stirring often, until soft, about 10 minutes. Remove from the heat.

2 Drain the pinto beans, reserving about ¼ cup of the liquid. In a food processor or blender, purée the beans, cooked onions and peppers, and just enough of the reserved bean liquid to make a thick, creamy spread. Add more salt and cayenne to taste.

3 Place the tortillas on an unoiled baking sheet. Spread each with half of the puréed beans and top with cheese. In a preheated 450° oven, bake until the cheese melts, about 5 minutes. Spread ½ cup of the cabbage or slaw mix on each tortilla and bake for another 5 minutes. Toss the tomatoes with the cilantro and sprinkle them on top of the cabbage. Bake for a couple of minutes, just until the tomatoes are hot.

VARIATIONS: Whole grain wraps or pita bread can be used in place of tortillas.

Use your favorite salsa instead of the chopped tomatoes and cilantro.

Instead of pintos, use any other beans such as red or black beans.

SERVING AND MENU IDEAS: Serve with Simple Guacamole (page 69). Have Latin Corn Soup (page 128) or Mellow Gazpacho (page 127) to start. Roasted Sweet Potatoes (page 299) are the ideal side dish.

OAXACAN TLAYUDA—PER 1 SERVING (OF 4)
Calories: 362, Protein: 17 g, Carbohydrate: 44 g, Dietary Fiber: 9 g, Total Fat: 15 g, Saturated Fat: 7 g, Monounsaturated Fat: 5 g, Cholesterol: 30 mg, Sodium: 739 mg

Broccoli Rabe and Beans

SERVES 4 AS A MAIN DISH, 8 AS A SIDE DISH | TIME: 20 MINUTES

In this quick and simple recipe, the pleasant bitterness of broccoli rabe, also known as raab or rapini, is quite delicious in contrast to the bland creaminess of the beans.

---

1 15-OUNCE CAN BUTTER BEANS

1 15-OUNCE CAN SMALL RED BEANS

1 BUNCH OF BROCCOLI RABE
(ABOUT 1 POUND)

1 TABLESPOON EXTRA-VIRGIN OLIVE OIL

4 GARLIC CLOVES, MINCED OR PRESSED

SALT AND GROUND BLACK PEPPER

---

1 Rinse both kinds of beans in a colander and set aside to drain.

2 Rinse the broccoli rabe well, and holding the bunch like a bouquet, slice off the bottom half-inch of stems and discard. Slice across the bunch into 1-inch-long pieces.

3 In a large skillet, warm the oil on medium-high heat. First, add the larger stems of broccoli rabe and cook for a couple of minutes. Then add the garlic and the rest of the broccoli rabe and cook, stirring frequently, until the broccoli rabe is wilted and bright green, about 6 minutes. Stir in the beans and cook until hot. Season with salt and pepper.

SERVING AND MENU IDEAS: Offer a cruet of extra-virgin olive oil at the table for drizzling just a touch more fruity richness on top of the finished dish. Serve with some whole grain bread and a tomato salad or pair with Couscous with Pistachios and Apricots (page 287).

BROCCOLI RABE AND BEANS—PER 1 SERVING (OF 8)
Calories: 259, Protein: 17 g, Carbohydrate: 39 g, Dietary Fiber: 16 g, Total Fat: 5 g, Saturated Fat: 1 g, Monounsaturated Fat: 3 g, Cholesterol: 3 mg, Sodium: 170 mg

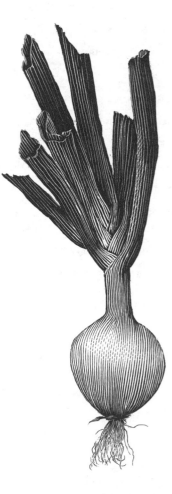

Down-home Black-eyed Peas

SERVES 4 TO 8 | YIELDS ABOUT 4 CUPS | TIME: 35 MINUTES

It's traditional in the Southern United States to serve black-eyed peas on New Year's Day for good luck. We like our black-eyed peas year-round. This dish is good warm, at room temperature, or chilled, and can be a main dish, side dish, or salad. The recipe calls for canned black-eyed peas, but if you want to use dried or frozen, see the variations at the end of the recipe.

1 TABLESPOON OLIVE OIL

1 CUP DICED ONIONS

1 CUP DICED CELERY

2 15-OUNCE CANS BLACK-EYED PEAS, UNDRAINED

1 TABLESPOON SOY SAUCE

1 CUP DICED GREEN, RED, OR YELLOW BELL PEPPERS

¼ CUP MINCED SCALLIONS

½ CUP CHOPPED FRESH CILANTRO

SALT AND GROUND BLACK PEPPER

1 In a saucepan on medium heat, warm the oil. Add the onions and celery and cook, stirring occasionally, until softened, about 10 minutes. Drain the black-eyed peas, reserving 1 cup of the liquid.

2 When the onions are soft, add the black-eyed peas and reserved liquid to the pan. Stir in the soy sauce and simmer on medium-high heat for 5 to 10 minutes.

3 Stir in the bell peppers, scallions, and cilantro, cover, remove from the heat, and let sit for 5 minutes. Add salt and black pepper to taste.

VARIATIONS: To cook dried black-eyed peas for this recipe, sort and rinse 1¼ cups (½ pound) of black-eyed peas. Place them in a saucepan with 6 cups of water, bring to a boil, and simmer until tender, about 45 minutes. For more tender skins, presoak in water overnight or all day, or cover with boiling water and soak for several hours. Or cook two 10-ounce packages of frozen black-eyed peas according to the package directions. Add the cooked peas and 1 cup of their cooking liquid to the softened onions and celery and proceed with the recipe.

To serve as a chilled salad, add 2 tablespoons lime or lemon juice and 2 tablespoons of extra-virgin olive oil just before serving.

SERVING AND MENU IDEAS: In winter, accompany this dish with Quinoa and Sweet Potatoes (page 284) or Maque Choux (page 309). In the summer, go with Watermelon Salad (page 99) and Sesame Flaxseed Cornbread (page 48). We can't think of a better dessert than Sweet Potato Pie with Pecan-Oat Crust (page 326).

DOWN-HOME BLACK-EYED PEAS—PER 1 SERVING (OF 8), ½ CUP *Calories: 108, Protein: 5 g, Carbohydrate: 17 g, Dietary Fiber: 4 g, Total Fat: 2 g, Saturated Fat: 0 g, Monounsaturated Fat: 1 g, Cholesterol: 0 mg, Sodium: 421 mg*

Chili Fest Chili

SERVES 6 TO 8 | YIELDS ABOUT 9 CUPS | TIME: ABOUT AN HOUR

Our city of Ithaca holds an outdoor Chili Fest in the freezing cold month of February, where local restaurants serve steaming tastes of their signature chilis. Our 2008 vegetarian Chili Fest chili has a kick that's complemented by its cool cilantro yogurt topping.

2 TABLESPOONS VEGETABLE OIL

1 CUP DICED ONIONS

2 CUPS DICED BELL PEPPERS

1 CUP DICED CARROTS

1 CUP DICED CELERY

1½ TABLESPOONS GROUND CUMIN

1 TABLESPOON GROUND CORIANDER

1 TEASPOON DRIED OREGANO

½ TEASPOON GROUND CINNAMON

¼ TEASPOON GROUND CLOVES

1 TABLESPOON PAPRIKA

1 TABLESPOON CANNED CHIPOTLES IN ADOBO SAUCE

1 28-OUNCE CAN DICED TOMATOES

1 TABLESPOON MOLASSES

2 15-OUNCE CANS RED KIDNEY BEANS, UNDRAINED

SALT

1 CUP PLAIN NONFAT YOGURT

3 TABLESPOONS CHOPPED FRESH CILANTRO

1 In a soup pot on high heat, warm the oil briefly and then add the onions and bell peppers and sauté for 5 minutes. Add the carrots and celery, reduce the heat to medium, cover, and cook until tender, about 5 minutes, stirring occasionally.

2 Stir in the cumin, coriander, oregano, cinnamon, cloves, and paprika, cover, and cook for 5 minutes, stirring occasionally so the spices won't stick.

3 Meanwhile, in a blender, purée the chipotles and adobo sauce with the tomatoes. Add the puréed tomatoes, the molasses, and the beans with their liquid, to the soup pot. Bring to a boil, reduce the heat, cover, and simmer, stirring often, for 30 minutes. Add salt to taste.

4 While the chili is cooking, in a small bowl, stir together the yogurt and cilantro and set aside.

5 Serve the chili topped with the cilantro yogurt.

VARIATIONS: Add tempeh: Cut 8 ounces of tempeh into ½-inch cubes. Warm a tablespoon of vegetable oil in a skillet on medium-high heat and cook the tempeh cubes, stirring often, until browned, about 5 minutes. Stir in a tablespoon of soy sauce. Add the browned tempeh to the chili just before serving.

Adjust the amount of chipotles to suit your taste for "hot." You can start with less and add more finely minced chipotles after the chili has simmered for 15 or 20 minutes.

Use 1 can of red kidney beans and 1 can of black beans.

SERVING AND MENU IDEAS: You may want a crisp salad, such as Mango Slaw (page 93) or Our Favorite Raw Slaw (page 267) for a nice contrast. For dessert have Butternut Cookies (page 334).

CHILI FEST CHILI—PER 1 SERVING (OF 8), 1 GENEROUS CUP *Calories: 210, Protein: 11 g, Carbohydrate: 34 g, Dietary Fiber: 8 g, Total Fat: 5 g, Saturated Fat: 1 g, Monounsaturated Fat: 2 g, Cholesterol: 1 mg, Sodium: 212 mg*

PASTA

ABOUT PASTA

Pasta is the first dish we think of for quick and easy, everyday at-home meals. Often, the topping can be prepared in the same amount of time it takes to boil water and cook the pasta. Dried pasta is economical, a pantry item that keeps almost indefinitely, and you could eat pasta every day of the year without repeating a dish.

Pasta is loaded with nutritional value. It's a good source of complex carbohydrates, B vitamins, protein (it contains six of the eight essential amino acids), and minerals, and it's low in fat, sodium, and calories. To make pasta dishes even more healthful, we created toppings full of vegetables, nuts, beans, and even fruit. We reversed the usual ratio of topping to pasta, and we cut back on the cheese just enough that you won't notice anything missing. Finally, we strongly recommend that you use whole grain pasta. In fact, we designed every pasta topping in this book to go with the hearty, nutty flavor of whole grain pasta.

Whole grain pasta has more flavor and is nutritionally superior to ordinary white flour pasta. Pastas made with whole grains are tastier now than they were in years past, and the variety available in supermarkets is still growing. We recommend whole wheat pastas made by DeCecco, Gia Russa, and Bionaturae. We also like rice, spelt, and buckwheat pastas.

The availability of gluten-free pasta opens up a whole wonderful category of food to those with restricted diets.

As a general rule, we prefer imported Italian pastas to those made by most domestic manufacturers. The Italian government enforces strict national standards for ingredients and manufacturing processes, standards that result in a superior product. For example, in Italy pasta is extruded through bronze dies, rather than the Teflon ones often used in this country, giving it a rougher, more porous surface. And when pasta is dried slowly at low temperatures, the protein is not denatured and the pasta is firmer when cooked.

There are a multitude of shapes and sizes of pasta. There is probably a whole aisle devoted to pasta in your supermarket, and although you may not find as large a variety of whole grain pasta shapes, there's probably enough to work with—and the selection is sure to grow. There's a certain logic applied to pairing sauces and toppings with particular shapes of pasta. Long strands such as spaghetti and linguini go well with smooth tomato sauces and pestos. Short, thicker pastas, such as fusilli, chioccide, and rigatoni, work best with hearty bean and chunky vegetable toppings. Bowl-shaped cuts, such as orecchiette and shells, are good for sauces with finely chopped vegetables, because the pasta catches and holds the vegetable pieces. That said, not having the perfect pasta shape would never stop us from going ahead with the sauce we want to make.

Cook pasta in a large pot with plenty of water so that it will return quickly to a boil after the pasta is added and so that the pasta has room to float freely, which helps it cook evenly and keeps it from sticking together. Use about four or five quarts of water per pound of pasta. Always salt the pasta cooking water; never add oil. Ease the pasta into rapidly boiling water, stir to separate, and cover the pot. When the water returns to a boil, remove the lid and stir again.

We don't always trust the cooking time listed on a pasta box; sometimes it's too long. You know when pasta is ready by tasting it. Start testing it several minutes before you expect it to be done so you'll be able to catch it when it's al dente—tender but with a firm bite. This is especially important for whole grain pastas, which tend to become too soft when overcooked.

We haven't been able to agree among ourselves about how much pasta is a reasonable serving size. Some of us want a quarter-pound of pasta for a serving at dinner, and that has been our recommendation in our other cookbooks. Others are satisfied with less, and some want more. When a pound of whole grain pasta is topped with plenty of a chunky vegetable sauce with beans or nuts or cheese, it will serve six, or even eight, hungry people handily, especially when the meal includes other dishes.

Pasta with Pistachio-Lemon Pesto

SERVES 4 TO 6 | YIELDS A GENEROUS CUP OF PESTO | TIME: 25 MINUTES

This piquant, interesting pesto is a snap to make while the pasta cooks. We like to use whole wheat linguini or spaghetti for this recipe.

---

1 POUND OF WHOLE GRAIN PASTA

10 OUNCES BABY SPINACH (ABOUT 6 CUPS PACKED)

PISTACHIO-LEMON PESTO

¼ CUP CHOPPED SHALLOTS

¼ CUP LEMON JUICE

⅓ CUP EXTRA-VIRGIN OLIVE OIL

1 CUP TOASTED SHELLED UNSALTED PISTACHIOS

SALT AND GROUND BLACK PEPPER

---

1 Bring a large covered pot of salted water to a boil. When the water boils add the pasta and cook until al dente. When the pasta is done, add the spinach to the pot and stir until just wilted. Reserve about a cup of the pasta cooking water, and then drain the pasta and spinach.

2 While the pasta cooks, make the Pistachio-Lemon Pesto: Place the shallots, lemon juice, olive oil, and pistachios in a blender or food processor and pulse, scraping down the sides with a spatula, until finely chopped, although it's fine if some of the pistachios remain whole.

3 Place the drained pasta and spinach in a serving bowl and toss with the pesto and enough of the reserved cooking water to coat the pasta. Season with salt and pepper to taste.

VARIATION: Use about 4 cups of baby arugula in place of the spinach.

SERVING AND MENU IDEAS: Serve with something light on the side, such as Quick-braised Snow Peas and Radishes (page 308), Pineapple and Tomato Salad (page 87), or steamed artichokes.

PASTA WITH PISTACHIO-LEMON PESTO—
PER 1 SERVING (OF 6) *Calories: 498, Protein: 16 g, Carbohydrate: 65 g, Dietary Fiber: 2 g, Total Fat: 23 g, Saturated Fat: 3 g, Monounsaturated Fat: 14 g, Cholesterol: 0 mg, Sodium: 13 mg*

PISTACHIO-LEMON PESTO (PESTO ONLY)—
PER 2 TABLESPOONS *Calories: 173, Protein: 3 g, Carbohydrate: 6 g, Dietary Fiber: 2 g, Total Fat: 16 g, Saturated Fat: 2 g, Monounsaturated Fat: 10 g, Cholesterol: 0 mg, Sodium: 2 mg*

Pasta with Broccoli Rabe and Beans

SERVES 4 TO 6 | TIME: 30 MINUTES

In this unpretentious Italian classic, the strong flavors of broccoli rabe, garlic, red pepper flakes, and olives really stand up to nutty whole wheat pasta. One or two of us might choose this soulful dish if we could have only one more meal.

> 8 OUNCES CHUNKY-SHAPED WHOLE GRAIN PASTA
>
> 2 POUNDS BROCCOLI RABE
>
> ¼ CUP OLIVE OIL
>
> 6 GARLIC CLOVES, THINLY SLICED
>
> ¼ TEASPOON RED PEPPER FLAKES
>
> ½ TEASPOON SALT
>
> 1 15-OUNCE CAN PINTO OR WHITE BEANS, RINSED AND DRAINED
>
> ½ CUP PITTED AND CHOPPED OIL-CURED BLACK OLIVES
>
> GROUND BLACK PEPPER

1 Bring a large covered pot of salted water to a boil. Add the pasta and cook until al dente. Reserve about ½ cup of the pasta cooking liquid, and then drain.

2 While the pasta cooks, chop the broccoli rabe (about 12 packed cups). In a soup pot on medium heat, warm the olive oil. Cook the garlic and red pepper flakes for a minute, and then add the broccoli rabe and salt. Cook, stirring often, until the broccoli rabe is tender. Remove from the heat, stir in the beans and the olives and cover.

3 In a serving bowl, stir together the pasta and broccoli rabe mixture, adding some of the reserved pasta cooking liquid if needed. Add black pepper to taste.

VARIATIONS: If you'd like a little extra spark, add a couple of tablespoons of lemon juice (although it may dull the bright green of the broccoli rabe).

Substitute your favorite beans.

SERVING AND MENU IDEAS: Top with toasted pine nuts and/or Parmesan or feta cheese, and serve with lemon wedges. Serve with a salad of fresh mozzarella and tomatoes, Watermelon Salad (page 99), or Roasted Beet Salad (page 92). Finish with Figs Baked with Chèvre and Pistachios (page 315).

PASTA WITH BROCCOLI RABE AND BEANS—
PER 1 SERVING (OF 6) *Calories: 323, Protein: 14 g, Carbohydrate: 45 g, Dietary Fiber: 8 g, Total Fat: 12 g, Saturated Fat: 2 g, Monounsaturated Fat: 8 g, Cholesterol: 0 mg, Sodium: 555 mg*

Japanese Noodles with Tomatoes

SERVES 2 OR 3 | TIME: 20 MINUTES

Extra-virgin olive oil is unexpectedly paired with dark sesame oil, soy sauce, and fresh summer tomatoes in this recipe, and it all works well together for a light supper or lunch. This simple dish can be served warm, at room temperature, or chilled. Soba noodles don't need to cook as long as most wheat pastas, so take care to catch them while they're still al dente.

8 OUNCES SOBA NOODLES (SEE NOTE)
2 TABLESPOONS DARK SESAME OIL
2 TABLESPOONS SOY SAUCE
1 TABLESPOON EXTRA-VIRGIN OLIVE OIL
2 CUPS DICED FRESH TOMATOES
¼ CUP SLICED SCALLIONS
GROUND BLACK PEPPER

NOTE: Soba noodles have a nutty flavor and delicate texture. Some Japanese soba noodles are made of 100 percent buckwheat flour and are a healthful, gluten-free alternative to wheat noodles, but are very delicate and overcook easily. Usually wheat is added to make a sturdier buckwheat noodle, so read the label if gluten is a concern.

1 Bring a large covered pot of salted water to a boil. Add the noodles and cook until al dente. Don't overcook. Drain the noodles, and if you're going to serve them cold, rinse with cold water.

2 While the noodles cook, in a serving bowl, stir together the sesame oil, soy sauce, olive oil, tomatoes, and scallions.

3 Add the cooked noodles and toss well. Sprinkle with black pepper. Serve warm, at room temperature, or chilled.

SERVING AND MENU IDEAS: For a heartier meal, add An Easy Baked Tofu (page 177) to the noodles. Green Beans with Ginger and Garlic (page 303) would be a good side dish.

JAPANESE NOODLES WITH TOMATOES—
PER 1 SERVING (OF 3) *Calories: 407, Protein: 13 g, Carbohydrate: 63 g, Dietary Fiber: 2 g, Total Fat: 14 g, Saturated Fat: 2 g, Monounsaturated Fat: 7 g, Cholesterol: 0 mg, Sodium: 1,009 mg*

Pasta with Summer Squash and Herbed Cheese

SERVES 4 TO 6 | TIME: 35 MINUTES

Garlic, lemon, and good fruity olive oil really boost the flavor of mild summer squash paired with tasty whole grain pasta. This pretty green and yellow dish dolloped with a vivid green herbed cottage cheese topping celebrates summer.

HERBED CHEESE

1 CUP SNIPPED CHIVES

1 CUP CHOPPED FRESH PARSLEY

2 TABLESPOONS EXTRA-VIRGIN OLIVE OIL

1 ½ CUPS LOW-FAT COTTAGE CHEESE

½ TEASPOON SALT

16 OUNCES CHUNKY-SHAPED WHOLE GRAIN PASTA

2 TABLESPOONS EXTRA-VIRGIN OLIVE OIL

6 GARLIC CLOVES, MINCED OR PRESSED

4 CUPS SLICED ZUCCHINI

4 CUPS SLICED YELLOW SQUASH

SALT AND GROUND BLACK PEPPER

¼ CUP LEMON JUICE

TOASTED PINE NUTS (OPTIONAL)

1 In a skillet on high heat, sauté the chives and parsley in the oil, stirring constantly for about a minute, until slightly wilted but still bright green. In a blender or food processor, purée the herbs, cottage cheese, and salt until smooth. Set aside.

2 Bring a large covered pot of salted water to a boil. When the water boils, stir in the pasta.

3 While the pasta cooks, in a soup pot on medium-high heat, warm the oil. Add the garlic, zucchini, and yellow squash and cook, stirring frequently, for about 5 minutes, until the squash is tender. Sprinkle with salt and pepper. Stir in the lemon juice and remove from the heat.

4 When the pasta is al dente, drain it and transfer to a large serving bowl. Top with the squash and then a large dollop of the herbed cheese. Sprinkle with pine nuts, if you wish. Pass the rest of the herbed cheese at the table.

SERVING AND MENU IDEAS: Serve with a platter of sliced many-colored heirloom tomatoes sprinkled with chopped basil, coarse salt, and cracked black pepper and drizzled with olive oil, and you won't need anything else, except maybe some good bread. Have Herbed and Spiced Fresh Fruit Popsicles (page 320) for dessert.

PASTA WITH SUMMER SQUASH AND HERBED CHEESE—PER 1 SERVING (OF 6) *Calories: 423, Protein: 21 g, Carbohydrate: 67 g, Dietary Fiber: 2 g, Total Fat: 11 g, Saturated Fat: 2 g, Monounsaturated Fat: 7 g, Cholesterol: 2 mg, Sodium: 224 mg*

Pasta with Broccoli

SERVES 4 | TIME: 30 MINUTES

We've been making pasta with broccoli for a long time, and over the years our recipe has evolved. Now we always use whole wheat pasta, both for its better nutrition and because it pairs well with assertive broccoli and garlic. And the proportion of broccoli to pasta is now reversed, so we probably ought to call the dish Broccoli with Pasta.

This is an everyday, at-home kind of recipe to make again and again, and we make many versions of it.

---

8 OUNCES CHUNKY-SHAPED WHOLE GRAIN PASTA

3 TABLESPOONS OLIVE OIL

4 CUPS CHOPPED BROCCOLI

2 TABLESPOONS MINCED GARLIC

½ TEASPOON SALT

⅛ TEASPOON GROUND BLACK PEPPER

1 CUP CRUMBLED FETA CHEESE

---

1 Bring a large covered pot of salted water to a boil. When the water comes to a boil, add the pasta and cook until al dente. Drain and place in a serving bowl.

2 While the pasta cooks, in a skillet, warm the oil on medium-high heat. Add the broccoli and cook, stirring frequently, for about 5 minutes. Add the garlic, salt, pepper, and a couple of spoonfuls of hot pasta cooking water. Cover, lower the heat, and steam until the broccoli is tender, about 5 minutes.

3 Top the pasta with the cooked broccoli and the crumbled feta.

VARIATIONS: Add a can of small red beans, rinsed and drained, or a cup of cooked fresh or frozen edamame.

Add about ½ cup of chopped kalamata olives.

Add ¼ teaspoon red pepper flakes.

Top with toasted walnuts or pine nuts.

Try it with pecorino Romano, ricotta salata, or Gorgonzola cheese.

Cook chopped red bell peppers with the broccoli or add a couple of chopped tomatoes at the end.

SERVING AND MENU IDEAS: Accompany this pasta with assorted olives, a tomato salad, and good bread. Then you'll be ready for an indulgent dessert such as Filo Nut Cigars (page 330).

PASTA WITH BROCCOLI—PER 1 SERVING (OF 4)
Calories: 417, Protein: 16 g, Carbohydrate: 50 g, Dietary Fiber: 2 g, Total Fat: 19 g, Saturated Fat: 7 g, Monounsaturated Fat: 9 g, Cholesterol: 33 mg, Sodium: 743 mg

Pasta with Tomato-Peach Sauce

SERVES 4 | YIELDS ABOUT 4 CUPS SAUCE | HANDS-ON TIME: 20 MINUTES | ROASTING TIME: 40 MINUTES

The inspiration for this unusual sweet-and-sour sauce comes from a summer dish served by the Stonecat Café, an eatery overlooking beautiful Seneca Lake in the little town of Hector, New York.

Although you can make the sauce with frozen peaches and hothouse tomatoes, its flavor is truly superb with fresh ripe peaches and succulent, juicy, just-picked tomatoes.

5 OR 6 SUN-DRIED TOMATOES

4 CUPS COARSELY CHOPPED TOMATOES

2 CUPS CHOPPED FRESH OR FROZEN PEELED PEACHES

1 CUP CHOPPED ONIONS

3 TABLESPOONS OLIVE OIL

½ TEASPOON SALT

⅛ TEASPOON GROUND CINNAMON

⅛ TEASPOON GROUND BLACK PEPPER

⅛ TEASPOON CAYENNE

1 TABLESPOON RED WINE VINEGAR

2 HEAPING TABLESPOONS CHOPPED FRESH TARRAGON

12 OUNCES CHUNKY-SHAPED WHOLE GRAIN PASTA

GRATED PARMESAN OR PECORINO ROMANO CHEESE

1 In a covered bowl, soak the sun-dried tomatoes in boiling water to cover for at least 15 minutes, until softened and plumped. Drain and chop the soaked sun-dried tomatoes.

2 In a lightly oiled 9 × 13-inch baking dish, stir together the sun-dried tomatoes, tomatoes, peaches, onions, olive oil, salt, cinnamon, black pepper, and cayenne. In a 450° oven, roast uncovered, stirring at least twice during cooking, until the ingredients have softened and thickened, about 40 minutes. When done, stir in the vinegar and tarragon.

3 When the sauce has been roasting for about 25 minutes, bring salted water to a boil in a large pot. Stir in the pasta and cook until al dente. Drain well.

4 To serve, divide the pasta among four warm bowls, spoon about a cup of the sauce on each serving, and top with grated cheese.

SERVING AND MENU IDEAS: Spinach Salad with Chèvre and Walnuts (page 84) is wonderful before or after the pasta.

PASTA WITH TOMATO-PEACH SAUCE—PER 1 SERVING (OF 4) *Calories: 476, Protein: 16 g, Carbohydrate: 84 g, Dietary Fiber: 4 g, Total Fat: 12 g, Saturated Fat: 2 g, Monounsaturated Fat: 8 g, Cholesterol: 0 mg, Sodium: 362 mg*

TOMATO-PEACH SAUCE ONLY—PER 1 SERVING (OF 4), 1 CUP *Calories: 178, Protein: 3 g, Carbohydrate: 20 g, Dietary Fiber: 4 g, Total Fat: 11 g, Saturated Fat: 2 g, Monounsaturated Fat: 8 g, Cholesterol: 0 mg, Sodium: 355 mg*

Pasta with Eggplant, Ricotta, and Walnuts

SERVES 4 TO 6 | TIME: 40 MINUTES

This pasta dish is enjoyed in households all over Sicily. The cinnamon is evidence of the Levantine influence in Sicilian cuisine.

---

1 TABLESPOON OLIVE OIL

2 CUPS CHOPPED ONIONS

½ TEASPOON SALT

1 MEDIUM EGGPLANT (ABOUT ¾ POUND)

¼ CUP WATER

12 OUNCES CHUNKY-SHAPED WHOLE GRAIN PASTA

1 15-OUNCE CONTAINER FAT-FREE RICOTTA

½ TEASPOON GROUND CINNAMON

½ CUP GRATED PARMESAN OR ASIAGO CHEESE

1 CUP CHOPPED FRESH BASIL AND/OR PARSLEY, LOOSELY PACKED

½ TEASPOON SALT

¼ TEASPOON GROUND BLACK PEPPER

2 CUPS DICED FRESH TOMATOES

½ CUP CHOPPED TOASTED WALNUTS

---

1 In a skillet on medium-high heat, warm the olive oil. Cook the onions and salt, stirring frequently, until lightly browned. Meanwhile, peel the eggplant, or don't, and cut it into ½-inch cubes. Add the eggplant to the onions and stir-fry for about 3 minutes. Then add the water, cover, reduce the heat to medium, and cook, stirring frequently, until the eggplant is tender, about 10 minutes.

2 Meanwhile, bring a large pot of salted water to boil, and cook the pasta until al dente.

3 While the pasta cooks, in a large serving bowl, mix together the ricotta, cinnamon, grated cheese, basil, salt, and pepper. When the pasta is al dente, reserve a cup of the cooking liquid, and then drain. Stir the drained pasta into the ricotta mixture, adding some pasta cooking liquid if needed to evenly coat the pasta. Stir in the cooked eggplant and onions and the fresh tomatoes.

4 Serve the pasta topped with the walnuts, and pass more grated cheese at the table.

VARIATIONS: To roast the onions and eggplant in the oven: Toss with the olive oil and salt and spread evenly on a lightly oiled baking sheet. Roast in a preheated 400° oven for 20 to 25 minutes, stirring once or twice, until the eggplant is tender and golden brown.

SERVING AND MENU IDEAS: Pair with a crisp, green salad dressed with flavorful Pear and Thyme Vinaigrette (page 110).

PASTA WITH EGGPLANT, RICOTTA, AND WALNUTS— PER 1 SERVING (OF 6) *Calories: 471, Protein: 23 g, Carbohydrate: 60 g, Dietary Fiber: 5 g, Total Fat: 18 g, Saturated Fat: 6 g, Monounsaturated Fat: 5 g, Cholesterol: 29 mg, Sodium: 422 mg*

Pasta with Ruby Chard and Cherries

SERVES 4 TO 6 | TIME: 40 MINUTES

This easy and interesting pasta is adapted from a recipe by the ever-sensible and inspiring food writer and cookbook author Jack Bishop. The earthy-tasting greens punctuated with sweet chewy nuggets of dried cherries combine well with the richness of toasted walnuts and flavorful whole wheat pasta. Hot pepper flakes, if you use them, add a warm bite.

½ CUP DRIED CHERRIES

16 OUNCES CHUNKY-SHAPED WHOLE GRAIN PASTA

2 BUNCHES RUBY CHARD (1½ TO 2 POUNDS)

¼ CUP EXTRA-VIRGIN OLIVE OIL

4 GARLIC CLOVES, MINCED OR PRESSED

1 TEASPOON SALT

GROUND BLACK PEPPER

PINCH OF RED PEPPER FLAKES (OPTIONAL)

¼ CUP CHOPPED TOASTED WALNUTS

GRATED PARMESAN CHEESE OR CRUMBLED RICOTTA SALATA CHEESE (OPTIONAL)

1 Bring a large covered pot of salted water to a boil. When the water comes to a rapid boil, ladle a few tablespoons of it into a bowl, add the dried cherries, and set aside to soak. Cook the pasta until al dente and drain.

2 While the water heats, rinse the chard and remove the bottom ½-inch of the stems. Cut the stems crosswise into ½-inch slices and set aside. Chop the leaves. (You should have about 9 cups of chopped leaves and 2 cups of stem slices.) Set aside.

3 While the pasta cooks, warm the oil in a large skillet or a soup pot on high heat. Add the chard stems and sauté for a minute. Add the garlic and the chard leaves and cook uncovered, stirring often, until the chard is limp but the leaves are still bright green, about 5 minutes. Stir in the salt and a sprinkling of black pepper, and add red pepper flakes, if you wish.

4 Drain the soaked cherries.

5 Divide the pasta into warm serving bowls and top with the garlicky chard, plump hot cherries, and toasted walnuts. Offer cheese at the table, if you like.

SERVING AND MENU IDEAS: Begin with Yellow Split Pea Dip (page 71) served with assorted crudités. Luscious Chocolate Bark (page 336), along with a red wine with a hint of cherry, may be the ideal dessert.

PASTA WITH RUBY CHARD AND CHERRIES—
PER 1 SERVING (OF 6) *Calories: 408, Protein: 14 g, Carbohydrate: 64 g, Dietary Fiber: 2 g, Total Fat: 14 g, Saturated Fat: 2 g, Monounsaturated Fat: 7 g, Cholesterol: 0 mg, Sodium: 636 mg*

Pasta with Sun-dried Tomatoes, Zucchini, and Beans

SERVES 4 | YIELDS ABOUT 8 CUPS | TIME: 30 MINUTES

Another of our quickly prepared pasta dishes that is satisfying and nourishing. This one is for garlic lovers: crunchy garlic tops the pasta and flavors the cooking oil. Green zucchini and parsley and red bits of sun-dried tomatoes make this pasta colorful.

½ CUP LIGHTLY PACKED SUN-DRIED TOMATOES (ABOUT 12)

8 OUNCES CHUNKY-SHAPED WHOLE GRAIN PASTA

5 LARGE GARLIC CLOVES

2 TABLESPOONS EXTRA-VIRGIN OLIVE OIL

1 MEDIUM ZUCCHINI CUT INTO MATCHSTICKS (ABOUT 3½ CUPS)

1 15-OUNCE CAN SMALL RED OR WHITE BEANS, UNDRAINED

¼ CUP CHOPPED FRESH PARSLEY

SALT AND GROUND BLACK PEPPER

GRATED PARMESAN OR PECORINO ROMANO CHEESE (OPTIONAL)

1 In a small pan on the stovetop or in a bowl in the microwave oven, bring to a boil the sun-dried tomatoes covered with water, then set aside until softened, at least 5 minutes. Bring a large covered pot of salted water to a boil. Add the pasta and cook until al dente. Reserve about a cup of the cooking water and then drain.

2 While the pasta cooks, cut the garlic into ⅛-inch-thick slices. (Cut uniform slices so it will cook evenly.) Warm the oil in a large skillet on medium heat, add the garlic, and cook carefully until golden and crisp but not brown. Use a slotted spoon to scoop out the cooked garlic and put it in a small bowl; set aside.

3 Increase the heat to medium-high, add the zucchini, and cook for a couple of minutes, stirring often. Drain the sun-dried tomatoes, chop them, and add them to the skillet with ¼ cup of the pasta cooking water. When the zucchini is almost tender, add the beans along with the liquid in the can, and cook until the beans are warm and the zucchini is tender. Stir in the parsley.

4 Toss the vegetables with the drained pasta, adding a little more of the reserved pasta cooking water if needed. Add salt and pepper to taste. Stir in the reserved garlic or use it to top each serving. Pass grated cheese at the table, if you wish.

INGREDIENT NOTE: Look for sun-dried tomatoes that have been preserved with salt and do not contain sulfites.

SERVING AND MENU IDEAS: Sample assorted olives to start. A crisp green salad would be a welcome accompaniment. End the meal with a couple of different kinds of cheese and fresh cherries or grapes.

PASTA WITH SUN-DRIED TOMATOES, ZUCCHINI, AND BEANS—PER 1 SERVING (OF 4) *Calories: 389, Protein: 16 g, Carbohydrate: 68 g, Dietary Fiber: 9 g, Total Fat: 8 g, Saturated Fat: 1 g, Monounsaturated Fat: 5 g, Cholesterol: 0 mg, Sodium: 521 mg*

Pasta with Grape Tomatoes and Feta

SERVES 4 TO 6 | TIME: 20 MINUTES

Have you had your lycopene today? Grape tomatoes are available year-round and their sweet flavor is intense enough to pair with salty feta for a fresh topping ready by the time the pasta cooks.

---

16 OUNCES CHUNKY-SHAPED WHOLE GRAIN PASTA

2 PINTS GRAPE TOMATOES (4 CUPS)

¼ CUP EXTRA-VIRGIN OLIVE OIL

6 LARGE GARLIC CLOVES, MINCED

¼ CUP CRUMBLED FETA CHEESE

GROUND BLACK PEPPER

---

1 Bring a large covered pot of salted water to a boil. Add the pasta and cook until al dente. Reserve about ½ cup of the pasta cooking liquid, and then drain.

2 While the pasta cooks, slice the tomatoes in half through the stem end and set aside. In a skillet on low heat, warm the olive oil. Add the garlic and cook until golden but not browned. Add the tomatoes, increase the heat to medium-high, and cook until the tomatoes have softened but are still fairly firm, about 5 minutes.

3 Transfer the drained pasta to a serving bowl. Toss the pasta with the crumbled feta, adding enough reserved cooking liquid to coat the pasta. Top with the tomato-garlic mixture. Season with black pepper to taste.

VARIATION: Add about 2 cups fresh or frozen chopped collards or spinach, or chopped fresh chard or kale to the pot of cooking pasta a few minutes before it's done, and then drain together.

SERVING AND MENU IDEAS: Lemony Zucchini with Bread Crumb Topping (page 301) or a simple green salad goes well with this.

PASTA WITH GRAPE TOMATOES AND FETA—
PER 1 SERVING (OF 6) *Calories: 386, Protein: 13 g, Carbohydrate: 63 g, Dietary Fiber: 1 g, Total Fat: 12 g, Saturated Fat: 2 g, Monounsaturated Fat: 7 g, Cholesterol: 6 mg, Sodium: 86 mg*

Pasta with Butternut Squash and Sage

SERVES 6 | YIELDS ABOUT 6 CUPS SAUCE | TIME: 50 MINUTES

Sweet butternut squash is complemented by savory fresh sage. This vegan sauce is a lovely golden color flecked with red and has a thick, creamy texture. Put it on nutty whole grain pasta and top it with salty cheese and toasted nuts and you have a dish with wonderful flavors.

2 TABLESPOONS OLIVE OIL

1½ CUPS CHOPPED ONIONS

½ TEASPOON SALT

3 CUPS CUBED PEELED BUTTERNUT SQUASH

1½ CUPS CHOPPED RED BELL PEPPERS

⅛ TEASPOON GROUND BLACK PEPPER

4 GARLIC CLOVES, MINCED OR PRESSED

½ TEASPOON DRIED THYME

¼ TEASPOON RED PEPPER FLAKES

PINCH OF GRATED NUTMEG

1½ CUPS VEGETABLE BROTH (SEE PAGE 33)

½ CUP DRY WHITE WINE

2 TABLESPOONS MINCED FRESH SAGE

16 OUNCES CHUNKY-SHAPED WHOLE GRAIN PASTA

CRUMBLED RICOTTA SALATA OR FETA CHEESE

CHOPPED TOASTED WALNUTS OR TOASTED PINE NUTS

1 In a soup pot on medium heat, warm the oil. Add the onions and salt and cook, stirring occasionally, until translucent, about 7 minutes. Stir in the squash, bell peppers, black pepper, garlic, thyme, red pepper flakes, nutmeg, broth, wine, and sage, cover, and bring to a boil. Reduce the heat and simmer uncovered until the squash is tender.

2 Meanwhile, bring a large covered pot of salted water to a boil. Add the pasta and cook until al dente. Drain the pasta, reserving about a cup of the cooking liquid.

3 In a blender, purée the cooked vegetables, adding some of the reserved pasta cooking liquid if needed to make a smooth sauce.

4 Serve the pasta topped with the sauce, and pass cheese and toasted nuts at the table.

VARIATION: The sauce can be thinned to make a delicious soup. Thin the puréed sauce with water or vegetable broth until it is the consistency you like.

SERVING AND MENU IDEAS: Delicious with Kale with Cranberries (page 298), broccoli rabe sautéed with garlic and olive oil, or Our Favorite Raw Slaw (page 267).

PASTA WITH BUTTERNUT SQUASH AND SAGE— PER 1 SERVING (OF 6) *Calories: 382, Protein: 13 g, Carbohydrate: 73 g, Dietary Fiber: 3 g, Total Fat: 6 g, Saturated Fat: 1 g, Monounsaturated Fat: 3 g, Cholesterol: 0 mg, Sodium: 207 mg*

SQUASH AND SAGE SAUCE ONLY—PER 1 CUP *Calories: 118, Protein: 2 g, Carbohydrate: 16 g, Dietary Fiber: 3 g, Total Fat: 5 g, Saturated Fat: 1 g, Monounsaturated Fat: 3 g, Cholesterol: 0 mg, Sodium: 201 mg*

Pasta with Caramelized Onions and Tomato Sauce

SERVES 4 TO 6 | TIME: 30 MINUTES

This is a luscious way to make pasta with tomato sauce more interesting. Onions and tomatoes go so well together and caramelized onions and feta are even better— nothing beats the combination of sweet and salty. Whole wheat penne or rigatoni is a good choice of pasta. Onions sliced lengthwise, from top to root end, hold their shape better than cross-cut onions.

---

4 TEASPOONS OLIVE OIL

8 CUPS SLICED ONIONS

16 OUNCES CHUNKY-SHAPED WHOLE GRAIN PASTA

2 CUPS OF YOUR FAVORITE TOMATO SAUCE (SEE NOTE)

¼ TEASPOON SALT

⅛ TEASPOON GROUND BLACK PEPPER

1 CUP CRUMBLED FETA CHEESE

NOTE: Our current favorite tomato sauce in a jar is Gia Russa brand tomato and basil sauce.

1 Warm the oil in a very large heavy skillet on medium heat. Add the onions and cook until very soft and golden, stirring frequently, for about 20 minutes.

2 While the onions cook, bring a large pot of salted water to a boil. When the water boils, stir in the pasta and cook until al dente.

3 When the onions are soft, stir in the tomato sauce, salt, and pepper and cook until hot.

4 When the pasta is ready, drain and transfer to a serving bowl. Stir in half of the cheese and all of the tomato-onion sauce. Top with the rest of the cheese.

VARIATION: Add about 6 to 8 ounces of vegetarian sausage, either crumbled sausage patties such as Yves brand veggie sausage patties, or sliced links such as Tofurkey brand vegetarian Italian sausages. Cook the sausage for a few minutes in a separate, lightly oiled saucepan or in the same pan with the softened onions. Add a teaspoon of ground fennel seeds to enhance the sausage flavor.

SERVING AND MENU IDEAS: This pasta will be nicely balanced by an interesting and complex salad such as Arugula, Kumquat, Walnut, and Fig Salad (page 95), or serve it with steamed green beans.

PASTA WITH ONIONS AND TOMATO SAUCE— PER 1 SERVING (OF 6) *Calories: 444, Protein: 18 g, Carbohydrate: 85 g, Dietary Fiber: 5 g, Total Fat: 7 g, Saturated Fat: 2 g, Monounsaturated Fat: 3 g, Cholesterol: 7 mg, Sodium: 620 mg*

ONIONS AND TOMATO SAUCE ONLY—PER ¾ CUP *Calories: 180, Protein: 7 g, Carbohydrate: 28 g, Dietary Fiber: 5 g, Total Fat: 6 g, Saturated Fat: 2 g, Monounsaturated Fat: 3 g, Cholesterol: 7 mg, Sodium: 614 mg*

Pasta with French Lentils and Kale

SERVES 4 | TIME: 50 MINUTES

This cold-weather pasta dish is robust with lentils and kale and the flavors of thyme and paprika. We suggest using a chunky pasta, such as orechiette, fusilli, or shells to "catch" the carrots and lentils.

---

1 CUP FRENCH GREEN LENTILS

3 CUPS WATER

8 OUNCES CHUNKY-SHAPED WHOLE GRAIN PASTA

3 TABLESPOONS OLIVE OIL

1½ CUPS CHOPPED ONIONS

3 GARLIC CLOVES, MINCED OR PRESSED

1½ TEASPOONS SALT

1 CUP DICED CARROTS

½ TEASPOON PAPRIKA OR SMOKED PAPRIKA

¼ TEASPOON RED PEPPER FLAKES

4 CUPS CHOPPED KALE

4 TEASPOONS MINCED FRESH THYME

2 CUPS DICED FRESH TOMATOES

GROUND BLACK PEPPER

GRATED PARMESAN OR PECORINO ROMANO CHEESE (OPTIONAL)

---

1 In a covered saucepan, bring the lentils and water to a simmer. Cook covered until tender but firm, about 20 minutes. Drain, cover, and set aside.

2 Meanwhile, bring a large covered pot of salted water to a boil. Add the pasta and cook until al dente. Reserve about a cup of the pasta cooking liquid, and drain.

3 While the pasta cooks, in a skillet on medium heat, warm the oil. Add the onions and cook for 3 to 4 minutes, stirring now and then, until softened. Add the garlic and salt, and cook until the onions are translucent, about 5 minutes. Stir in the carrots, paprika, and red pepper flakes and cook until the carrots are tender, about 5 minutes. Add the kale and about ½ cup of the reserved pasta cooking water and cook until the kale is tender, adding more water if needed. Stir in the thyme and tomatoes and remove from the heat.

4 In a serving bowl, toss together the cooked lentils, the pasta, and the vegetables. Add salt and pepper to taste. Pass grated cheese at the table, if you wish.

SERVING AND MENU IDEA: Serve with a little salad of crisp cucumbers splashed with a bit of balsamic vinegar and sprinkled with salt.

PASTA WITH FRENCH LENTILS AND KALE—PER 1 SERVING (OF 4) *Calories: 549, Protein: 25 g, Carbohydrate: 92 g, Dietary Fiber: 19 g, Total Fat: 12 g, Saturated Fat: 2 g, Monounsaturated Fat: 8 g, Cholesterol: 0 mg, Sodium: 357 mg*

Spaghetti Aglio, Olio, e Prezzemolo

SERVES 4 TO 6 | TIME: 20 MINUTES

In Italy, this spaghetti is a favorite late-night pick-me-up, sometimes called *pasta al Vesuvio* (inflamed spaghetti). Our version isn't peppery-hot enough to be called volcanic, but there is a bit of bite from the generous amounts of garlic and parsley and a little kick from the lemon zest and the red pepper flakes. This pasta is a favorite of ours at almost any time of day.

The simple, assertive topping can be made in the time it takes to cook the pasta. We like to use flat-leafed Italian parsley, for its smoother texture and stronger taste.

16 OUNCES WHOLE GRAIN SPAGHETTI OR LINGUINE

½ CUP EXTRA-VIRGIN OLIVE OIL

6 GARLIC CLOVES, MINCED

1 CUP CHOPPED FRESH PARSLEY

2 TABLESPOONS TOASTED PINE NUTS (OPTIONAL)

1 TABLESPOON GRATED LEMON ZEST

½ TEASPOON RED PEPPER FLAKES, OR MORE TO TASTE

½ TEASPOON SALT

GROUND BLACK PEPPER

GRATED PARMESAN OR PECORINO ROMANO CHEESE (OPTIONAL)

1 Bring a large covered pot of salted water to a boil. Add the pasta and cook until al dente.

2 Meanwhile, in a skillet on low heat, warm the olive oil. Add the garlic and cook for a minute or two until golden. Add the parsley, pine nuts if using, lemon zest, and red pepper flakes, and cook until the parsley is wilted but still bright green, about 2 minutes. Stir in the salt and a pinch of black pepper. Cover and set aside.

3 When the pasta is done, drain it and place in a serving bowl. Add the parsley mixture to the pasta and toss to coat. Pass grated cheese at the table, if you wish.

SERVING AND MENU IDEAS: In the summer, serve this spaghetti with a fresh mozzarella and tomato salad and then have chilled fresh fruit. In winter, serve it with Herbed Vegetable Packets (page 197) or Maple-glazed Root Vegetables (page 307).

SPAGHETTI AGLIO, OLIO, E PREZZEMOLO—
PER 1 SERVING (OF 6) *Calories: 433, Protein: 12 g, Carbohydrate: 59 g, Dietary Fiber: 1 g, Total Fat: 19 g, Saturated Fat: 3 g, Monounsaturated Fat: 13 g, Cholesterol: 0 mg, Sodium: 206 mg*

Pasta with Winter Pesto

SERVES 4 TO 6 | YIELDS 1 GENEROUS CUP OF PESTO | TIME: 25 MINUTES

We decided to go nuts with this pesto! It's packed with three kinds of nutrient-rich nuts. Dulse flakes (see pages 162–163) provide the salty note usually played by a hard cheese in a more traditional pesto. Made with whole wheat pasta and topped with parsley and fresh tomatoes for a tasty and colorful contrast, this is a filling dish especially welcome in cold weather.

16 OUNCES WHOLE GRAIN PASTA (SEE NOTE)

WINTER PESTO

1 CUP CHOPPED FRESH TOMATOES

3 GARLIC CLOVES, PRESSED OR CHOPPED

½ CUP TOASTED ALMONDS, COARSELY CHOPPED

⅓ CUP TOASTED WALNUTS, COARSELY CHOPPED

¼ CUP TOASTED PINE NUTS

2 TABLESPOONS DULSE FLAKES

2 TEASPOONS GROUND FENNEL SEEDS

¼ TEASPOON SALT

⅛ TEASPOON GROUND BLACK PEPPER

3 TABLESPOONS OLIVE OIL

1 CUP DICED FRESH TOMATOES

CHOPPED FRESH PARSLEY

GRATED PARMESAN CHEESE (OPTIONAL)

NOTE: This pesto is fine with any shape of pasta; our favorite for it is whole wheat spaghetti.

1 Bring a large covered pot of salted water to a boil. Add the pasta, and cook until al dente. Drain the pasta, reserving about a cup of the cooking liquid.

2 While the pasta cooks, make Winter Pesto: In a food processor, whirl the tomatoes, garlic, toasted nuts, dulse flakes, fennel, salt, black pepper, and olive oil until you have a thick smooth paste. Add more salt and pepper to taste.

3 Transfer the drained pasta to a serving bowl. Toss the pasta with the Winter Pesto, adding enough of the reserved cooking liquid to help the pesto coat the pasta. Top with the tomatoes and parsley. Offer grated cheese at the table, if you wish.

VARIATIONS: Add ½ cup of grated Parmesan cheese, and omit the dulse flakes or not.

We love this pesto made with all three nuts, but sometimes we make it with only one or two kinds of nuts (1 heaping cup).

SERVING AND MENU IDEA: Serve with Roasted Sweet Potatoes (page 299) and a salad of greens dressed simply with olive oil and lemon juice.

PASTA WITH WINTER PESTO—PER 1 SERVING (OF 6)
Calories: 484, Protein: 16 g, Carbohydrate: 64 g, Dietary Fiber: 3 g, Total Fat: 22 g, Saturated Fat: 2 g, Monounsaturated Fat: 11 g, Cholesterol: 0 mg, Sodium: 111 mg

WINTER PESTO ONLY—PER 2 TABLESPOONS
Calories: 163, Protein: 4 g, Carbohydrate: 5 g, Dietary Fiber: 2 g, Total Fat: 16 g, Saturated Fat: 2 g, Monounsaturated Fat: 8 g, Cholesterol: 0 mg, Sodium: 89 mg

Vegetarian Pasta Bolognese

SERVES 6 | YIELDS ABOUT 7 CUPS SAUCE | TIME: ABOUT AN HOUR

In so many Italian-American homes, there's a pot of sauce simmering on a back burner almost every day. Well, this is that sauce, except we've crammed it full of diced vegetables—and tofu!

VEGETARIAN BOLOGNESE SAUCE

¼ CUP EXTRA-VIRGIN OLIVE OIL

2 CUPS DICED ONIONS

⅛ TEASPOON RED PEPPER FLAKES (OPTIONAL)

1 TEASPOON DRIED OREGANO

5 GARLIC CLOVES, MINCED OR PRESSED

2 CUPS DICED EGGPLANT

1 CUP DICED CARROTS

3 CUPS DICED MUSHROOMS

1 TEASPOON SALT

8 OUNCES FIRM TOFU, DICED OR CRUMBLED

1 CUP DICED RED BELL PEPPERS

1 15-OUNCE CAN DICED TOMATOES

½ CUP DRY RED WINE

2 TABLESPOONS TOMATO PASTE

⅛ TEASPOON GROUND BLACK PEPPER

⅓ CUP CHOPPED FRESH BASIL

16 OUNCES CHUNKY-SHAPED WHOLE GRAIN PASTA

GRATED PARMESAN CHEESE (OPTIONAL)

1 To make the sauce, warm the olive oil in a soup pot on medium heat. Add the onions, red pepper flakes if using, oregano, and garlic and cook, stirring occasionally, until the onions are translucent, about 10 minutes. Add the eggplant, carrots, mushrooms, and salt, cover, and cook for 5 minutes. Add the tofu and bell peppers, cover, and cook for 5 minutes. Stir in the tomatoes, wine, tomato paste, and black pepper. Simmer uncovered for 15 minutes, stirring occasionally. Stir in the basil.

2 While the sauce is simmering, bring a large pot of salted water to a boil. Add the pasta and cook until al dente. Drain the pasta and serve topped with the sauce and grated cheese, if you wish.

SERVING AND MENU IDEAS: Sprinkle with chopped fresh parsley or arugula. This hearty pasta cries out for something crisp and light, such as a leafy green salad or crudités. You'll probably want crusty bread. Finish with a fruity dessert, perhaps Simply Baked Fruit (page 319).

VEGETARIAN PASTA BOLOGNESE—PER 1 SERVING (OF 6) *Calories: 462, Protein: 18 g, Carbohydrate: 76 g, Dietary Fiber: 5 g, Total Fat: 12 g, Saturated Fat: 2 g, Monounsaturated Fat: 7 g, Cholesterol: 0 mg, Sodium: 522 mg*

VEGETARIAN PASTA BOLOGNESE SAUCE ONLY— PER 1 CUP *Calories: 198, Protein: 6 g, Carbohydrate: 19 g, Dietary Fiber: 5 g, Total Fat: 11 g, Saturated Fat: 1 g, Monounsaturated Fat: 7 g, Cholesterol: 0 mg, Sodium: 516 mg*

STEWS

Spanish Stew

SERVES 3 OR 4 | YIELDS 6 GENEROUS CUPS | TIME: 50 MINUTES

Sunny, bright flavors set this hearty, colorful stew apart. We like it best when topped with a dollop of Romesco Sauce.

2 TABLESPOONS OLIVE OIL

1½ CUPS CHOPPED ONIONS

1½ CUPS CHOPPED RED OR YELLOW BELL PEPPERS

2 GARLIC CLOVES, MINCED OR PRESSED

½ TEASPOON SALT

2 BAY LEAVES

½ TEASPOON DRIED THYME

2 TEASPOONS SWEET PAPRIKA

¼ TEASPOON RED PEPPER FLAKES

½ CUP DRY SHERRY

1½ CUPS CUBED PEELED SWEET POTATOES OR WINTER SQUASH

1 15-OUNCE CAN DICED TOMATOES

½ CUP WATER

2 CUPS GREEN BEANS CUT IN HALF

1 15-OUNCE CAN BUTTER BEANS, DRAINED

ROMESCO SAUCE (PAGE 74)

1 In a soup pot on medium heat, warm the olive oil and cook the onions, bell peppers, and garlic for about 5 minutes, stirring often, until the vegetables soften. Add the salt, bay leaves, thyme, paprika, and red pepper flakes, and cook for 3 minutes or so; stir often and lower the heat if necessary to avoid scorching. Add the sherry, sweet potatoes, tomatoes, and water, cover and bring to a boil; then lower the heat and simmer for 5 minutes.

2 Add the green beans and butter beans and simmer until the green beans and sweet potatoes are tender but firm, 10 to 15 minutes.

3 Remove the bay leaves, and add more salt to taste. Top each serving with a dollop of Romesco Sauce.

SERVING AND MENU IDEAS: If you don't top the stew with Romesco Sauce, try chopped Spanish olives and/or hard-boiled eggs. Serve this filling stew with a crisp green salad, such as Curly Endive with Hazelnuts, Raspberries, and Manchego (page 85), Spinach Salad with Chèvre and Walnuts (page 84), or Arugula, Kumquat, Walnut, and Fig Salad (page 95).

SPANISH STEW—PER 1 CUP *Calories: 207, Protein: 7 g, Carbohydrate: 32 g, Dietary Fiber: 9 g, Total Fat: 5 g, Saturated Fat: 1 g, Monounsaturated Fat: 3 g, Cholesterol: 0 mg, Sodium: 224 mg*

Italian Stew with Winter Squash and Chickpeas

SERVES 4 TO 6 | YIELDS ABOUT 8 CUPS | TIME: 1 HOUR

Every single ingredient in this colorful stew is nutritious. (A few are often on those regularly released lists of "top ten super foods.") But to enjoy such a flavorful, hearty melange, you probably don't need to know that you're getting potassium, iron, lycopene, beta-carotene, calcium, protein, fiber, folic acid, and vitamins A and C, among other good things.

3 CUPS CHOPPED ONIONS

1½ TEASPOONS SALT

2 TABLESPOONS OLIVE OIL

6 GARLIC CLOVES, MINCED OR PRESSED

½ TEASPOON GROUND CORIANDER

½ TEASPOON DRIED THYME

¼ TEASPOON GROUND BLACK PEPPER

2 CUPS WATER

2 CUPS DICED PEELED BUTTERNUT SQUASH

1 15-OUNCE CAN CHICKPEAS, DRAINED

1 28-OUNCE CAN DICED TOMATOES

1 CUP DICED CARROTS

½ CUP DICED BELL PEPPERS (OPTIONAL)

5 CUPS CHOPPED KALE (SEE NOTE)

1 TABLESPOON CHOPPED FRESH BASIL

2 TEASPOONS RED WINE VINEGAR

NOTE: Bunches of kale vary noticeably in weight and in the amount of yellowing or wilted leaves and large center stems. You'll probably need about a pound of kale to get about 5 cups of sorted, stemmed, and chopped kale.

1 In a soup pot on medium-high heat, cook the onions and salt in the oil, stirring often, until very soft and beginning to caramelize, 12 to 15 minutes.

2 Add the garlic, coriander, thyme, and black pepper and stir for a minute. Stir in the water, squash, chickpeas, tomatoes, carrots, and bell peppers. Cover and bring to a boil. Reduce the heat and simmer until the vegetables are tender, about 15 minutes.

3 Stir in the kale, cover, and simmer for 5 to 10 minutes, until the greens are tender but still bright green. Stir in the basil and vinegar.

SERVING AND MENU IDEAS: This dish is a complete meal with the addition of a simple green salad and bread, or when served over quinoa, polenta, or brown rice. A Mediterranean-style dessert is most appropriate, perhaps Figs Baked with Chèvre and Pistachios (page 315) or simply fresh fruit and cheese.

ITALIAN STEW WITH WINTER SQUASH AND CHICKPEAS—PER 1 CUP *Calories: 315, Protein: 14 g, Carbohydrate: 53 g, Dietary Fiber: 14 g, Total Fat: 7 g, Saturated Fat: 1 g, Monounsaturated Fat: 3 g, Cholesterol: 0 mg, Sodium: 488 mg*

Thai Red Curry

SERVES 4 | YIELDS ABOUT 7 CUPS | TIME: 50 MINUTES

A delectable curry that is well paired with brown rice or whole grain pasta to soak up the highly flavored sauce.

8 OUNCES FIRM TOFU, CUT INTO ¾-INCH CUBES

2 TABLESPOONS SOY SAUCE

1 TABLESPOON GRATED PEELED GINGER ROOT

4 TEASPOONS VEGETABLE OIL

3 GARLIC CLOVES, MINCED

¼ CUP MINCED SHALLOTS OR ONIONS

1 TABLESPOON THAI RED CURRY PASTE (SEE NOTE)

1 14-OUNCE CAN COCONUT MILK

1 CUP WATER

2 KEIFFER LIME LEAVES (OPTIONAL)

1 CUP ¼-INCH-THICK DIAGONALLY SLICED CARROTS

3 CUPS BITE-SIZED CAULIFLOWER FLORETS

1 CUP CUT GREEN BEANS (2-INCH PIECES)

1 RED OR YELLOW BELL PEPPER, CUT INTO 2-INCH STRIPS

½ CUP CHOPPED FRESH BASIL OR CILANTRO OR BOTH

1 TABLESPOON LIME JUICE

1   In a bowl, toss together the tofu cubes, soy sauce, and 1 teaspoon of the grated ginger. Set aside for at least 10 or 15 minutes while you prepare the vegetables. Then drain the tofu cubes, reserving the marinade.

2   In a skillet on medium heat, warm 2 teaspoons of the oil and add the drained tofu cubes. Cook for about 5 minutes, stirring occasionally, until the tofu is golden. Set aside.

3   In a soup pot on medium-high heat, warm the remaining 2 teaspoons of oil, add the remaining 2 teaspoons of ginger and the garlic, shallots, and red curry paste, and cook for about a minute, stirring constantly to prevent scorching. Stir in the coconut milk, water, and lime leaves, if using, and bring to a boil on high heat. Stir in the carrots and cauliflower, bring back to a boil, reduce the heat, and simmer for 5 minutes. Add the green beans and simmer for 2 minutes. Add the bell peppers, basil, tofu cubes, and reserved marinade. Return to a simmer for 2 or 3 minutes, until all of the vegetables are crisp-tender. Stir in the lime juice and add salt and more curry paste to taste.

NOTE: Know your curry paste. Hotness varies, so start modestly—you can add more later.

VARIATIONS: Substitute your favorite vegetables for those we call for in this recipe, but try for a variety of colors. Try sweet potatoes for the carrots, asparagus or snow peas for the green beans. Baby corn and straw mushrooms are good additions.

SERVING AND MENU IDEAS: Serve on brown rice or whole grain pasta, garnished with lime wedges and topped with chopped peanuts or cashews.

THAI RED CURRY—PER 1 CUP *Calories: 215, Protein: 6 g, Carbohydrate: 13 g, Dietary Fiber: 4 g, Total Fat: 17 g, Saturated Fat: 12 g, Monounsaturated Fat: 2 g, Cholesterol: 0 mg, Sodium: 326 mg*

Hot and Sour Tofu and Cabbage Stew

SERVES 6 TO 8 | YIELDS ABOUT 12 CUPS | TIME: 35 MINUTES

With a variety of tastes, this easy, wholesome stew makes a great simple supper. The flavors intensify as it simmers. Make it as hot and/or sour as you like by adding more chili paste and/or vinegar.

1 TABLESPOON VEGETABLE OIL

2 CUPS CHOPPED ONIONS

1 GREEN BELL PEPPER, CHOPPED

6 CUPS CHOPPED CABBAGE

2 CUPS VEGETABLE BROTH (SEE PAGE 33)

1 28-OUNCE CAN DICED TOMATOES

3 TABLESPOONS SOY SAUCE

2 TEASPOONS CHINESE CHILI PASTE, OR TO TASTE

2 TABLESPOONS CIDER VINEGAR OR WHITE VINEGAR

1 TABLESPOON GRATED PEELED GINGER ROOT (OPTIONAL)

1 CAKE OF FIRM TOFU (ABOUT 16 OUNCES)

GROUND BLACK PEPPER

1 In a soup pot on medium-high heat, warm the oil and cook the onions, bell peppers, and cabbage, stirring frequently, for 8 to 10 minutes, until the onions are translucent and the cabbage is beginning to wilt.

2 Stir in the broth, tomatoes, soy sauce, chili paste, vinegar, and ginger, if using. Cut the tofu into small cubes (about ½-inch) and add to the stew. Cover and bring to a simmer. Simmer for about 10 minutes. Add black pepper to taste.

SERVING AND MENU IDEAS: Serve with whole grain bread or on brown rice. After the hot and sour stew, something sweet is in order. Try Simply Baked Fruit (page 319) or Pineapple-Cinnamon Popsicles (page 321).

HOT AND SOUR TOFU AND CABBAGE STEW—PER 1 CUP *Calories: 72, Protein: 4 g, Carbohydrate: 10 g, Dietary Fiber: 3 g, Total Fat: 2 g, Saturated Fat: 0 g, Monounsaturated Fat: 1 g, Cholesterol: 0 mg, Sodium: 275 mg*

Tempeh Bourgignon

SERVES 4 TO 6 | YIELDS ABOUT 6 CUPS | TIME: 45 MINUTES

Not only is tempeh low in fat and high in fiber and protein, it also has the wonderful ability to soak up flavors. Mushrooms, red wine, and fresh thyme give this stew richness and depth.

3 TABLESPOONS OLIVE OIL

1 ½ CUPS CHOPPED ONIONS

4 GARLIC CLOVES, MINCED OR PRESSED

2 BAY LEAVES

½ TEASPOON SALT

½ CUP CHOPPED CELERY

1 CUP CHOPPED CARROTS

1 CUP CHOPPED FENNEL BULB

4 CUPS COARSELY CHOPPED MUSHROOMS

8 OUNCES TEMPEH, CUT INTO ½-INCH CUBES

½ CUP DRY RED WINE

1 15-OUNCE CAN DICED TOMATOES

1 TABLESPOON DIJON MUSTARD (OPTIONAL)

2 TABLESPOONS MINCED FRESH THYME

¼ TEASPOON GROUND BLACK PEPPER

1 TABLESPOON SOY SAUCE

CHOPPED FENNEL FRONDS OR FRESH PARSLEY (OPTIONAL)

1 In a soup pot on medium heat, warm the olive oil and cook the onions, garlic, bay leaves, and salt for about 5 minutes. Add the celery, carrots, fennel, and mushrooms and cook, stirring frequently, until the mushrooms begin to release juice, about 10 minutes.

2 Stir in the tempeh, red wine, and tomatoes, and bring to a boil. Reduce the heat and simmer, covered, for about 15 minutes, stirring occasionally.

3 Stir in the Dijon mustard if using, the thyme, black pepper, and soy sauce and simmer, covered, for about 5 minutes. When the stew is done, stir in chopped fennel fronds or parsley, if desired.

SERVING AND MENU IDEAS: This stew is great served with a hearty bread to sop up the juices. A salad of sharp-tasting greens such as arugula or frisee would be good. Or think French and serve with Celeriac Apple Slaw (page 94).

TEMPEH BOURGIGNON—PER 1 CUP *Calories: 181, Protein: 9 g, Carbohydrate: 15 g, Dietary Fiber: 3 g, Total Fat: 10 g, Saturated Fat: 2 g, Monounsaturated Fat: 5 g, Cholesterol: 0 mg, Sodium: 397 mg*

Oaxacan Green Mole Stew

SERVES 6 | YIELDS ABOUT 2 CUPS MOLE | YIELDS ABOUT 10 CUPS STEW WITH MOLE | TIME: 45 MINUTES

This Moosewood version of Oaxacan mole verde has a fabulous complexity and depth. We incorporate herbs and spices readily available in North American groceries.

STEW

1 TABLESPOON OLIVE OIL

2½ CUPS CHOPPED ONIONS

2 GARLIC CLOVES, MINCED OR PRESSED

2 TEASPOONS GROUND FENNEL SEEDS

2 CUPS GREEN BEANS CUT INTO 2-INCH PIECES

4 CUPS SLICED ZUCCHINI AND/OR YELLOW SQUASH (¼-INCH-THICK SEMICIRCLES)

1½ CUPS FRESH OR FROZEN CORN KERNELS

2 15-OUNCE CANS SMALL WHITE BEANS, RINSED AND DRAINED

1 CUP WATER

MOLE VERDE

1 13-OUNCE CAN TOMATILLOS, DRAINED

½ CUP PACKED FRESH PARSLEY

½ CUP PACKED FRESH CILANTRO

3 GARLIC CLOVES, ROUGHLY CHOPPED

2 FRESH CHILES, CHOPPED

1 TABLESPOON LIME JUICE

1 TEASPOON GROUND CUMIN

¼ TEASPOON GROUND CINNAMON

⅛ TEASPOON GROUND BLACK PEPPER

⅛ TEASPOON GROUND CLOVES

1   Warm the oil in a soup pot on medium-high heat. Add the onions, cover, and cook for 8 minutes until golden-translucent, stirring occasionally. Stir in the garlic, fennel, and green beans and cook for 5 minutes, stirring frequently. Add the squash, corn, white beans, and water. Cover and bring to a simmer, then lower the heat to medium and cook until the squash begins to soften, about 5 minutes.

2   Meanwhile, combine all of the mole ingredients in a blender or food processor and whirl until very smooth. When the squash is just tender, pour the green mole sauce into the stew, return to a simmer, and cook for 10 minutes. Add salt to taste.

VARIATION: Use fresh tomatillos (about a pound). Remove the husks, cut in half, and place in a shallow baking dish, cut side up and in a single layer. Roast in a preheated 450° oven for 30 to 35 minutes, until soft.

SERVING AND MENU IDEAS: Really delicious topped with crumbled tortilla chips and sour cream or grated cheese. Or serve with Sesame Flaxseed Cornbread (page 48) or on brown rice. Good on the side are Watermelon Salad (page 99) or a green salad with Avocado Citrus Dressing (page 109). For dessert, something mild and creamy, like Our Healthiest Cheesecake Pie (page 332).

OAXACAN GREEN MOLE STEW—PER 1 CUP
Calories: 182, Protein: 9 g, Carbohydrate: 34 g, Dietary Fiber: 8 g, Total Fat: 3 g, Saturated Fat: 0 g, Monounsaturated Fat: 1 g, Cholesterol: 0 mg, Sodium: 20 mg

MOLE VERDE ONLY—PER ⅓ CUP   *Calories: 33, Protein: 1 g, Carbohydrate: 6 g, Dietary Fiber: 2 g, Total Fat: 1 g, Saturated Fat: 0 g, Monounsaturated Fat: 0 g, Cholesterol: 0 mg, Sodium: 8 mg*

Japanese Winter Stew

SERVES 4 TO 6 | YIELDS ABOUT 8 CUPS | TIME: 50 MINUTES

The base of this light yet nourishing and filling winter vegetable stew is a classic Japanese broth flavored with kombu seaweed and dried shiitake mushrooms. Miso enhances umami, and chiles and ginger add warmth.

---

1 TABLESPOON VEGETABLE OIL

2 CUPS DICED ONIONS

1 FRESH CHILE, MINCED

1 TABLESPOON GRATED PEELED GINGER ROOT

SALT

4 CUPS WATER

2 PIECES KOMBU SEAWEED
(5 OR 6 INCHES LONG) (SEE PAGE 162)

6 DRIED SHIITAKE MUSHROOMS

1 CUP PEELED AND DICED TURNIPS

3 CUPS PEELED AND DICED SWEET POTATOES

1 SMALL BUNCH OF MUSTARD GREENS
(ABOUT 4 CUPS CHOPPED)

1 CAKE OF FIRM TOFU (ABOUT 16 OUNCES)

¼ CUP LIGHT MISO

---

1 In a soup pot on medium heat, warm the vegetable oil. Add the onions, chiles, and ginger and sprinkle with salt. Cook, stirring frequently, until the onions begin to soften, about 5 minutes. Add the water, kombu, and shiitakes. Cover the pot, increase the heat, and bring to a near boil. Add the turnips and sweet potatoes and simmer covered until the vegetables are tender, about 10 minutes.

2 Meanwhile, remove the center ribs of the mustard greens and chop the leaves. Cut the tofu into bite-sized cubes.

3 Remove the kombu pieces and the shiitakes. When the shiitakes are cool enough to handle, squeeze the liquid into the pot. Remove the stems; dice the caps and add to the pot.

4 Add the greens and tofu to the pot. In a cup, stir the miso with enough of the stew's broth to make a smooth sauce and then stir into the pot. After adding the miso, don't let the stew boil.

VARIATION: In place of mustard greens, use fresh or frozen collards or spinach.

SERVING AND MENU IDEAS: Garnish with scallions and a few drops of dark sesame oil. For a little extra flavor and brightness, add a splash of mirin, vinegar, or lemon juice to each bowl of stew. Serve small bowls of plain brown rice to accompany the brothy stew. Cooked beets with Umeboshi Dressing (page 108) is an interesting side dish. For dessert have Simply Baked Fruit (page 319).

JAPANESE WINTER STEW—PER 1 CUP *Calories: 147, Protein: 7 g, Carbohydrate: 22 g, Dietary Fiber: 4 g, Total Fat: 4 g, Saturated Fat: 0 g, Monounsaturated Fat: 1 g, Cholesterol: 0 mg, Sodium: 381 mg*

Vegetable Stew with Gremolata

SERVES 4 TO 6 | YIELDS ABOUT 10 CUPS | TIME: 50 MINUTES

Gremolata is a simple herb condiment made with parsley and lemon zest. Its bright flavor adds complexity to this stew.

GREMOLATA

GRATED ZEST OF 2 LEMONS

1½ CUPS MINCED FRESH PARSLEY

2 GARLIC CLOVES, MINCED OR PRESSED

½ TEASPOON SALT

⅛ TEASPOON GROUND BLACK PEPPER

VEGETABLE STEW

2 TABLESPOONS OLIVE OIL

2 CUPS CHOPPED ONIONS

3 GARLIC CLOVES, MINCED OR PRESSED

2 CUPS DIAGONALLY SLICED CARROTS (CUT IN HALF LENGTHWISE IF LARGE)

2 FRESH FENNEL BULBS, SLICED (ABOUT 4 CUPS)

1 TABLESPOON DRIED MARJORAM

2 TEASPOONS DRIED THYME

1 CUP WATER

1 CUP DRY WHITE WINE

1 15-OUNCE CAN QUARTERED ARTICHOKE HEARTS, UNDRAINED

1 BELL PEPPER, CUT INTO 1-INCH CHUNKS

1 15-OUNCE CAN WHITE BEANS

2 TEASPOONS SALT

¼ TEASPOON GROUND BLACK PEPPER

2 CUPS FRESH OR FROZEN EDAMAME

1 To make the gremolata, stir together the lemon zest, parsley, garlic, salt, and pepper. Set aside.

2 Heat the oil in a soup pot on medium heat. Add the onions and garlic, cover, and cook for about 3 minutes. Add the carrots, fennel, marjoram, thyme, water, wine, and artichoke hearts. Cover and bring to a boil. Reduce the heat to a simmer and cook covered until the carrots are just crisp-tender. Add the bell peppers and simmer for a minute; then add the white beans (undrained), salt, and black pepper. Simmer until the stew is hot.

3 A few minutes before serving, add the edamame and cook until tender. Top each bowl of stew with gremolata.

VARIATION: For the edamame, substitute green peas or diagonally sliced sugar snap peas, asparagus, snow peas, or green beans.

SERVING AND MENU IDEAS: Serve with whole grain bread and a fine cheese. Follow the stew with Whole Grain Crêpes Filled with Chocolate and Walnuts (page 328) or Silken Chocolate Pudding (page 335).

VEGETABLE STEW WITH GREMOLATA—PER 1 CUP
Calories: 211, Protein: 8 g, Carbohydrate: 26 g, Dietary Fiber: 9 g, Total Fat: 8 g, Saturated Fat: 1 g, Monounsaturated Fat: 4 g, Cholesterol: 0 mg, Sodium: 670 mg

VEGANISM

The word "vegan" was coined by Donald Watson of Britain to describe a vegetarian who neither eats nor uses animal products. Watson was born in 1910 and lived to be ninety-five years old. He produced a newsletter called *The Vegan News,* which described veganism as "the practice of living on fruits, nuts, vegetables, grains, and other wholesome non-animal products."

A vegan diet of plant-based foods is more restricted than the usual vegetarian diet. Vegetarians do not eat meat, poultry, seafood, or fish. Vegans, in addition to eliminating animal protein, do not eat animal products such as eggs, dairy products, and honey. Strict vegans do not wear or use animal by-products such as leather, fur, silk, wool, or cosmetics and soaps derived from animal products. Other commonly avoided animal by-products include gelatin, lanolin, rennet, whey, beeswax, and shellac.

People decide to be vegan for health, environmental, and ethical reasons. Commonly cited reasons for choosing to be a vegan are 1) ethical or moral convictions regarding animal rights and the inhumane conditions often associated with meat production, 2) concern for the environment, 3) a belief that a vegan diet is healthful, and

4) spiritual or religious beliefs and practices that support or dovetail with vegan principles.

Of particular concern to many vegans are the widely criticized practices involved in factory farming and animal testing, and the intensive use of land and other resources required for animal farming. One point of view is that animal agriculture takes a devastating toll on the earth and is an inefficient way of producing food; vegans extend this criticism to the egg and dairy industries as well as the meat industry.

Vegan diets have been credited with lowering the risk of heart attack, colon cancer, prostate cancer, high blood pressure, high cholesterol, and stroke. By simply not eating meat, dairy products, and eggs, vegans avoid consuming food that contains substances such as growth hormones and antibiotics, which are often given to intensively farmed animals in countries where this is legal. Because they are similar to human hormones, growth promoters such as anabolic steroids that are used in cattle farming in the United States may negatively affect human fetal and child development. Although investigations are not yet conclusive, the use of such growth promoters is illegal throughout much of Europe.

It is important that vegans learn how

to satisfy all of the body's many nutritional needs within the framework of the vegan diet, and heed mainstream guidelines regarding balanced and adequate nutrition standards.

The key to a nutritionally sound vegan diet is variety. A healthy and varied vegan diet includes fruits, vegetables, plenty of leafy greens, whole grain products, nuts, seeds, and legumes. Good vegan sources of protein include potatoes, whole wheat bread, rice, broccoli, spinach, almonds, peas, beans, peanut butter, tofu, soymilk, lentils, and kale. Iron-rich foods include soybeans, lentils, blackstrap molasses, kidney beans, chickpeas, black-eyed peas, seitan, Swiss chard, tempeh, black beans, prune juice, beet greens, tahini, peas, figs, bulghur, bok choy, raisins, watermelon, and millet. Iron absorption is greatly enhanced by eating foods containing vitamin C along with foods containing iron.

Vegan diets can be low in levels of calcium, iodine, omega-3 fatty acids, and vitamins B_{12} and D. Vegans are advised to eat high-calcium foods, such as fortified soymilk, fortified orange juice, dark green vegetables, blackstrap molasses, and tofu processed with calcium sulfate, and take a calcium supplement as necessary (although most research suggests that dietary calcium is preferred over supplements). In countries where salt is not iodized, vegans may need to take a vegan multivitamin that contains iodine, or regularly eat kelp, a common seaweed high in iodine. To ensure adequate B_{12} intake, the Vegan Society, among others, recommends that vegans consistently eat foods fortified with B_{12} or take a B_{12} supplement. Fortified soymilk is a good source of vitamin D for vegans. Adequate amounts of vitamin D may also be obtained by spending twenty to forty minutes every few days in outdoor sunlight.

Over the years, the proportion of Moosewood recipes that are vegan has steadily increased, both in the restaurant and in our cookbooks. This is because our taste has changed—this is the food we like to eat now. It tastes better than rich, cheesy foods, and we're convinced that eating fewer animal products is better for us, better for the environment, and better for the cows, pigs, and chickens.

Mushroom, Peanut, Tofu Stew with Greens

SERVES 4 TO 6 | YIELDS ABOUT 12 CUPS | TIME: 45 MINUTES

For more than three decades at Moosewood Restaurant, we've made variations of this stew, and this is our latest favorite. The combination of tomatoes, ginger, and ground peanuts is common to the cuisines of many countries in West Africa. In this spin-off, we've added chunks of chewy mushrooms and smooth tofu, and we think that this hearty, rich stew makes a satisfying and nourishing supper or lunch all by itself. Leftovers are even more delicious.

1 TABLESPOON VEGETABLE OIL

2 CUPS CHOPPED ONIONS

1 ½ CUPS CHOPPED CELERY

1 TEASPOON SALT

4 CUPS SLICED MUSHROOMS
(CREMINI OR WHITE)

2 TABLESPOONS GRATED PEELED GINGER
ROOT

1 28-OUNCE CAN DICED TOMATOES

3 CUPS WATER

1 CAKE OF FIRM TOFU (ABOUT 16 OUNCES),
DICED

3 CUPS CHOPPED FRESH OR FROZEN
COLLARDS OR KALE

½ CUP PEANUT BUTTER

¼ TO ½ CUP CHOPPED FRESH CILANTRO

1 In a soup pot on medium heat, warm the oil. Add the onions, celery, and salt, cover, and cook until soft, about 10 minutes. Stir in the mushrooms and ginger and cook covered, stirring occasionally, for 10 minutes.

2 Add the tomatoes, water, and tofu and bring to a boil. Reduce the heat, cover, and simmer gently for 5 minutes. Add the greens, cover, and cook, stirring now and then, until the greens are tender, about 10 minutes.

3 Meanwhile, in a small bowl, stir together the peanut butter and about 2 cups of the hot broth until smooth. When the greens are tender, stir the peanut butter and the cilantro into the pot. Add more salt to taste.

VARIATIONS: For a delicate sweetness, add a 20-ounce can of crushed pineapple when you add the tomatoes and water.

For the greens, use chard, spinach, or cabbage. If you use cabbage, add it with the tofu.

Add Tabasco or other hot pepper sauce to taste.

SERVING AND MENU IDEAS: This stew is satisfying—it doesn't call out for rice or bread. If you need more to make a meal, have fresh fruit, a green salad, or sliced cucumbers dressed with some vinegar. Or try Mango Pickles (page 68) on the side.

MUSHROOM, PEANUT, TOFU STEW WITH GREENS—
PER 1 CUP *Calories: 203, Protein: 10 g, Carbohydrate: 11 g, Dietary Fiber: 4 g, Total Fat: 14 g, Saturated Fat: 2 g, Monounsaturated Fat: 7 g, Cholesterol: 0 mg, Sodium: 333 mg*

Bulgarian Lentil and Vegetable Stew

SERVES 4 TO 6 | YIELDS ABOUT 10 CUPS | TIME: 55 MINUTES

Earthy lentils, meaty mushrooms, and lots of vegetables and herbs add up to an especially hearty and satisfying stew, perfect for chilly weather.

½ CUP FRENCH GREEN LENTILS

1 BAY LEAF (OPTIONAL)

1 GARLIC CLOVE

3 CUPS WATER

2 TABLESPOONS OLIVE OIL

1½ CUPS CHOPPED ONIONS

1 CUP CARROTS CUT INTO 1-INCH CHUNKS

½ TEASPOON SALT

3 CUPS COARSELY CHOPPED CABBAGE

2 CUPS RED OR YELLOW BELL PEPPERS CUT INTO 1-INCH CHUNKS

4 CUPS SLICED OR QUARTERED CREMINI OR OTHER MUSHROOMS (8 OUNCES)

1 TABLESPOON SWEET PAPRIKA

1 TEASPOON CHOPPED FRESH ROSEMARY

½ TEASPOON RED PEPPER FLAKES OR ¼ TEASPOON CAYENNE

1 28-OUNCE CAN DICED TOMATOES

¼ CUP RED WINE OR SHERRY

2 TABLESPOONS CHOPPED FRESH DILL

GROUND BLACK PEPPER

1 In a small pan, bring to a boil the lentils, bay leaf if using, garlic, and water. Reduce the heat to low and simmer until the lentils are tender, 20 to 30 minutes. Remove the bay leaf and drain the lentils.

2 Meanwhile, in a soup pot on medium-high heat, warm the olive oil and cook the onions, carrots, and salt for about 5 minutes, stirring frequently. Add the cabbage and bell peppers, cover, and cook on medium-low heat for 10 minutes.

3 Add the mushrooms, paprika, rosemary, and red pepper flakes, and cook for a minute, stirring to prevent the spices from sticking. Add the tomatoes and wine, cover, and simmer until the vegetables are tender, 10 to 15 minutes. Stir in the dill and cooked lentils. Add black pepper and more salt to taste.

VARIATIONS: French lentils, also called *lentilles de Puy,* are pretty, but regular brown lentils are also fine for this stew.

Substitute small cauliflower florets for the cabbage.

Add some chopped celery with the onions, or diced parsnips with the cabbage.

Substitute thyme or marjoram for the rosemary.

SERVING AND MENU IDEAS: Top with yogurt, sour cream, or crumbled feta. Great served with bread or toasted pita, or on a bed of rice or noodles.

BULGARIAN LENTIL AND VEGETABLE STEW—
PER 1 CUP *Calories: 117, Protein: 5 g, Carbohydrate: 18 g, Dietary Fiber: 6 g, Total Fat: 3 g, Saturated Fat: 0 g, Monounsaturated Fat: 2 g, Cholesterol: 0 mg, Sodium: 141 mg*

Three Sisters at Four Corners Stew

SERVES 4 TO 6 | YIELDS ABOUT 9 CUPS | TIME: 45 MINUTES

We've named this not-so-traditional stew for the trio of corn, beans, and squash that Navajos call the "three sisters," and also for the place where four states (Arizona, Utah, New Mexico, Colorado) meet, a place that's adjacent to Navajo country. A traditional Navajo stew would not include olives or edamame, but we like them in this stew, so there you are. A good stew for both hot weather and wintertime.

Many stews improve with age, and this one ages well, but it is particularly delicious right out of the pot as soon as it's hot, while the corn and edamame are still fresh and sweet. Leftovers make a great side dish.

---

3 OR 4 CUPS PEELED AND CUBED BUTTERNUT SQUASH (ABOUT 1 POUND)

3 CUPS CHOPPED ONIONS

2 TABLESPOONS OLIVE OIL

1 RED BELL PEPPER, DICED

1 FRESH CHILE, MINCED

3 GARLIC CLOVES, MINCED OR PRESSED

¾ TEASPOON SALT

⅛ TEASPOON GROUND BLACK PEPPER

1 CUP WATER

1 TABLESPOON GROUND CUMIN

1 TEASPOON DRIED THYME OR 1 TABLESPOON MINCED FRESH

2 CUPS CHOPPED FRESH TOMATOES

2 CUPS SHELLED FRESH EDAMAME OR 1 16-OUNCE PACKAGE FROZEN

2 CUPS FRESH OR FROZEN CORN KERNELS

½ CUP CHOPPED GREEN OR BLACK OLIVES

CHOPPED FRESH PARSLEY (OPTIONAL)

GRATED SHARP CHEDDAR CHEESE (OPTIONAL)

1 In a soup pot on high heat, cook the squash and onions in the oil for 5 minutes, stirring constantly. Add the bell peppers, chiles, garlic, salt, black pepper, and water, lower the heat to medium, cover, and cook until the peppers soften, about 5 minutes.

2 Stir in the cumin, thyme, tomatoes, edamame, corn, and olives. Cover and cook, stirring frequently, until the vegetables are tender, about 15 minutes. Serve topped with parsley and grated cheese, if desired.

VARIATIONS: Instead of edamame, use field peas or other beans: red, black, pinto, white, kidney, black-eyed peas, and so on.

It's good with lima beans, but frozen limas don't do well cooking in a sauce that includes tomatoes, so if you're using frozen limas, cook them separately and then add to the stew.

In place of fresh tomatoes, use a 15-ounce can of diced tomatoes.

SERVING AND MENU IDEAS: This is delicious on brown basmati rice, whole wheat couscous, quinoa, or polenta, or serve with warm corn tortillas or Sesame Flaxseed Cornbread (page 48). This stew makes an excellent side dish for Spinach Quesadillas (page 187). Peaches grow well in the desert canyons of the Southwestern United States, and they are the perfect dessert to follow this stew.

THREE SISTERS AT FOUR CORNERS STEW—PER 1 CUP *Calories: 156, Protein: 6 g, Carbohydrate: 23 g, Dietary Fiber: 5 g, Total Fat: 6 g, Saturated Fat: 1 g, Monounsaturated Fat: 3 g, Cholesterol: 0 mg, Sodium: 324 mg*

Summer Pistou

SERVES 6 TO 8 | YIELDS ABOUT 10 CUPS STEW, 1⅓ CUPS PESTO | TIME: 55 MINUTES

The flavors of this hearty and colorful vegetable and bean stew are intensified with a fresh pesto of almonds, parsley, and basil.

STEW

2 TABLESPOONS OLIVE OIL

1½ CUPS CHOPPED ONIONS

1 GARLIC CLOVE, MINCED OR PRESSED

1½ CUPS CHOPPED RED OR YELLOW BELL PEPPERS

2 CUPS GREEN BEANS CUT INTO 2-INCH PIECES

1½ CUPS WATER OR VEGETABLE BROTH (SEE PAGE 33)

4 CUPS CHOPPED YELLOW SUMMER SQUASH

1 28-OUNCE CAN DICED TOMATOES

2 15-OUNCE CANS RED BEANS OR WHITE BEANS (OR 1 OF EACH), UNDRAINED

½ TEASPOON SALT

¼ TEASPOON GROUND BLACK PEPPER

ALMOND-HERB PESTO

1 CUP TOASTED ALMONDS

1 PACKED CUP FRESH BASIL

2 PACKED CUPS FRESH PARSLEY

2 GARLIC CLOVES, PRESSED

5 TABLESPOONS EXTRA-VIRGIN OLIVE OIL

¼ TEASPOON SALT

2 TABLESPOONS LEMON JUICE

2 TO 3 TABLESPOONS WATER

1 To make the stew: Warm the olive oil in a soup pot on medium heat, add the onions, and cook for about 10 minutes. Add the garlic and bell peppers and cook for 3 to 4 minutes. Add the green beans and water and simmer for 6 to 8 minutes. When the green beans are bright green and crisp-tender, add the yellow squash, tomatoes, and red beans, and return to a simmer. Cook until all of the vegetables are tender. Add the salt and pepper.

2 To make the pesto: In a food processor, pulverize the almonds. Add the basil, parsley, garlic, olive oil, salt, and lemon juice, and pulse until well-blended. Add water if needed for the consistency you like.

3 Top each bowl of stew with a generous dollop of pesto.

VARIATIONS: Substitute zucchini for summer squash.

This stew can be served without the pesto. Just before serving, add some chopped fresh parsley and basil and stir in lemon juice to taste.

SERVING AND MENU IDEAS: With this stew, have bread, cheese, and fruit. Or a salad.

SUMMER PISTOU (STEW ONLY)—PER 1 CUP
Calories: 162, Protein: 8 g, Carbohydrate: 27 g, Dietary Fiber: 7 g, Total Fat: 3 g, Saturated Fat: 1 g, Monounsaturated Fat: 2 g, Cholesterol: 0 mg, Sodium: 149 mg

ALMOND-HERB (PESTO ONLY)—PER 2½ TABLESPOONS
Calories: 231, Protein: 6 g, Carbohydrate: 7 g, Dietary Fiber: 4 g, Total Fat: 22 g, Saturated Fat: 3 g, Monounsaturated Fat: 15 g, Cholesterol: 0 mg, Sodium: 85 mg

Tunisian Chickpea Stew

SERVES 4 TO 6 | YIELDS ABOUT 8 CUPS | TIME: 40 MINUTES

This stew of butternut squash, red bell peppers, chickpeas, and tomatoes is rich in the aromas and flavors of garlic, cumin, coriander, caraway, and hot peppers, a combination frequently found in Tunisian cuisine.

---

1 TABLESPOON OLIVE OIL

2 CUPS CHOPPED ONIONS

½ TEASPOON SALT

2 TABLESPOONS MINCED OR PRESSED GARLIC

1 OR 2 FRESH CHILES, MINCED

2 TEASPOONS GROUND CUMIN

2 TEASPOONS GROUND CORIANDER

1 TEASPOON CARAWAY SEEDS, WHOLE OR GROUND

½ TEASPOON GROUND BLACK PEPPER

4 CUPS PEELED AND CUBED BUTTERNUT SQUASH

1 CUP WATER OR VEGETABLE BROTH (SEE PAGE 33)

1 BELL PEPPER, DICED (RED, ORANGE, YELLOW, OR GREEN)

1 15-OUNCE CAN CHICKPEAS, RINSED AND DRAINED

1 15-OUNCE CAN DICED TOMATOES

2 TABLESPOONS SOY SAUCE

¼ CUP CHOPPED FRESH CILANTRO

---

1 In a soup pot on medium heat, warm the oil. Add the onions and salt, cover, and cook until the onions soften, about 7 minutes, stirring occasionally.

2 Add the garlic, chiles, cumin, coriander, caraway, and black pepper and cook for another 2 minutes, stirring often. Add the butternut squash and stir to coat with the spices. Add the water and stir well. Cover, bring to a simmer, and cook for 7 minutes.

3 Add the bell peppers, cover, and gently simmer for another 7 minutes. Stir in the chickpeas, tomatoes, soy sauce, and cilantro and simmer until the squash is quite tender. If the stew is gently simmered for an extra 15 to 20 minutes, the flavors develop and mellow.

VARIATION: For a soupier stew that's delicious served with warm flatbread, use a 12-ounce package of frozen puréed winter squash in place of fresh butternut squash. Add the bell peppers with the spices and cook for 3 or 4 minutes. Add the water and frozen squash, increase the heat to medium-high, cover, and return to a simmer. Add the chickpeas and tomatoes and return to a simmer. Stir in the soy sauce and cilantro and simmer on low heat for at least 10 minutes.

SERVING AND MENU IDEAS: Garnish with feta cheese and olives and serve with whole wheat pita bread. Or serve on whole wheat couscous or brown rice and top with toasted almonds and/or hard-boiled eggs. A small salad of sliced cucumbers or grated carrots with Shallot Vinaigrette (page 111) makes a crisp counterpoint. Then bring on a fabulous dessert, such as Fruit and Nut Truffles (page 314), to linger with over tea.

TUNISIAN CHICKPEA STEW—PER 1 CUP *Calories: 281, Protein: 13 g, Carbohydrate: 49 g, Dietary Fiber: 13 g, Total Fat: 5 g, Saturated Fat: 1 g, Monounsaturated Fat: 2 g, Cholesterol: 0 mg, Sodium: 411 mg*

RAW FOOD

RAW FOODS

Bookstores are well stocked with raw food books, and raw food restaurants are springing up all across the country, testaments to the popularity of this diet. Uncooked, nonprocessed plant foods form the basis of the raw food diet. Heating food over 116° is believed to destroy enzymes that may aid both digestion and nutrient absorption. Cooking is also thought to diminish the "life force," and in some cases the nutritional value, of food. So the raw diet consists largely of unprocessed organic foods: fresh fruits and vegetables, sprouts, seeds, nuts, raw legumes, dried fruit, seaweed, purified water, and young coconut water (juice).

The most important goal of raw food preparation is enzyme preservation. Raw or "living" foods are full of enzyme activity. Enzymes help you digest food and are the catalysts for metabolic reactions such as cell division, the work of the immune system, and brain activity. Raw foodists believe that when food is cooked, the perfect natural enzymes in the food are destroyed or denatured.

While critics of the raw food diet agree that some enzymes are killed when food is cooked, they consider this inconsequential because the body has digestive enzymes of its own. In addition, recent research shows that some phytochemicals are more easily absorbed by the body when food is cooked; carotenoids in carrots and lycopene in tomatoes, for example. Raw foodists counter that every raw food contains the perfect mix of enzymes needed to digest that particular food completely.

For well over a hundred years, there have been people practicing various raw food diets with the belief that this way of eating is one of the healthiest choices available. Early proponents include Arnold Ehret, an influential naturopath; Ann Wigmore and Viktoras Kulvinskas, the two founders of the Hippocrates Health Institute; and Norman Walker, who advocated drinking fresh-squeezed juices and who lived to be ninety-nine. Typically today, to be considered a raw foods follower, at least 75 percent of your diet must be "living" or raw.

Most of the evidence for the benefits of raw food is anecdotal. Adherents report that they feel detoxed, vibrant, and energetic. They believe strongly that there are health benefits beyond the benefits of simply eating a diet high in fruits, vegetables, nuts, and seeds. There is a sizable group of dedicated raw food eaters who believe that they regained their health by adopting the diet when other forms of standard medical care failed. Other health benefits may be weight loss, better digestion, increased energy, improved skin tone, and a reduced risk of diabetes, some cancers, and heart disease.

But there are researchers who question the advisability of a raw food diet. Some think that the human body has changed in response to eating primarily cooked foods, and that our bodies are no longer suited to digest primarily raw foods. Biological anthropologist Richard Wrangham has investigated eating patterns in current and historical cultures. He says, "We evolved to eat cooked foods. Raw food eating is not systematically practiced anywhere in the world, except for people in urban settings who are philosophically committed to raw food."

The raw food diet is low in sodium and fats and high in potassium, magnesium, phytochemicals, folate, and fiber.

Raw foods may contain bacteria or parasites that cause food-borne illnesses, and cooking can reduce the danger of disease, because it kills many bacteria. So when foods are uncooked, thorough cleaning and proper storage are essential.

We didn't include raw foods on our Moosewood menus until a few years ago, when a new young cook came to work in our kitchen. Kelly Serbonich was a chef for years at the Hippocrates Health Institute, known for its raw diet, and she has coauthored a raw food "cook" book. Some special equipment is helpful for preparing raw meals; Kelly brought in her own dehydrator and a special spiral slicer, tools we didn't have in our kitchen.

Several preparation techniques make raw foods more digestible and add variety to meals: juicing fruits and vegetables, soaking nuts and dried fruit, sprouting seeds, grains, and beans, and blending, puréeing, or dehydrating certain foods. If you're considering a raw diet, it will be helpful to stock your kitchen with a few useful devices such as a juice extractor, rotary grater, mandoline, and a dehydrator that dries foods at a temperature lower than 116°.

Since most raw dishes are made from scratch and many contain ingredients that should be soaked or sprouted, a considerable commitment of time is necessary to sustain a healthy raw food diet. Some ingredients may be hard to find locally, but can be ordered or sourced online.

For raw food recipes beyond the few we offer here, we recommend *Healthful Cuisine* by Anna Maria Clement, Ph.D., N.M.D., L.N.C., with Kelly Serbonich, and *Raw: The Uncook Book: New Vegetarian Food for Life* coauthored by Erika Lenkert and Juliano Brotman. Brotman's Los Angeles restaurant has made him a West Coast celebrity chef. Some raw food books, filled with recipes for attractive dishes, are listed in the bibliography on page 339.

The raw recipes in this book are just a small sampler, a teaser. None require special ingredients or special equipment, only a blender and food processor. If you don't wish to try an entirely raw meal, you can enjoy these tasty dishes along with cooked foods.

Green Soup

YIELDS 4 CUPS | TIME: 30 MINUTES

Fresh flavor and a wonderful shade of green. This soup will be smoother if you peel the apple and the cucumber.

1 CUP NONCHLORINATED WATER

½ CUP FRESH ORANGE JUICE

¼ CUP FRESH LEMON JUICE

1 AVOCADO

1 APPLE

1 CUCUMBER

8 OUNCES FRESH SPINACH,
LARGE STEMS REMOVED (ABOUT 4 CUPS)

1 SCALLION, CHOPPED

½ TEASPOON GROUND DRIED SEAWEED
(WAKAME, DULSE, OR ARAME)
(SEE PAGES 161–63)

1 TEASPOON LIGHT MISO

PINCH OF SEA SALT

1 GARLIC CLOVE, MINCED OR PRESSED
(OPTIONAL)

½ TEASPOON MINCED FRESH CHILES
(OPTIONAL)

1 Put the water, orange juice, and lemon juice in a blender.

2 Cut the avocado in half through the stem end, remove the pit, and with a spoon, scoop the flesh into the blender.

3 Peel the apple or not, core it, and coarsely chop. Peel the cucumber or not, and coarsely chop. Add to the blender with the rest of the ingredients and whirl until smooth. Serve right away.

SERVING AND MENU IDEAS: Garnish with nasturtiums, fresh mint, or sprigs of dill. Pair this zesty soup with Raw "Tacos" (page 268), Cauliflower "Tabouli" (page 269), or Arugula, Kumquat, Walnut, and Fig Salad (page 95) for a fabulous raw meal. It makes a stimulating starter for many cooked dishes, such as New World Pizza (page 188), Skillet Barbecue Tofu in a Pita (page 139), or Oaxacan Tlayuda (page 219).

GREEN SOUP—PER 1 CUP *Calories: 138, Protein: 4 g, Carbohydrate: 17 g, Dietary Fiber: 6 g, Total Fat: 8 g, Saturated Fat: 1 g, Monounsaturated Fat: 5 g, Cholesterol: 0 mg, Sodium: 104 mg*

Our Favorite Raw Slaw

SERVES 4 TO 6 | YIELDS ABOUT 6 GENEROUS CUPS | HANDS-ON TIME: ABOUT 20 MINUTES
MARINATING TIME: AT LEAST 30 MINUTES

This is such a quintessential dish in "living cuisine" that it will be welcome in any raw food meal. It's also an excellent slaw to serve as a side dish with cooked foods. It is colorful, crunchy, and very tasty, and is high in calcium and vitamins A and C. It's best when you have tender, young kale.

3 TABLESPOONS OLIVE OIL

2 TABLESPOONS CIDER VINEGAR

½ TEASPOON SALT

⅛ TEASPOON GROUND BLACK PEPPER

1 ½ TEASPOONS MINCED FRESH THYME

DASH OF CAYENNE

3 CUPS VERY FINELY CHOPPED KALE, RIBS REMOVED

1 CUP MINCED RED CABBAGE

1 ½ CUPS GRATED CARROTS

1 CUP GRATED APPLES

1 In a cup, whisk together the oil, vinegar, salt, pepper, thyme, and cayenne. Set aside.

2 In a bowl, toss the kale, cabbage, carrots, and apples. Pour on the marinade, stir well, and let sit at room temperature for at least 30 minutes. Add more pepper and/or fresh thyme to taste.

3 Serve at room temperature or chilled.

VARIATIONS: Sprinkle with sunflower seeds and/or top with sprouts.

SERVING AND MENU IDEAS: For a great lunch, pair with Sweet Potato, Apple, and Chipotle Soup (page 132). Serve alongside Pasta with Butternut Squash and Sage (page 238), Mushroom-Barley "Risotto" (page 280), or Spinach, Beans, and Tomatoes on Cheese Toast (page 144).

OUR FAVORITE RAW SLAW—PER 1 SERVING (OF 6), 1 CUP *Calories: 92, Protein: 1 g, Carbohydrate: 7 g, Dietary Fiber: 1 g, Total Fat: 7 g, Saturated Fat: 1 g, Monounsaturated Fat: 5 g, Cholesterol: 0 mg, Sodium: 212 mg*

Raw "Tacos"

SERVES 6 | YIELDS ABOUT 1¼ CUPS SUNFLOWER SEED "CHEESE" AND 2 CUPS FILLING | TIME: 45 MINUTES

It seems that almost every raw food "cook" book offers nut mixtures to replace the protein of meat and cheese in conventional cooking, and there's almost always a recipe called "tacos" or "burritos" in which to use those mixtures. Here's our version. Lettuce leaves replace the usual tortilla shells. The zesty walnut and sun-dried tomato filling combines nicely with the spicy sunflower seed "cheese." Together they make a tasty although somewhat messy-to-eat taco.

SUNFLOWER SEED "CHEESE"

1 CUP SUNFLOWER SEEDS

1 GARLIC CLOVE, MINCED OR PRESSED

2 TABLESPOONS SOY SAUCE (SEE NOTE)

½ CUP CHOPPED FRESH PARSLEY

¼ CUP CHOPPED FRESH CILANTRO

¼ CUP FRESH LEMON JUICE

2 TABLESPOONS NONCHLORINATED WATER

½ TO 1 FRESH CHILE, MINCED

WALNUT AND SUN-DRIED TOMATO FILLING

1 CUP SUN-DRIED TOMATOES, SOAKED

2 CUPS WALNUTS

2 GARLIC CLOVES, MINCED OR PRESSED

1½ TEASPOONS SOY SAUCE

1 TEASPOON GROUND CUMIN

1 TEASPOON GROUND CORIANDER

6 LARGE ROMAINE LETTUCE LEAVES

1 Soak the sun-dried tomatoes for the filling in warm water until softened, at least ½ hour.

2 While the sun-dried tomatoes soak, prepare the "cheese." In a food processor, whirl the sunflower seeds until crumbly. In a bowl, combine the ground sunflower seeds with the garlic, soy sauce, parsley, cilantro, lemon juice, water, and chiles, and mix well. Set aside.

3 To make the filling, drain and chop the soaked sun-dried tomatoes. In a food processor, whirl the walnuts until ground. Add the sun-dried tomatoes, garlic, soy sauce, cumin, and coriander, and pulse until it becomes a thick paste.

4 To assemble a "taco," spread about ⅓ cup of the walnut and sun-dried tomato filling along the rib of a lettuce leaf, spread with a generous dollop of sunflower "cheese," and fold the sides of the leaf up and over the filling. Eat by hand.

INGREDIENT NOTE: Nama Shoyo brand soy sauce is preferred by raw food adherents because it is not pasteurized. It contains wheat.

VARIATIONS: Use Brazil nuts in place of the sunflower seeds for a richer flavor.

Use smaller Romaine or Boston lettuce leaves: more leaves, less filling on each leaf.

SERVING AND MENU IDEAS: Embellish the "tacos" with corn, olives, tomatoes, and/or avocados. Use the sunflower seed "cheese" as a filling for vegetables such as red bell peppers, tomatoes, hollowed-out cucumber halves or avocado halves.

SUNFLOWER SEED "CHEESE"—PER 1 TABLESPOON
*Calories: 44, Protein: 2 g, Carbohydrate: 2 g,
Dietary Fiber: 1 g, Total Fat: 4 g, Saturated Fat: 0 g,
Monounsaturated Fat: 1 g, Cholesterol: 0 mg,
Sodium: 92 mg*

**WALNUT AND SUN-DRIED TOMATO FILLING—
PER ¼ CUP** *Calories: 184, Protein: 5 g,
Carbohydrate: 8 g, Dietary Fiber: 3 g, Total Fat: 17 g,
Saturated Fat: 2 g, Monounsaturated Fat: 2 g,
Cholesterol: 0 mg, Sodium: 199 mg*

Cauliflower "Tabouli"

SERVES 4 TO 6 | YIELDS ABOUT 4 CUPS | TIME: 15 MINUTES

When this raw food salad is freshly made, it is very much like traditional bulghur tabouli in both appearance and taste.

---

4 CUPS CAULIFLOWER FLORETS

¼ CUP FRESH LEMON JUICE

½ CUP EXTRA-VIRGIN OLIVE OIL

½ TEASPOON GROUND BLACK PEPPER

½ TEASPOON SALT

1 CUP MINCED FRESH PARSLEY

¼ CUP CHOPPED SCALLIONS

1 TABLESPOON CHOPPED FRESH MINT
OR 1 TEASPOON DRIED

1 CUP DICED TOMATOES

2 GARLIC CLOVES, MINCED OR PRESSED

In a food processor, pulse the cauliflower until about the size of grains of bulghur. Transfer to a serving bowl, add all of the other ingredients, and stir until well mixed. Add more salt and pepper to taste. Serve at room temperature or chilled, but it's best when served soon after you make it.

VARIATIONS: Add finely chopped cucumbers, red bell peppers, and/or black olives.

SERVING AND MENU IDEAS: For an attractive raw meal, pair this salad with Green Soup (page 266) and serve bunches of purple grapes for dessert. With cooked foods, try Cauliflower "Tabouli" with Greek Black-eyed Peas (page 218) or Greener Spanakopita (page 186).

**CAULIFLOWER "TABOULI"—PER 1 SERVING (OF 6),
⅔ CUP** *Calories: 187, Protein: 2 g, Carbohydrate: 6 g,
Dietary Fiber: 2 g, Total Fat: 18 g, Saturated Fat: 3 g,
Monounsaturated Fat: 13 g, Cholesterol: 0 mg,
Sodium: 212 mg*

Winter Squash "Rice Mexicali"

SERVES 10 | YIELDS ABOUT 5 CUPS | TIME: 30 MINUTES

Raw foodists often make dishes that mimic conventional cooked versions. Winter squash can be processed to resemble rice, and in this dish it looks like a pretty Spanish rice. We've made it with both acorn and butternut squash; acorn squash yields rice-size pieces that are drier and stay more separate, while the easier-to-peel butternut squash is brighter in color and its "rice" is more moist.

Pulse the squash cubes in a food processor in small batches to make pieces the size of cooked grains of rice. In a serving bowl, stir the tomatoes, parsley, cilantro, red onions, garlic, and salt throughout the squash "rice." Add black pepper to taste.

SERVING AND MENU IDEAS: For a whole meal of raw foods, serve on a bed of salad greens with cucumber or bell pepper slices, pitted olives, fresh avocado cubes, sprouts, slivered nuts, and/or tomatillos. This dish makes a good side salad for Southwestern Black Bean Burgers (page 154) or Spinach Quesadillas (page 187).

WINTER SQUASH "RICE MEXICALI"—PER 1 SERVING (OF 10), ½ CUP *Calories: 33, Protein: 1 g, Carbohydrate: 8 g, Dietary Fiber: 2 g, Total Fat: 0 g, Saturated Fat: 0 g, Monounsaturated Fat: 0 g, Cholesterol: 0 mg, Sodium: 238 mg*

---

4 CUPS PEELED AND CUBED BUTTERNUT OR ACORN SQUASH

2 CUPS CHOPPED FRESH TOMATOES

3 TABLESPOONS CHOPPED FRESH PARSLEY

2 TABLESPOONS CHOPPED FRESH CILANTRO

1 TABLESPOON MINCED RED ONIONS

1 GARLIC CLOVE, MINCED OR PRESSED

1 TEASPOON SALT

GROUND BLACK PEPPER

Date-Nut Fruit Smoothies

SERVES 2 | YIELDS ABOUT 2 CUPS | TIME: 10 MINUTES

These substantial and nutritious smoothies are just sweet enough. Serve them for breakfast, snack, or even dessert. Dates are the most common sweetener in living cuisine because they are unprocessed and naturally delicious. Raw foodies often soak nuts before using because soaking activates enzymes that make nuts easier to digest, and it also neutralizes phylates in the nut bran that inhibit mineral absorption.

In a blender, whirl all of the ingredients at high speed until smooth, 30 to 60 seconds.

NOTE: If your blender doesn't handle the nuts and dates (if there are chunks in your smoothie, and you don't like them), try soaking the nuts and/or dates first: soak in water to cover plus a couple of inches for 1 to 2 hours.

SERVING AND MENU IDEAS: For a raw breakfast, serve with apple slices and sunflower seeds. And if you're not a raw foodist, these smoothies are really good with Breakfast Muffins (page 52) or Blueberry and Almond Quick Bread (page 51). To serve as dessert, pour the smoothie into tall, chilled glasses and garnish with fresh fruit or serve with cookies.

BANANA ORANGE DATE-NUT SMOOTHIE

1 CUP FRESH ORANGE JUICE

¼ CUP BRAZIL NUTS

1 RIPE BANANA

6 DATES, CHOPPED

STRAWBERRY DATE-NUT SMOOTHIE

1½ CUPS STEMMED STRAWBERRIES

3 TABLESPOONS RAW ALMOND BUTTER OR PEANUT BUTTER

6 DATES, CHOPPED

½ CUP NONCHLORINATED WATER

½ CUP FRESH ORANGE JUICE

BANANA ORANGE DATE-NUT SMOOTHIE—
PER 1 SERVING (OF 2), 1 CUP
Calories: 293, Protein: 5 g, Carbohydrate: 47 g, Dietary Fiber: 5 g, Total Fat: 12 g, Saturated Fat: 3 g, Monounsaturated Fat: 4 g, Cholesterol: 0 mg, Sodium: 3 mg

STRAWBERRY DATE-NUT SMOOTHIE—
PER 1 SERVING (OF 2), 1 CUP *Calories: 285, Protein: 5 g, Carbohydrate: 39 g, Dietary Fiber: 5 g, Total Fat: 15 g, Saturated Fat: 1 g, Monounsaturated Fat: 9 g, Cholesterol: 0 mg, Sodium: 112 mg*

GRAINS

WHOLE GRAINS

When Moosewood Restaurant opened back in 1973, there were a few small voices championing the benefits of eating whole grains instead of refined grains, and they made sense to us. We preferred the taste of whole grains, although none of us fully understood their health benefits. Every day since day one, whole wheat bread and brown rice have been on our menu.

Fast-forward thirty-five years. Today, the Food and Drug Administration (FDA), the United States Department of Agriculture (USDA), and most nutritional and medical authorities say that eating whole grains in conjunction with other foods that are low in saturated fats (fruits, vegetables, beans) may help reduce the risk of heart disease and certain cancers. On the basis of evidence culled from studies involving over 300,000 participants, the FDA and USDA recommend eating two and a half servings of whole grains daily (a serving is one cup of whole grain cereal or cooked grain, or a slice of whole grain bread). Further analysis of these studies by the Yale and Harvard schools of public health revealed that a regular diet of whole grain products is also associated with a reduced risk of type 2 diabetes and gastrointestinal disorders. There is accumulating evidence that eating whole grains can help control weight gain, which has been tied to the above conditions.

The average American eats just one half of a serving of whole grains daily. Could it be that consumers are unaware of the metabolic and protective benefits of whole grains, benefits not supplied by other foods? Cornell University nutrition researcher Dr. Rui Hai Liu succinctly explains this process: "Different plant foods have different phytochemicals. These substances go to different organs, tissues, and cells, where they perform different functions. What your body needs to ward off disease is this synergistic effect, this teamwork, that is produced by eating a wide variety of plant foods, including whole grains."

So what are whole grains? With minor exceptions, they are whole seeds of grasses that have been cultivated for food, like brown rice, barley, millet, wheat groats, spelt berries, and quinoa. The term also refers to whole seeds that have been cracked, like bulghur, or rolled and flaked, like oats for oatmeal, or ground into flour or meal, like wheat, rye, buckwheat, and corn.

Scientists believe that the health benefits of grains involve every part of the seeds. The seed (also known as the kernel, groat, or berry) is composed of three parts. The outer layer is the bran that houses the grain's fiber and most of its rich store of B vitamins, minerals, and protein. The largest portion of the grain is the endosperm, which primarily supplies complex carbohydrates, protein, and a small amount of B vitamins. The smallest segment is the germ, a rich repository of antioxidant vitamins and minerals, healthful unsaturated oils, and a host of phytonutrients that support antioxidant activity and are catalysts for many essential physiological processes. The bran and germ of whole grains are particularly valuable sources of the essential minerals selenium, manganese, magnesium, and copper, all of which are in short supply in the average American diet.

When grains are refined, as are white flour and white rice, the bran and germ are largely removed through the milling and polishing process. The endosperm remains, and from the endosperm we get complex carbohydrates—but a host of other nutrients have been lost in the refining process. What about "enriched" or "fortified" white flour products and white rice—can't they be as healthful as whole grain products? By law in the United States, refined grain products must be enriched by reintroducing vitamins B_1 and B_2 and iron, though not at their original levels. There are at least four other B vitamins and seven nutrients, fiber, and essential fatty acids (omega-6 and omega-3) that are reduced by half during refining and

not replaced. Second, there is debate about the food value of isolated chemical nutrients that are reintroduced into a food. Does that nutrient have the same value as in its natural state, and can it perform the same synergistic, protective, and enzymatic functions, especially if many of its cohorts are out of proportion, or in some cases absent?

The vitamins, minerals, fiber, and phytochemicals largely concentrated in the bran and the germ are thought to be protective of the heart and vascular system, and are associated with reduced risk of certain cancers, type 2 diabetes, and weight gain. The fiber and phytonutrients in whole grains have been found to lower and control cholesterol levels and thereby contribute to heart health. The fiber in whole grains is associated with colon health. A review of colonoscopy reports found that patients who regularly ate whole grains had many fewer precancerous polyps than those whose diets did not regularly include whole grains. Other nutrients found in the germ of whole grains that have been associated with cancer prevention are antioxidants and anti-inflammatories, specifically vitamin E and selenium.

The bran fiber also slows down the metabolism of complex carbohydrates, which may protect against overeating and the development of insulin resistance. Fiber reduces overeating in part because of the satiety experienced when food sticks around longer in the stomach, but also because without the fiber (as in refined grains), metabolism is much quicker, triggering an insulin response followed by a dramatic drop in glucose and then a surge of hunger. People who consumed the majority of their fiber from whole grains were 49 percent less likely to gain weight when compared to the group that ate mostly refined grains. Surges in hunger beg for quick fixes, and that often means more refined carbs; this continuous triggering may cause exhaustion of the insulin response, which is thought to be responsible for type 2 diabetes.

These are compelling reasons to make the transition from refined grains to whole grains, but also, whole grains just plain taste good. There may be a period of adjustment if you've eaten mostly refined grains, but soon you'll appreciate the variety and depth of flavor of a food group that you may have considered just filler. You may find yourself enjoying your carbohydrates more and eating less of them.

BARLEY

Barley has a rich, nut-like flavor and an appealing chewy, pasta-like consistency. The most common forms of barley are hulled and pearled. The inedible outermost hull of the grain is all that is removed in hulled barley, sometimes called "dehulled barley." This makes for a chewier grain that requires more soaking and cooking, that is more nutritious than pearled barley.

Pearled barley is produced by various degrees of polishing. In the case of small, round, whitish pearled barley, the grain's bran layer and parts of its inner endosperm layer are removed in addition to the outermost hull. Pearled barley is less chewy and cooks faster than hulled barley. Look in the natural foods store or the bulk section of the supermarket for larger, brown-colored pearled barley that is less polished. Hull-less barley is an heirloom variety that is easily threshed free from the hull and so requires less processing.

Barley contains more fiber than any other grain. One cup of cooked hulled barley provides 54 percent of the USDA's recommended daily allowance for fiber and 52 percent of the recommended daily allowance for selenium, a potent antioxidant. Our new vegetable barley soups are hands-down favorites among our customers. And we love the barley "risotto" we developed for this book (page 280). See pages 18–19 for basic cooking information. Barley is wheat-free but not gluten-free.

BROWN RICE

Brown rice is our mainstay at Moosewood: it's our "daily bread." We use all varieties— short grain, medium grain, long grain, basmati, and jasmine. We serve rice with beans and curries; we make pilafs for side dishes and stuffed vegetables. Then there are rice salads, rice puddings, and layers of rice in our casseroles and gratins. Of all grains, brown rice is the highest in vitamin E. It is wheat-free and gluten-free.

BUCKWHEAT (KASHA)

Nutty, creamy, and comforting, buckwheat is botanically a fruit, and so it is a good choice for people with wheat sensitivities or gluten allergies. The protein in buckwheat is high quality; it contains all eight essential amino acids. Try our Kasha-stuffed Peppers (page 191).

CORN

Corn can be eaten fresh, dried as popcorn, or ground into flour or meal for polenta, cornbread, and tortillas. People who are concerned about glycemic load (see page 46, The Glycemic Index) may want to seek out blue corn products, because blue corn has 20 percent more protein than white or yellow corn and 8 percent less starch. Corn is wheat-free and gluten-free.

MILLET

If you've never eaten millet, try our Curried Millet on page 286. Millet is a nutty-tasting grain that carries spices well. It cooks in just twenty minutes, and when cooked with extra water, makes a tasty, buttery breakfast cereal. Millet is wheat-free and gluten-free.

OATS

Oats are a favorite breakfast for many of us, both cooked as hot cereal and as the principal component in Granola (page 40). At Moosewood, we use oats in our dessert fruit crisps and crumbles. Oatmeal is a good source of omega-6 and omega-3 fatty acids and a rich source of protein. Two cups of cooked oats supplies the FDA's recommended daily allowance for protein. Oats are wheat-free, but most oats contain gluten because most oat crops are contaminated by crops in adjacent fields. When that can be controlled, oats are gluten-free. If gluten is a problem, look for Bob's Red Mill or other rolled oats labeled gluten-free; otherwise, assume the oats contain gluten.

QUINOA

In the history of grains eaten in the United States, quinoa is a newcomer, though it could not be more ancient. Quinoa has been a staple Peruvian grain for millennia. It was, for a period, banned by the imperialist Spanish and

Portuguese who sought cultural dominance by, among other impositions, outlawing the native diet. But quinoa is back, and it is a gift. It is a complete form of protein with a profile similar to casein (milk protein). It is lightly textured, low-fat, and packed with nutrients. Quinoa is wheat-free and gluten-free.

RYE

Many of us are most familiar with rye in rye bread. Although most rye breads are a blend of refined white flour and rye flour, the rye in rye bread is a very good thing: rye is not easily separated from its bran and germ so whatever its form, it is pretty much always a whole grain. By volume, rye has two to four times the fiber of most grains, fruits, and vegetables. Rye is available in berries (whole grains), flakes (similar to rolled oats), and flour. Rye flakes can be cooked into a hot, satisfying cereal. Rye is wheat-free but not gluten-free.

SPELT

Spelt is another relative newcomer to North American markets that has, in fact, been around for centuries. Although spelt is a variety of wheat and can be used in all the ways that wheat is used (spelt bread, bagels, muffins, pretzels, and pasta), many people with wheat sensitivities can eat spelt products without negative reactions. Some people have speculated that this is so because spelt is a hardier grain than wheat and does not need the same applications of pesticides, or maybe it is a different enough variety that it doesn't cause an allergic response. Modern-day spelt is truer to its original form—it has not been hybridized as extensively as wheat—and as a result, spelt's nutritional profile is broader. It contains some nutrients at higher levels than wheat and some nutrients that wheat does not supply.

WHOLE WHEAT

Whole wheat comes in many forms besides flour for bread. Our customers are always grateful for the appearance of whole wheat pasta and couscous on the menu. We use cracked wheat or bulghur in many of our main dish grain salads, in pilafs for side dishes, in stuffed vegetables, and in casseroles.

Mock Risotto Primavera

SERVES 4 TO 6 | YIELDS ABOUT 8 CUPS | TIME: 35 MINUTES

This recipe makes a lovely rice dish packed with colorful vegetables. We love Italian risottos for easy, homey, one-pot meals. The creamy texture of traditional risotto comes from the starches released by arborio white rice during cooking and stirring. But white rice is bereft nutritionally. At Moosewood we prefer more nutritious whole grain brown rice, but it just won't make risotto.

Then we discovered that we can approximate risotto with instant brown rice, creamy neufchâtel, and Parmesan cheese.

1 TABLESPOON OLIVE OIL

2 CUPS DICED ONIONS

4 GARLIC CLOVES, MINCED OR PRESSED

2 CUPS INSTANT BROWN RICE (SEE NOTE)

3 CUPS VEGETABLE BROTH (SEE PAGE 33)

1 CUP DICED CARROTS

2 CUPS THINLY SLICED ASPARAGUS

1 CUP DICED RED BELL PEPPERS

2 CUPS DICED ZUCCHINI

1 CUP FRESH OR FROZEN GREEN PEAS

4 OUNCES NEUFCHÂTEL CHEESE

¼ CUP GRATED PARMESAN CHEESE

¼ CUP CHOPPED CHIVES OR SCALLIONS

SALT AND GROUND BLACK PEPPER

1 In a large saucepan on medium-high heat, warm the olive oil. Add the onions and sauté for a couple of minutes. Add the garlic and rice and stir until the rice is well coated with oil. Pour in the broth, cover, and maintain medium-high heat for 5 minutes.

2 Add the carrots, asparagus, bell peppers, and zucchini to the saucepan, but don't stir them into the rice: let them sit on top. Continue to cook uncovered for 5 minutes. Add the peas and stir everything together. Add the neufchâtel and stir until it has melted and is evenly distributed. Remove from the heat and stir in the grated cheese and the chives. Season with salt and pepper to taste.

INGREDIENT NOTE: Instant brown rice is a relatively new-to-the-market rice that takes about 10 minutes to cook. Look for plain instant brown rice; avoid flavor packets and microwave or boil-in bags. Instant brown rice has a lighter texture than long-cooking brown rice.

SERVING AND MENU IDEAS: A leafy green salad with Shallot Vinaigrette (page 111) provides a nice contrast to creamy Mock Risotto Primavera.

MOCK RISOTTO PRIMAVERA—PER 1 SERVING (OF 6), 1⅓ CUPS *Calories: 248, Protein: 10 g, Carbohydrate: 34 g, Dietary Fiber: 6 g, Total Fat: 9 g, Saturated Fat: 4 g, Monounsaturated Fat: 4 g, Cholesterol: 18 mg, Sodium: 402 mg*

Mushroom Barley "Risotto"

SERVES 4 | YIELDS ABOUT 5 CUPS | TIME: ABOUT 1 HOUR

Barley substitutes well for arborio rice in this robust mock risotto. Like arborio, barley cooks slowly and creates a moist, creamy texture as it softens, but the cooked barley grains are larger. This dish is full of mushrooms simmered in white wine and seasoned with herbs. We use a combination of cremini and white mushrooms to add interest, but either type alone works fine.

3 TABLESPOONS OLIVE OIL

1 CUP FINELY CHOPPED ONIONS

1 GARLIC CLOVE, CHOPPED

3 TO 4 CUPS SLICED CREMINI AND/OR WHITE MUSHROOMS (ABOUT 10 OUNCES)

1 TEASPOON SALT

½ TEASPOON DRIED THYME

½ TEASPOON MINCED FRESH ROSEMARY

1 TABLESPOON SOY SAUCE

¼ TEASPOON BLACK PEPPER

½ CUP WHITE WINE

1 CUP "NATURAL" PEARLED BARLEY (SEE NOTE)

3 CUPS WATER

CHOPPED FRESH PARSLEY (OPTIONAL)

GRATED PARMESAN, PECORINO ROMANO, OR ASIAGO CHEESE (OPTIONAL)

1 Warm the olive oil in a saucepan on medium heat. Add the onions and garlic, cover, and cook for about 5 minutes. Stir in the mushrooms and salt, cover, and cook until the mushrooms start to give off liquid, about 5 minutes.

2 Stir in the thyme, rosemary, soy sauce, pepper, wine, barley, and water, cover, and bring to a boil. Then lower the heat and simmer uncovered, stirring every 10 minutes or so, for 30 minutes or more (see Note), until the barley is tender and the texture creamy. Add water if needed during the cooking process.

3 Serve sprinkled with parsley and topped with grated cheese, if desired.

NOTE: Look for brown-colored pearled barley in a natural foods store or the bulk section of a large supermarket (not the small, round, white, very polished pearled barley that has less nutritive value, flavor, and texture). In our experience, the cooking time of different barleys varies significantly; 30 minutes for some natural pearled barleys and 1½ hours for Bob's Red Mill pearled barley. To reduce cooking time, soak the barley for 2 to 12 hours and then drain well.

SERVING AND MENU IDEAS: Lovely side dishes for Mushroom Barley "Risotto" are Roasted Beet Salad (page 92), Celeriac Apple Slaw (page 94), Roasted Brussels Sprouts and Pecans (page 300), or Kale with Cranberries (page 298). Try Our Healthiest Cheesecake Pie (page 332) for dessert.

MUSHROOM-BARLEY "RISOTTO"—PER 1 SERVING (OF 4) *Calories: 152, Protein: 3 g, Carbohydrate: 22 g, Dietary Fiber: 5 g, Total Fat: 5 g, Saturated Fat: 0 g, Monounsaturated Fat: 3 g, Cholesterol: 0 mg, Sodium: 296 mg*

Ratatouille Rice

SERVES 4 | YIELDS 8 TO 9 CUPS | TIME: 40 MINUTES

This colorful dish is filled with sunny Mediterranean vegetables. Neufchâtel adds a lot of richness without a lot of fat.

1 28-OUNCE CAN DICED TOMATOES

1 BAY LEAF

3 CUPS COOKED BROWN RICE

3 TABLESPOONS NEUFCHÂTEL CHEESE

¼ CUP GRATED PECORINO ROMANO CHEESE OR CRUMBLED FETA CHEESE

1 TABLESPOON OLIVE OIL

1½ CUPS FINELY CHOPPED ONIONS

3 CUPS DICED RED AND/OR GREEN BELL PEPPERS (1-INCH DICE)

3 CUPS DICED YELLOW SUMMER SQUASH AND/OR ZUCCHINI (1-INCH DICE)

1 SMALL EGGPLANT, CUT INTO 1-INCH CUBES (3 TO 4 CUPS)

3 GARLIC CLOVES, MINCED OR PRESSED

½ TEASPOON DRIED THYME

½ TEASPOON DRIED OREGANO

1 TEASPOON SALT

GROUND BLACK PEPPER

1 In a covered saucepan on low heat, warm the tomatoes, bay leaf, and rice, stirring occasionally and taking care not to scorch. When the rice is hot, stir in the cheeses, remove the pan from the heat, and set aside until the vegetables are done.

2 While the rice heats, warm the olive oil in a soup pot on medium heat. Cook the onions and peppers for about 4 minutes. Add the squash and cook for a few minutes more. Add the eggplant, garlic, thyme, oregano, and salt and cook, stirring occasionally, until the vegetables are tender, about 7 minutes. Add black pepper to taste.

3 Add the rice to the vegetables and stir well.

VARIATIONS: If you make rice just for this dish, add a pinch of saffron to the cooking water. Or add a pinch of saffron to the rice and tomatoes while it heats.

Add a splash of wine to the rice and tomatoes.

Top with chopped fresh basil.

RATATOUILLE RICE—PER 1 SERVING (OF 4)
Calories: 360, Protein: 12 g, Carbohydrate: 61 g, Dietary Fiber: 11 g, Total Fat: 9 g, Saturated Fat: 3 g, Monounsaturated Fat: 4 g, Cholesterol: 12 mg, Sodium: 737 mg

Polenta Domes with Garlicky Greens

SERVES 4 | TIME: 45 TO 50 MINUTES, WITH PREPARED TOMATO SAUCE

This dish looks and tastes great. You'll need four ovenproof 6- or 8-ounce custard cups, ramekins, or soup cups for making the "domes." You can make the polenta domes ahead of time and then reheat them in the oven while you cook the kale and heat the tomato sauce.

POLENTA DOMES

3 CUPS WATER

1 GARLIC CLOVE, MINCED OR PRESSED

¼ CUP DICED SUN-DRIED TOMATOES

½ TEASPOON SALT

SPRINKLING OF GROUND BLACK PEPPER AND/OR RED PEPPER FLAKES

1 CUP WHOLE GRAIN CORNMEAL (SEE PAGE 22)

2 TEASPOONS OLIVE OIL OR EXTRA-VIRGIN OLIVE OIL

¼ CUP GRATED PARMESAN OR CHEDDAR CHEESE (OPTIONAL)

GARLICKY GREENS

2 TABLESPOONS OLIVE OIL

3 OR 4 GARLIC CLOVES, MINCED OR PRESSED

8 TO 10 CUPS CHOPPED KALE (SEE NOTE)

½ TEASPOON SALT

¼ CUP WATER

1 CUP CREAMY TOMATO SAUCE (PAGE 78) OR YOUR FAVORITE TOMATO SAUCE

GRATED PARMESAN OR CHEDDAR CHEESE (OPTIONAL)

1 For the polenta domes: In a heavy saucepan, bring to a boil the water, garlic, sun-dried tomatoes, salt, and pepper. While whisking, add the cornmeal in a thin steady stream and whisk until smooth. Continue to cook on low heat, stirring often, until the polenta is thick and creamy, about 10 minutes. Stir in the olive oil and the cheese, if using. Immediately pour into 4 lightly oiled 6- or 8-ounce ovenproof cups in equal portions and set aside at room temperature until firm, about 10 minutes. Keep warm in a 200° oven.

2 For the greens: Warm the olive oil in a soup pot on medium-high heat. Add the garlic and cook until it begins to sizzle. Add the kale, salt, and water. Cover and cook, stirring often, until the kale is tender but still bright green, about 10 minutes. (The cooking time will depend on the tenderness of your kale.) Add more water if necessary to prevent sticking. Add salt to taste.

3 Meanwhile, heat the tomato sauce.

4 To serve, spread some kale on each dinner plate, invert a cup of polenta over each plate of kale and give it a little shake to plop the "polenta dome" onto the center of the kale. Top with Creamy Tomato Sauce and pass grated cheese at the table, if you wish.

NOTE: Bunches of fresh kale are different weights and have larger or smaller center stems and more or fewer yellowing or wilted leaves, so it's hard to tell you how much to buy. In our experience, 1½ to 2 pounds will yield 8 to 10 packed cups after sorting, stemming, and chopping.

VARIATIONS: At Moosewood Restaurant, we usually go Italian with this recipe, but you could go Mexican and top the domes with some salsa and fresh cilantro.

Other greens that are good are Swiss chard, collards, and broccoli rabe.

Use chopped olives in place of the sun-dried tomatoes.

Replace the greens with roasted or sautéed vegetables.

SERVING AND MENU IDEAS: Pomegranate Carrots (page 302) work well as a side dish. Have Chocolate Bark (page 336) to finish.

POLENTA DOMES ONLY—PER 1 SERVING (OF 4), 1 DOME
Calories: 140, Protein: 3 g, Carbohydrate: 26 g, Dietary Fiber: 3 g, Total Fat: 3 g, Saturated Fat: 0 g, Monounsaturated Fat: 2 g, Cholesterol: 0 mg, Sodium: 378 mg

GARLICKY GREENS ONLY—PER 1 SERVING (OF 4)
Calories: 180, Protein: 8 g, Carbohydrate: 24 g, Dietary Fiber: 5 g, Total Fat: 8 g, Saturated Fat: 1 g, Monounsaturated Fat: 5 g, Cholesterol: 0 mg, Sodium: 393 mg

Quinoa and Sweet Potatoes

SERVES 4 TO 6 | YIELDS ABOUT 4 CUPS | TIME: 35 MINUTES

Here's a tremendously versatile vegan side dish. Its simple, savory, light nutty flavor makes it a good complement to a wide variety of main dishes. For anyone on a wheat-free diet, it is a great replacement for the bread or couscous that might accompany a stew.

This recipe includes our favorite way to embellish the basic dish, but we also like it plain or dressed up with other herbs and seasonings.

BASIC RECIPE

¾ CUP QUINOA

1 TABLESPOON OLIVE OIL

1 CUP DICED ONIONS

½ TEASPOON SALT

2 CUPS DICED, PEELED SWEET POTATOES

1⅔ CUPS WATER

OUR FAVORITE ELABORATION

2 CUPS LIGHTLY PACKED FINELY CHOPPED FRESH SPINACH

2 TABLESPOONS TOASTED PINE NUTS

¼ CUP CURRANTS

1 TABLESPOON MINCED SCALLIONS

1 TABLESPOON LEMON JUICE

SALT AND GROUND BLACK PEPPER

1 Rinse and drain the quinoa in a fine-meshed strainer to remove any residue of the grains' bitter coating.

2 Warm the oil in a covered saucepan. Add the onions and salt and cook on low heat, stirring now and then, until the onions are transparent, about 8 minutes. Add the sweet potatoes, water, and drained quinoa, cover, and bring to a simmer. Lower the heat and simmer gently for 15 to 20 minutes, until the sweet potatoes are tender and the liquid has been absorbed. Remove from the heat. Stir well and add salt and pepper to taste.

3 To prepare our favorite elaboration, just before removing from the heat, stir in the spinach, pine nuts, currants, scallions, and lemon juice. Let sit for 5 minutes. Season to taste with salt and pepper.

BASIC RECIPE VARIATIONS: Add minced fresh chiles and/or garlic along with the onions.

Stir in chopped fresh parsley, basil, cilantro, and/or scallions or chives before serving.

Garnish with toasted almonds or sesame seeds.

Add a squeeze of fresh lemon or lime juice or a drizzle of soy sauce.

SERVING AND MENU IDEAS: The basic recipe of Quinoa and Sweet Potatoes is perfect under Oaxacan Green Mole Stew (page 251) or next to Southwestern Black Bean Burger (page 154) or Maque Choux (page 309). Our favorite elaboration of the dish is good with Down-home Black-Eyed Peas (page 221) or Tofu Mole (page 182).

QUINOA AND SWEET POTATOES—PER 1 SERVING (OF 6), ¾ CUP *Calories: 151, Protein: 4 g, Carbohydrate: 26 g, Dietary Fiber: 3 g, Total Fat: 4 g, Saturated Fat: 0 g, Monounsaturated Fat: 2 g, Cholesterol: 0 mg, Sodium: 247 mg*

Red Fried Rice

SERVES 4 TO 6 | YIELDS 6 GENEROUS CUPS | TIME: ABOUT 1 HOUR

Red vegetables and spices give this fried rice brilliance of color as well as depth of flavor. Pungent sun-dried tomatoes add chewiness, cherry tomatoes a juicy tang, and bell peppers and onions their distinctive presence. A sprinkling of toasted nuts finishes the dish with a rich, crunchy topping.

2 CUPS BROWN BASMATI OR LONG-GRAIN BROWN RICE

2½ CUPS WATER

12 SUN-DRIED TOMATOES (ABOUT ⅔ CUP)

1 MEDIUM RED ONION

1 MEDIUM RED BELL PEPPER

12 CHERRY TOMATOES

2 TABLESPOONS VEGETABLE OIL

⅛ TEASPOON RED PEPPER FLAKES
OR ¼ TEASPOON CHINESE CHILI PASTE

1 TEASPOON PAPRIKA

3 GARLIC CLOVES, MINCED OR PRESSED

2 TABLESPOONS GRATED PEELED GINGER ROOT

½ TEASPOON SALT

1 CUP SLICED SCALLIONS

⅓ CUP CHOPPED FRESH BASIL

2 TABLESPOONS DRY SHERRY (OPTIONAL)

2 TABLESPOONS SOY SAUCE

CHOPPED TOASTED ALMONDS, PECANS, OR WALNUTS

1 In a saucepan with a tight-fitting lid, bring the rice and water to a boil. Lower the heat and simmer for 35 to 45 minutes, until the water has been absorbed and the rice is tender.

2 Meanwhile, in a small pan on the stovetop or in a bowl in the microwave oven, bring to a boil the sun-dried tomatoes covered with water, and then set aside until softened, about 5 minutes. Drain the sun-dried tomatoes and chop them. Quarter and slice the red onion, dice the bell pepper, and halve the cherry tomatoes. Place all the ingredients near the stovetop.

3 In a wok or a large skillet on medium heat, warm the oil, red pepper flakes, and paprika. Stir in the onions, garlic, ginger, and salt and cook, stirring occasionally, until the onions soften, about 7 minutes. Add the bell peppers and sun-dried tomatoes and cook until the peppers are tender, about 5 minutes.

4 Add the scallions and the cooked rice and stir until everything is well mixed. Stir in the basil, cherry tomato halves, sherry if using, and soy sauce. Serve topped with toasted nuts.

SERVING AND MENU IDEAS: Pair with something light and green, such as Azuki Bean and Spinach Soup (page 124), Green Beans with Ginger and Garlic (page 303), or a green salad.

RED FRIED RICE—PER 1 SERVING (OF 6), 1 CUP
Calories: 313, Protein: 7 g, Carbohydrate: 57 g, Dietary Fiber: 4 g, Total Fat: 7 g, Saturated Fat: 1 g, Monounsaturated Fat: 3 g, Cholesterol: 0 mg, Sodium: 488 mg

Curried Millet

SERVES 4 | YIELDS ABOUT 3 CUPS | TIME: 35 MINUTES | | SITTING TIME: 10 TO 15 MINUTES

Millet is high in protein and gluten-free. This golden millet dish is bright with flecks of green herbs and glistening black currants. Serve it on its own, as a side dish, as a bed for stew or beans, or as a stuffing for bell peppers, tomatoes, or zucchini.

1 TABLESPOON VEGETABLE OIL
½ TEASPOON BLACK MUSTARD SEEDS (OPTIONAL)
½ CUP MINCED ONIONS
¾ CUP MILLET
½ TEASPOON GROUND TURMERIC
½ TEASPOON GROUND CINNAMON
¼ TEASPOON GROUND CARDAMOM
¼ TEASPOON SALT
⅛ TO ¼ TEASPOON RED PEPPER FLAKES OR CAYENNE
1½ CUPS WATER OR VEGETABLE BROTH (SEE PAGE 33)
¼ CUP CURRANTS
¼ CUP CHOPPED FRESH CILANTRO OR PARSLEY (OPTIONAL)

1 In a saucepan on medium-high heat, warm the oil and then add the mustard seeds, if using, and cook until they begin to pop, about 2 minutes. Add the onions right away so the mustard seeds won't burn and cook for about 3 minutes. Add the millet and stir constantly until fragrant, about 3 minutes. Add the turmeric, cinnamon, cardamom, salt, and red pepper flakes and cook for a minute, stirring constantly. Pour in the water, cover, and bring to a boil. Reduce the heat to low and simmer until the liquid has been absorbed and the millet is tender, about 20 minutes.

2 Stir in the currants and the cilantro, if using, and fluff with a fork. Cover and let sit for 10 to 15 minutes. Stir to fluff again. Serve hot, at room temperature, or chilled.

VARIATIONS: Use scallions instead of onions.

Use 1½ teaspoons of your favorite curry powder in place of the spices in the recipe.

Replace the currants with chopped raisins, dried cranberries, or dried apricots.

Use coconut milk in place of ½ cup of the water or broth.

SERVING AND MENU IDEAS: Top with plain nonfat yogurt and your favorite chopped toasted nuts—we suggest almonds or pistachios. Serve this versatile dish with Tropical Lime Tofu (page 179) and Pineapple and Tomato Salad (page 87). Or serve as part of an Indian meal, with Curried Yellow Pepper Soup (page 115), Kale with Sweet Potatoes (page 305), or Baked Sweet Potatoes with Indian Stuffing (page 196).

CURRIED MILLET—PER 1 SERVING (OF 4), ¾ CUP
Calories: 192, Protein: 5 g, Carbohydrate: 32 g, Dietary Fiber: 4 g, Total Fat: 5 g, Saturated Fat: 1 g, Monounsaturated Fat: 2 g, Cholesterol: 0 mg, Sodium: 183 mg

Couscous with Pistachios and Apricots

SERVES 3 OR 4 | YIELDS ABOUT 4 CUPS | TIME: 15 MINUTES

Whole wheat couscous has a nutty flavor that is enhanced by the addition of nuts, seeds, vegetables, fruits, and herbs. In this dish we combine it with the fresh flavors of parsley and mint and the sweetness of apricots and green peas.

---

1 TABLESPOON OLIVE OIL

1 CUP WHOLE WHEAT COUSCOUS

¼ TEASPOON SALT

1 CUP BOILING WATER

½ CUP CHOPPED DRIED APRICOTS

1 CUP FRESH OR THAWED FROZEN GREEN PEAS

¼ CUP CHOPPED FRESH PARSLEY

2 TABLESPOONS CHOPPED FRESH MINT

½ CUP TOASTED SHELLED PISTACHIOS

In a small covered pot on very low heat, warm the oil and stir in the couscous and salt. Stir in the boiling water and cover. After 5 minutes, stir in the apricots and peas. Cover and leave on the heat until the apricots begin to soften and the couscous is soft and chewy, about 2 minutes. Remove from the heat and stir in the parsley, mint, and pistachios. Add more salt to taste.

VARIATION: In place of pistachios, use toasted sunflower seeds or pumpkin seeds, or chopped toasted almonds or cashews.

SERVING AND MENU IDEAS: Serve this couscous as a side dish for Pomegranate-glazed Tofu (page 179), or Spinach-Tofu Burgers (page 153). Or serve alongside a soup, such as Watercress and Cauliflower Soup (page 116) or Greek Tomato-Yogurt Soup (page 125).

COUSCOUS WITH PISTACHIOS AND APRICOTS— PER 1 SERVING (OF 4), 1 CUP *Calories: 351, Protein: 12 g, Carbohydrate: 54 g, Dietary Fiber: 7 g, Total Fat: 11 g, Saturated Fat: 1 g, Monounsaturated Fat: 6 g, Cholesterol: 0 mg, Sodium: 158 mg*

Wild Rice Pilaf with Chestnuts

SERVES 4 | YIELDS ABOUT 3½ CUPS | TIME: 55 MINUTES

Chestnuts and wild rice give this pilaf a nutty flavor and gentle sweetness. It's great for autumn and winter holiday meals.

Chestnuts are virtually fat-free and their calories are derived largely from complex carbohydrates, earning them the nickname "the grain that grows on a tree." Remember this recipe when whole chestnuts that you can roast yourself are available.

It's been said that before the chestnut blight hit North America at the turn of the twentieth century, a squirrel could travel from New England to Georgia by hopping from tree to tree without touching any species other than the chestnut. There are newer disease-resistant varieties that we hope will bring chestnut trees back to North America.

RICE

½ CUP LONG-GRAIN BROWN RICE

¼ CUP WILD RICE

1 TEASPOON VEGETABLE OIL

1¼ CUPS WATER

3 BAY LEAVES

¼ TEASPOON SALT

PILAF VEGETABLES

1 TABLESPOON VEGETABLE OIL

1 CUP DICED ONIONS

1 CUP DICED CELERY

½ TEASPOON DRIED THYME

1 TEASPOON CHOPPED FRESH ROSEMARY

¼ TEASPOON SALT

½ CUP DRY WHITE WINE

1½ TO 2 CUPS COARSELY CHOPPED ROASTED FRESH CHESTNUTS OR DRY-PACKED CHESTNUTS (SEE NOTE)

GROUND BLACK PEPPER

NOTE: To roast fresh chestnuts for this recipe, you'll need about 32 fresh chestnuts, but while you're at it, roast more because they're so good to snack on. On the flat side of each chestnut, carve an *X* with the tip of a paring knife. Place the nuts *X* side down on a baking sheet or in an ovenproof pan. Roast in a preheated 400° oven for about 30 minutes. They're done when the shell cracks open easily when pressed between your thumb and index finger and the nut meat feels tender. Wrap a towel around the roasted chestnuts for about 15 minutes to steam them and make peeling easier. Squeeze each chestnut open and then peel off both the shell and the coarse membrane that covers the nut.

You can also use dry-packed chestnuts in a jar, usually found in the baking section of the supermarket. In our local store, we can find Haddon House brand in a 7.4-ounce jar, which makes about 1½ cups chopped. There is no need to roast dry-packed chestnuts.

1 To make the rice, rinse and drain the brown rice and wild rice. In a saucepan on high heat, stir the drained rice in the oil for a moment, then add the water, bay leaves, and salt. Cover and bring to a boil, then lower the heat to a very gentle simmer. Cook until the rice is tender and the water has been absorbed, about 45 minutes.

2 Meanwhile, prepare the pilaf vegetables. In a skillet or saucepan on medium heat, warm the oil. Add the onions, celery, thyme, rosemary, and salt and cook, stirring occasionally, for about 15 minutes. If the vegetables start to brown, lower the heat to medium-low. Add the wine and increase the heat to a rapid simmer. Cook until the wine has been absorbed, about 5 minutes. Remove from the heat.

3 When the rice is done, stir the chestnuts into the onions and celery and cook just until hot. Remove the bay leaves from the cooked rice and stir the rice into the vegetables. Add pepper to taste.

SERVING AND MENU IDEAS: This pilaf is nice with any autumn meal. Try it with Maple-glazed Root Vegetables (page 307), or Root Vegetable Hash (page 165). For an attractive light meal pair it with a colorful side dish or two, such as Kale with Cranberries (page 298), Pomegranate Carrots (page 302), or Roasted Sweet Potatoes (page 299). You can also use it as a filling for baked winter squash.

WILD RICE PILAF WITH CHESTNUTS—PER 1 SERVING (OF 4), GENEROUS ¾ CUP *Calories: 295, Protein: 5 g, Carbohydrate: 50 g, Dietary Fiber: 4 g, Total Fat: 6 g, Saturated Fat: 1 g, Monounsaturated Fat: 3 g, Cholesterol: 0 mg, Sodium: 317 mg*

Fourteen Ways to Embellish Brown Rice

At Moosewood, plain brown rice is our daily bread. But often we add extras to rice for tasty side dishes. We use both plain and embellished rice as a bed for burritos, beans, tofu, stews, and roasted or steamed vegetables.

Basic Recipe: Plain Rice

YIELDS 3 CUPS | HANDS-ON TIME: 10 MINUTES
SIMMERING TIME: ABOUT 45 MINUTES

> 1 CUP RINSED AND DRAINED BROWN RICE
>
> 2 TEASPOONS OLIVE OIL
>
> SCANT ½ TEASPOON SALT
>
> 1 ½ CUPS WATER

In a saucepan on high heat, stir together the rice, oil, and salt, and cook for a minute, stirring constantly. Add the water and bring to a boil. Reduce the heat to very low (use a heat diffuser if you have one), stir once, and simmer covered until tender, about 45 minutes. If you like softer rice, add ¼ to ½ cup more water.

Embellishments

ONION-HERB RICE

Before adding the rice to the saucepan, cook ⅓ cup diced onions and the salt in the oil, stirring constantly. Stir in ½ teaspoon of your favorite dried herb (thyme, tarragon, and oregano are our favorites) and then the water. Or stir 2 or 3 teaspoons chopped fresh herbs into the cooked rice.

SAFFRON RICE

Crumble a pinch (⅛ to ¼ teaspoon) of saffron into the rice when you add the water. Remember, a little goes a long way. Saffron Rice is also good with onions. Cook ⅓ cup diced onions in the oil before adding the raw rice.

INDIAN RICE

Add 3 whole cloves, 3 cardamom pods, and a cinnamon stick with the water. Remove them when the rice is done. A pinch of saffron adds another dimension to this aromatic rice.

COCONUT RICE

Replace half of the water with unsweetened coconut milk. Or add ½ cup unsweetened dried coconut with the raw rice. We often add ½ teaspoon ground turmeric for a golden hue.

GINGER RICE

Add 3 slices fresh ginger root and a garlic clove with the water, and then remove them when the rice is done.

SESAME RICE

Add ¼ cup sesame seeds with the raw rice and omit the salt. To the cooked rice, add 1 teaspoon dark sesame oil and soy sauce to taste.

GINGER-SESAME RICE

With the rice, add ¼ cup sesame seeds and omit the salt, and add 3 slices fresh ginger root and a garlic clove with the water. To the cooked rice, add 1 teaspoon dark sesame oil and soy sauce to taste.

JEWELED RICE

To the Ginger Rice, Sesame Rice, or Ginger-Sesame Rice, add about ⅓ cup diced red bell peppers and ⅓ cup green peas during the last 10 minutes of simmering. When the rice is done, toss in ¼ to ⅓ cup sliced scallions. Lovely!

ZESTY RICE

Add a generous teaspoon of freshly grated lemon, orange, or lime zest with the raw rice.

SOUTH-OF-THE-BORDER RICE

When you cook the raw rice in the oil, add ½ teaspoon cumin seeds, 1 garlic clove, and 1 small chile pepper. When the rice is done, remove the garlic and chile and stir in 1 cup diced fresh tomatoes and 1 or 2 tablespoons chopped fresh cilantro.

WILD RICE PILAF

In place of ⅓ cup of the brown rice, use ⅓ cup wild rice. When you add the rice to the pot, add ½ teaspoon dried thyme or rosemary or 1 teaspoon minced fresh herbs, and a garlic clove. When the rice is done, stir in ¼ cup minced fresh parsley.

RED RICE PILAF

Replace ⅓ cup of the brown rice with ⅓ cup wehani or other red rice. With the raw rice, add a bay leaf and ¼ teaspoon red pepper flakes or cayenne. When the rice is done, stir in ¼ cup chopped pecans and 2 or 3 tablespoons chopped scallions. Remove the bay leaf before serving.

ITALIAN RICE

Add ¼ cup diced sun-dried tomatoes with the water. When the rice is cooked, stir in 1 or 2 tablespoons chopped fresh basil. Top with 2 or 3 tablespoons toasted pine nuts just before serving.

FRUIT AND NUTS RICE

Toss the cooked rice with ¼ cup currants or chopped apricots or other dried fruit, and ¼ cup chopped toasted nuts.

BASIC RECIPE: PLAIN RICE—PER ½ CUP
Calories: 128, Protein: 2 g, Carbohydrate: 24 g, Dietary Fiber: 1 g, Total Fat: 2 g, Saturated Fat: 0 g, Monounsaturated Fat: 1 g, Cholesterol: 0 mg, Sodium: 195 mg

SIDE VEGETABLES

DARK LEAFY GREENS

Sweet, bitter, earthy. Smooth, mellow, mild. Pungent, peppery, spicy, sharp. The nuanced flavors of leafy greens can be described and debated in a way similar to cheese, coffee, and wine. Collards, spinach, bok choy, and chard are mild-flavored greens. Kale and cabbage are somewhere in the middle, and escarole, arugula, watercress, broccoli rabe, and turnip and mustard greens are more aggressive. We love them all.

Young plants have smaller, more tender, and milder-flavored leaves, and they can be used in just about anything. Mature leaves are bigger and may be tougher and more strongly flavored. They are very useful in long-simmered stews and for wrapping around fillings. In general, the darker the color, the more nutritious the green, but remember that because various types of greens have different nutritive profiles, it's a good idea to eat a variety of greens—don't get stuck on just one. When cooked, greens retain their nutrients and in some cases the nutrients are more easily absorbed.

Dark green leafy vegetables are perhaps the most nutrient-rich of all foods. The list of the most commonly identified vitamins and minerals found in greens is impressive, and greens are a rich source of minerals including iron, calcium, potassium, and magnesium, and vitamins including K, C, E, and many Bs. Their phytonutrients include carotenoids, lutein, and zeaxanthin (for healthy aging) as well as amino fatty acids. Greens are low in carbohydrates and high in fiber, making them slow to be digested with little impact on blood sugar levels.

Besides promoting general good health, a long list of medical benefits is connected to greens, including protection against: age-related cognitive decline, arthritis and other inflammatory diseases, osteoporosis, heart disease, cataracts and macular degeneration, diabetes, lung disease, anemia, and colon, skin, and other cancers. The list could go on and on, but the point is well taken: Eat your greens—lots of them and in a wide variety.

ARUGULA

Arugula has a medium-green hue and flat, long-stemmed leaves with lobes something like an oak leaf. Its flavor is described as sharp, spicy, peppery, warm, and pungent, and its mildness or assertiveness is quite variable from crop to crop. It's one of those flavors that becomes addictive, with many delicious applications, both raw and cooked.

BOK CHOY

Also called pak choi, bok choy has long, dark green leaves with ivory- or light green-colored stalks that are flattened and celery-like and remain crisp when cooked. The flavor is similar to cabbage. Baby bok choy is harvested after about a month and is smaller, more tender, and delicate in flavor.

BROCCOLI RABE

Also called raab or rapini, broccoli rabe has long, thin broccoli-like stalks with leafy greens and small florets that you chop up and cook all together. Broccoli rabe has a pungent, somewhat bitter flavor.

CABBAGE

Cabbage is one of the most widely grown vegetables on earth. Technically, the cabbage family, Cruciferae, includes green, red, and savoy cabbage, and also broccoli, kale, turnips, cauliflower, and various Chinese greens. When we say cabbage in recipes, we mean green cabbage, unless we specify red, savoy, or Chinese. Cabbage can be steamed, stir-fried, sautéed, braised, boiled, pickled, and fermented. Cabbage is obviously very versatile, with a clean, sweet flavor when cooked properly.

CHARD

We've tried not to go on too much about chard here, but there's just so much to love about it! Its flavor is mild, sweet, and earthy, its leaves are dark and succulent, and its stalks are delicious, too. At the farmers' market, you may find huge bouquets of different colors of chard: dark green, light green, red, orange, yellow, russet. The most common types are Swiss chard and ruby or red chard. Swiss chard has glossy green leaves and somewhat flattened white ribs. Ruby chard is similar, but with bright or deep red stalks and veins. The edges of the leaves are curled and they are usually 10 to 18 inches long. Cooked chard has a soft, velvety texture and that distinctive earthy taste. In the garden, chard flourishes all summer and fall, still fresh and bright long after spinach has bolted and gone to seed.

Chard gets excellent marks for its concentrations of vitamin K, vitamin A, vitamin C, magnesium, manganese, potassium, iron, vitamin E, and dietary fiber, and it is a good or very good source of copper, calcium, vitamin B_2, vitamin B_6, protein, phosphorus, vitamin B_1, zinc, folate, biotin, niacin, and pantothenic acid.

COLLARDS

Collard greens outrank broccoli, spinach, and mustard greens in nutritional value. Broad, smooth, substantial dark green leaves that become tender with a mild, likable, somewhat grassy flavor when cooked.

ESCAROLE

Choose crisp green heads with large, loose bunches of sturdy, ragged-edged green leaves. The flavor is mild to pleasingly bitter, and it is delicious in combination with sweet vegetables.

KALE

The dark, leafy green that we cook most often in the restaurant is kale. We see many varieties: some are curly, some darker green, and some have a red, blue, or purple patina. Like chard, kale flourishes in the garden all summer and fall, and we've even brushed off snow and enjoyed it in the winter. Kale is a powerhouse of calcium, fiber, vitamins, and minerals and is very often on "super foods" lists. Kale's substantial leaves become tender when cooked, and its flavor has presence, pleasantly mellow but not really mild.

MUSTARD GREENS

Graced with bright green, frilly, almost delicate leaves with a nippy mustard flavor and perfume, mustard greens might also be described as radish-like. Served alone, its pungency can be overwhelming, but it gives a delightful hint of spiciness when mixed with milder greens or added to soups and stews, particularly with beans and sweet vegetables.

SALAD GREENS

You can make a wonderful salad filled with visual and textural interest and plenty of color and flavor with just salad greens, a little oil and lemon, and salt. Add a few fresh herbs and it's spectacular.

Arugula: flavors from mild and nutty to peppery hot

Butter crunch, Boston, Bibb lettuces: soft, velvety leaves with delicate flavors

Endive: succulent and bittersweet, with a velvety crunch

Frisée, also called *curly endive:* crisp and textural with a bittersweet taste

Loose-leaf lettuces (red leaf, green leaf, ruby, oakleaf): soft, loosely connected leaves with mild and delicate flavors

Mâche: succulent, rounded leaves with a nutty flavor and smooth texture

Mizuna: striking-looking dark green, feathery, serrated leaves with a mild mustard flavor

Radicchio: beautiful cranberry color with white veins, mildly bitter

Romaine lettuce: long, upright green leaves with a crisp texture and mild flavor

Tatsoi: small paddle-shaped leaves with pale green stalks, often included in mesclun salad mixes

SPINACH

Spinach needs no introduction here. The creator of Popeye was onto something when he made spinach Popeye's power food. Its rich, dark green color is a marker of the wealth of nutrients within.

TURNIP GREENS

Turnip leaves are slightly fuzzy with a sharp flavor. They are an acquired taste for many people.

WATERCRESS

Look for delicate, green, heart-shaped leaves clustered on long, thin stalks with a pungent, peppery, spicy flavor. An aquatic plant, it grows wild in all fifty states. Watercress is extremely perishable, but incredibly nutritious: it has three times the calcium of spinach, is comparable to carrots for vitamin A, and is high in copper, iron, magnesium, vitamin C, and the B vitamins.

Kale with Cranberries

SERVES 4 TO 6 | YIELDS ABOUT 3 CUPS | TIME: 20 MINUTES

We love kale, and not only because it always appears on those lists of top ten super foods. Try this simple preparation, flavored with garlic and tart-sweet dried cranberries.

---

8 CUPS CHOPPED KALE, PACKED (SEE NOTE)

1 TABLESPOON OLIVE OIL

3 GARLIC CLOVES, MINCED OR PRESSED

¼ CUP CHOPPED DRIED CRANBERRIES

¼ CUP WATER

½ TEASPOON SALT

¼ TEASPOON GROUND BLACK PEPPER

NOTE: Bunches of kale vary significantly in weight, and in the size and quantity of large center stems and yellowed or wilted leaves, so it's hard to suggest how much fresh kale you'll need for 8 cups chopped after sorting and stemming. In our experience, you'll probably need about 1½ pounds.

Rinse and drain the kale. In a soup pot or large skillet on high heat, warm the olive oil. Add the garlic and still damp kale and sauté, stirring constantly, until the kale wilts significantly. Add the cranberries and water, cover, lower the heat to medium, and cook, stirring occasionally, until the kale is tender and dark green. The time depends upon the tenderness of the kale, but probably about 5 minutes. Stir in the salt and pepper.

VARIATIONS: Replace the kale with collard greens. Cooking time will depend on how young, fresh, and tender the collards are.

Omit the dried cranberries.

SERVING AND MENU IDEAS: This delicious green side dish is quite versatile. Serve it with Italian Sweet Potato Gratin (page 199), Kasha-Stuffed Peppers (page 191), or Wild Rice Pilaf with Chestnuts (page 288). It is also good with Vegetable Tofu Scramble (page 181), Mushroom-Barley "Risotto" (page 280), and Pasta with Butternut Squash and Sage (page 238).

KALE WITH CRANBERRIES—PER 1 SERVING (OF 6)
Calories: 70, Protein: 2 g, Carbohydrate: 11 g, Dietary Fiber: 2 g, Total Fat: 3 g, Saturated Fat: 0 g, Monounsaturated Fat: 2 g, Cholesterol: 0 mg, Sodium: 223 mg

Roasted Sweet Potatoes

SERVES 4 TO 6 | HANDS-ON TIME: 10 MINUTES | BAKING TIME: 15 TO 30 MINUTES

Because they are so sweet and delicious, you might not guess that sweet potatoes are so nutritious. They are filled with potassium, fiber, iron, antioxidants, and vitamins A, C, B$_6$, and E, and yet they are low in calories; a medium-sized sweet potato is about 145 calories. In fact, they were rated the number one vegetable for nutrition by the Center for Science in the Public Interest.

One of our favorite simple side dishes is roasted sweet potatoes, because it's so easy to make and so delicious and nutritious, and besides it goes so well with so many other foods.

---

2 LARGE SWEET POTATOES (ABOUT 2 POUNDS)

2 TABLESPOONS OLIVE OIL

½ TEASPOON SALT

GROUND BLACK PEPPER

---

1 If the skins are firm and smooth, just remove any spots and little dried-up roots; otherwise, peel the sweet potatoes. Cut them into chunks, sticks, slices, or half-moons.

2 In a bowl, toss the sweet potato pieces with the olive oil and salt. Spread on a lightly oiled baking sheet and sprinkle with black pepper. Bake in a 400° oven, stirring once or twice, until the sweet potatoes are tender and crisping on the edges, 15 to 30 minutes, depending on the size of the pieces.

VARIATIONS: Add chopped fresh or dried herbs such as rosemary, thyme, or marjoram.

Add ground cumin and coriander or curry powder.

Add cayenne or hot pepper sauce.

SERVING AND MENU IDEAS: Roasted Sweet Potatoes are a favorite to serve beside any number of dishes. Just to mention a few: Green Eggs, No Ham (page 58), Oaxacan Tlayuda (page 219), Broccoli Rabe and Beans (page 220), Cabbage with Fermented Black Beans (page 171), and Saucy Miso Tofu (page 178).

ROASTED SWEET POTATOES—PER 1 SERVING (OF 6)
Calories: 157, Protein: 2 g, Carbohydrate: 27 g, Dietary Fiber: 4 g, Total Fat: 5 g, Saturated Fat: 1 g, Monounsaturated Fat: 3 g, Cholesterol: 0 mg, Sodium: 269 mg

Roasted Brussels Sprouts and Pecans

SERVES 4 | YIELDS ABOUT 4 CUPS | TIME: 30 MINUTES

Roasting Brussels sprouts has become our hands-down favorite way of cooking them. We toss them in a lemony dressing and add some toasted nuts for a festive side dish.

1 POUND BRUSSELS SPROUTS

1½ TABLESPOONS OLIVE OIL

¼ TEASPOON SALT

DRESSING

2 TABLESPOONS MINCED RED ONIONS OR SHALLOTS

1 TEASPOON DIJON MUSTARD

1 TABLESPOON LEMON JUICE

1½ TABLESPOONS OLIVE OIL

SALT AND GROUND BLACK PEPPER

½ CUP TOASTED PECANS OR WALNUTS

1 Cut off the bottoms of the Brussels sprouts stems and remove any yellow or dry outer leaves. Cut the Brussels sprouts in half lengthwise and toss with the olive oil and the salt. Place them cut side down on a lightly oiled baking sheet. Bake in a preheated 375° oven until just tender and lightly browned on the cut side, 12 to 18 minutes, depending on the size of the sprouts.

2 Meanwhile, make the dressing: In a serving bowl, whisk together the red onions, mustard, lemon juice, and olive oil. Stir in the roasted Brussels sprouts and sprinkle with pepper and more salt to taste. Just before serving, toss with the toasted nuts.

SERVING AND MENU IDEAS: This delicious dish goes well alongside Root Vegetable Hash (page 165), Mushroom-Barley "Risotto" (page 280), Winter Squash Stuffed with Two-Rice Pilaf (page 198), and Kasha-stuffed Peppers (page 191).

ROASTED BRUSSELS SPROUTS AND PECANS—
PER 1 SERVING (OF 4) *Calories: 232, Protein: 5 g, Carbohydrate: 12 g, Dietary Fiber: 5 g, Total Fat: 20 g, Saturated Fat: 2 g, Monounsaturated Fat: 13 g, Cholesterol: 0 mg, Sodium: 188 mg*

Lemony Zucchini with Bread Crumb Topping

SERVES 2 | TIME: 25 MINUTES

This delicious side dish enhances lightly sautéed lemony zucchini with the delightful crunch of toasted bread crumbs.

At Moosewood, we serve freshly baked bread from a local bakery, which we slice to order for our customers. This results in many leftover bread ends and pieces, so one of our regular kitchen tasks is to make bread crumbs. We whirl the leftover bread pieces in the food processor and then dry out the crumbs in the oven until they're nice and toasty. When the bread crumbs are cool, we bag them and put them into the freezer. The bread crumbs are handy when we make tofu burgers, strudels, and casseroles, and to top a dish like this one.

BREAD CRUMB TOPPING

1 TABLESPOON OLIVE OIL

1 GARLIC CLOVE, MINCED OR PRESSED

½ CUP TOASTED WHOLE WHEAT BREAD CRUMBS

¼ TEASPOON SALT

¼ TEASPOON DRIED MARJORAM OR OREGANO (OPTIONAL)

LEMONY ZUCCHINI

2 PACKED CUPS GRATED ZUCCHINI

½ TEASPOON SALT

1 TABLESPOON OLIVE OIL

2 GARLIC CLOVES, MINCED OR PRESSED

½ TEASPOON GRATED LEMON ZEST

1 TABLESPOON LEMON JUICE

GROUND BLACK PEPPER

1 Prepare the bread crumb topping: Heat the olive oil in a skillet on medium heat. Add the garlic, bread crumbs, salt, and herbs, if using, and stir constantly until the bread crumbs begin to darken and become crisp, 2 or 3 minutes. Remove and set aside.

2 To drain liquid from the grated zucchini before cooking it, mix it with the salt, place in a colander in the sink or over a bowl, and let sit for at least 5 minutes. Then, with your hands or the back of a large spoon, press more liquid from the zucchini.

3 In the same skillet you used to toast the bread crumbs, heat the olive oil. Add the garlic and zucchini and cook on medium-high heat, stirring often, until the zucchini is tender, about 3 minutes. Remove from the heat, stir in the lemon zest and lemon juice, and season with pepper. Serve in a bowl, topped with the bread crumbs.

SERVING AND MENU IDEAS: This dish goes with summer foods and with foods of the sunny Mediterranean. Try it with Greek Lentil Burgers (page 155) or on the side of Greek Vegetable Pie (page 204).

LEMONY ZUCCHINI WITH BREAD CRUMB TOPPING— PER 1 SERVING (OF 2) *Calories: 213, Protein: 4 g, Carbohydrate: 18 g, Dietary Fiber: 3 g, Total Fat: 15 g, Saturated Fat: 2 g, Monounsaturated Fat: 10 g, Cholesterol: 0 mg, Sodium: 1,027 mg*

Pomegranate Carrots

SERVES 4 | YIELDS ABOUT 2 CUPS | TIME: 30 MINUTES

These deeply colored carrots are delightfully sweet yet tart, and they're simple to make. Pomegranates and carrots are both nutrient rich.

1 TABLESPOON OLIVE OIL

3½ CUPS CARROTS SLICED DIAGONALLY INTO ¼-INCH-THICK SLICES

½ TEASPOON GROUND CORIANDER

¼ TEASPOON SALT

1 CUP UNSWEETENED POMEGRANATE JUICE

1 CINNAMON STICK OR A PINCH OF GROUND CINNAMON (OPTIONAL)

GROUND BLACK PEPPER

CHOPPED FRESH PARSLEY OR MINT

1 In a skillet or saucepan on medium-high heat, warm the olive oil, add the carrots, and cook for 5 minutes, stirring frequently. Add the coriander and salt and stir for a minute, then add the pomegranate juice and cinnamon, if using. Simmer uncovered on medium-low heat for about 15 minutes, stirring frequently, until the juice has reduced and the carrots are tender. Add black pepper to taste. Remove the cinnamon stick before serving.

2 Serve topped with parsley or mint.

SERVING AND MENU IDEAS: These tasty carrots go well with Quinoa and Collard Leaf Dolmas (page 200), Greener Spanakopita (page 186), Mediterranean Eggplant Casserole (page 205), and Italian Lentils (page 217).

POMEGRANATE CARROTS—PER 1 SERVING (OF 4)
Calories: 128, Protein: 2 g, Carbohydrate: 24 g, Dietary Fiber: 4 g, Total Fat: 4 g, Saturated Fat: 1 g, Monounsaturated Fat: 3 g, Cholesterol: 0 mg, Sodium: 225 mg

Green Beans with Ginger and Garlic

SERVES 4 | YIELDS ABOUT 4 CUPS | TIME: 25 MINUTES

Green beans are wonderful with the flavors of garlic, ginger, and sesame oil. In this brilliant green side dish, the ginger matchsticks, fried until crisp, are little bursts of flavor.

1 POUND GREEN BEANS
1 TABLESPOON OLIVE OIL
1 TABLESPOON DARK SESAME OIL
2-INCH PIECE OF PEELED GINGER ROOT, CUT INTO SMALL MATCHSTICKS
1 TABLESPOON MINCED GARLIC
SALT
LEMON WEDGES (OPTIONAL)

1 Snip off the stem ends of the green beans. Steam the green beans until tender and bright green, about 5 minutes. Set aside.

2 Warm the olive oil and sesame oil in a small skillet on medium-high heat. Add the ginger matchsticks and stir-fry for a minute. Add the garlic and stir-fry until the ginger and garlic are golden brown and the ginger is crisp. Remove from the heat and toss with the steamed green beans. Sprinkle with salt and garnish with lemon wedges, if you wish. Serve hot or at room temperature.

SERVING AND MENU IDEAS: Serve beside Curried Red Lentil Burgers (page 151), Egg Foo Yung (page 63), or noodles topped with Toasted Sesame Sauce (page 77). They'll add a new dimension to Japanese Noodles with Tomatoes (page 230) or Curried Tofu and Mango Salad (page 88).

GREEN BEANS WITH GINGER AND GARLIC— PER 1 SERVING (OF 4) *Calories: 97, Protein: 2 g, Carbohydrate: 9 g, Dietary Fiber: 2 g, Total Fat: 7 g, Saturated Fat: 1 g, Monounsaturated Fat: 4 g, Cholesterol: 0 mg, Sodium: 7 mg*

Mashed Cauliflower with Shallots

SERVES 4 | YIELDS ABOUT 3 CUPS | TIME: 25 MINUTES

Who could have guessed that mashed cauliflower would taste so good? It has a light texture and mild flavor, it cooks quickly, and best of all, it has the comforting quality of mashed potatoes without blood-sugar-spiking simple carbs.

---

1 HEAD OF CAULIFLOWER, TRIMMED AND CHOPPED

2 TABLESPOONS OLIVE OIL

¼ CUP MINCED SHALLOTS

2 GARLIC CLOVES, MINCED OR PRESSED

½ TEASPOON SALT

¼ TEASPOON GROUND BLACK PEPPER

½ CUP FINELY CHOPPED SCALLIONS

¼ CUP MINCED FRESH PARSLEY

GRATED PARMESAN, ASIAGO, OR SHARP CHEDDAR CHEESE (OPTIONAL)

---

1 Steam the cauliflower until very tender, about 7 minutes. Put in a shallow bowl and set aside.

2 Warm the oil in a small skillet on medium-high heat and sauté the shallots, garlic, salt, and pepper until the shallots have softened. Add to the bowl of cauliflower and mash with a potato masher. Stir in the scallions and parsley. Stir in grated cheese, if desired.

SERVING AND MENU IDEAS: This is a light and lovely side dish for a burger, perhaps the Greek Lentil Burger (page 155), or for one of our Four Stovetop Tofus (pages 178–180). Paired with An Easy Baked Tofu (page 177) and Quick-braised Snow Peas and Radishes (page 308), it makes an appealing spring meal.

MASHED CAULIFLOWER WITH SHALLOTS—
PER 1 SERVING (OF 4) *Calories: 110, Protein: 4 g, Carbohydrate: 11 g, Dietary Fiber: 4 g, Total Fat: 7 g, Saturated Fat: 1 g, Monounsaturated Fat: 5 g, Cholesterol: 0 mg, Sodium: 338 mg*

Kale with Sweet Potatoes

SERVES 6 | YIELDS ABOUT 4 CUPS | TIME: 35 MINUTES

This super healthful, colorful side dish combines two of our favorite nutrient-rich vegetables.

4 CUPS DICED PEELED SWEET POTATOES (½-INCH CUBES)

2 TABLESPOONS OLIVE OIL

1 TEASPOON BLACK MUSTARD SEEDS

2 GARLIC CLOVES, MINCED OR PRESSED

¼ TEASPOON RED PEPPER FLAKES

1 TEASPOON CURRY POWDER

8 CUPS CHOPPED KALE (SEE NOTE)

½ TEASPOON SALT

2 TABLESPOON WATER

1 TABLESPOON SOY SAUCE

GROUND BLACK PEPPER

NOTE: Depending upon how large the center stems are and how much waste there is due to yellowing or wilted leaves, you'll probably need about 1½ pounds of kale for 8 cups cleaned and chopped.

1 Steam the sweet potatoes until tender, about 5 minutes. Set aside.

2 Warm the oil in a large pot on medium heat. Add the mustard seeds, and when they start to pop, add the garlic and red pepper flakes. Stir for a few seconds. Add the curry powder, kale, and salt. Stir constantly until the kale wilts, about 2 minutes. Add the water, cover, and cook on low heat until the kale is tender, 5 to 8 minutes.

3 Stir in the sweet potatoes and soy sauce and add black pepper to taste.

SERVING AND MENU IDEAS: This makes a nice meal with Curried Millet (page 286) and Tropical Lime Tofu (page 179).

KALE WITH SWEET POTATOES—PER 1 SERVING (OF 6)
Calories: 167, Protein: 5 g, Carbohydrate: 28 g, Dietary Fiber: 5 g, Total Fat: 5 g, Saturated Fat: 1 g, Monounsaturated Fat: 3 g, Cholesterol: 0 mg, Sodium: 432 mg

Cabbage Braised in Red Wine

SERVES 4 TO 6 | YIELDS ABOUT 5 CUPS | TIME: ABOUT 75 MINUTES

A long, gentle simmer brings out the sweet and savory flavors of this deep plum-colored side dish; the taste is reminiscent of a hearty cabbage borscht.

---

2 TABLESPOONS VEGETABLE OIL

1 CUP CHOPPED RED ONIONS

5 CUPS THINLY SLICED RED CABBAGE

1½ CUPS GRATED APPLES

1 CUP DRY RED WINE

¼ CUP BALSAMIC VINEGAR

1 TEASPOON DRIED THYME

1 TEASPOON SALT

¼ TEASPOON GROUND BLACK PEPPER

2 TABLESPOONS RAISINS

---

1 In a soup pot on low heat, warm the oil. Add the onions, cover, and cook until they begin to soften, about 5 minutes. Increase the heat to medium-high, add the cabbage, and cook, stirring constantly, for 2 or 3 minutes.

2 Add the apples, red wine, vinegar, thyme, salt, pepper, and raisins and stir until the liquid begins to simmer. Lower the heat, cover, and simmer gently, stirring every 10 minutes or so until the cabbage is very soft, about an hour.

3 Serve hot or at room temperature.

VARIATIONS: Substitute red wine vinegar for balsamic vinegar.

For a sweeter dish, add 2 more tablespoons of raisins.

Add 1 teaspoon of rubbed sage.

SERVING AND MENU IDEAS: Sweet and sour cabbage provides a piquancy that is welcome next to milder fare. Try it with Kasha-stuffed Peppers (page 191), Wild Rice Pilaf with Chestnuts (page 288), or Winter Squash Stuffed with Two-Rice Pilaf (page 198). It is also good with Mushroom-Barley "Risotto" (page 280), Italian Sweet Potato Gratin (page 199), or Roman Grain and Mushroom Soup (page 120).

CABBAGE BRAISED IN RED WINE—PER 1 SERVING (OF 6), GENEROUS ¾ CUP *Calories: 131, Protein: 2 g, Carbohydrate: 16 g, Dietary Fiber: 2 g, Total Fat: 5 g, Saturated Fat: 0 g, Monounsaturated Fat: 3 g, Cholesterol: 0 mg, Sodium: 414 mg*

Maple-glazed Root Vegetables

SERVES 6 | YIELDS ABOUT 6 CUPS | HANDS-ON TIME: 25 MINUTES | ROASTING TIME: 50 TO 55 MINUTES

These sweet, savory, and aromatic vegetables of red, deep orange, and dark purple make a wonderfully satisfying side dish on a frosty autumn or winter day. Serve as a novel side dish at Thanksgiving.

3 TABLESPOONS OLIVE OIL

1 TEASPOON DRIED THYME

1 TEASPOON RUBBED SAGE

1 TEASPOON MINCED FRESH ROSEMARY

12 CUPS VEGETABLES CUT INTO CHUNKS OR SLICES SOMEWHAT BIGGER THAN BITE-SIZED, IN ANY PROPORTION YOU LIKE. WE SUGGEST:

   3 MEDIUM SWEET POTATOES

   3 MEDIUM CARROTS

   3 MEDIUM BEETS

   1 LARGE ONION

   1 MEDIUM RED BELL PEPPER

MAPLE GLAZE

2 TABLESPOONS PURE MAPLE SYRUP

2 TABLESPOONS CIDER VINEGAR OR RICE VINEGAR

1 TABLESPOON OLIVE OIL

SALT AND GROUND BLACK PEPPER

1 In a large bowl, whisk together the oil, thyme, sage, and rosemary. Toss the vegetable chunks with the herbed oil until well coated. Spread evenly in a single layer on an unoiled baking sheet. In a 400° oven, roast the vegetables for 30 minutes. Remove from the oven and stir. Return to the oven and roast until the vegetables are tender, 10 to 15 minutes.

2 Meanwhile, make the maple glaze: in a cup or small bowl, stir together the maple syrup, vinegar, and oil. When the vegetables are tender, drizzle them with the glaze, sprinkle with salt and pepper, and stir until well coated. Roast for another 10 minutes.

SERVING AND MENU IDEAS: Grated feta is a delicious topping. Serve this dish with Tofu, Leek, and Almond Stuffed Portabellas (page 193), Mushroom Barley "Risotto" (page 280), Wild Rice Pilaf with Chestnuts (page 288), or Vegetable Tofu Scramble (page 181). Maple-glazed Root Vegetables are good with spicy Southwestern dishes, such as Southwestern Scramble (page 39), Migas (page 59), and Southwestern Black Bean Burgers (page 154).

MAPLE-GLAZED ROOT VEGETABLES—PER 1 SERVING (OF 6) *Calories: 212, Protein: 3 g, Carbohydrate: 31 g, Dietary Fiber: 5 g, Total Fat: 9 g, Saturated Fat: 1 g, Monounsaturated Fat: 7 g, Cholesterol: 0 mg, Sodium: 99 mg*

Quick-braised Snow Peas and Radishes

SERVES 4 | TIME: 10 MINUTES

Peas are sweet, radishes are sharp, mustard is pungent, and orange juice is citrusy-sweet. Together, the flavors are scrumptious. The color and the flavor of this elegant dish are best when it is served right away.

> 1 ORANGE
>
> 1 TEASPOON DIJON MUSTARD
>
> ½ TEASPOON SALT
>
> 1 TEASPOON VEGETABLE OIL
>
> ½ POUND SNOW PEAS, ENDS AND STRINGS REMOVED
>
> ¾ CUP VERY THINLY SLICED RADISHES

Grate the orange peel for about ½ teaspoon zest. Set aside. Squeeze the orange for about ⅓ cup strained juice. Whisk the mustard and salt into the orange juice. Warm the oil in a saucepan on medium heat. Add the snow peas and radishes and stir for a minute. Add the orange juice, cover, and cook for 3 to 4 minutes, until the snow peas are bright green and crisp-tender. Stir in the orange zest.

VARIATION: Also delicious made with sugar snap peas.

SERVING AND MENU IDEAS: Serve as a quick, crisp side dish for Spinach-Tofu Burgers (page 153), Egg White Omelet with Herbs (page 60), or Pasta with Pistachio-Lemon Pesto (page 228).

QUICK-BRAISED SNOW PEAS WITH RADISHES—PER 1 SERVING (OF 4) *Calories: 48, Protein: 2 g, Carbohydrate: 7 g, Dietary Fiber: 2 g, Total Fat: 1 g, Saturated Fat: 0 g, Monounsaturated Fat: 1 g, Cholesterol: 0 mg, Sodium: 317 mg*

Maque Choux

SERVES 4 TO 6 | YIELDS ABOUT 4 CUPS | TIME: 25 MINUTES

This American Indian–influenced Cajun side dish of stewed tomatoes, corn, and okra has many regional variations. *Maque choux* is pronounced "mock shoe" and is probably a French spelling of the sound of the Indian name for a similar dish.

1 TABLESPOON OLIVE OIL

1 CUP CHOPPED ONIONS

¼ TEASPOON SALT

1 TABLESPOON MINCED OR PRESSED GARLIC

1 FRESH CHILE, MINCED

2 CUPS FRESH, FROZEN, OR DRAINED
CANNED CORN KERNELS (SEE NOTE)

2 CUPS FROZEN CUT OKRA

2½ CUPS DICED FRESH TOMATOES
OR 1 15-OUNCE CAN DICED TOMATOES

¼ CUP WATER

1 TEASPOON DRIED OREGANO

¼ TEASPOON DRIED THYME

⅛ TEASPOON GROUND BLACK PEPPER

MINCED SCALLIONS

GRATED SMOKED CHEDDAR CHEESE
(OPTIONAL)

1   Warm the oil in a saucepan on medium heat. Add the onions and salt, and cook, stirring occasionally, until the onions have softened, about 7 minutes.

2   Add the garlic and chiles and cook for 3 minutes. Stir in the corn, okra, tomatoes, water, oregano, thyme, and pepper. Cover and bring to a boil, then lower the heat and simmer for 10 minutes, stirring often.

3   Serve topped with scallions, and smoked cheese, if desired.

NOTE: If you have fresh corn, after cutting the kernels off the cob, scrape the pulp and milk from the cobs into the saucepan for a nice creaminess.

VARIATIONS: Substitute chopped green bell peppers for the okra.

Add black-eyed peas, field peas, or lima beans.

SERVING AND MENU IDEAS: Offer Tabasco or other hot sauce at the table. Serve Maque Choux on the side with Down-home Black-eyed Peas (page 221), or try it with Tempeh-Quinoa Burgers (page 152) or Caribbean Stuffed Sweet Potatoes (page 195). For a main dish, serve it on rice, grits, polenta, with Quinoa and Sweet Potatoes (page 284), or with Sesame Flaxseed Cornbread (page 48).

MAQUE CHOUX—PER 1 SERVING (OF 6) *Calories: 104, Protein: 3 g, Carbohydrate: 19 g, Dietary Fiber: 4 g, Total Fat: 3 g, Saturated Fat: 0 g, Monounsaturated Fat: 2 g, Cholesterol: 0 mg, Sodium: 113 mg*

DESSERTS

Pomegranate Gel with Fruit

SERVES 6 TO 8 | YIELDS 8 CUPS | HANDS-ON TIME: 15 MINUTES | CHILLING TIME: AT LEAST 1 HOUR

A deep burgundy-colored pomegranate "gelatin" studded with fresh strawberries and dried cherries. Using agar agar as the gelling agent makes it vegetarian.

Pomegranates, besides being beautiful and delicious, contain higher concentrations of antioxidants than blueberries, cranberries, or red wine.

---

6 CUPS POMEGRANATE JUICE BLEND (SEE NOTES)

---

6 TABLESPOONS AGAR AGAR FLAKES OR 2 TABLESPOONS AGAR AGAR POWDER (SEE PAGE 18)

¼ CUP DRIED CHERRIES

---

3 CUPS SLICED FRESH STRAWBERRIES

---

2 TABLESPOONS PURE MAPLE SYRUP OR AGAVE NECTAR (OPTIONAL)

½ TEASPOON PURE VANILLA EXTRACT (OPTIONAL)

In a nonreactive saucepan, combine the pomegranate juice and agar agar. Bring to a boil, and then reduce the heat and simmer for about 5 minutes, stirring frequently, until the agar agar has dissolved. Remove from the heat and stir in the dried cherries, strawberries, and maple syrup and vanilla, if using. Pour into a serving bowl or dessert cups. Chill for at least an hour.

NOTES: Pure pomegranate juice may be too tart for most palates. We like a blend of pomegranate and apple juice for this recipe.

You can find agar agar flakes or powder at most natural foods stores.

After combining the juice and agar agar, you can also set it aside for about 15 minutes, and then bring to a boil and stir for just a minute or two, until it dissolves.

SERVING AND MENU IDEAS: Serve this whenever you think your grandmother would have served red Jell-O with fruit. This updated recipe still has a homey, retro appeal.

POMEGRANATE GEL WITH FRUIT—PER 1 SERVING (OF 8), 1 CUP *Calories: 102, Protein: 2 g, Carbohydrate: 26 g, Dietary Fiber: 2 g, Total Fat: 1 g, Saturated Fat: 0 g, Monounsaturated Fat: 0 g, Cholesterol: 0 mg, Sodium: 5 mg*

Cantaloupe with Fresh Raspberry Sauce

SERVES 4 TO 6 | YIELDS ABOUT ½ CUP SAUCE | TIME: 10 MINUTES

A simple elegant, refreshing, and beautiful dessert. Thin, bite-sized pieces of cantaloupe are fanned out on plates and drizzled with a lovely red sauce.

FRESH RASPBERRY SAUCE

6 OUNCES FRESH RED RASPBERRIES

1 TEASPOON SUGAR

1 TEASPOON LEMON JUICE

1 SMALL RIPE CANTALOUPE

1 In a blender, purée the raspberries with the sugar and lemon juice. Pour the purée into a fine-meshed sieve over a bowl and mash with the back of a spoon; you should have about ½ cup of raspberry sauce in the bowl and about a tablespoon of seeds left in the sieve.

2 Cut the cantaloupe in half through the stem and blossom ends. Peel and seed each half and cut it into wedges lengthwise. Then cut crosswise into thin slices; they'll be fan shaped.

3 On individual dessert plates, fan out slightly overlapping cantaloupe slices and drizzle with the raspberry sauce.

SERVING AND MENU IDEAS: This pretty fruit is not just for dessert. Serve it for breakfast or brunch, or as an appetizer or salad. Fresh Raspberry Sauce is delicious on Whole Grain Pancakes (page 38), French toast, and Maple Banana Oatmeal (page 41), and it's also quite nice on sliced peaches or stirred into yogurt.

FRESH RASPBERRY SAUCE ONLY—PER 1 SERVING, 4 TEASPOONS *Calories: 18, Protein: 0 g, Carbohydrate: 4 g, Dietary Fiber: 2 g, Total Fat: 0 g, Saturated Fat: 0 g, Monounsaturated Fat: 0 g, Cholesterol: 0 mg, Sodium: 0 mg*

CANTALOUPE ONLY—PER 1 SERVING, ⅙ OF A SMALL CANTALOUPE *Calories: 25, Protein: 1 g, Carbohydrate: 6 g, Dietary Fiber: 1 g, Total Fat: 0 g, Saturated Fat: 0 g, Monounsaturated Fat: 0 g, Cholesterol: 0 mg, Sodium: 12 mg*

Fruit and Nut Truffles

YIELDS ABOUT 36 TRUFFLES | HANDS-ON TIME: 1 HOUR | CHILLING TIME: AT LEAST 20 MINUTES

Naturally sweet dried fruit is combined with nuts, citrus, cinnamon, and cocoa and then rolled in fragrant toasted coconut. These tasty truffles make a lovely dessert or snack.

---

1 CUP PITTED DATES

1 CUP UNSULFURED DRIED APRICOTS

½ CUP DRIED CRANBERRIES, DRIED CHERRIES, OR RAISINS

1 CUP WATER

1 ½ TEASPOONS GRATED ORANGE ZEST

1 ½ TEASPOONS GRATED LEMON ZEST

1 ½ TABLESPOONS LEMON JUICE

½ CUP GROUND TOASTED WALNUTS

½ CUP GROUND TOASTED ALMONDS

1 TEASPOON GROUND CINNAMON

3 TABLESPOONS UNSWEETENED COCOA POWDER

2 TABLESPOONS CONFECTIONERS' SUGAR, SIFTED

½ CUP TOASTED UNSWEETENED SHREDDED COCONUT

---

1 Place the dates, dried apricots, dried cranberries, and water in a saucepan, cover, and simmer on medium-low heat until softened, about 10 minutes. Drain, reserving the liquid. Purée the cooked fruit in a food processor, adding only as much of the reserved liquid as needed to make a smooth thick paste.

2 In a mixing bowl, combine the orange zest, lemon zest, and lemon juice. Add the puréed fruit and the walnuts, almonds, cinnamon, cocoa, and confectioners' sugar and mix well. By the tablespoonful, form the fruit and nut mixture into balls about an inch in diameter. Roll each ball in the toasted coconut and arrange the truffles in a single layer on a serving platter.

3 Chill for at least 20 minutes before serving. With longer chilling, the flavor develops and the truffles become more firm.

NOTES: Stored in a container in the refrigerator, these truffles will keep for 3 weeks. If you pile them in layers, put waxed paper between the layers to prevent sticking.

SERVING AND MENU IDEAS: One or two of these are a lovely conclusion to a Mediterranean meal; serve with a demitasse of espresso, or with a glass of port on a wintry evening. They are also a healthful lunchbox treat or an afternoon pick-me-up and wonderful with a cup of Ginger Orange Tea (page 44).

FRUIT AND NUT TRUFFLES—PER 1 TRUFFLE (OF 36)
Calories: 48, Protein: 1 g, Carbohydrate: 8 g, Dietary Fiber: 1 g, Total Fat: 2 g, Saturated Fat: 1 g, Monounsaturated Fat: 1 g, Cholesterol: 0 mg, Sodium: 4 mg

Figs Baked with Chèvre and Pistachios

SERVES 4 TO 6 | YIELDS 12 FIGS | HANDS-ON TIME: 20 MINUTES | BAKING TIME: 12 MINUTES

Here's an easy, pretty finale that has it all: It's sweet, tart, salty, chewy, creamy, and crunchy all at once. We like to serve these luscious little fig flowers while they're still warm and the filling is creamy. They can be prepared ahead of time and refrigerated until you're ready to bake them.

---

12 LARGE DRIED FIGS

1 TEASPOON GRATED ORANGE OR LEMON ZEST

½ CUP CHÈVRE CHEESE

1 TABLESPOON HONEY

2 TABLESPOONS FINELY CHOPPED SALTED PISTACHIOS

---

1 Cut the stems off the figs. Slice them down to, but not through, the bottoms in an *X* pattern. Press apart the quarters of each fig so that it looks a bit like an open flower. Place the fig flowers in a lightly oiled baking pan large enough to hold them upright in a single layer.

2 Stir the zest into the chèvre. Spoon a dollop into each fig. Drizzle each with honey and sprinkle the top with pistachios. Bake in a preheated 400° oven for 10 to 12 minutes. These are best served straight from the oven. Don't let them sit in a warm oven because they'll dry out and become tough.

SERVING AND MENU IDEAS: These figs are delectable after a Middle Eastern or Mediterranean meal. Serve with steaming coffee or tea. And we do love them for brunch.

FIGS BAKED WITH CHÈVRE AND PISTACHIOS— PER 1 SERVING (OF 6), 2 FIG "FLOWERS" *Calories: 110, Protein: 4 g, Carbohydrate: 15 g, Dietary Fiber: 2 g, Total Fat: 5 g, Saturated Fat: 2 g, Monounsaturated Fat: 1 g, Cholesterol: 9 mg, Sodium: 60 mg*

Apple-Blueberry Crumble

SERVES 8 | HANDS-ON TIME: 15 MINUTES | BAKING TIME: 45 TO 50 MINUTES

At Moosewood Restaurant, we serve a fruit crumble almost every day. This version, with antioxidant-rich fruits and heart-healthy oats and nuts, is wheat-free and vegan (unless, of course, you top the warm crumble with a scoop of vanilla ice cream, its perfect complement).

The crumble topping is good on other fruit combos, too. Try apple and blackberry, pear and cranberry, or peach and strawberry. Frozen berries or sliced fruit can be used, without being defrosted. We like to double or triple the topping recipe so we'll have some to freeze, making it really easy to throw together a fruit dessert anytime. The topping can go straight from freezer to oven.

FRUIT FILLING

3 CUPS PEELED AND SLICED APPLES

3 CUPS FRESH OR FROZEN BLUEBERRIES

1 TEASPOON GROUND CINNAMON

1 TABLESPOON CORNSTARCH

⅓ CUP PURE MAPLE SYRUP (OR ONE OF THE SWEETENERS IN THE VARIATIONS)

CRUMBLE TOPPING

½ CUP ROLLED OATS

½ CUP WHOLE GRAIN CORNMEAL (SEE PAGE 22)

½ CUP CHOPPED WALNUTS OR PECANS

¼ CUP BROWN SUGAR (OR ONE OF THE SWEETENERS IN THE VARIATIONS)

1 TEASPOON GROUND CINNAMON

¼ TEASPOON SALT

¼ CUP VEGETABLE OIL

1 In a bowl, stir together the apple slices, blueberries, cinnamon, cornstarch, and maple syrup. Spread into an unoiled nonreactive 7 × 11-inch baking pan or a 9-inch square baking pan. Bake in a preheated 375° oven until bubbling, about 30 minutes.

2 While the fruit bakes, make the crumble topping. In a bowl, combine the oats, cornmeal, chopped nuts, brown sugar, cinnamon, and salt. Add the oil and stir until well mixed.

3 When the fruit has baked for 30 minutes, remove it from the oven. Stir the fruit to settle it into the dish a little, top with the crumble mixture, and return it to the oven for 15 to 20 minutes, until the fruit looks thick and the topping has crisped and browned.

4 Serve hot, warm, or at room temperature.

VARIATIONS: For the fruit filling, in place of maple syrup use ¼ cup brown sugar, ⅓ cup thawed frozen apple juice concentrate, or about ¼ teaspoon powdered stevia (see page 31).

For the crumble topping, in place of the brown sugar, use ¼ teaspoon powdered stevia, or ⅓ cup maple syrup or thawed frozen apple juice concentrate. If you use maple syrup or apple juice concentrate, the crumble mixture will be quite moist.

Add 2 tablespoons of ground sunflower seeds or flaxseeds to the topping.

SERVING AND MENU IDEAS: Apple-Blueberry Crumble seems like such an all-American dessert but it's really at home with many cuisines. Served warm, it's a wonderful finale for brunch.

APPLE-BLUEBERRY CRUMBLE—PER 1 SERVING (OF 8)
Calories: 271, Protein: 3 g, Carbohydrate: 40 g, Dietary Fiber: 4 g, Total Fat: 13 g, Saturated Fat: 1 g, Monounsaturated Fat: 5 g, Cholesterol: 0 mg, Sodium: 80 mg

Fig and Pecan Baked Apples

SERVES 4 | HANDS-ON TIME: 25 MINUTES | BAKING TIME: 30 TO 60 MINUTES

As you can imagine, we've baked many kinds of apples in our long tenure at Moosewood, and every year it seems that new heirloom varieties and hybrids are available in our market to try. We've learned that both the amount of time any one apple needs to bake and its tendency to explode when you're not looking are unpredictable. We prefer to use locally grown and organic apples. For this dish we've tried Gala, Honey Crisp, Pink Lady, Mutsu, Cortland, Ida Red, Braeburn, and Northern Spy, and they're all good. Try apple varieties that are available in your area.

6 LARGE DRIED FIGS
⅔ CUP APPLE OR PEAR JUICE
1 ORANGE
4 LARGE APPLES
¼ CUP CHOPPED PECANS
¾ TEASPOON GROUND CINNAMON
4 TEASPOONS PURE MAPLE SYRUP

1 In a small pan on the stovetop or in a bowl in the microwave oven, bring the figs and juice to a boil. Set aside for 5 to 10 minutes to soften.

2 Grate the peel of the orange, reserve 1 teaspoon of the zest, and juice the orange.

3 Cut the apples in half from stem to blossom end, core them, and place cut side up in a nonreactive baking pan.

4 Remove the figs from the soaking liquid and stir the orange juice into the liquid. Coarsely chop the figs and combine them with the orange zest, pecans, and cinnamon. Mound the fig and nut mixture in the cavities of the apple halves. Pour the soaking liquid into the baking pan. Drizzle ½ teaspoon of maple syrup over the cut surface of each apple half, but not over the filling.

5 Cover the pan with foil and bake in a preheated 400° oven for 30 minutes. Uncover and check the apples for softness—they will most likely require another 10 to 15 minutes of baking, or more. Baked apples are best when very soft, and even when they've exploded, they taste good.

6 After removing the apples from the oven, spoon some of the pan juices over them. Serve warm, at room temperature, or cold.

VARIATIONS: Instead of apple or pear juice, use peach, mango, or apricot juice.

Instead of pecans, use walnuts or almonds. Or, no nuts at all—just add one or two more figs.

FIG AND PECAN BAKED APPLES—PER 1 SERVING (OF 4), 2 APPLE HALVES *Calories: 243, Protein: 2 g, Carbohydrate: 52 g, Dietary Fiber: 8 g, Total Fat: 6 g, Saturated Fat: 1 g, Monounsaturated Fat: 3 g, Cholesterol: 0 mg, Sodium: 5 mg*

Simply Baked Fruit

SERVES 4 | HANDS-ON TIME: 15 MINUTES | BAKING TIME: 35 TO 40 MINUTES

A bit of sweetener, lemon, and vanilla give a surprising lift to fruit without masking its own delightful flavor. Use this simple, homey preparation all year with an ever-changing cast of seasonal fresh fruit; it's a delightful way to get more fruit into your diet. We're very fond of pure maple syrup as a sweetener. It's a local product from the multitude of sugar maple trees that thrive here in upstate New York (and that are botanically related to the striped maple or moosewood tree).

> **2 TABLESPOONS PURE MAPLE SYRUP**
>
> **2 TEASPOONS LEMON JUICE**
>
> **1 TEASPOON PURE VANILLA EXTRACT**
>
> **PINCH OF SALT**
>
> **5 CUPS PEELED AND SLICED APPLES, OR A MIXTURE OF APPLES AND PEARS**

1 In a small bowl, mix together the maple syrup, lemon juice, vanilla, and salt. In a nonreactive 9-inch square baking pan, combine the fruit and the syrup mixture.

2 Bake in a preheated 400° oven, stirring once or twice, until the fruit is tender, 35 to 40 minutes.

VARIATIONS: Use softer fruits like peaches, plums, apricots, pineapple, and mangoes. They will be tender in about 15 minutes. If you use plums or apricots, both of which can be rather tart, halve the amount of lemon juice in the recipe.

SERVING AND MENU IDEAS: For dessert, serve plain, over yogurt, under ice cream, or layered with Granola (page 40) in a parfait glass. At breakfast or brunch, serve on Whole Grain Pancakes (page 38) or Maple Banana Oatmeal (page 41).

SIMPLY BAKED FRUIT—PER 1 SERVING (OF 4)
Calories: 96, Protein: 0 g, Carbohydrate: 25 g, Dietary Fiber: 2 g, Total Fat: 0 g, Saturated Fat: 0 g, Monounsaturated Fat: 0 g, Cholesterol: 0 mg, Sodium: 1 mg

Herbed and Spiced Fresh Fruit Popsicles

EACH FLAVOR YIELDS ABOUT 8 POPSICLES | HANDS-ON TIME: ABOUT 10 MINUTES
FREEZING TIME: 6 HOURS OR OVERNIGHT

The flavors of these delicious "mom & pop-sicles" aren't what you might expect so open your mind, stick out your tongue, and say "Mmmm." We designed these popsicles for grown-ups, but our kids like them, too. All of the purées make delicious smoothies. For slushies, freeze in ice cube trays and then whirl the frozen cubes in a food processor.

Honeydew and Basil Popsicles

YIELDS ABOUT 3 CUPS, ABOUT 8 POPSICLES

Delectable. For a grown-up version, add ⅓ cup of Midori or other melon liqueur and reduce the sugar to taste.

4 CUPS HONEYDEW MELON CUBES

¼ CUP CHOPPED FRESH BASIL

¼ CUP LEMON OR LIME JUICE

1 TABLESPOON SUGAR, OR MORE OR LESS
TO TASTE, OR ¼ TO 1 TEASPOON STEVIA
POWDER (SEE NOTE)

PINCH OF SALT

Whirl all of the ingredients in a blender until smooth, and then whirl on high speed for about a minute until very smooth and "creamy" (this whips the purée and gives the popsicles a softer texture). Pour into popsicle molds and freeze for at least 6 hours.

NOTE: The sweetening strength of stevia powders varies considerably, making it impossible to give an exact amount that will sweeten to the level intended. If you know the sweetening power of the stevia you're using, estimate the amount that will work. Otherwise, start at the lower end of the range called for, and add more stevia to taste. See page 31 for more information.

VARIATIONS: Add fresh mint instead of basil.

In place of lemon juice and sugar or stevia, use ½ cup frozen lemonade concentrate.

HONEYDEW AND BASIL POPSICLES—PER 1 SERVING
(OF 8) *Calories: 39, Protein: 1 g, Carbohydrate: 10 g, Dietary Fiber: 1 g, Total Fat: 0 g, Saturated Fat: 0 g, Monounsaturated Fat: 0 g, Cholesterol: 0 mg, Sodium: 15 mg*

Pineapple-Cinnamon Popsicles

YIELDS ABOUT 3 CUPS, ABOUT 8 POPSICLES

The riper and sweeter the pineapple, the more luscious the flavor. In the blender, the purée will become "creamy." Pour into the molds and put in the freezer right away; if you're delayed, whirl again in the blender before freezing.

3 CUPS RIPE FRESH PINEAPPLE CHUNKS

¼ CUP FRESH ORANGE JUICE

½ TEASPOON GROUND CINNAMON

DASH OF SALT

Whirl all of the ingredients in a blender until smooth, and then whirl on high speed for about a minute until very smooth and "creamy" (this whips the purée and gives the popsicles a softer texture). Pour into popsicle molds and freeze for at least 6 hours.

PINEAPPLE-CINNAMON POPSICLES—PER 1 SERVING (OF 8) *Calories: 32, Protein: 0 g, Carbohydrate: 8 g, Dietary Fiber: 1 g, Total Fat: 0 g, Saturated Fat: 0 g, Monounsaturated Fat: 0 g, Cholesterol: 0 mg, Sodium: 1 mg*

Mango-Parsley Popsicles

YIELDS ABOUT 2 CUPS, ABOUT 6 POPSICLES

A surprisingly compelling flavor—if you like it, you'll keep coming back to it. This tastes like midsummer to us.

½ CUP LOOSELY PACKED, ROUGHLY CHOPPED PARSLEY

2 RIPE MANGOES

Whirl all of the ingredients in a blender until smooth, and then whirl on high speed for about a minute until very smooth and "creamy" (this whips the purée and gives the popsicles a softer texture). Pour into popsicle molds and freeze for at least 6 hours.

VARIATION: Use a 15-ounce can of mango slices or a 14-ounce package of frozen mango pulp and reduce the parsley to ¼ cup.

NOTE: If your mango isn't perfectly ripe and sweet with a velvety texture, add ¼ cup frozen orange juice or lemonade concentrate.

MANGO-PARSLEY POPSICLES—PER 1 SERVING (OF 6) *Calories: 38, Protein: 0 g, Carbohydrate: 10 g, Dietary Fiber: 1 g, Total Fat: 0 g, Saturated Fat: 0 g, Monounsaturated Fat: 0 g, Cholesterol: 0 mg, Sodium: 4 mg*

Ice Pops

Using small paper or plastic cups as molds for Ice Pops is practical. They're easy to fill and easy to unmold, and they serve several purposes while the kids eat the pops: the cup can catch drips, it's a handy "storage container" when a kid needs both hands for something, and if half a pop is enough, the rest can go back in the cup and back into the freezer for later. Use aluminum foil to cover each cup and to hold the stick upright while the pop freezes. Tongue depressors or jumbo craft sticks make good sticks for small children; they're easier for a small hand to grip.

LEMON OR LIME

2 CUPS WATER

¼ CUP LEMON OR LIME JUICE

1 TEASPOON STEVIA POWDER, OR TO TASTE (SEE NOTE ON PAGE 320)

½ CUP RASPBERRIES OR DICED STRAWBERRIES

PEACH

1 CUP PEACH JUICE

½ CUP VANILLA SOYMILK OR ALMOND MILK

½ CUP FRESH OR FROZEN PITTED HALVED CHERRIES OR PEACH CHUNKS

PINEAPPLE

1 CUP PINEAPPLE JUICE

1 CUP VANILLA SOYMILK OR ALMOND MILK

½ CUP FRESH OR FROZEN BLUEBERRIES OR RASPBERRIES

Combine the liquid ingredients and stevia, if using. Divide the fruit equally among 4 to 6 molds. Pour the liquid into the molds over the fruit. Freeze until firm, 2 to 4 hours.

VARIATIONS: Mix and match fruits and fruit juices; thicker juices or nectars, such as peach, apricot, pear, and pineapple are especially good. We don't recommend using raw apples or pears, but most other fruits work well.

LEMON OR LIME—PER 1 SERVING (OF 6) *Calories: 8, Protein: 0 g, Carbohydrate: 3 g, Dietary Fiber: 1 g, Total Fat: 0 g, Saturated Fat: 0 g, Monounsaturated Fat: 0 g, Cholesterol: 0 mg, Sodium: 3 mg*

PEACH—PER 1 SERVING (OF 6) *Calories: 33, Protein: 1 g, Carbohydrate: 7 g, Dietary Fiber: 1 g, Total Fat: 0 g, Saturated Fat: 0 g, Monounsaturated Fat: 0 g, Cholesterol: 0 mg, Sodium: 10 mg*

PINEAPPLE—PER 1 SERVING (OF 6) *Calories: 48, Protein: 2 g, Carbohydrate: 9 g, Dietary Fiber: 1 g, Total Fat: 1 g, Saturated Fat: 0 g, Monounsaturated Fat: 0 g, Cholesterol: 0 mg, Sodium: 17 mg*

SUGARS

Ah, sweetness! It is probably the first taste sensation we encounter in life, from mother's milk or infant formula. Our five taste senses—sweet, sour, bitter, salty, and umami (a savory, meaty sensation)—protect us from inedible or toxic foods, bring us pleasure, and help us stay healthy.

In health as well as in illness, our bodies continually work to maintain and restore balance, a process often manifested in our changing taste for certain foods. An obvious example is our pull toward the vitamin C-rich, sweet and sour astringency of orange juice or lemony tea to soothe a sore throat or a bad cold, often in amounts and strengths that we would find intolerable when well. This taste bud "intelligence" also explains why sweet, rich pastries and confections seem to beg for the bitter, acidic quality of strong coffee or tea. Attending to the full spectrum of tastes increases our enjoyment of each, and is the secret of fine cooking.

Much has been written about the ill effects of overconsumption of sugar and other sweeteners. In addition to obesity, adult-onset diabetes, and poor dental health, researchers have accumulated data that indicate that too much sugar and refined carbohydrates (which metabolize as simple sugars) may

also contribute to osteoporosis, increased cholesterol levels, and depression of the immune system.

And yet our desire for sweet-tasting food seems to be growing. One worrisome trend in the marketplace is the addition of sweeteners to traditionally savory processed foods. Everyday foods on grocery shelves are becoming sweeter. This trend is not only increasing the amount of sugar we ingest, but also changing our idea of what is "sweet enough." If, as writer Michael Pollan suggests, we were to eat only foods our great-grandmothers would have recognized, a piece of fruit would taste wonderfully sweet and be very satisfying. Now, however, sugar is such a common ingredient that the baseline for sweet has risen, and our palates insist on a greater degree of sweetness than ever before.

As a result of our accelerating taste for sweet and, ironically, also our concern about health and healthful foods, the market now offers us more kinds of sweeteners than ever before. Although many bear the label "natural" or "unrefined," nutritionists and food chemists seem to agree that all concentrated sweeteners, be they white or brown sugar, honey, molasses, maple syrup, corn syrup, concentrated fruit juice sweeteners, malted barley syrup, or evaporated cane juice crystals, are metabolized as sugar and will ultimately enter the bloodstream as glucose; too much of any sweetener can cause problems. The claim that less-refined sweeteners have important trace vitamins and minerals is not regarded as credible by food scientists, given the low level of these nutrients in sweeteners. Organic products do have the benefit of being pesticide-free. And there is some agreement that fruit sweeteners, including honey, do not ignite the same "trigger effect" that white sugar does: a craving for more of something sweet.

There is strong motivation for all of us to watch the amount of sweeteners we eat, and we can get help from our other taste senses. Understanding that our yens are often a dance of opposites in service of balance, and that moderation in one area will invite moderation in another, can be a good place to start. That large bag of something salty, like potato chips, creates an insistent desire for something sweet and acidic, like soda. So if you want to curtail your sweet tooth, watch your salt, and vice versa.

Another good thing to remember is that sugar does not contain the B vitamins necessary for its metabolism, and when the vitamins are absent, our bodies extract them from their own stores. So it is always a good idea to include a vitamin B-rich whole grain like oats, whole wheat flour, or brown rice in a sweet dish.

At Moosewood, we use sweeteners in many of our desserts and—judiciously—in some of

our savory dishes to achieve the balance of flavors that will produce the most delicious outcome. We use different sweeteners in different dishes because sweeteners have distinct qualities that interact with other ingredients and spices, as well as their own unique flavors and textures.

We try to minimize our use of refined sugar in the restaurant, reserving it mostly for desserts, and we use it very, very sparingly in the recipes in this cookbook. We're always open to trying new techniques and substitutes for concentrated sugar. We look for ways to make the most of the natural sweetness of fruits and vegetables. We caramelize onions, for instance, which nicely balances the acidity of tomatoes in tomato sauce. We roast and grill vegetables and fruits to develop and concentrate their natural sugars.

We use fruit purées to replace or reduce the need for sweeteners. In one of our popular vegan chocolate cakes, we've begun substituting banana purée for some of the sugar and oil, with good results. We developed a recipe for this cookbook with a whole ripe pear or apple blended into the salad dressing to give a sweet, creamy quality. We use 100 percent fruit juice as a sweetener in desserts, dressings, curries, and more. Unsweetened fruit preserves flavor some of our filo desserts and summer fruit mousses, and serve as filling for layer cakes and whole grain cookies.

We use pure New York State maple syrup instead of corn syrup in pecan and walnut pies, tarts, and bars and to sweeten cranberry applesauce. It is a wonderful and flavorful substitute for sugar in whipped cream. For this book we developed a glistening, delicious dish of root vegetables glazed with a touch of maple syrup.

A local beeman, Joe Rowland, delivers honey to Moosewood in a 60-pound tub as well as in small refillable honey bear squeeze bottles. Honey has a strong taste, and its taste and strength vary depending on the blossoms the bees visit. In general, fall and winter honey is stronger and darker than that produced in the spring and summer. We always offer honey to our customers in the restaurant, and many of them love it in honey lemon tea, one of our signature beverages.

Molasses is a thick, dense sweetener, a by-product of the sugar refining process. It adds boldness to the dishes it sweetens. In baking and cooking it stands up to the challenge of strong, sweet, and hot spices. We use it in barbecued tofu, roasted vegetable glazes, and some of our Caribbean- and African-inspired bean dishes.

Brown sugar is granulated white sugar that is made moister and given an earthy flavor by the addition of molasses. We use brown sugar in baking when a dominant ingredient will be enhanced by or can support its stronger flavor. It is also used in baking when a moist or fudgier texture is sought. In cooking, it adds flavor and depth as well as sweetness.

Turbinado sugar is a brown sugar with larger crystals that do not melt as easily as traditional brown sugar. In the restaurant we roll cookies in it so they have a sparkly, crunchy topping, and we use it to decorate lattes and cappuccinos.

White sugar is our choice when a sweetener is needed to enhance but not alter a dessert's structural integrity and delicate synergy of tastes. Likewise, we occasionally use white sugar in savory dishes to balance sour or bitter ingredients but without changing their essential flavors.

Stevia has been used as a sweetener for centuries but is relatively new to the U.S. market. We don't use stevia for cooking in the restaurant, but we experimented with it for this cookbook. Some of us use it at home as a sugar substitute because we want to avoid aspartame and other artificial sweeteners. See page 31 for more information about stevia.

Agave nectar is a high-fructose sugar derived from the agave plant. The plants grow in Mexico and are in the same family as blue agave, from which tequila is made. We don't use agave in the restaurant and didn't experiment with it for this cookbook, although some of us use it at home.

Sweet Potato Pie with Pecan-Oat Crust

SERVES 8 | YIELDS 1 9-INCH PIE | HANDS-ON TIME: 40 MINUTES | BAKING TIME: 45 TO 50 MINUTES

We think this pie is a good candidate for an autumn or a winter holiday dessert. It's made with favorite flavors of the season: sweet potatoes, pecans, and maple syrup. Buttermilk and beaten egg whites make the filling lighter.

CRUST

⅔ CUP PECANS, WALNUTS, OR ALMONDS

⅔ CUP ROLLED OATS (NOT QUICK-COOKING OR INSTANT)

2 TABLESPOONS PURE MAPLE SYRUP

2 TABLESPOONS VEGETABLE OIL

PINCH OF SALT

FILLING

1½ CUPS MASHED COOKED SWEET POTATOES (SEE NOTE)

½ TEASPOON GROUND NUTMEG

½ TEASPOON GROUND CINNAMON

½ TEASPOON SALT

½ CUP PURE MAPLE SYRUP

⅔ CUP BUTTERMILK OR PLAIN NONFAT YOGURT

2 TABLESPOONS WHOLE WHEAT FLOUR

2 LARGE EGGS

1 To make the crust: In a food processor, whirl all of the crust ingredients until the mixture is finely ground. Scrape into a 9-inch pie plate and use your fingers to press into an even thickness across the bottom and up the sides of the plate. Set aside.

2 To make the pie filling: Place the mashed sweet potatoes in a food processor. Add the nutmeg, cinnamon, salt, maple syrup, buttermilk, and flour. Separate the eggs, adding the yolks to the food processor and placing the whites in a separate bowl. Purée the sweet potato mixture until smooth, and place in a mixing bowl.

3 Beat the egg whites until stiff peaks form. With a spatula, gently fold the whites into the sweet potato filling. Pour the filling into the pie crust and bake in a preheated 350° oven until the filling is set and the center feels firm, about 45 minutes. Allow the pie to cool to room temperature before serving.

NOTE: About 1 pound of sweet potatoes will yield about 3 cups of raw chunks which, after cooking and mashing, will make just about the right amount for this recipe. If you have a little more than 1½ cups, go ahead and use it all for the filling. Then if it is too much for the pie shell, bake the extra in a custard cup.

SERVING IDEAS: Serve plain or topped with vanilla frozen yogurt or ice cream.

SWEET POTATO PIE WITH PECAN-OAT CRUST—
PER 1 SERVING (OF 8) *Calories: 257, Protein: 5 g, Carbohydrate: 35 g, Dietary Fiber: 2 g, Total Fat: 12 g, Saturated Fat: 1 g, Monounsaturated Fat: 6 g, Cholesterol: 53 mg, Sodium: 223 mg*

Apple and Dried Fruit Strudel

SERVES 8 | HANDS-ON TIME: 30 MINUTES | BAKING TIME: 30 TO 35 MINUTES

This moist, flaky dessert strudel boasts a filling of walnuts, dried cranberries, and apricots—all nutritional stars that have made the food headlines in recent years. It has no added sugar or honey, no butter, uses whole wheat filo, and it's deliciously satisfying, especially straight from the oven.

FRUIT FILLING

1¼ CUPS PEELED AND FINELY DICED APPLES

¼ CUP CHOPPED DRIED APRICOTS

¼ CUP CHOPPED RAISINS

¼ CUP CHOPPED DRIED CRANBERRIES

1 TEASPOON LEMON JUICE

1 TEASPOON GROUND CINNAMON

⅛ TEASPOON GRATED NUTMEG

PINCH OF GROUND ALLSPICE

PASTRY LAYERS

4 13 × 17-INCH SHEETS WHOLE WHEAT FILO (SEE PAGE 23)

4 TO 5 TABLESPOONS OLIVE OIL OR VEGETABLE OIL

½ CUP GROUND TOASTED WALNUTS

1 In a bowl, mix together all of the fruit filling ingredients and set aside.

2 Place 2 sheets of filo on a flat dry surface with one of the short ends closest to you. Brush the top sheet lightly with oil. Spread half of the fruit filling over half of the filo sheet, leaving a 2-inch border uncovered at the edges. Sprinkle ¼ cup of the walnuts over the filling. Fold the uncovered half of the sheets of filo over the filling and brush the top with oil. Press around the edges to lightly seal; this keeps the filling from oozing out. Starting at the short end nearest you, roll the filo into a log. Place the log seam-side down on a lightly oiled or parchment-paper-lined baking sheet. Brush the log with oil and slice 3 vents crosswise, evenly spaced across the top. Make another log with the two remaining sheets of filo.

3 Bake in a preheated 375° oven for 30 to 35 minutes, until hot and golden. Cool for at least 5 minutes, and then slice through the cuts you have made in the filo to get 8 pieces.

VARIATIONS: Use other dried fruit, such as dates, pears, currants, cherries, blueberries.

SERVING IDEAS This impressive-looking dessert needs nothing more than a cup of coffee or tea to accompany it, but it does look awfully pretty with a sprinkling of confectioners' sugar across the top.

APPLE AND DRIED FRUIT STRUDEL—PER 1 SERVING (OF 8) *Calories: 129, Protein: 2 g, Carbohydrate: 20 g, Dietary Fiber: 2 g, Total Fat: 5 g, Saturated Fat: 1 g, Monounsaturated Fat: 2 g, Cholesterol: 0 mg, Sodium: 51 mg*

Whole Grain Crêpes Filled with Chocolate and Walnuts

YIELDS ABOUT 14 CRÊPES | HANDS-ON TIME: 40 MINUTES | BAKING TIME: 10 MINUTES

Chocolate and walnuts make an easy and delectable filling for these light yet satisfying crêpes. And the crêpes make tasty wrappers for an array of dessert or savory fillings; see our menu ideas.

CRÊPES

2 LARGE EGGS

1 CUP MILK

¼ CUP WATER

1 CUP WHOLE WHEAT FLOUR (SEE NOTES)

½ TEASPOON SALT

½ TEASPOON BAKING POWDER

½ TEASPOON PURE VANILLA EXTRACT (OPTIONAL)

VEGETABLE OIL OR SPRAY

FILLING

1 CUP WALNUTS

1 CUP SEMISWEET CHOCOLATE CHIPS

1 Place the eggs, milk, water, flour, salt, baking powder, and vanilla, if using, in a blender. Whirl until smooth and evenly colored. Use a spatula to scrape the sides of the blender jar if needed.

2 Lightly oil or spray an 8- or 9-inch skillet (use a crêpe pan or a skillet with sloping sides), and place on medium-high heat for a minute or two to warm. Pour a scant ¼ cup of the batter into the pan, and swirl it around by tipping the pan to evenly coat the bottom and up the sides. Cook for about a minute, until the crêpe is set and the edge is lightly browned. Using a spatula, carefully loosen the edges, then flip the crêpe and cook the second side until golden brown, about a minute. Stack the cooked crêpes on a plate. In most skillets, cooking the crêpes is easier if you lightly spray or oil the skillet before cooking each crêpe. Repeat until the batter is used up (stir the batter occasionally to make sure it stays well mixed).

3 To fill the crêpes: Whirl the walnuts and chocolate in a food processor until coarsely chopped. Spread about 2 tablespoons of the filling in a 3-inch-wide strip across the center of a crêpe to within an inch of the sides. Fold the left and right sides over the filling, followed by the top and bottom flaps. Place in a lightly oiled baking dish, seam-side down.

4 Cover the pan with foil and bake in a preheated 350° oven for 10 minutes, until the chocolate has melted and the crêpes are warm. They can also be heated in a microwave oven.

NOTES: Use traditional whole wheat flour, whole wheat pastry flour, or white whole wheat flour, but not whole wheat bread flour.

The batter keeps in the refrigerator for a day or two; stir well before using. Crêpes can be made in advance and then filled and baked when you're ready to serve them. Cooked crêpes keep for three days when well covered and refrigerated, or for a couple of months frozen in a freezer bag.

SERVING AND MENU IDEAS: These crêpes make an excellent dessert, breakfast, or brunch filled with all-fruit spread or preserves mixed with yogurt. Or try them filled with Simply Baked Fruit (page 319). They're also fine unfilled as a stack of pancakes layered with lightly sweetened fresh berries.

For lunch or a light supper, fill crêpes with a savory filling such as Vegetable Cream Cheese (page 45), or one of our Two Nut-free Pestos (page 79), Winter Pesto (page 242), or Pistachio-Lemon Pesto (page 228). When you make crêpes for a savory filling, omit the optional vanilla.

WHOLE GRAIN CRÊPES FILLED WITH CHOCOLATE AND WALNUTS—PER 1 SERVING (OF 14), 1 CRÊPE WITH 2 TABLESPOONS FILLING *Calories: 159, Protein: 4 g, Carbohydrate: 16 g, Dietary Fiber: 2 g, Total Fat: 10 g, Saturated Fat: 3 g, Monounsaturated Fat: 2 g, Cholesterol: 31 mg, Sodium: 122 mg*

CRÊPE ONLY—PER 1 CRÊPE *Calories: 48, Protein: 3 g, Carbohydrate: 7 g, Dietary Fiber: 1 g, Total Fat: 1 g, Saturated Fat: 0 g, Monounsaturated Fat: 0 g, Cholesterol: 31 mg, Sodium: 118 mg*

Filo Nut Cigars

YIELDS 32 PASTRIES | HANDS-ON TIME: 45 MINUTES | BAKING TIME: 20 MINUTES

In this Moosewood adaptation of a Greek confection, we use whole wheat filo pastry and two kinds of nutritious nuts, and replace some of the sugar with all-fruit apricot preserves. Then we bake, not fry, our "cigars." Honey syrup, which contains citrus juices and spices, gives a bright, sweet, fruity finish to these very tasty pastries.

Paper-thin whole wheat filo is pleasantly light and bakes to a crisp, flaky texture. It also provides whole grain goodness and a wonderful flavor.

---

1 ORANGE

2 CUPS FINELY CHOPPED TOASTED WALNUTS

2 CUPS FINELY CHOPPED TOASTED ALMONDS

¼ CUP APRICOT ALL-FRUIT PRESERVES

1½ TEASPOONS GROUND CINNAMON

1 TEASPOON GROUND CLOVES (OPTIONAL)

1 TEASPOON GROUND GINGER

½ TEASPOON SALT

¼ CUP BROWN SUGAR, TURBINADO SUGAR, OR HONEY

⅓ CUP OLIVE OIL

8 13 × 17-INCH SHEETS WHOLE WHEAT FILO (SEE PAGE 23)

HONEY SYRUP

½ CUP HONEY

½ CUP ORANGE JUICE

1 TABLESPOON LEMON JUICE

½ TEASPOON GROUND CINNAMON

¼ TEASPOON GROUND CLOVES (OPTIONAL)

¼ TEASPOON GROUND GINGER

---

1 Grate the orange rind for 2 teaspoons of zest, and juice the orange for 3 tablespoons of juice. In a mixing bowl, combine the orange zest and juice, the nuts, preserves, cinnamon, cloves if using, ginger, salt, and sugar. Set aside.

2 Place the stack of filo sheets on a dry work surface with one of the short sides closest to you. Lightly brush the top sheet with oil. Lift the bottom edge of the sheet and fold it over to about 5 inches from the top, to make a double thickness in the bottom half of the sheet. Brush with oil. About 2 inches from the bottom fold, evenly spread about ½ cup of the nut mixture in a line running from side to side. Pull the folded edge of the filo up over the filling and roll into a log. Brush the outside of the log with oil and slice it into quarters to make four "cigars." Place them on a lightly oiled baking sheet.

3 Repeat with the remaining 7 sheets of filo to make 32 pastries in all.

4 Bake in a preheated 350° oven until golden brown, about 20 minutes.

5 Meanwhile, combine all of the syrup ingredients in a small saucepan and bring to a boil. Lower the heat and simmer, stirring occasionally, for about 8 minutes to reduce the liquid a bit.

6 When you remove the pastries from the oven, transfer them to a serving tray and drizzle with the hot honey syrup. Stored in a container at room temperature, Filo Nut Cigars will keep for a week.

SERVING IDEAS: Filo Nut cigars are a sweet and satisfying dessert, perfect with tea or coffee as well as a great midafternoon pick-me-up. Serve garnished with fresh orange slices.

FILO NUT CIGARS—PER 1 PASTRY (OF 32)
Calories: 160, Protein: 3 g, Carbohydrate: 13 g, Dietary Fiber: 2 g, Total Fat: 12 g, Saturated Fat: 1 g, Monounsaturated Fat: 5 g, Cholesterol: 0 mg, Sodium: 40 mg

Our Healthiest Cheesecake Pie

SERVES 6 TO 8 | YIELDS ONE 9-INCH PIE | YOGURT CHEESE DRAINING TIME: 4 TO 24 HOURS
HANDS-ON TIME: 20 MINUTES | BAKING TIME: 30 TO 40 MINUTES | CHILLING TIME: ABOUT 2 HOURS

If you've given up cheesecake because it's too high in fat and calories, here's a recipe to try. Stevia, a plant-derived sweetener, combines with tangy yogurt cheese in this creamy, dense cheesecake pie that has significantly less of the fat and calories that put cheesecake on the "avoid completely" heart-healthy lists in health and food magazines. Making this dessert takes some planning, but the actual hands-on time is brief enough to schedule into a busy day. It is even better after a day or two in the refrigerator.

---

1 QUART (4 CUPS) PLAIN NONFAT YOGURT

½ CUP WHOLE GRAIN GRAHAM CRACKER CRUMBS

2 TABLESPOONS OLIVE OIL

8 OUNCES NEUFCHÂTEL CHEESE, AT ROOM TEMPERATURE

1 TABLESPOON PURE VANILLA EXTRACT

¼ TO 1½ TEASPOONS STEVIA POWDER, OR MORE TO TASTE (SEE NOTE)

3 LARGE EGGS

NOTE: The sweetening strength of stevia powders varies considerably, making it impossible to give an exact amount that will sweeten to the level intended. If you know the sweetening power of the stevia you're using, estimate the amount that will work. Otherwise, start at the lower end of the range called for, and add more stevia to taste. See page 31 for more information.

1 Place a colander or sieve lined with overlapping coffee filters or several layers of cheesecloth inside a large bowl. Spoon the yogurt into the colander, cover, and refrigerate for 4 to 24 hours. Discard the liquid that collects in the bowl. The longer the yogurt drains, the thicker the yogurt cheese. For this recipe, 24 hours is ideal. Covered and refrigerated, yogurt cheese will keep for several days.

2 When the yogurt cheese is ready, preheat the oven to 300° and lightly oil a 9-inch pie plate. Combine the graham cracker crumbs and oil in a bowl. Press the crumbs evenly over the bottom of the pie plate.

3 In a food processor, whirl the yogurt cheese, neufchâtel, and vanilla until very smooth. Whirl in the stevia powder. Taste, and add more stevia for more sweetness if necessary. Add the eggs and process until fully incorporated. Pour the filling into the pie plate.

4 Bake for 30 to 40 minutes, until the edges are set and the center jiggles only slightly. Remove from the oven and cool to room temperature; cover and refrigerate until completely chilled, 1 to 2 hours.

SERVING IDEAS: Serve with fresh berries or peach slices or Fresh Raspberry Sauce (page 313) or Simply Baked Fruit (page 319).

OUR HEALTHIEST CHEESECAKE PIE—
PER 1 SERVING (OF 8) *Calories: 226, Protein: 13 g, Carbohydrate: 15 g, Dietary Fiber: 0 g, Total Fat: 13 g, Saturated Fat: 5 g, Monounsaturated Fat: 5 g, Cholesterol: 103 mg, Sodium: 266 mg*

Oatmeal Cookies

YIELDS ABOUT 2 DOZEN | HANDS-ON TIME: 30 MINUTES | BAKING TIME: 15 MINUTES

We minimized the sugar in this soft and chewy cookie and found that doing so highlights the rich sweet-tart flavors of dark chocolate, walnuts, and cranberries. A couple of these cookies will satisfy a craving for a snack in midafternoon, on a long car trip, or on a hike through the woods.

2 TABLESPOONS BUTTER, AT ROOM TEMPERATURE

2 TABLESPOONS VEGETABLE, OLIVE, WALNUT, OR HAZELNUT OIL

⅓ CUP BROWN SUGAR

1 TEASPOON PURE VANILLA EXTRACT

1 LARGE EGG

½ CUP WHOLE WHEAT PASTRY FLOUR

¼ TEASPOON BAKING SODA

½ TEASPOON SALT

1½ CUPS ROLLED OATS (NOT QUICK-COOKING OR INSTANT)

½ CUP SEMISWEET CHOCOLATE CHIPS

½ CUP CHOPPED DRIED CRANBERRIES

½ CUP CHOPPED WALNUTS

1 In a bowl, with an electric mixer or a whisk, beat the butter and oil until well blended and smooth. Beat in the sugar and vanilla until creamy. Add the egg and beat until creamy and smooth. Sift the flour, baking soda, and salt into the bowl and stir until well blended. Stir in the oats, chocolate chips, cranberries, and nuts. The batter will be chunky.

2 Line 2 baking sheets with parchment paper. (Lightly oiled baking sheets work, but parchment paper is better for removing the baked cookies.) Drop a dozen rounded tablespoonfuls of the dough, evenly spaced, on each sheet. You may need to use your fingers to clump the dough together. Press each spoonful of dough down with a fork dipped in water.

3 Bake in a preheated 350° oven for about 10 minutes, until the cookies are light brown around the edges. Remove the cookies and place them on a wire rack to cool. Store in a covered container.

VARIATIONS: You can substitute almonds, pecans, cashews, or hazelnuts for the walnuts.

Dried chopped blueberries, raisins, or apricots can replace the dried cranberries.

SERVING IDEAS: Probably the best thing with to these cookies is a tall glass of ice-cold milk.

OATMEAL COOKIES—PER 1 SERVING (OF 24), 1 COOKIE *Calories: 98, Protein: 2 g, Carbohydrate: 12 g, Dietary Fiber: 1 g, Total Fat: 5 g, Saturated Fat: 2 g, Monounsaturated Fat: 2 g, Cholesterol: 11 mg, Sodium: 69 mg*

Butternut Cookies

YIELDS ABOUT 3 DOZEN SMALL COOKIES | HANDS-ON TIME: 20 MINUTES | BAKING TIME: 10 TO 15 MINUTES

These cakey little cookies are crisp when they come out of the oven and then soft in a few hours. Guilt-free treats—high in beta-carotene, omega-3s, whole grains, and fiber—they passed the test of our kid testers who thought they were really yummy and are hoping to find them often in their lunchboxes.

1½ CUPS PURÉED COOKED BUTTERNUT SQUASH (SEE NOTES)

⅓ CUP PACKED BROWN SUGAR

½ CUP OLIVE OIL

1 LARGE EGG, LIGHTLY BEATEN

1 TEASPOON PURE VANILLA EXTRACT

2 CUPS WHOLE WHEAT FLOUR (SEE NOTES)

1 TEASPOON GROUND CINNAMON

1 TEASPOON BAKING POWDER

½ TEASPOON BAKING SODA

½ TEASPOON SALT

½ CUP CHOPPED TOASTED WALNUTS, ALMONDS, PEANUTS, OR PECANS

½ CUP SEMISWEET CHOCOLATE CHIPS

½ CUP CHOPPED RAISINS OR DRIED CRANBERRIES

½ CUP SUNFLOWER SEEDS OR CHOPPED PUMPKIN SEEDS

2 TABLESPOONS SESAME SEEDS (OPTIONAL)

1 In a bowl, mix together the squash, sugar, oil, egg, and vanilla. In a separate bowl, sift together the flour, cinnamon, baking powder, baking soda, and salt. Fold the flour mixture into the squash mixture until well blended. Stir in the nuts, chocolate chips, dried fruit, sunflower seeds and sesame seeds, if using. Drop by heaping teaspoonfuls onto two large unoiled baking sheets, about 18 cookies per pan. Space the cookies evenly giving them a bit of room to spread as they bake.

2 Bake in a preheated 375° oven for 10 to 15 minutes, until slightly browned on the bottom. Use a spatula to move the cookies to a wire rack to cool. Store in a covered container.

NOTES: If you don't happen to have leftover cooked butternut squash on hand, pick up a 12-ounce package of frozen winter squash at the market and let it thaw. It'll work just fine.

Use whole wheat regular flour or pastry flour, but not bread flour.

VARIATION: These cookies are chock-full of stuff; if you don't have all of the extras (nuts, chocolate chips, dried fruit, and sunflower or pumpkin seeds) on hand, it's okay to increase the quantity of what you do have as a substitute.

BUTTERNUT COOKIES—PER 1 SERVING (OF 36), 1 COOKIE *Calories: 103, Protein: 2 g, Carbohydrate: 11 g, Dietary Fiber: 2 g, Total Fat: 6 g, Saturated Fat: 1 g, Monounsaturated Fat: 3 g, Cholesterol: 6 mg, Sodium: 69 mg*

Silken Chocolate Pudding

SERVES 6 | YIELDS ABOUT 2½ CUPS | HANDS-ON TIME: 20 MINUTES | CHILLING TIME: AT LEAST AN HOUR

This rich, smooth, glossy high-protein dessert can be just what you crave after a light, mostly-vegetables meal. Okay, maybe you could crave it anytime. The richness comes from both chocolate and, surprisingly, silken tofu. It is quickly and easily made—no standing and stirring over a hot stove. And it's vegan!

1 CAKE OF SILKEN TOFU (ABOUT 16 OUNCES)

3 TABLESPOONS CONFECTIONERS' SUGAR

8 OUNCES SEMISWEET CHOCOLATE

6 TABLESPOONS WATER

3 TABLESPOONS UNSWEETENED COCOA POWDER

1 TEASPOON PURE VANILLA EXTRACT

1 In a food processor, whirl the tofu and confectioners' sugar until well blended. In a double boiler, a small pan on low heat, or in a microwave oven, warm the chocolate, water, cocoa, and vanilla until the chocolate melts. Stir until thoroughly mixed. Pour the chocolate sauce into the food processor with the sweetened whipped tofu, and whirl again until very smooth and silky.

2 Spoon the pudding into 6 serving cups. Chill for at least an hour.

SERVING IDEAS: Serve topped with chopped toasted hazelnuts, almonds, peanuts, or walnuts.

SILKEN CHOCOLATE PUDDING—PER 1 SERVING (OF 6) *Calories: 245, Protein: 6 g, Carbohydrate: 31 g, Dietary Fiber: 3 g, Total Fat: 14 g, Saturated Fat: 7 g, Monounsaturated Fat: 4 g, Cholesterol: 0 mg, Sodium: 9 mg*

Chocolate Bark

YIELDS ABOUT 16 PIECES | HANDS-ON TIME: 20 MINUTES | COOLING TIME: 30 TO 60 MINUTES

Chocolate Bark is quick and easy to make and just a little piece can satisfy your sweet tooth. It makes a fine gift. We love the flavor of those little strips of orange peel in this chocolate.

---

1 ORANGE

12 OUNCES 60–70% CACAO DARK
SEMI-SWEET OR BITTERSWEET CHOCOLATE
(SEE PAGE 21)

1 CUP COARSELY CHOPPED TOASTED NUTS,
SUCH AS WALNUTS, ALMONDS,
OR HAZELNUTS

½ CUP CHOPPED DRIED FRUIT,
SUCH AS CHERRIES, CRANBERRIES,
OR APRICOTS

⅛ TEASPOON COARSE SALT

---

1 Smoothly line a 9 × 13-inch baking pan with parchment paper, waxed paper, or aluminum foil.

2 With a sharp knife or vegetable peeler, pare thin slices of the peel from half of the orange and cut into very thin strips about ½ inch long, to make 1 tablespoon. Set aside.

3 Heat the chocolate in a double boiler or in an ovenproof bowl set over a pan of simmering water. Stir just until melted and smooth, being careful not to let any water get into the chocolate. Stir in half of the orange peel, half of the nuts, and all of the dried fruit, and immediately pour into the prepared pan. Spread the chocolate mixture evenly. Sprinkle with the salt and top with the remaining orange peel and nuts. Press down lightly to set the nuts in the chocolate.

4 Refrigerate for about 30 minutes until firm, or let harden at room temperature for a couple of hours. Break or cut into pieces. Store in a covered container at room temperature or refrigerated.

SERVING AND MENU IDEAS: With a tin of Chocolate Bark at the ready, you can bring out a fabulous dessert anytime you come to the end of a meal and wish there were just a little sweet something to cap it off. Serve with fresh fruit, such as cherries, pears, or oranges, or with coffee or a dessert wine.

VARIATIONS: Omit the salt.

Try lemon peel instead of orange peel, or no peel at all.

Use pistachios or chopped cashews, peanuts, macadamia nuts.

Use chopped raisins or dried figs as the fruit, or leave the fruit out altogether.

Flavor with ¼ teaspoon ground cinnamon or a dash of cayenne.

CHOCOLATE BARK—PER 1 PIECE (OF 16),
ABOUT 1½ OUNCES *Calories: 176, Protein: 2 g, Carbohydrate: 18 g, Dietary Fiber: 2 g, Total Fat: 12 g, Saturated Fat: 5 g, Monounsaturated Fat: 2 g, Cholesterol: 1 mg, Sodium: 20 mg*

Hot Chocolate

SERVES 2 TO 4 | YIELDS ABOUT 2½ CUPS | TIME: 10 MINUTES

Now that we know that dark chocolate contains antioxidant-rich flavonoids that promote cardiovascular health, shopping for chocolate has become increasingly interesting because supermarkets carry dozens of selections, with different countries of origin, varying percentages of cacao, and distinctive qualities of flavor and texture. The healthful phytonutrients are in the cacao. In general, the more cacao in the chocolate, the less sugar and fat it contains. We recommend organic chocolate with 60% to 75% cacao content.

2 CUPS UNSWEETENED ALMOND MILK, RICE MILK, OR SOYMILK

3 TO 4 OUNCES GOOD-QUALITY DARK BITTERSWEET OR SEMI-SWEET CHOCOLATE, FINELY CHOPPED

In a saucepan on low heat, warm the milk, stirring occasionally and being careful not to let it boil. Add the chopped chocolate and stir constantly until melted and evenly dispersed.

VARIATIONS: Cow's milk works in this recipe, too.

Add 1 to 2 tablespoons of your favorite liqueur, such as amaretto, Grand Marnier, or Kahlúa.

Add 1 to 2 tablespoons of brandy or rum.

Sprinkle with ground cinnamon.

SERVING AND MENU IDEAS: Hot chocolate is a sensual and stimulating drink for breakfast or brunch, a much appreciated after-school treat, and a simple, sophisticated, and satisfying dessert.

HOT CHOCOLATE (MADE WITH RICE MILK)—
PER 1 SERVING (OF 4), ABOUT ⅔ CUP *Calories: 182, Protein: 2 g, Carbohydrate: 2 g, Dietary Fiber: 2 g, Total Fat: 8 g, Saturated Fat: 4 g, Monounsaturated Fat: 3 g, Cholesterol: 0 mg, Sodium: 46 mg*

METRIC AND OTHER EQUIVALENCIES

IMPERIAL MEASUREMENTS

Theoretically, both the United Kingdom and Canada use the metric system, but older recipes rely on the "imperial" measurement system, which differs from standard U.S. measurements in its liquid ("fluid") measurements:

U.S.	IMPERIAL
2.5 ounces	¼ cup
5 ounces	½ cup ("gill")
10 ounces	1 cup
20 ounces	1 pint
40 ounces	1 quart

LIQUID EQUIVALENCIES

U.S.	METRIC
¼ teaspoon	1.25 milliliters
½ teaspoon	2.5 milliliters
1 teaspoon	5 milliliters
1 tablespoon	15 milliliters
1 fluid ounce	30 milliliters
¼ cup	60 milliliters
⅓ cup	80 milliliters
½ cup	120 milliliters
1 cup	240 milliliters
1 pint (2 cups)	480 milliliters
1 quart (4 cups)	960 milliliters (.96 liter)
1 gallon (4 quarts)	3.84 liters

DRY MEASURE EQUIVALENCIES

U.S.	METRIC
1 ounce (by weight)	28 grams
¼ pound (4 ounces)	114 grams
1 pound (16 ounces)	454 grams
2.2 pounds	1 kilogram (1,000 grams)

RESOURCES

BOOKS

Agatson, Arthur M.D. *The South Beach Diet Cookbook*. Rodale, 2004. Popular recipes that emphasize "good fats and good carbohydrates."

Albi, Johnna and Catherine Walthers. *Greens Glorious Greens!* St. Martin's Press, 1996. Recipes and information on buying and preparing thirty-five different greens.

Baird, Lori, editor. *The Complete Book of Raw Food*. Healthy Living Book, 2004. Encyclopedic collection of recipes from fifty raw food chefs.

Bishop, Jack. *Vegetables Every Day*. HarperCollins, 2001. A comprehensive A-to-Z guide to the bounty of produce, with recipes.

Campbell, T. Colin. *The China Study*. Benbella Books, 2005. A comprehensive study of nutrition that deals with long-term health, diet, and weight loss.

Clement, Anna Maria, Ph.D., and Kelly Serbonich. *Healthful Cuisine*. Healthful Communications, 2007. Excellent raw food recipes and information cowritten by Kelly Serbonich, a chef at Moosewood.

Jenkins, Nancy Harmon. *The Mediterranean Diet Cookbook*. Bantam Books, 1994. Recipes from a healthful food culture with a focus on plentiful vegetables, fruits, legumes, and grains, with olive oil as the principal fat.

Kingsolver, Barbara. *Animal, Vegetable, Miracle*. HarperCollins, 2007. Well-written memoir of a family who consumes only food raised at their own or neighboring farms.

Madison, Deborah. *Local Flavors: Cooking and Eating from America's Farmer's Markets*. Broadway Books, 2002. A cross-country tour of regional recipes and locavore favorites.

Nabhan, Gary Paul. *Coming Home to Eat: The Pleasures and Politics of Local Foods*. W. W. Norton, 2002. A celebration of food and thoughts on the food industry.

Nestle, Marion. *Food Politics: How the Food Industry Influences Nutrition and Health*. University of California Press, 2007. How corporate control limits our choices.

———. *What to Eat*. North Point Press: Farrar, Straus, and Giroux, 2006. Thoroughly and engagingly researched advice that covers the full array of consumer choices.

Phyo, Ani. *Ani's Raw Food Kitchen*. Marlowe & Company, 2007. Raw food recipes that are accessible and easy to follow.

Pollan, Michael. *In Defense of Food, An Eater's Manifesto*. Penguin Press, 2008. We like the main message: Eat real food, not too much, mostly plants.

———. *The Omnivore's Dilemma, A Natural History of Four Meals*. Penguin Press, 2007. Fascinating portrayal of our dynamic coevolutionary relationship with the handful of plant and animal species we depend on.

Somerville, Annie. *Everyday Greens*. Scribner, 2003. Recipes using an essential food source.

UC Berkeley Wellness Letter. Wellness Foods A to Z. Rebus, 2002. An encyclopedic guide for the health conscious.

Vegetarian Times Complete Cookbook.
HarperCollins, 2003. A-to-Z recipes for all
occasions, from the well-known magazine.

Weil, Andrew, M.D. *Eating Well for Optimum
Health.* Quill: HarperCollins, 2000. A guide to
food, diet, and nutrition with recipes, menus, and
advice for chronic ailments.

WEBSITES

General Health

www.whfoods.com Information on the world's
healthiest foods from a nonprofit organization.

www.nuthealth.com/library A thorough source for
all you might want to know about nuts.

www.nal.usda.gov/fnic Department of Agriculture
food and nutrition information center.

www.health.harvard.edu Health newsletters from
Harvard University with a wide range of focuses,
including nutrition.

www.johnshopkinshealthalerts.com Information
from Johns Hopkins University that includes
health-related nutrition.

www.consumerreports.org/health Information on
foods, supplements, and health.

Advocacy

www.worldwatch.org Worldwatch focuses on the
challenges of climate change, resource degradation,
population growth, and poverty and presents
strategies for achieving a sustainable society.

www.sustainabletable.org Sustainable Table was
created in 2003 to help consumers understand
the problems with our food supply, offer viable
solutions and alternatives, and celebrate the joy of
food and eating.

www.ams.usda.gov/farmersmarkets Lets you search
for farmers' markets across the United States.

www.localharvest.org A nationwide directory of
small farms, farmers' markets, and other local food
sources.

www.foodroutes.org A national nonprofit dedicated
to reintroducing Americans to their food—the seeds
it grows from, the farmers who produce it, and the
routes that carry it from the fields to our tables.

www.mbayaq.org/cr/seafoodwatch.asp Seafood
Watch is a program of Monterey Bay Aquarium
designed to raise consumer awareness about the
importance of buying seafood from sustainable
sources. Recommendations about which seafood
to buy or avoid, helping consumers to become
advocates for environmentally friendly seafood.

www.organicconsumers.org Health, food safety, fair
trade, genetic engineering, environmental and farm
policies, and other topical issues.

www.slowfoodusa.org An organization that
promotes a transformation in food policy,
production practices, and market forces.

www.ediblecommunities.com A network of
regionally produced magazines that connect
people with local resources in their communities
throughout the United States and Canada.

www.vegetarianresourcegroup.org Restaurant
guide, recipes, nutritional information, education,
and more.

Allergies

www.foodallergy.org Education, advocacy, and
research for food allergies.

www.livingwithout.com Gluten-free and dairy-free
recipes.

www.medicinenet.com/food allergy/article.htm A
medical perspective on food allergies.

INDEX

ABOUT THE AUTHORS

Most Moosewood Collective members have worked at Moosewood since the mid-1970s and our newest partners joined the collective in the early 1990s, so we've been together between sixteen and thirty-six years. That is remarkable to us, and somewhat incredible to others, but it doesn't explain the strength of our relationships, or the staying power of our business. It's cooking and sharing good food that keeps us going.

Our process for writing books is collaborative. Some of us like to develop recipes by ourselves, cooking several variations on a theme at home, and others prefer to develop ideas in small teams, meeting in each other's kitchens. But we all share the food we've developed with our cookbook partners (and neighbors, friends, and family) for taste testing and advice. And finally, we give each polished recipe at least one last test to make sure we have an easy-to-follow, accurate recipe, ready for home cooks.

Eleven of the nineteen Moosewood Collective members worked directly on this cookbook: Joan Adler, Ned Asta, Laura Branca, Linda Dickinson, Susan Harville, David Hirsh, Nancy Lazarus, Sara Wade Robbins, Myoko Maureen Vivino, Lisa Wichman, and Kip Wilcox.

We believe that delicious, healthful food begins with fresh, natural ingredients. We get excellent produce, milk, and cheese delivered to the restaurant year-round (from the large, regional Syracuse market and from smaller local farmers as well). This is the food that has inspired our more than two thousand recipes. We love to cook and we love to eat flavorful, fresh food. We hope you'll find lots to inspire you in this book.

NY COALITION FOR
HEALTHY SCHOOL FOOD

Moosewood and the authors of this book have donated one percent of their earnings from *Cooking for Health* to the New York Coalition for Healthy School Food (NYCHSF) Fresh Fruit and Vegetable Snack Program, which serves fresh fruit and vegetable snacks in the classroom each morning and afternoon to children at the Beverly J. Martin School in the Ithaca City School District, in Ithaca, NY, where Moosewood Restaurant is located. The program focuses on local and organic produce as much as possible. Students, parents, and teachers are thrilled with the program. Surprising the adults, kids are eating kale, bok choy, broccoli, turnips, arugula, and beets with no dressings or dips. They can't get enough fruit.

NYCHSF also has pilot projects in Corning and Harlem. NYCHSF is partnering with New York City Office of School Food to create plant-based recipes, in support of the NYC Wellness Policy, which states they will offer and promote plant-based entrees. NYCHSF has created resources including posters, a music CD by Jay Mankita (http://www.cdbaby.com/cd/jaymankita5), food activity cards to show how much fat and sugar are in various foods, and a fantastic website.

For more information or to make a donation to this wonderful program go to: www.healthyschoolfood.org

Moosewood Restaurant's Imaginatively Delicious Vegetarian Fare...Now Available Nationwide!

Our organic refrigerated soups and frozen entrées are now available in supermarkets and natural foods stores across the country.

www.moosewoodfoods.com

EAT YOUR GREENS...

and your yellows and oranges, your blues and
purples, and your blacks and reds and browns!

*It's a great time to eat well. Farmers' markets filled with local and organic
vegetables are sprouting up everywhere, and supermarkets are spilling over
with whole grain choices, bigger and better produce sections, and a variety of
healthier convenience foods. Cooking for both health and pleasure has made
creating this, our twelfth cookbook, a wonderful experience. What always
remains fresh and constant is the joy we find in cooking and delight in eating.*

—From the Introduction

Moosewood, Inc., and the authors of this book have donated one percent of
their earnings from the sale of this book to the New York Coalition for Healthy
School Food Fresh Fruit and Vegetable Snack Program that serves fresh
fruit and vegetable snacks in the morning and afternoon to schoolchildren at the
Beverly J. Martin School in the Ithaca City School District.

SIMON &
SCHUSTER
PAPERBACKS

EBOOK EDITION ALSO AVAILABLE

MEET THE AUTHORS, WATCH VIDEOS AND MORE AT
SimonandSchuster.com
THE SOURCE FOR READING GROUPS

JACKET DESIGN BY PATTI RATCHFORD • COVER ART BY SCOTT MCKOWEN

1109

$24.99 U.S.
$32.99 Can.

ISBN 978-1-4165-4887-4

PRINTED IN THE U.S.A